PRACTICING THE PATH

PRACTICING THE PATH

A Commentary on the *Lamrim Chenmo*

YANGSI RINPOCHE

Foreword by Geshe Lhundub Sopa
Preface by Lama Zopa Rinpoche
Translated by Tsering Tuladhar (Ven. Tsenla)
Edited by Miranda Adams

Wisdom Publications • Boston

Wisdom Publications
199 Elm Street
Somerville, MA 02144 USA
www.wisdompubs.org

Library of Congress Cataloging-in-Publication Data
Yangsi Rinpoche.
    Practicing the path : a commentary on the Lamrim Chenmo / Yangsi
  Rinpoche ; foreword by Geshe Lhundub Sopa ; preface by Lama Zopa
  Rinpoche ; translated by Tsering Tuladhar ; edited by Miranda Adams.
      p.   cm.
    ISBN 0-86171-346-X (pbk. : alk. paper)
    1. Tsoṅ-kha-pa Blo bzaṅ-grags-pa, 1357–1419 Lam rim chen mo.
  I. Tuladhar, Tsering. II. Adams, Miranda. III. Title.
  BQ7950.T754L344439 2003
  294.3'444—dc21   2003008088

ISBN 0-86171-346-X

First Edition
08 07
6   5   4   3   2

Cover design: Nita Ybarra
Interior design: Gopa and Ted2, Inc. using Adobe Garamond fonts, 10.75/14

Wisdom Publications' books are printed on acid-free paper
and meet the guidelines for the permanence and durability
set by the Council of Library Resources.

Printed in Canada

# CONTENTS

Note: A comprehensive outline of the commentary with page references
can be found on pages 489–97.

FOREWORD

I AM VERY HAPPY to see the publication of this book on Tsongkhapa's *Lamrim Chenmo*. The lamrim is the essence of all the Buddhist teachings, and shows how to put into practice all of the various scriptures: Hinayana, Mahayana, and Tantrayana. Although there are many different sutras and tantras by the Buddha, and many commentaries on these, the lamrim arranges the entire path in stages, in a practical manner, so that individuals can go from the beginning all the way up to enlightenment.

As is well known, *lam* means "path" in Tibetan and *rim* means "stages." The great teacher Atisha summarized all the Buddhist scriptures in his *Lamp for the Path to Enlightenment,* the root text for the lamrim tradition. His text divides beings' spiritual perspectives into three levels: beginning, intermediate, and finally, highest. Based on that division, the *Lamp for the Path* shows how to begin, explaining the main activities and emphasis of that initial stage. When that is fully developed and a practitioner reaches the intermediate level, the *Lamp for the Path* describes the meditations and emphasis at that stage. Finally, it describes the practice of the highest beings, the Mahayanists. Of these three levels, the first two mainly emphasize how an individual can be liberated from misery or from an impure life, while the third emphasizes liberating others, starting with one's own dear mother. Seeing all beings as equal to one's dear mother, one develops the wish to liberate them all. The third level presents the ideal way to liberate them.

There is no sentient being who does not want to be free from misery. Each one of us wants peace and happiness, and particularly everlasting peace and happiness. Yet we do not know how to bring that about, due to ignorance and the other delusions, which obstruct knowledge. As Shantideva says:

Although they wish to escape suffering
They run straight to the causes of suffering.
Although they wish happiness, out of ignorance
They destroy their own happiness, as if it were their enemy.

All the teachings of the Buddha, either directly or indirectly, were taught for the sake of wisdom, to free sentient beings from misery so that they may attain the highest goal of lasting happiness. Although 84,000 different teachings were taught for these purposes, the lamrim arranges those practices to make it easier to grasp and actualize their essential meaning. By condensing and arranging them in an orderly way, the lamrim teachings include the sequence, the variety, and the essence of all the teachings of the Buddha.

As Je Tsongkhapa says in his short lamrim text, the *Condensed Meaning*:

These stages on the path to enlightenment
Fulfill all the aims of the nine types of beings without exception.
Their instructions, a wish-fulfilling gem,
Gather together the rivers of thousands of excellent texts.
Thus they are indeed an ocean of glorious good explanation.

Since Je Tsongkhapa's *Lamrim Chenmo,* the great exposition on the lamrim, is an extremely deep teaching, it is possible to give numerous different explanations of it. Thus, even though many others have commented on the text before, I feel it will be of great benefit for people to have this detailed explanation by Yangsi Rinpoche.

Geshe Lhundub Sopa

EDITOR'S PREFACE

THIS BOOK IS COMPOSED of teachings from Yangsi Rinpoche's commentary on Lama Tsongkhapa's *Lamrim Chenmo* given February–April, 2000 at Tushita Meditation Center in Dharamsala, India. The entire scope of teachings has made its way into this book, although in editing for print much of the repetition has been cut. This is a traditional commentary in the sense that Rinpoche followed the outline of the root text more or less faithfully and touched on all of its key points. It is not a traditional commentary in the sense that Rinpoche diverged from the root text considerably at many points, supporting the given topic with related or source material from significant Indian and Tibetan sources outside of the *Lamrim Chenmo,* which itself, in root form, makes extensive use of secondary sources to support its presentation of the path. Rinpoche teaches in this commentary how the lamrim tradition is like a key opening all the doors of the Buddhist scriptures—with the understanding of the main points of the lamrim, one is able to contextualize and understand any text within the tradition, and likewise is able to understand all of the main points of practice on the path to enlightenment. With this commentary, I hope, the reader will be able to do likewise.

In transforming this commentary from an oral teaching to a written text, I attempted to leave Venerable Tsenla's exquisite translation of Rinpoche's words as pristine as possible while maintaining consistency and clarity and making the necessary syntactical reorganization to present a coherent written text. All of the points that were ambiguous in translation were checked and clarified under Rinpoche's guidance, as were most of the quotations. Also, some of the original material has been sorted and re-

ordered from the presentation that was given in the course in order to follow Lama Tsongkhapa's outline as faithfully as possible.

I have documented the source material that was used both by Rinpoche
in his preparation for the course and myself in the editing process as accu-
rately as possible, although Rinpoche did use a massive body of commentary to support these teachings and I am certain that some of them were
overlooked. Also, due to time constraints I was unable to catalogue the texts
in the bibliography to the detail that I would have liked, and for that, and
for any other inevitable mistakes that may appear in the edited text, I take
complete responsibility and offer my most sincere and heartfelt apologies.

Many thanks to the staff of Tushita Meditation Center, especially Sally
Barraud, the former director, and Venerable Tsomo for their kindness in
organizing and facilitating the lamrim course from beginning to end.
Thanks to Venerable Rita for her unrivaled skill and compassion in leading the course and all its participants through the entire two months, and
to Venerable Tsenla for her beautiful translation of Rinpoche's words.
Thanks to all those participants of the course and others who transcribed
the entire set of tapes from the teachings on a daily basis—without your
effort this manuscript would never have even been begun. Thanks as well
to Nick Ribush, for his kind advice and ongoing encouragement of this
project. Thanks to David Kittelstrom from Wisdom for overseeing the
project and especially for reviewing the final section. Thanks to those others who read various parts of the manuscript in its various drafts—Ann
Chavez and Carl Yoder, and especially to Louise Light, for her formative
critique as well as for her love and support, and to my Dharma sister
Lhundup Damcho, whose readings of various sections of this text were
invaluable, and for her ever-present mentoring, protection, and friendship. Thanks to my father and mother for their inspiration and encouragement in the world of making books. Also, I would like to thank the
precious teacher Lama Zopa Rinpoche for requesting that this course be
taught and for his inspiration as a shinning light on the path to enlightenment in our world.

And most of all, I offer my deepest gratitude to Yangsi Rinpoche, who
not only teaches the lamrim but lives it through every action of his body,
speech, and mind. I offer my most humble thanks for the hours spent
patiently answering my many questions and painstakingly explaining the

unclear points of the commentary as I worked through the text, for the many hours of listening to edited drafts being read aloud, and for allowing me this opportunity to spend so much time immersed in these teachings, the one medicine for the suffering of sentient beings in the world. I hope and pray that every sentient being may one day come under the close guidance and care of such a perfect virtuous friend.

Tenzin Namdrol (Miranda Adams)
the 25th day of the 10th Tibetan month of the Water Horse Year, 2129
Deer Park
Madison, Wisconsin USA

PREFACE

by Lama Zopa Rinpoche

Dear readers of this precious lamrim teaching,

THE REASON WE NEED TO PRACTICE DHARMA is because we all need happiness. All of us—even the insects that can be seen only through a microscope—keep busy, running to achieve happiness. In this world people use so many thousands of methods to be healthy, to have a long life, to be harmonious, to have success in business, to have wealth and material prosperity. People use so many thousands of methods to have a good reputation and power in this life, to make themselves beautiful, to be loved by others, and to have friends. However, even though they use so many thousands of methods, all of these methods are external, while in fact the originator fulfilling the wishes for happiness and any success is the mind—one's own mind. The actual root of all happiness and suffering comes from within, from one's own mind. That is the main cause.

The pure mind unstained by ignorance, anger, and attachment and the good heart that cherishes and benefits others produce all temporary and ultimate happiness. The mind stained by ignorance, anger, attachment, and self-cherishing thought is the originator of all of the problems of our past, present, and future lives. Negative thoughts not only produce one's own suffering, but also harm others.

The positive, healthy, peaceful, inner-happy mind, on the other hand, not only gives you all temporal and ultimate happiness, it also stops you from harming all living beings and instead causes you to benefit all living beings—especially when there is the good heart, letting go of "I" and cherishing others. This mind causes all temporal and ultimate happiness for yourself and also fulfills the wishes of sentient beings equaling the limitless sky. It causes temporary and ultimate happiness—happiness in this and all future lives as long as one is in samsara, the ultimate happiness of liberation from samsara, and the peerless happiness of enlightenment.

Therefore you can see that, even thinking in terms of your own happiness, since you dislike even the smallest discomfort that you may experience in a dream, there is the greatest urgency to practice Dharma immediately, which means to transform your mind into a positive, healthy mind with virtuous thoughts. When the mind is transformed from a negative, impure, unhealthy, and disturbed state, you achieve all your own happiness and numberless sentient beings also achieve happiness. But as long as there is no change to the mind, as long as the mind does not become Dharma, no matter how much you try all those other external means, you will encounter obstacles and problems in life, one after another.

There will be so many difficulties in your life and so much unhappiness and misery in your heart. Your inner life will be filled only with suffering, depression, guilt, disappointment, and anguish. No matter how much education, and intelligence you have, and no matter how much extensive knowledge you have acquired, your inner life and your heart will always be empty and you will feel unhappiness. There will always be jealousy, pride, anger, desire, self-centered mind, and so forth, and these will always torture and abuse you, not giving you any freedom or peace.

Your mind has every potential because your mind has buddha-nature. Not only that, but you also have a precious human body qualified with eight freedoms and ten endowments that allows you to make use of this buddha-nature. Therefore, you have all the potential to become free forever from every problem, including the cycle of death and rebirth and all the sufferings between—old age, sickness, the suffering of being unable to get the objects you desire, and the suffering of, even after obtaining them, being unable to experience satisfaction because of the worry and fear of losing them. You can not only become free from the suffering of pain, but also you can become free forever from the suffering of change—from the suffering experience of the temporary samsaric pleasures which are only in the nature of suffering. You can also become free forever from pervasive compounded suffering. Wherever you reincarnate in the six realms, not just in the evil-gone realms—the realms of the hell beings, hungry ghosts, and animals—but also in the realms of the happy transmigratory beings—the humans, suras, asuras, and even the form and formless realms where there is no suffering of pain and suffering of change—in all these realms you are under the control of karma and the contaminated seeds of delusion. That is why all of these realms are in the nature of suffering.

The seeds of delusion are within the aggregates. They are carried by the consciousness and they compound suffering by causing delusions to rise, which motivate karma and create samsara again. In order to cease the cause of all suffering—delusions and karma—you need to actualize the remedy, the antidote, which is the complete path to liberation within your own mind. Therefore, in order to make this most precious life, which is found just once, most meaningful, of course you must practice Dharma. But it is not enough to practice Dharma just to cause happiness in the next life, nor is it sufficient to practice Dharma to achieve liberation. Rather, you must practice Dharma in order to achieve enlightenment so that you can liberate all sentient beings from suffering and lead them to enlightenment.

For this, you need to actualize the cause of enlightenment, and that has to be a path that is unmistaken and complete. Just knowing one meditation, such as Vipassana, and practicing only that your whole life cannot produce enlightenment. With that alone, you cannot even free yourself from the suffering of samsara because even to do this you need to actualize the whole path of method and wisdom. Also, spending your whole life meditating on the conventional nature of the mind, the mere clarity of mind—with just that alone you cannot be liberated from samsara.

Even when you practice a complete path, that path must not be chaotic and random. If it is complete but chaotic and random you cannot achieve enlightenment, which means you cannot do perfect work for sentient beings. Therefore, you have to practice the whole path to enlightenment and you must do so in the correct order.

The lamrim is a Mahayana teaching for a fortunate being to go to enlightenment. It is well expounded by the Two Great Charioteers, Nagarjuna and Asanga. It was originally composed by Lama Atisha who was the crown of the great pandit-scholars and highly-attained ones of India. When Buddhism had become corrupt in Tibet due to much misunderstanding and confusion regarding the practices of sutra and tantra, Lama Atisha wrote the *Lamp for the Path to Enlightenment,* which integrates the Hinayana path, the Mahayana-Paramitayana path, and the Mahayana-Mantrayana path. He arranged all of these teachings taught by the Buddha into a graduated practice, showing that they are not contradictory to one another, but rather that they are all necessary for one person to achieve enlightenment.

The lamrim is the essence of Lama Atisha's understanding and realization of the path to enlightenment. It is also the essence of the understanding and realization of the Dharma King of the Three Realms, Lama Tsongkhapa, who wrote the most extensive commentary to Lama Atisha's *Lamp for the Path to Enlightenment*. This lamrim text contains the essence of all the 84,000 teachings of the Buddha without anything missing and all of this is set up in a graduated practice for one person.

If you do not take the opportunity to practice a most precious teaching such as this lamrim, the graduated path, then even if you have stable single-pointed concentration that can last for eons, there is nothing special about it because with that attainment alone the highest you can hope to achieve is the formless realm—another samsaric realm. Even if you have psychic powers, such attainments are nothing special because even intermediate-state beings have clairvoyance—as do lower realm beings such as pretas, ordinary spirits, and hell beings. Even if you are a human being and you can fly, that is nothing special, because birds and insects can also fly.

Also, actualizing the lamrim, the stages of the path to enlightenment, is a completely new experience, something we have never had before. It is not something that we have repeated many times in the past. Without lamrim realizations, such as the renunciation of samsara, none of the actions we do become the cause to achieve liberation from samsara—not even our spiritual practices. Without the lamrim realizations, such as the right view, none of our actions, including our spiritual practice, become a remedy to samsara—so we cannot eliminate the root of samsara. Without bodhichitta, none of our actions in daily life become the cause to achieve enlightenment, so we cannot achieve enlightenment. Without lamrim, even tantric practice cannot become Dharma—spiritual practice—and there is the danger that it may become a cause of rebirth in the lower realms of the hell beings, hungry ghosts, or animals.

One Kadampa Geshe said that when you read the lamrim it shakes the whole 84,000 teachings of the Buddha. Why? Because the lamrim is the heart of the entire Buddhadharma.

ABOUT LAMA TSONGKHAPA

This book is Yangsi Rinpoche's commentary on the *Lamrim Chenmo,* or *Great Treatise on the Stages of the Path to Enlightenment,* by Lama Tsongkhapa, which was completed in 1402, near Reting in Tibet. Reting is a very important holy place. It was the seat of Lama Atisha's translator Dromtonpa—the continuity of whose reincarnation is His Holiness the Dalai Lama—and the place where the Kadampa tradition began. Lama Tsongkhapa gave this commentary on the stages of the path to enlightenment in a hermitage very near Reting, and that is also where he wrote it down.

Lama Tsongkhapa is the crown of the learned, highly attained ones in the snow land of Tibet. This is expressed in the prayer called *Migtsema,* which Lama Tsongkhapa wrote for his guru, Lama Rendawa. Initially, Lama Tsongkhapa offered this prayer to his guru, but Lama Rendawa responded by offering it back, remarking that it was more appropriate for Lama Tsongkhapa himself.

Lama Tsongkhapa received teachings from Manjushri directly as disciple and guru. He consulted with Manjushri, who is the embodiment of all the Buddha's wisdom, and with his guidance clarified every subtle point of sutra and tantra. He clarified what had not been realized before and he cut and eliminated all wrong understandings and doubts. Therefore, whatever is Lama Tsongkhapa's understanding—this commentary itself as well as many other philosophical teachings on sutra and tantra—can also be said to be a teaching of Manjushri. Not only that, but there is a whole story that Lama Tsongkhapa himself *is* Manjushri.

One of these stories explains that Lama Tsongkhapa's mother gave birth to him on the road as she was taking animals to the mountain. After giving birth, she did not look after him but left him there and continued on with the animals. When she returned, she thought the baby would have been eaten, but instead he was completely protected—sheltered by ravens. After this, she took the baby back home. From the spot where the blood dropped as the baby was born a sandalwood tree arose, and its leaves are imprinted with one hundred thousand images of Manjushri's holy body as well as with the syllable *Dhi.* People take the skin off this tree and give it to women who are pregnant because eating it makes it easy for them to give birth. When we went to Tibet fifteen years ago, an English nun named

Sarah saw the syllables very clearly on the tree when the bark was peeled off by a Western monk who knew the story. At that time, the caretaker got upset because he felt that the way the monk was touching the holy tree was not respectful. The caretaker explained to them that scientists had come to investigate how the syllables could get into the tree through the bark, but they could not explain it.

Therefore, it can be said that Lama Tsongkhapa's teachings *are* Manjushri's teachings. And Lama Tsongkhapa is also the embodiment of Chenrezig, Vajrapani, and Maitreya. There are other stories that prove this.

Lama Tsongkhapa's *Lamrim Chenmo* is an incredibly clear, moving-the-mind teaching. As far as the preliminaries are concerned, since details are also explained by other lamas, Lama Tsongkhapa emphasized with just a few words the vital points that make up the practices to collect extensive merit and bring very powerful purification. Lama Tsongkhapa put the greatest amount of effort and time into clarifying points and eliminating misunderstandings where previous famous meditators made mistakes. Especially, he clarified and eliminated misunderstandings about the emptiness of the four schools and particularly the most subtle one, the Prasangika school view of emptiness, which explains that while phenomena are empty, they exist merely by being labeled by mind, and that while they exist they are empty. Lama Tsongkhapa gave so much clarification and explanation on this incredible Middle Way view, devoid of the two extremes of nihilism and eternalism. He eliminated all wrong views which harm the acceptance of karma, the law of cause and effect. Other well-known meditators and learned ones had a wrong view of reality—of the emptiness of phenomena—which harmed the law of cause and effect because they were unable to put together that while cause and effect functions it is empty, and that while it is empty cause and effect functions. This is the Middle Way, and without realizing the Middle Way view of emptiness, which is the Prasangika view, you cannot cut the root of ignorance forever.

For example, the Hashang view negates not only the delusions, but any thought that arises, bad or good—even loving-kindness, compassion, and bodhichitta, which bring peace and happiness for oneself up to enlightenment and which bring peace and happiness including enlightenment to numberless other sentient beings. Generally speaking, all of sentient beings' past, present, and future happiness arise from bodhichitta.

Lama Tsongkhapa also gave extensive clarification on the very important points of tantra that previous yogis did not clarify, such as clear light and the illusory body.

Some of Lama Tsongkhapa's incomparable teachings are the *Lamrim Chenmo, The Medium Treatise on the Stages of the Path, Essence of Eloquence: Distinguishing the Interpretable and the Definitive Meanings,* and *Commentary to Nagarjuna's "Root Wisdom."* Then, *Ngagrim Chenmo,* or the *Great Treatise on the Stages of the Path to Tantra,* the *Graduated Completion Stage,* the *Clear Light,* and the *Good Explanation of the Golden Garlands.* Through his use of valid reasoning and quotations, Lama Tsongkhapa gave an extremely clear explanation of the Buddhadharma—sutra and tantra. He made it so easy for sentient beings to have correct understanding and practice, and to have realization without confusion. Even the late head of the Nyingma School, His Holiness Dudjom Rinpoche, commented in his *History of the Tibetan Four Mahayana Traditions,* while treating the history of the Gelug tradition, that Lama Tsongkhapa gave the clearest explanation of Buddhism.

Therefore, you readers of this commentary will certainly derive immense benefit from it—even if you have read other lamrim texts. Even if you have read elaborate lamrim texts such as *Liberation in the Palm of Your Hand,* which presents the complete teachings in a simple and clear way, still when you read the *Lamrim Chenmo* there is so much richness in it, like cream, and so much depth and profundity. It is so moving for the mind—every line and every word is like this. Nothing is meaningless. This is generally the quality of Lama Tsongkhapa's work, how he presents the teachings—giving a very wide view and depth. He clarifies all of the very important points of the practice, and that is why his writings are so beneficial for the minds of those who are practicing and why many ascetic meditators, even renounced monks, carry the *Lamrim Chenmo* wherever they go.

Wherever you are in the world—on a very isolated mountain or under the ocean—study and meditate and allow your mind to become the stages of the path to enlightenment by putting this into practice. This makes life so meaningful. Living life like this is the richest life, the best life. This is the way to get out—it is the best way to get out of the ocean of samsaric suffering that we have been drowning in from time without beginning.

ABOUT THE AUTHOR, YANGSI RINPOCHE

Yangsi Rinpoche is the incarnation of a very well-known Lharampa Geshe who was outstanding among the well-learned ones of the greatest monasteries of Tibet—Sera, Ganden and Drepung—where Buddhist philosophy was studied in extensive depth, covering all the five major texts and after that learning tantra extensively. His name was Geshe Ngawang. He was the teacher of Geshe Sopa Rinpoche, who among the great teachers is an extremely rare one, most outstanding. Geshe Sopa was a professor at the University of Wisconsin since 1967 and is also the guru of Lama Yeshe and myself, taking care of me for around thirty years by teaching Dharma and other things.

The very clear proof that Yangsi Rinpoche is Geshe Ngawang's incarnation is that when his teacher, the ex-Abbot of the Lower Tantric College, Geshe Drubtob-la, was teaching Yangsi Rinpoche Madhyamaka, Geshe Drubtob-la remembered that in the past Geshe Ngawang-la had given him a very subtle and vital explanation on one of the points and that this special explanation was not in the text. Gen Drubtob-la was struggling to recall what it was and then Yangsi Rinpoche very easily brought up that point. That made Gen Drubtob-la feel certain that Yangsi Rinpoche was the *real* Geshe Ngawang-la, and even though he is one of the most learned teachers of sutra and tantra at Sera Monastery, Gen Drubtob-la cried.

Yangsi Rinpoche entered Kopan Monastery and lived there for around five years before going to study at Sera Monastery. He completed his studies at Sera Je, took the examination, and received a Lharampa Geshe degree. He studied extremely well and because of that this book will also help your understanding.

The other most important quality of Yangsi Rinpoche is that he has done very good guru devotion practice. That does not mean always reciting prayers, such as *Migtsema* and the guru's mantra. It means correctly devoting to the guru with thought and action—for example, practicing the nine attitudes of correctly devoting to the spiritual friend as explained by Lama Tsongkhapa. Because of his very good practice of guru devotion, this book can be of great benefit to tame the mind and soften the heart, and to bring realizations. If one has broken the *samaya* with the guru then it is difficult for the disciple to generate realizations and to have successful practice. Also, the disciple might receive pollution and make the same mistake. So in the monasteries, those who really understand well and correctly the practice of devotion to the spiritual friend also understand that this is the most important thing in order to achieve realizations of the path to enlightenment and to complete the works for self and the works for others.

I thank the author Yangsi Rinpoche and also the readers of this book.

I, Thubten Zopa, bearing the name of the incarnation of the Lawudo Lama, the very least follower of Shakyamuni Buddha, dictated this to a student, the English nun Sarah at Aptos House, Kachoe Dechen Ling, November 2002.

PART 1

Introduction to the Lamrim

INTRODUCTION TO THE TEXT

ALTHOUGH IT IS COMMON to view the attainment of enlightenment as the supreme accomplishment of the Buddhist path, it is important to keep in mind that the supreme purpose of that accomplishment is to benefit sentient beings in the most extraordinary way. Once we become enlightened, we will be completely empowered and fully able to bring about the ultimate benefit of others. In contrast, the way we are now, at most we are able to benefit others only temporarily.

To understand enlightenment we need to understand *nirvana,* or liberation, which means freedom from cyclic existence. In order to understand nirvana, we need to understand the conventional level of cyclic existence, which in turn requires an understanding of consciousness. *Samsara,* or cyclic existence, does not refer to our land or our house or our things. Samsara refers to the mental afflictions and the negative thoughts that bind us to this tiresome cycle of birth, death, and rebirth. Everything in the Buddhadharma depends on the understanding of consciousness, as it is the mind itself that imprisons us in cyclic existence, and the mind itself that liberates us.

According to the teachings of Buddha, the way that things ordinarily appear to our minds is fundamentally mistaken. Problems, difficulties, and hardships arise in our lives because of these basic misconceptions, because we are not able to see things the way that they actually are. According to Buddhism, we perceive the things and events in our lives from a totally obscured perspective. What we experience from this perspective is known as conventional existence. All of our problems arise because we grasp the conventional nature of things as being ultimately true.

Therefore, Buddhist philosophy is not just intellectual thought or theory. The Buddhist point of view is, ultimately, the antidote to all of our pain and problems. Its foremost objective is to eliminate the suffering in our minds.

In order to attain enlightenment, we must understand the path that leads to that state. The teachings on the graduated path to enlightenment, or the *lamrim,* help us do just that. Perhaps some of you have heard lamrim teachings already; others may be brand new. Regardless, there are two important things that I would like you to keep in mind as you study this text. The first is that it is essential that you try to integrate these teachings with your mind. There should not be a gap between your mind and the teachings at any point. If there is such a gap, although it may be possible for you to derive some sort of intellectual understanding of the teachings, you will not be able to apply them to your experience and you will not get very far on the path. If, however, you receive the teachings on the lamrim with the firm intention to put them into practice and improve your mind, you will be building a house with a perfect foundation, and you will reap the rewards later on.

The second point that you should consider is your motivation to receive these teachings. If you do virtuous activities with attachment, or with a mind distracted by the eight worldly concerns, the results will not be pure. If you engage in violent activities without compassion, even in the context of your tantric practice, these activities become nonvirtuous. If you take teachings on the profound path of wisdom or the extensive path of method with thoughts of pride or jealousy, your otherwise positive actions become polluted. As Lama Atisha says, if the roots of the plant are poisonous, then the trunk, the branches, the leaves, the flowers, and the fruits will also be poisonous. And when the roots of the tree are medicinal, the rest of the tree will be medicinal as well. In the same way, if your motivation is rooted in nonvirtue and negativity, your actions will also be nonvirtuous, and if your motivation is rooted in the wish to benefit others, your actions will be beneficial as well.

Studying the blessed teachings of Lama Tsongkhapa only in order to increase your intellectual understanding is a mistake. Studying with the expectation of worldly gain in this life is also absolutely wrong. Even studying with aspirations for the next life—hoping to obtain a precious human rebirth or free yourself from the difficulties of cyclic existence—is not correct. You must consider: which is more important—one person's happiness, or the happiness of all beings? Clearly, it is a great mistake to focus on your own comfort and happiness alone, without considering others. From beginningless time you have suffered in cyclic existence due to the thought "I must be happy." This concern for the self has been the basis of all of your downfalls. Thinking in this way for numberless lifetimes, you have thus far accomplished nothing.

From the *Eight Verses of Mind Training,* by the Kadam Geshe Langri Tangpa:

> By thinking of all sentient beings
> As even better than wish-granting gems
> For accomplishing the highest aim
> May I always consider them precious.

If you are able to practice as this text advises, you will naturally begin to cherish others, and eventually develop the wish to devote yourself entirely to working for their benefit. This thought is the foundation of the entire graduated path to enlightenment.

The *Eight Verses* also says:

> Wherever I go, with whomever I go
> May I see myself as the lowest of all, and
> From the depth of my heart
> May I consider others to be supremely precious.

The practice of seeing oneself as "the lowest of all" is fundamental to your practice of lamrim. This way of thinking is not intended to demean you. Rather, seeing yourself as the one of least importance, and others as the most important, is in fact one of the most advantageous ways of thinking. On the basis of this thought you can establish the foundation of happiness and develop bodhichitta, which will enable you to attain liberation and enlightenment. If you do not understand and grasp this essential principle of the spiritual path, then no matter how elaborate or decorative your practice might be, it will be meaningless.

Most of us actually have the wish to benefit sentient beings. We pray and we meditate on compassion and bodhichitta and so forth. But ultimately, if we don't uproot our self-cherishing mind even a little, no matter how much we meditate on kindness, the only benefit we will receive is a good feeling. This applies to any kind of long retreat, listening to teachings, as well as taking any of the three classes of vows.[1] In general, everyone has some wish to benefit others, some wish to make their lives useful. But in order to actually accomplish this, we must let go of our sense of self-importance. Ego-grasping is the greatest obstacle to the wish to benefit others. The more we can diminish the self-cherishing mind, the purer and more fruitful our wish to benefit others will become.

Trying to become aware of exactly how much we are cherishing ourselves is the perfect practice for the beginner. Coming to the recognition of the depth and the grossness of our self-cherishing mind early on in the path is essential. Perhaps, rather than doing so many sessions of deity yoga, it would be more useful for us to do a session meditating on the way we have promoted the self-cherishing mind in the past, a session on how much we are promoting the self-cherishing mind at the moment, and a session on how much we plan to promote the self-cherishing mind in the future. This would be an extremely good way to start ourselves off on the path.

It is very easy for us to recognize the way in which someone else is cherishing themselves, but it is also very easy for us to forget that we are doing the same thing! However, the fact that we are capable of recognizing self-cherishing in others shows that we are indeed capable of seeing it. Therefore, we only have to change the object from another person to ourselves. When we are able to do that, we have the basis upon which we can train our minds.

The objective of Lama Tsongkhapa's *Lamrim Chenmo,* or the *Great Treatise on the Stages of the Path to Enlightenment,* is to eliminate the self-cherishing mind. Once that objective is in focus, we can begin on the path to liberation and enlightenment.

Let me clarify one point. I do not mean to say that I, myself, am this kind of perfect practitioner. I am exactly the same as you—I see another person's self-cherishing quite clearly, but I am unaware of how it manifests in my own actions of body, speech, and mind. Therefore, I would like to make it clear that I am not giving this commentary on this text because I am confident that I have understood it and can practice it, or because I feel that I know all of the intricate details of the lamrim. Rather, I am going on the strength of the faith and the trust that since this is the wish of our teacher, Lama Zopa Rinpoche, it fulfills some necessity, and thereby will have some beneficial result.

FOUR METHODS TO TEACH THE LAMRIM

I, myself, have had teachings on the lamrim many times. I have received the teachings on the *Lamrim Chenmo* from His Holiness Yongdzin Ling Rinpoche, His Holiness the Dalai Lama's senior tutor. I have also received teachings on the eight lamrim texts from His Holiness the Dalai Lama himself. Although I cannot say that I have grasped all the teachings exactly as His Holiness has taught them, I do have the confidence that I have received the blessing of the oral transmission.

It is stated in Lama Tsongkhapa's *Three Principal Paths* that the essence of all the teachings of Buddha is contained within the three turnings of the wheel of Dharma. The lamrim, in turn, takes the heart of the three turnings and makes it available for one individual to practice. Through understanding and meditating on lamrim, it is possible to realize renunciation, bodhichitta, and emptiness. Once you have studied lamrim, you hold the key that opens the door to the entire expanse of the teachings.

It is important to understand that the practice of the graduated path to enlightenment is not something exclusive to the teachings of Lama Tsongkhapa. Nor is it correct to say that the lamrim tradition began with Lama Tsongkhapa as such, because all of these teachings have their source in the teachings of Buddha himself. Nor should you think that lamrim is something exclusive to the Gelug tradition. Perhaps some of you are even wondering if you have to be a follower of the Gelug tradition to practice the lamrim. The answer to this is no. The point of the lamrim is not to make you a Gelugpa. The point of the lamrim is to improve your mind, develop your compassion, and eliminate your grasping at true existence. To think that practicing the lamrim makes you a Gelugpa is another support for your ignorance. The lamrim is the path and practice for individuals of the three scopes—the small, medium, and great scope—and the subject matter is common to the Nyingma, Kagyu, Sakya, and Gelug traditions.

In our everyday lives, before we make a material purchase, we examine the quality of whatever it is we are planning to buy. Of course, no matter how big a mistake we make in the purchase of a material item, that loss will only affect us for a short time. But if, when choosing a spiritual path, we fail to analyze or research the path we plan to adopt and then make a mistake, that mistake can affect us much more deeply.

Buddha advised:

Bhikshus and wise ones,
As gold is burnt, cut, and rubbed
Take my advice by examining my speech well—
Not [merely] for the sake of respect.

These words advise us to check the validity of the Buddhadharma before accepting any of these practices as our own path. This is an important point, and we should take care to do this to the best of our ability. We can test the validity of the teachings by examining whether or not those that are categorized as the actual presentation can be faulted by valid cognition, whether or not those that are categorized as slightly hidden teachings can be faulted by inferential valid cognition, and whether or not those that are categorized as extremely hidden phenomena can be faulted by the inferential cognition of belief. It is important to understand the way these cognitions function in order to be able to apply proper analysis. We will discuss this topic further later on.

According to tradition, there are four methods by which the lamrim teachings are commonly presented.

The first method, which is recommended for beginners, is known as direct explanation. In this method of presentation, the teacher clarifies each point of the outline explicitly and in detail in order to help the student develop a clear and complete understanding. A faultless understanding is essential to fruitful meditation. It is commonly said that we must begin on the path by listening extensively.[2] From this listening we can develop an understanding of the teachings, and through this understanding we can cultivate meditation. There is no food for meditation if we do not have understanding, and there is no understanding if we have not listened.

In the second method of presenting the lamrim, the teacher points out the faults and mistakes in the mind of the student directly and then teaches their antidotes.

In the third method of presentation, the teacher gives instructions based on his or her own spiritual experience and realization of the subjects.

The fourth method of presentation is the gradual method. A student being trained in this manner may first be instructed on the subject of precious human rebirth and then sent away to meditate upon it. Until the student shows signs of having generated a complete experience of that subject, the next topic will not be taught. This method takes months and years, for which we don't have time.

This commentary will be given primarily according to the first method of presentation.

BRIEF HISTORY OF THE LAMRIM

The *Lamrim Chenmo* is the most elaborate explanation on the graduated path to enlightenment that exists within the Gelug tradition. It is unique in that it utilizes scriptural authority in addition to perfect logic and reasoning in order to clarify all doubts on the subject matter. The result of this is that whatever understanding of Dharma that the student gains from studying this text is unshakable.

Traditionally, there are eight great lamrim texts. Three were composed by Lama Tsongkhapa: the *Great Treatise on the Stages of the Path to Enlightenment,* the *Medium Treatise on the Stages of the Path to Enlightenment,* and the *Small Treatise on the Stages of the Path to Enlightenment.* Two lamrims in conjunction with the tantric path were composed by the Panchen Lamas: the *Quick Path* by Panchen Losang Chokyi Gyaltsen, and the *Blissful Path* by Panchen Losang Yeshe. As well, there are two lamrim texts composed by the Third and Fifth Dalai Lamas: *Essence of Refined Gold* by the Third, and its commentary *Instruction From Manjushri,* which was composed by the Fifth. The eighth is the lamrim text composed by Dakpo Ngawang Drakpa which is known as the *Essence of Eloquent Sayings.*

Lama Tsongkhapa composed the *Lamrim Chenmo* in the late part of his life, around the age of forty-seven. After completing his summer retreat in Tibet in a place known as Reting, Lama Tsongkhapa composed the prayers of request to the lineage lamas of the lamrim, at which time it is said that he had a direct vision of the lineage lamas, which means that he actually saw them in the same way that we see one another now. In this vision, the lineage lamas appeared to dissolve one by one into each other, until eventually all of them dissolved into the great pandit Lama Atisha. Lama Atisha then pledged his commitment to support and help Lama Tsongkhapa with the composition and teaching of the text. Then Lama Atisha in turn absorbed into Lama Tsongkhapa himself.

Lama Tsongkhapa was also known to have direct visionary experiences of Manjushri. In one of these instances, Manjushri taught him the subject matter of the *Three Principal Paths,* which is a short text in which the instructions on developing renunciation, bodhichitta, and the wisdom realizing emptiness are presented in a very skillful, precise manner. Later, when Lama Tsongkhapa was composing the *Lamrim Chenmo,* Manjushri challenged him, saying that there was no need, as the entire path to enlightenment was already set forth in the *Three Principal Paths.* Lama Tsongkhapa explained that in order to create an even more profound presentation, he wished to combine the subject matter of the *Three Principal Paths* with the structure of Lama Atisha's *Lamp for the Path to Enlightenment,* in which the method of practicing the path is organized into the framework of the three scopes.

During the actual composition of the text, Lama Tsongkhapa wrote the sections on the small, medium, and the great scope of the *Lamrim Chenmo* straight through up until the section on superior insight. When he reached that section he stopped, doubting whether writing it would be of benefit. At that point, Manjushri appeared to him and advised that he continue, saying that it would be moderately beneficial, even if not greatly beneficial.

Five Preeminent Qualities

The *Lamrim Chenmo* is praised for possessing five preeminent qualities. The first is its manner of explanation—that it contains Manjushri's explanations of renunciation, bodhichitta, and wisdom, and that this subject matter is further enriched by the structure of the three scopes as presented in Lama Atisha's *Lamp for the Path to Enlightenment.* The second preeminent quality of the text is the unmistaken order in which the topics are set forth. The third quality is the excellence of those who requested that it be taught. This refers to the disciples of Lama Tsongkhapa who were renowned for their knowledge, their realizations, their goodness of heart, and their diligence in the spiritual path. The fourth quality is the auspiciousness of the place where it was written—Reting was actually named by Shakyamuni Buddha in the sutras as a place where, in the future, the teachings on the profound and the extensive path would arise and flourish. The last quality is the auspiciousness of the entourage. This refers to the two heart disciples of Lama Tsongkhapa who were present when the composition of the *Lamrim Chenmo* took place.[3]

HOW TO TEACH THE LAMRIM

There are two schools of thought regarding the basis upon which to begin the activity of teaching the lamrim. The first, in accordance with the tradition as established in the ancient monastic university of Nalanda, which was renowned for its many great learned masters and accomplished practitioners, states the prerequisite of three purities. These are the purity of the teacher's speech, the purity of the student's mind, and the purity of the subject matter.

The purity of the teacher's speech means that there must be no mistakes on the part of the teacher in explaining the sequence of the path.

The purity of the motivation of the student means that the students should ensure that they are not listening to the teachings with the wish to become learned and well known for their expertise in the subject. They must also be free of the motivation of coming to the teachings in order to look for mistakes in the presentation, or with a feeling of competitiveness toward their peers.

The purity of the Dharma means that the subject matter must be unmistaken and complete in all aspects. This refers to the fact that the authority of the two lineages of method and wisdom should be established through the lineage masters and rooted in the teachings of Buddha himself.

The second school of thought regarding the basis upon which to begin the teaching of the lamrim is in accordance with the great monastic university of Vikramashila. In this method, the preeminent qualities of the author and the Dharma itself are explained, so that one might develop respect and appreciation for these instructions. Since, in present times, we tend not to examine the meaning of the Dharma, but only look at the words, and since we are less likely to rely on the Dharma itself, but rather depend too much on the person, the Vikramashila system is perhaps the most suitable for us. Therefore, I will begin my explanation of the text with a discussion of these points.

THE OPENING STANZAS

I prostrate to the Guru Manjushri.

Body produced from millions of excellent virtues,
Speech fulfilling the wishes of countless sentient beings,
Mind seeing all objects of knowledge as they exist,
I prostrate to Buddha Shakyamuni.

According to custom, a philosophical text in the Tibetan tradition begins with lines of praise, the author's commitment to complete the writing, and words of encouragement for the student to study and practice the subject matter.

The praise may be dedicated to Manjushri, or to all the buddhas and bodhisattvas, or to any of them. The object of praise depends on the subject matter: texts from the Vinaya Pitaka traditionally begin with a praise to Shakyamuni Buddha; texts from the Sutra Pitaka traditionally begin with lines of praise to the buddhas and bodhisattvas; and texts from the Abhidharma Pitaka often begin with lines of praise to Manjushri. Alternatively, we can say that when the praise is directed to Shakyamuni Buddha, it indicates that the subject of the text will be the higher training in ethics. When the praise is directed to the buddhas and bodhisattvas, the subject matter will be the higher training in concentration. When a text begins with praise to Manjushri, the subject matter will be the training in higher wisdom.

The *Lamrim Chenmo* begins with the words, "Namo Guru Manjughoshaya," which is a line of homage in Sanskrit. The Sanskrit is used in order create a connection to the source language in the mind of the reader, to encourage receptivity to the blessings of this particular text, and also to establish the authority of the text as having been translated from the original language. The translation of this particular Sanskrit line is: "To the guru, Manjushri, I prostrate." Arya Manjushri and Lama Tsongkhapa had an extremely close relationship, that of direct teacher and disciple. Lama Tsongkhapa received extensive teachings from Arya Manjushri on both the profound view of wisdom and the extensive method of conduct, and thus he offers the first line of praise to Arya Manjushri, his guru. The second line of praise is offered to the body of Shakyamuni Buddha. This is followed by praise of the speech, which fulfills all the wishes of sentient beings, and praise of the holy mind of Buddha, which sees all existence exactly as it is.

These lines of praise are meant to indicate to us that enlightenment is not self-arisen, but rather results from causes and conditions that are virtuous by nature. These causes and conditions are the determination to emerge from cyclic existence, or the mind of renunciation, the wish to attain enlightenment solely for the welfare of others, or the mind of bodhichitta, and the wisdom realizing emptiness. These, in turn, come forth as a result of extensive listening to the teachings, cultivation of the understanding of the teachings, and subsequent meditation upon them. The result of the complete accumulation of the merit of virtue and the merit of wisdom is an enlightened holy body, holy speech, and holy mind. If we reflect in this way on the significance of these lines of praise, a sense of faith and respect will arise easily, and there will be much greater meaning in the praise and prostrations that we offer.

The next stanzas of praise in the *Lamrim Chenmo* are offered to Arya Manjushri and Arya Maitreya, and then to Nagarjuna and Asanga, who are considered the great revivers of the teachings of Buddha. The main lineage of the profound path of wisdom begins with Manjushri and is passed to Nagarjuna. In the same way, the lineage of the extensive path of method is passed from Shakyamuni Buddha to Maitreya and then to Asanga. Nagarjuna came about four hundred years after the passing of Buddha, and Asanga came about five hundred years after that. Both were foretold by Buddha. These two lineages were eventually combined in Lama Atisha, who is regarded as the treasury of the essential advice of Buddha.

The last verse of praise pays homage to the "eyes that view all the vast teachings"—the spiritual teachers: Lama Tsongkhapa, all the direct and indirect lineage gurus, the Kadampas[4] of the textual lineage, and the Kadampas of the instruction lineage. These lineage holders and one's own root guru are considered to be the supreme gateway to liberation.

The next stanza addresses Lama Tsongkhapa's personal reasons for undertaking the writing of this text and his pledge of commitment to writing it. Earlier we discussed the external conditions that contributed to its writing: the auspicious place of Reting, Arya Manjushri's involvement, the auspicious gathering, and so forth. In addition to that, the internal conditions were Lama Tsongkhapa's strong wish to clarify the ignorance of sentient beings, his wish to show that the various teachings of Buddha are the one medicine eliminating all suffering, and his wish to complete the offering of practice to his teachers.

The promise to compose the text is followed by the presentation of the description of the disciple who is qualified to receive these teachings. Such a disciple must be blessed with a perfect human rebirth, must have the wish to make that rebirth meaningful, and must possess a mind not darkened by bias. He or she must also be honest and blessed with the ability to discriminate between what is right and what is wrong.

THE EXCELLENT QUALITIES
OF THE AUTHOR

IN THE OUTLINE OF THE ROOT TEXT, the first topic is establishing the excellent qualities of the author in order to substantiate the authentic source of the teachings. The second topic is knowing the excellent qualities of the Dharma in order to generate respect for the instructions. The third is how to teach and listen to the Dharma. And the fourth is the actual advice guiding the disciple on the stages of the path to enlightenment.

All of the Dharma is rooted in the teachings of Shakyamuni Buddha. Over time, Buddha's teachings have been further clarified by the great commentaries of the Indian masters, which in turn have been meditated upon by great yogis who not only practiced, but also actually achieved the experiences of those practices. These three criteria assure us of the excellent qualities of the Dharma. The *Lamrim Chenmo* was composed by Lama Tsongkhapa, but has its source in the *Sutra on the Perfection of Wisdom,* the explicit teachings on wisdom given by Buddha himself. As a commentary to the *Sutra on the Perfection of Wisdom,* Maitreya wrote *Ornament of Clear Realization,* which focuses on the method aspects of the path. Then Lama Atisha wrote *Lamp for the Path to Enlightenment,* a commentary on *Ornament of Clear Realization,* which establishes the path and practice for individuals of three scopes, or three levels of capacity. However, Lama Atisha's *Lamp for the Path to Enlightenment* is very, very abbreviated—it is only about three pages long. Thus, for the benefit of the beings of future generations, Lama Tsongkhapa wrote this extremely detailed explanation of Lama Atisha's *Lamp for the Path to Enlightenment* called the *Great Treatise on the Stages of the Path to Enlightenment,* or the *Lamrim Chenmo.*

In a manner of speaking, we can say that the composer of *Lamp for the Path to Enlightenment* is also the composer of the *Lamrim Chenmo.* Of course, if we were to debate it, we would have to accept that this is not directly so, since it is clear that Lama Atisha did not actually compose the *Lamrim Chenmo*. However, some scholars say that Lama Tsongkhapa is the same mental continuum, or the reincarnation, of Lama Atisha. And others say that rather it is because the meaning of the *Lamrim Chenmo* is no different than the meaning of Atisha's text that Lama Atisha can be considered the author of both.

The *Lamrim Chenmo* begins with the discussion of its composer in order to inspire us to develop faith, which is the basis upon which our minds will transform. The lineage masters of the text are mentioned in order to create the understanding that the result of spiritual practice does not arise out of nowhere. When we reflect on the biography of any one of these great spiritual masters, we see that each has an exemplary life story characterized by the extensive training and practice that enabled the attainment of realizations. These names are not mentioned merely in order to authenticate this particular subject matter. The subject matter of the lamrim totally validates itself.

LAMA ATISHA

Lama Atisha's ordination name was Dipamkara Sri Jñana. "Lama Atisha," as he is known in Tibet, was a name offered by Jangchub Oe, the Tibetan who invited Lama Atisha to Tibet. The name Atisha means "most excellent one." Lama Atisha was the crown jewel of all the learned beings of ancient India; he had the most extensive knowledge, the most extensive compassion, and was the most excellent in every aspect. In this presentation of the biography of the teacher, first we will discuss the perfect circumstances into which he took birth. Secondly, we will discuss the many ways that he studied and acquired knowledge. And thirdly, we will discuss how he put all this knowledge into service to benefit others.

Lama Atisha was born in Bengal, in the eastern part of present day India, around the year 982 C.E. He was born the second son of three into a royal family. From his youth he was known for his exceptionally altruistic mind and his incredibly good nature. From as young as ten years old, Lama Atisha naturally felt a sense of refuge in the Buddha, Dharma, and Sangha. He understood the nature of refuge perfectly, as well as all the qualities of the objects of refuge, and at a young age he was able to explain them all for the benefit of others.

As a prince, Lama Atisha was brought up to take over the leadership of his father's kingdom. However, in his biography it is stated that from a young age he had many dreams in which wisdom beings spoke to him, warning him that it would be a terrible loss if he were to become totally distracted by the quagmire of worldly existence. As a result, Lama Atisha sought out the spiritual path, and studied with the most excellent teachers of the time, such as Lama Rahula Gupta Aradhuti. He became extremely proficient in the study and practice of all the teachings of Buddha in both the Sutrayana and the Tantrayana. At the age of twenty-nine, Lama Atisha took the vows of full ordination from the Mahasangika abbot Shilarakita. From that point forward, his practice of ethics became extremely inspired. Even when traveling Lama Atisha carried a stupa, and upon creating any small nonvirtue, he purified it immediately in front of the holy object.

Throughout the course of his life, Lama Atisha was known to have studied with 157 great masters. And yet, even after such extensive study with so many teachers, Lama Atisha still wondered, "What is the quickest way to attain enlightenment?" This question led him to Lama Serlingpa, from whom he learned the various techniques for cultivating bodhichitta and the principles of thought transformation, and trained in the precepts of the bodhisattva vow. Lama Atisha completed the common training in concentration through the nine stages of placing the mind, took tantric vows, and, through his secret practice of the generation stage, Lama Atisha obtained the level of uncommon single-pointed concentration. On the basis of this he accomplished the wisdom of the combined practice of superior insight and concentration, which are common to the outer schools, as well as the uncommon wisdom practice of the completion stage.

Through the course of his study and practice Lama Atisha generated bodhichitta, and then returned to India where he taught extensively. He was renowned for his excellence in dialectics, and in Bodhgaya he had great debates with practitioners of other schools, emerging victorious time and again. Within the Buddhist schools, Lama Atisha corrected and cleared away all doubts and wrong views, and was well respected by all the philosophers of the time. In this way he accomplished many activities of benefit for sentient beings and the Dharma.

During the time of Lama Atisha, the Dharma was very well established in India, but in Tibet there was a lot of controversy surrounding it. Initially, the teachings of Buddha were brought into Tibet by various Dharma kings who acted as patrons. Later on, there was a particular king in Tibet known as Langdharma who was opposed to Buddhism and made it his life's mission to destroy it. After he passed away, the teachings were slowly revived in Tibet, but with its revival there arose a lot of distortion and misunderstanding as to what exactly Dharma was. At that time in Tibet, people who studied sutra did not accept tantra, and people who had some understanding of the tantric teachings did not accept the teachings of the sutras at all. They had no idea how to combine these two aspects of Buddha's instructions into a single path to enable one individual to attain enlightenment.

During this time, King Lha Lama Yeshe Oe sent some of the best young scholars from Tibet to India to study, and wished to invite the most exceptional teachers from India to Tibet to re-establish Buddhism. In the course of his travel to India to extend this invitation, Lha Lama Yeshe Oe himself was captured, held hostage, and eventually executed. His relative Jangchub Oe then sent the great translator and scholar Naktso Lotsawa to India with an offering of gold to extend the invitation to Lama Atisha. Eventually Naktso Lotsawa and his company of scholars managed to meet with Lama Atisha, and told him of the miserable condition of the Dharma in Tibet and of the incredible lengths that Lha Lama Yeshe Oe and Jangchub Oe had taken to benefit the Dharma, and invited Lama Atisha to come to Tibet.

Upon hearing their story, Lama Atisha said that he would think about their request. He then petitioned his monastery, and was granted permission to go on the condition that he return to India within three years. During this time, Lama Atisha had a vision of Arya Tara in which she told him that a trip to Tibet would bring forth great benefit. In particular, Arya Tara told him that if he met with a lay disciple there, together they could accomplish much for the Dharma and sentient beings. However, Arya Tara also told Lama Atisha that if he made the trip to Tibet, his life would be shortened by twenty years. But Lama Atisha decided that if his presence in Tibet would bring such incredible benefit for Dharma and sentient beings, it would be worthwhile.

When Lama Atisha arrived in Tibet, Jangchub Oe requested teachings that would benefit beings by way of instructions on cause and effect and bodhichitta. Jangchub Oe did *not* request the quickest method to attain enlightenment, but rather the type of teachings that would most benefit the people at that time—a means of practice by which they could incorporate the entire scope of the teachings of both sutra and tantra into their spiritual path. Thus, Lama Atisha was inspired to compose *Lamp for the Path to Enlightenment,* which is the root of all the lamrim teachings. This is why *Lamp for the Path* begins with the words "At the instigation of the fortunate disciple Jangchub Oe."

Most of us have taken a great many empowerments, initiations, and oral transmissions of various tantric deities. And yet in actuality, the profound practices of tantra can only be established upon the foundation of the training in the three paths. In general, we say that we have received such and such an initiation of such and such a deity, and so forth. In reality, however, the level of empowerment received is only in accordance with the level of the practitioner. Merely being in the audience when the empowerment is going on does not mean that we receive it. Practitioners who have spontaneous renunciation mind, spontaneous wisdom knowing emptiness, and spontaneous great compassion definitely receive the perfect empowerment. If, however, we are able to generate renunciation, wisdom, and compassion only with great effort, we take the initiation on another level. Then again, if we are totally ignorant of renunciation, wisdom, and compassion, we receive the empowerment at the level of a blessing.

If we take an initiation with the motivation of achieving long-term benefit for ourselves and for other sentient beings, it is definitely possible that we can experience a positive result. But sometimes in the Tibetan community people do not have this motivation, but rather feel great enthusiasm for empowerments and long-life initiations where there are lots of blessed things to drink and take home. People feel as if they receive some kind of blessing from the initiating lama simply for being there. However, their interest in practicing the three paths or learning about the lamrim is not as great. This way of thinking has not yet taken hold in Western communities, and we should take care not to let this happen in the future.

Of course, when we hear about attaining enlightenment "quickly and even more quickly," as it says in the tantric texts, naturally we are drawn to the concept. Yet in order to accomplish such a result, we must create its causes. The concept of bliss and emptiness that is taught in tantra is founded in the sutra teachings. The teachings on the perfection of wisdom in the sutras are exactly the same as those in tantra—as taught by Nagarjuna, all phenomena are merely labeled and empty of inherent existence by the reasoning of dependent arising. In order to ensure that the levels of our practice are in accordance with our capacity, the study of the Sutrayana is essential.

To return to Lama Atisha, although he had promised to spend only three years in Tibet, he was continuously requested by his main disciple Dromtonpa to stay longer. Despite this, at the end of the three years, Lama Atisha began his journey home, but was barred from crossing into India by a local war at the border. Thus, in accordance with Dromtonpa's request, Lama Atisha remained in Tibet after all.

Eventually, Naktso Lotsawa returned to India with Lama Atisha's composition of *Lamp for the Path to Enlightenment.* It was traditional in the ancient monasteries of the time for the great learned masters to compose writings that were then presented and examined before their peers. If a particular composition met all expectations, the text was highly praised. However, if a text contradicted scriptural authority or logic, it was totally disregarded. Lama Atisha's *Lamp for the Path to Enlightenment* was presented at such a yearly event and was unanimously commended, with the comment that Lama Atisha would never have written such a text as this had he remained in India, because there was absolutely no reason for him to do so since Dharma was already so well established. Lama Atisha had written this extremely beautiful text on the stages of the path to enlightenment in order to suit the circumstances of the Tibetan people. All the Indian masters of that time praised this work and said that Lama Atisha's presence in Tibet had been no less beneficial than his presence in India, and thereby allowed him to remain there. By that writing in itself, they felt that Lama Atisha's time had been truly well spent.

Perhaps you feel I am only telling a story, but actually this is a very meaningful story. To hear a biography such as this one is very beneficial, since knowing the life stories of such teachers can inspire you to remember their kindness in ensuring that the Dharma exists in your life today. In the present there is a great danger of forgetting the effort and determination of the past great masters. If you think about their kindness, you will develop faith, which will make your mind suitable to receive blessings. Also, by remembering the kindness of such eminent teachers as Lama Atisha and their incredibly wondrous, virtuous work in the service of the Dharma and sentient beings, you will accumulate great stores of merit. The biographies of the great teachers of the past should serve as examples upon which to model your own practice.

LAMA TSONGKHAPA

When we contemplate the eminent qualities of the author of the *Lamrim Chenmo* itself, Lama Tsongkhapa, we should be aware of the extensive listening, study, and meditation that he engaged in, and the internal experience of those practices that he accomplished. In *Lines of Experience,* Je Tsongkhapa says: "I, the yogi, practice this way. You who are interested in liberation should practice likewise." It is in the context of knowing the way in which he practiced that we establish his greatness.

In the time of Shakyamuni Buddha, Lama Tsongkhapa was born as a brahmin. During this lifetime, he offered Buddha a crystal rosary and made prayers that he would be able to benefit sentient beings and spread the teachings of Buddha without concern for personal hardship and so on. As a result of these prayers, Lama Tsongkhapa was born into the world in eastern Tibet around the year 1357. At the age of three he took his first lay vows, and at eight he took the vows of a novice monk. When he was sixteen years old, Lama Tsongkhapa came to Central Tibet to further his education.

Later in his life, having studied and practiced extensively, Lama Tsongkhapa developed the wish to travel to India to increase his understanding of the *Madhyamaka*, or Middle Way, view, and also of the Guhyasamaja and Chakrasamvara tantras. While he was considering leaving Tibet, he was warned by an Indian yogi that travel to India would bring him renown as a scholar and abbot, but would hinder his ability to benefit sentient beings by shortening his lifespan considerably. Therefore, Lama Tsongkhapa remained in Tibet in order to be of the greatest possible benefit to others.

Although he studied the philosophy of the Madhyamaka extensively, to ordinary observation Lama Tsongkhapa manifested the appearance of having difficulty ascertaining the final difference between the views of the two Madhyamaka schools. On the advice of Arya Manjushri, he undertook extensive purification and accumulation practice at Ulca Choling, south of Lhasa, on the basis of which he clarified all doubts and realized the perfect Madhyamaka view. It was following this that he began the composition of the *Lamrim Chenmo*.

The Gelug tradition, which considers Lama Tsongkhapa its founder, derives its name from the monastery that Lama Tsongkhapa built in Tibet called Ganden. The Tibetan word *Gelugpa* means "practitioner of the system of Ganden." Also, in earlier times, those practitioners who were particularly strong in the tradition of Vinaya, or the practice of ethics, wore small yellow hats. It is said that Lama Tsongkhapa thought this was auspicious, and thus wore a yellow hat himself. The tradition of calling Gelug practitioners the "Yellow Hats" thus derives from this. Yellow hats are still worn today in the Gelug tradition for ceremonies and special events.

THE GREATNESS OF THE DHARMA

T HERE ARE TWO WAYS of approaching our study of the Dharma. We can listen to and study the teachings seeking to overcome our negative thoughts, or we can listen to and study the teachings with the wish to acquire an intellectual knowledge of the subject matter, without interest in dealing with our emotions. The correct way to study a spiritual path is with the intention to use the knowledge we gain to subdue our negative states of mind. It can sometimes happen that a person develops a very good understanding of a spiritual path and is able to explain it quite well, but is unable to actually put it into practice.

For example, in Tibet there was a geshe who was very learned in many subjects, but unfortunately was unable to put his learning into practice. After he passed away he was reborn as a ghost with a donkey's head, donkey's hooves, and a human's body.

In Tibet before 1959, students of the major schools would gather in the winter for a great debate. They would have six weeks of serious study of Dharmakirti's *Commentary on the "Compendium on Valid Cognition,"* a text on logic and reasoning. The winter in Tibet is very cold, so all the monks would put their upper robes over their heads to keep warm. It was said during those times that it was particularly important to win the midnight debate sessions, because you could never be certain with whom you were debating since all the monks had covered heads. You could be debating with the donkey-headed monk and not know it, and in that situation a loss could create a lot of obstacles. However, if you came out victorious, it was considered very auspicious, and your wisdom was sure to increase. In the evening all the monks would gather together in a circle before the debating session, and each monk would have to clap his hands. A particular monk would clap, then the one next to him would clap, and so on, all the way around the circle. This was also a way to check for the donkey-monk, as he couldn't clap—for he had no hands.

Therefore, in the monasteries if a person studies very well, but cannot put that study into practice, we sometimes joke that that person will be reborn as a donkey-headed monk.

FOUR GREAT QUALITIES

The lamrim is especially renowned for having as its main objective the purpose of subduing the mind of its negativities. There are four great qualities of the lamrim teachings, which demonstrate how they can benefit us.

The first is that when we understand the lamrim, all of the teachings of Buddha—the sutras, the tantras, the teachings on the perfection of wisdom, and so forth—appear to our minds as complementary. Superficially, the views of the four philosophical views of Buddhism—the Sautrantika, Vaibashika, Chittamatra, and the Madhyamaka schools—may sometimes appear contradictory. But for someone who is truly interested in cultivating the pure view of ultimate truth, understanding the Vaibashika view becomes a condition enabling that person to understand the Sautrantika view; understanding the Sautrantika view becomes a condition enabling that person to understand the Chittamatra view; and understanding the Chittamatra view becomes a condition enabling the correct comprehension of the Madhyamaka view.

We all regard the wisdom that realizes emptiness as something very, very important, and we have a great wish to develop our understanding of it. If we go about it correctly, we study the views of the four schools in the above order. If we do so, when we eventually begin our study of the Madhyamaka view, our understanding will be very solid and pure because our foundation is so strong. However, if we focus on the Prasangika viewpoint alone, without examining the other schools, we actually do not have a very sound basis for developing that wisdom. In particular, if we do not have a clear idea of the object to be negated from the point of view of the lower schools, it will be difficult to have a clear picture of the object to be negated from the point of view of the higher schools. According to the view of the Prasangika-Madhyamika, or the Middle Way-Consequentialists, the object to be negated is very, very subtle and very difficult to apprehend without understanding the grosser objects to be negated of the lower schools.

We can understand that all the Buddha's teachings are complementary in terms of one person's path to enlightenment by using the analogy of a tree. The fruit—the ultimate attainment—is enlightenment. Some of the teachings are the root, some are the branches, some are the trunk, some teachings are the leaves, and so forth. All of them together lead to the fruit. That is how it should appear. The study of lamrim empowers us to see the noncontradictory nature of all the various aspects of the teachings. This is the first greatness of the teachings.

The second greatness of the lamrim teachings is that they allow us to realize all of Buddha's teachings as personal advice. While it may be very easy for us to perceive *some* of the subjects within the lamrim as clear counsel for our practice, when we begin to study the philosophical explanations of the view and so forth, we may find ourselves thinking that this is merely a great deal of intellectual information, and we may feel that it is difficult for us to see how they relate to our lives. We might feel that one part of the teachings is intended to serve us solely as an intellectual experience, while another part is intended for practice. If we differentiate the Dharma into parts that are practiced and parts that are solely informative, we are making a big mistake. Whatever the scripture or whatever the explanation, there is no such differentiation. To think that any portion of the teachings is not to be practiced means that we are incurring the transgression of abandoning the Dharma. Moreover, if we are unable to see some of the teachings as personal instruction, it is hard for us to have faith and respect for them, and we run the risk of coming to disregard these teachings, or thinking less of them, or creating the profoundly negative karma of abandoning the Dharma altogether.

For example, there is no doubt that the cultivation of the altruistic mind of bodhichitta, that is, renouncing self and cherishing others, is a subject that is meant to be practiced. What is the origin of this subject? Maitreya's *Ornament of Clear Realization* says that cultivating the mind of bodhichitta is only for the benefit of others, and in order to fulfill the wishes of this mind of bodhichitta, we have to attain enlightenment. What is the source of this explanation? Its source is the sutras, the teachings of Buddha himself.

All of the teachings of Buddha should appear as a form of practice for us to undertake. To have studied Dharma very extensively but be unable to apply it to our own lives is like training a horse to race, and then taking it to the racetrack and letting it run all over the place. Once the teachings appear as personal advice, as instruction for us to practice, we have the basis to generate realizations. The lamrim is like the reins of the horse that guide it in the right direction, and the philosophical explanations are the horse itself. The sign that we have really grasped the lamrim is that we are able to derive a very clear understanding of whatever philosophical text we study, based on our background in lamrim.

You can go about studying the lamrim in two ways. One way is to study the lamrim first, and having grasped all its main points, continue on to study the scriptures that further expand upon those points. In this way the lamrim becomes like a key that opens all the volumes of scripture, and the other texts further clarify the points as explained in the lamrim. The second way is to study the scriptures very extensively first, and then study the points of the lamrim using this background knowledge.

For example, in order to develop a more profound understanding of the section on superior insight in the *Lamrim Chenmo,* we need to rely upon the explanations given in texts such as *Root Wisdom of the Middle Way,* by Nagarjuna, and *Illumination of the Thought of the Middle Way,* by Lama Tsongkhapa. These texts contain detailed commentary that can help us to develop our understanding of superior insight. Likewise, in order to gain a more profound understanding of the section on calm abiding in the *Lamrim Chenmo,* we can turn to commentaries on the meditative states and the formless realms, such as the *Ornament for the Mahayana Sutras* and *Ornament of Clear Realization,* two of the five texts by Maitreya. In order to gain understanding of the depth and profundity of the practices of bodhichitta, the four noble truths, the twelve links of dependent origination, or cause and effect, again we should rely on the explanations in *Ornament of Clear Realization* and the second section of Dharmakirti's *Commentary on the "Compendium on Valid Cognition."* To really come to understand impermanence, we should study the first section of *Commentary on the "Compendium on Valid Cognition,"* which contains an in-depth explanation of the logic and reasoning of subtle impermanence. Of course, the lamrim itself explains these points, but studying the additional commentaries will allow us to comprehend the full depth and profundity of the subjects.

I am not telling you all of this to overwhelm you. There are different traditions as regards the approach to explaining the scriptures. Among the lineage masters there are the Kadampas of the instruction lineage and the Kadampas of the textual lineage. The Kadampas of the textual lineage use the resources of many scriptures to explain the finer points of one particular subject in great detail. I've heard it said that the Gelug tradition tends to follow the Kadam tradition that studies the scriptures extensively.

The third greatness of the lamrim is that through our studies of this path we are able quickly to realize the ultimate intention of Buddha. What is the ultimate intention of Buddha? What does Buddha want us to practice and understand? What is Buddha teaching us? As stated in many prayers and practices, the essence of the teachings is contained in the three principal paths: renunciation, bodhichitta, and the wisdom that realizes emptiness. These are the paths that have been praised by all the buddhas and bodhisattvas. These three paths are the ultimate intention of Buddha, and the lamrim—the graduated path to enlightenment—is what enables us to realize them quickly.

The fourth greatness is that the study of the lamrim will cause us to spontaneously cease mistaken actions. This refers in particular to the mistaken action of abandoning Dharma.

These four great qualities should encourage us to study and practice the lamrim. If we don't understand the benefits, we may lack enthusiasm or interest in this path. By coming to appreciate the extraordinary qualities of the lamrim, our studies become meaningful, the understanding that we generate in relation to our studies becomes meaningful, and the meditations that we engage in on this basis become meaningful as well.

HOW TO TEACH AND
LISTEN TO THE DHARMA

IN ORDER TO INSPIRE US to listen and study, the next points address the benefits of teaching and listening to the Dharma.

HOW TO LISTEN TO THE DHARMA

We listen to teachings in order to learn how to protect ourselves from our own nonvirtue and negativity. The teachings of the path and practice of the small scope protect us from the limited mentality whereby we work only for the benefit of this one brief lifetime. The teachings of the path and practice of the medium scope protect us from being attached to the temporary pleasures of cyclic existence. The teachings of the path and practice of the great scope protect us from getting caught up in the attainment of our own individual liberation alone. The teachings of Madhyamaka philosophy protect us from the two extreme views: the view of total nonexistence, and the view of eternalism. In the same way, the teachings of the path and practice of the Mahayana protect us from the extremes of cyclic existence and nirvana's peace. Through listening, we attain liberation. Whatever listening that we do—whether it be listening to lamrim teachings or to the various philosophical explanations of the path—the goal of every moment of it is to attain enlightenment, and the purpose of that attainment is to benefit sentient beings.

We make a lot of mistakes in our life due to not knowing. The first step to eliminating this pattern is to listen. Listening gives us the insight into what to eliminate and what to cultivate in our practice. It is the best way to increase our wisdom, intellect, and insight. As our wisdom and insight increase, our ignorance will lessen. It should be very clear to us that we do all this listening for the purpose of being able to implement the teachings in our life. Whatever we listen to, we should then try to integrate into our thoughts and actions. Through such means we can free ourselves from the prison of karma and delusions.

Through listening we develop the force of understanding, and through the force of understanding we cultivate the force of meditation. It is through the force of meditation that we become able to cultivate the antidotes to the delusions that bind us to cyclic existence. If we have only a little experience listening, then we will have only a little understanding, and thereby very little meditation and very little cultivation of the antidote. Results are dependent on their causes. If the cause of listening is extensive, deep, and profound, then our understanding will be deep and profound, and our meditation too will be deep and profound. Also, if we listen to the teachings with an attitude of faith and respect, the mind of faith becomes a condition for our listening to bear fruit.

The Three Faults of Container

In the *Lamrim Chenmo,* the advice on listening is given within the context of abandoning the three faults of container and cultivating the six discriminating attitudes. The three faults of container are established on the basis of the container of our own minds. Our minds should not be like a container with a hole, a container that is upside-down, or a container that is dirty.

A container with a hole cannot keep anything inside. In the same way, we should not listen to the teachings with a mind that does not hold them—if the nectar of the Dharma is poured in and nothing remains in our mind, we possess the first fault of the container. We should listen with our eyes looking at the teacher, our body facing the teacher, our ears hearing the words of the teacher, and so forth.

An upside-down container is being physically present, but mentally someplace else, like in front of the computer sending an email.

A dirty container is, for example, listening to the lamrim teachings with a selfish motivation, such as the wish to achieve more happiness for oneself alone.

The Six Discriminating Attitudes

The activity of listening should also be adorned with the ornament of the six discriminating attitudes. These are recognizing oneself as a patient, recognizing the teachings as the medicine or the treatment, recognizing the teacher as the physician, recognizing that diligent practice will cure the sickness, recognizing Buddha as a holy being, and recognizing that the Dharma should be preserved for a long time.

The first of the six is the discriminating attitude whereby one sees oneself as a sick person. On the path of the small scope, the thought of clinging to this lifetime is the sickness that afflicts us. On the path of the medium scope, the sickness is the thought of clinging to the wish for the happiness of future lives within cyclic existence—whether a human rebirth or rebirth in the form or formless realms. On the path of the great scope, the sickness is the self-cherishing thought of clinging to individual liberation from cyclic existence. In a more general sense, when we look at ourselves as a sick person, the sickness can refer to our failings and mistakes in terms of the lamrim. For example, in the first stage of the path our attitudes of despising, disregarding, or being faithless and disrespectful toward our spiritual teachers is the sickness. If we are able to ascertain our failings in relation to each of the subjects of the lamrim, whatever teaching we are listening to will automatically become the medicine.

When we recognize the sickness, and when we are introduced to the teachings as the antidote or the medicine, we automatically understand the third discriminating attitude: seeing the teacher as the physician. Even if we cannot see a spiritual teacher as an enlightened being, if we see the teachings as the antidote to our ailments, we will naturally see the teacher as the physician.

Please remember that you should not limit the practice of the six discriminating attitudes to those times when you are formally listening to teachings. Rather, you should apply them at all times, whether you are sitting in teachings or whether you are meditating in your room.

Although most of us could probably say that we have listened to many teachings, if we have failed to apply the six discriminations, we are not really getting the taste of what we have heard. Even if we listen to every possible teaching, if we lack the attitude of the six discriminations, our mind can shut down toward Dharma. It is really important that we do not let this happen. If we develop this shut-down mentality toward the lamrim in particular, we will become totally helpless. Normally we use water to put out fire, but if we create a mental barrier against the lamrim, then it is as if the water itself has caught fire, and there is no remedy for that.

The six discriminations may appear minor because no great explanation accompanies them, but actually they are essential to learning the Dharma. The benefits of the study of the Dharma will be carried forward lifetime after lifetime. Therefore, we should try to make whatever study we engage in effective, right up until the time of our death. All of the teachings that we have heard should manifest in our actions and in our mind. If our relationship with the study of Dharma never moves past the level of mere information, it's like eating only the skin of a piece of fruit, without ever tasting the flesh inside. Of course, the skin of the fruit has a pleasant taste, but the inside of the fruit is much richer.

By following the first four of the six discriminating attitudes, we are able to generate the fifth, which is seeing Buddha as a holy being. Buddha is considered a holy being because he recognized the subject matter of the lamrim, practiced it, attained the result, and taught what he had learned and experienced. Therefore Buddha is considered the source of the Dharma. We should try to train our minds to recognize this to be true. Additionally, according to the advice of Pabongka Rinpoche, we should try to see the person from whom we are receiving the teachings on the lamrim as a holy being as well.

Having seen the value of the Dharma in our life through the previous five methods, we realize that just as it has been greatly beneficial for us, it could also be beneficial for others. By the force of that thought, we generate the attitude of wishing the Dharma to be long preserved for the benefit of sentient beings, which is the sixth discriminating attitude.

Many Western students have experienced the sixth discriminating attitude to some degree. Although people from the West in general don't seem to have many physical problems, you do have many mental problems. Having received great benefit through the force of the Dharma teachings, you are inspired to bring the teachings to your own countries, to benefit all of your friends and others who are suffering. This is the sixth of the six attitudes: wanting the Dharma to be long preserved for the benefit of others.

HOW TO TEACH THE DHARMA

Again I would like to mention that I am not explaining the points of the path to you here with the idea that I have extensive knowledge or great understanding that I want to share with you. Rather, I am taking this opportunity to explain because in explaining, I have the opportunity to look into the mirror of the teachings and see the image of all my own failings and mistakes. Likewise, as you listen, the Dharma teachings should be like a mirror in which all of the mistakes and failings of your own body, speech, and mind are reflected.

From the side of the teacher expounding the Dharma, the Dharma should be taught with the awareness of its benefits, with respect for the Dharma, and with the knowledge of the difference between suitable and unsuitable students.

Benefits

In the *Sutra of the Inconceivable Mind,* it is stated that there are twenty benefits of explaining the Dharma. Of these twenty benefits, the first six benefits are in the karmic category of what we call results which are similar to the cause.

The first benefit of the six is that by teaching the Dharma to others you are able to keep the ideas fresh in your mind, meaning that you will not forget the Dharma.

The second benefit is that your knowledge becomes experiential. For example, by explaining a subject such as emptiness over and over again, you begin to understand it very clearly in your own mind. On this basis you can develop the wisdom of meditation, and your intellectual knowledge will become an experience.

The third benefit is gaining knowledge or intellect. If you have the experiential knowledge gained through meditation, you would of course also have attained the ordinary intellectual knowledge of the subject matter.

The fourth benefit is that whatever knowledge you have acquired becomes very firm and stable through the process of teaching it. Let's say, for example, that you are training in the bodhisattva's path and someone comes along and says: "This is an incredible, admirable path that you are undertaking, but it's extremely difficult and you are better off working toward individual liberation." If your knowledge is not stable, you may be persuaded to abandon training in the bodhisattva's path. In the same way, if you are trying to realize the highest philosophical view of the emptiness of inherent existence, and someone comes along and tries to encourage you to accept a lower view, if your knowledge is not firm and stable, you may be convinced. If someone talked you out of a Prasangika viewpoint into a Svatantrika viewpoint it wouldn't be so harmful, but if someone talked you out of a higher viewpoint into a viewpoint such as the view of nothingness, where the method is to empty the mind of any kind of focus or intention, it could cause a lot of trouble. If, however, your knowledge of that subject matter has become very firm through teaching it, you are less likely to be persuaded.

The fifth benefit is that through the analysis you naturally engage in while teaching, whatever you have learned through correct assumption becomes the wisdom of inferential valid cognition.

The sixth benefit is that as you become familiar with this conceptual wisdom, it becomes the direct perception of seeing, of meditation, and so forth.

Each of the first six benefits arises from the previous one. Again, these six benefits are the results that are similar to the cause, and the cause is teaching Dharma itself.

The seventh through tenth benefits are the results of separation, which means that due to explaining Dharma, you will be separated from certain negative actions.

The seventh, eighth, and ninth benefits are that teaching lessens the three effects of your poisonous minds: the obsessive mind of attachment, the aggressive mind of anger and hatred, and the mind of ignorance.

The tenth benefit is that because your delusions have been comparatively weakened, your mind comes under their control less frequently.

The eleventh to the nineteenth benefits are in the category of the immediate results of teaching the Dharma.

The eleventh is that you come under the care of all the buddhas and bodhisattvas.

The twelfth is that you come under the protection of all the Dharma protectors.

The thirteenth is that even the worldly gods will help you, so that your power, influence, and magnificence will be enhanced.

The fourteenth benefit is that when you teach the Dharma without any expectations of material gifts, reputation, or respect, other people will not criticize you.

The fifteenth is that you come under the loving care of your spiritual teachers and become an object of faith and trust for your spiritual friends.

The sixteenth benefit is that your speech becomes ethical and virtuous, naturally free from the vices of speaking harsh words and so forth.

The seventeenth is that as a result of this, your own wisdom is enhanced, and when you are in the company of many other learned people, you have a sense of fearlessness and confidence in yourself.

The eighteenth is that you will have more and more happiness of mind.

The nineteenth benefit is that when you teach Dharma with a pure motivation, you become an object of praise and admiration in the eyes of even those individuals who have attained very high levels of the paths and grounds.

The twentieth benefit is categorized as the ripening result: due to practicing the generosity of giving the Dharma, in future lifetimes you will always enjoy and never lack the teachings.

When you speak of the Dharma to others, at a minimum you should have experienced the certainty of faith that arises from extensive listening. Of course, if you have the certainty arising from understanding, that is even better. And if you have the certainty arising from extensive meditation, that is the very best. At first, when you have the opportunity to talk about the Dharma to somebody new, you might find that you feel a sense of hesitation or worry that you might make mistakes. That thought is sometimes rooted in the eight worldly dharmas, whereby you concern yourself with your own reputation and so forth. If instead, you can consider this activity a practice that you are undertaking on the advice of your spiritual teachers, and as long as you have the basic motivation to completely benefit others, you will be able to overcome your doubts and hesitation.

Generating Respect for the Dharma and the Teacher

The next point in the text concerns generating respect for the Dharma and the teacher. Welcoming the teacher with incense and so forth and making a special formal seat for him or her is not just a Tibetan tradition.

It is a mode of conduct that has existed since the time of Buddha himself. We show such respect out of consideration for the preciousness of the Dharma that is being taught.

Also, before receiving teachings we should remember to remove any obstacles that may exist by recalling the meaning of emptiness and reciting the short sutra on the perfection of wisdom, the *Heart Sutra*. This may seem strange to you, as on the one hand we talk about taking all sentient beings as the objects of our compassion, while on the other hand, upon teaching texts and giving empowerments, we chase away interferers. So what is really going on when we offer the gift of a ritual torma cake, or recite the *Heart Sutra* and clap our hands to remove obstacles? When we do these things, we are trying to eliminate the negative mind that grasps the "I" and the manifestations of the three poisonous states of mind that may appear in the form of interferences. These are the obstacles that we are targeting. In reality, we are removing states of mind, as opposed to targeting sentient beings. Sentient beings, it is understood, are always the object of our compassion.

Those Whom We Should Teach and Those Whom We Should Not Teach

The next point is differentiating between those whom we should teach and those whom we should not teach. The sutras say that it is not appropriate to give Dharma teachings without first being requested to do so. To talk about the Dharma to somebody who doesn't wish to hear it is like advertising on television. Even if someone does make such a request, we are still advised to consider whether that individual is a suitable receptacle for the teachings or not. In general, we should not offer the Dharma to people who have no aspiration, no interest, or have not asked.

It is further advised that it is better not to talk about Dharma to someone who is just standing around, or lying around, to someone who is seated higher than you and in grandeur, or while taking a walk. Teaching in these types of situations is considered disrespectful since the mind is not favorably turned toward the Dharma at these times.

At the end of the teachings we should always make extensive dedications for the long existence of the teachings in this world, and the well-being and enlightenment of all sentient beings.

When we teach and listen to the Dharma correctly, this effort in itself will purify all of our past negative karma of disrespecting Dharma. It will also prevent us from creating further negative karmic obscurations in relation to the Dharma. However, if we talk about the most profound topics of the Dharma but lack the proper motivation, the correct action, and the completion of the action, rather than being an antidote to the negative states of mind, whatever we do will only become a support for them.

PART 2

*The Foundation of
Practicing the Lamrim*

Relying on the Spiritual Teacher

HOW TO RELY ON THE SPIRITUAL TEACHER

According to the outline of the root text, the next heading is the actual advice for guiding a disciple on the stages of the path to enlightenment. The first topic within that larger topic is the root of the path, the practice of guru devotion. On the basis of having cultivated guru devotion, the second topic is the instruction on the proper way to practice devotion through our thoughts and actions. These points are explained in a very detailed manner so that we might generate certainty with respect to this subject through extensive listening and understanding, and later gain certainty through meditation using scriptural authority, logic, and reasoning.

The basis of the entire path to enlightenment is rooted in the practice of pure guru devotion, free of mistakes. Making the path a reality in our life is completely dependent upon our reliance on a spiritual teacher. If we are interested in Dharma only on an intellectual or academic level, we will be unable to see the importance of this practice. But as we try to apply the spiritual path to our own lives, as we learn to make the teachings a part of our own experience, the conviction of the necessity of relying upon a spiritual teacher will arise without effort.

Guru devotion is the practice that makes it possible for the path to take root within our minds and for whatever realizations that we have already generated to continue to develop. Our root guru is the source of all of the realizations of the path, from generating calm abiding and bodhichitta, to generating wisdom within our minds. Even to accomplish ordinary things in this life—to gain expertise in the labor of our worldly existence—we must depend upon a teacher who shows us the skills involved in that particular work. If we have to rely upon an instructor to develop even the simple skills of this life, consider how much more important it is to rely upon a teacher in order to accomplish a goal such as enlightenment.

Once we understand the need to practice pure devotion in order to train the mind, we will be able to appreciate the benefits of practicing, the disadvantages of not practicing, and the faults of incurring a breach in our guru devotion practice. We will be able to reflect on the points of training the mind to see the spiritual teacher as Buddha, understand the necessity of doing so, and be assured that it is within our capacity to cultivate this kind of view.

If we wish only to train in the paths of the small or the medium scope, it is not necessary to generate the realizations of guru devotion as explained in the lamrim. But if we wish to train in the entire graduated path to enlightenment, the causal vehicle of the six perfections, and the resultant vehicle of secret mantra to attain the enlightened state of Vajradhara, it is essential to cultivate the realizations of guru devotion as explained here.

I would like to draw your attention to the fact that the early sections of the lamrim include extensive explanations on the generation of loving-kindness, great compassion, and so on. Following this is detailed commentary on the practices of the six perfections, calm abiding meditation, and superior insight. If the intention of the lamrim were to guide the disciple singularly through the Sutrayana, it would seem logical that the section on the great scope would also include extensive explanation on the ten grounds and the five paths of a bodhisattva. It would also include more extensive explanation on complete purification practices according to the Sutra vehicle. But the *Lamrim Chenmo* is not organized this way. This shows that the intent of this text is to guide the disciple through the stages of the path to the practice of Vajrayana, and to the result of Vajradhara's enlightenment.

My own thought is that we all want to attain enlightenment in this short life. To achieve enlightenment as soon as possible, we must practice Vajrayana. In order to practice Vajrayana, we need the foundation of the three principal paths of renunciation, bodhichitta, and the wisdom that realizes emptiness. We also need the firm foundation of guru devotion. If we look at it from this perspective, we will see that training in the practice of guru devotion is very, very important. Of course, if we don't wish to attain enlightenment as soon as possible, then we can think about it.

According to the path of the individual vehicle, there is no requirement to see the spiritual teacher as an actual buddha. According to this path, there is benefit in being able to practice in accordance with the instructions of the spiritual teacher. Conversely, there is harm in not practicing in accordance with the instructions of the spiritual teacher. In the same way, being able to practice in accordance with the instructions of Buddha brings benefit, and not doing so brings harm. Since the harm and the benefit are the same in relation to both Buddha and our own spiritual teacher, in the individual vehicle the spiritual teacher is regarded *like* a buddha but not *as* a buddha. For those merely wishing to attain individual liberation, it is not necessary to regard the spiritual teacher as an actual buddha. However, as we train in the great vehicle and then in the resultant vehicle of the Vajrayana, the progression of our realizations depends much more upon our faith in the guru, and thus we are encouraged to begin training our minds in this practice early on in the stages of the path.

The individual that we consider to be our teacher, our lama, and our guru should not be just any ordinary individual. There are many qualities that the teacher must have in order to fulfill this role in which so much trust is placed. In the same way, there are also qualifications that the student relying upon a spiritual teacher should fulfill. Finally, there are specifications about how the relationship between such a qualified teacher and such a qualified student should be established.

Qualities of the Spiritual Teacher

The *Ornament for the Mahayana Sutras* by Maitreya lists ten qualities that one should seek in a spiritual teacher.

The first is that the mind of the spiritual teacher be completely subdued by the training in ethics, by the vows of individual liberation, and by the bodhisattva vows. Although it is not specifically mentioned, we could also say that the spiritual teacher's mind should be well subdued by the practice of living in the tantric vows.

The second quality is that the mind of the spiritual teacher be peaceful, subdued by the higher training in concentration.

The third quality is that the mind of the spiritual teacher be extremely peaceful, subdued by the higher training in wisdom.

The fourth quality is that the teacher must be more knowledgeable in the subject matter than the disciple. For example, although Lama Atisha held the view of a higher philosophical school than his teacher Lama Serlingpa, from the point of view of the knowledge of instruction of bodhichitta, Lama Serlingpa was more proficient.

The fifth quality is that the spiritual teacher possess joyful perseverance in the acts of benefiting others.

The sixth quality is that the spiritual teacher be rich in bearing all of the oral transmissions of the sutras and tantras. If the teacher lacks the richness of the collection of oral transmissions, he or she will be hindered in his or her capacity to benefit sentient beings.

The seventh quality that the teacher should possess is the direct realization of emptiness, or at the very least the inferential realization of emptiness. A while ago I took a trip to Virginia to give refuge vows to a man in prison. This man wanted to ask me some questions first, so he asked me, "Have you realized emptiness?" He was quite young, maybe around twenty years old. Well, I don't have any realization of emptiness, but I told him I have studied a little bit and so on. After we finished everything I was curious where he had gotten the idea to ask this question. The young man said that he had read it in a lamrim text.

The eighth quality is that the teacher is skilled in expressing him- or herself in order to be able to guide disciples.

The ninth quality is that the teacher is able to lovingly care for the disciple.

The tenth quality that a qualified spiritual teacher should possess is not being easily fed up by having to repeat things.

With these considerations in mind, you may begin to see that for a lama to claim many disciples is not an easy thing. In accordance with the instructions of Buddha, even if the disciple falls sick, the spiritual teacher should be there to care for him or her.

When I was young, I had to memorize a great deal, and one day as I was memorizing a text a senior monk asked a young monk who was in the same room, "Do you want to become a rinpoche?"[5] The senior monk told him, "If you become a rinpoche, you will be treated very well, and be well taken care of," and so forth, but still this young monk was not convinced. He thought and thought, and finally he said no, he didn't want to become a rinpoche. He made his decision very clear, and then the senior monk said, "Why? Why don't you want to become a rinpoche?" And the young monk said, "So much studying, no chance to play!"

But seriously, there really is a lot of responsibility. People give you their trust. People totally depend upon you to be their cause for enlightenment. If you make some slight mistake, one human being's whole life can be destroyed. It's not an easy job. Therefore, if anyone has the wish to teach Dharma, in any place, please be aware of that responsibility.

In summary, a Mahayana spiritual teacher should be able to teach the practices of the three paths without mistake. Also the teacher must be skillful, able to guide disciples faultlessly on the three paths, and adept in the methods to guide them. If the teacher is not skillful in this way, then despite all of his or her knowledge, that teacher will not be able to impart this knowledge to others. Besides being knowledgeable, unmistaken, and skillful in guiding disciples on the three paths, the spiritual teacher should embody bodhichitta. Without bodhichitta, the teacher will be unable to induce the stream of blessings of the Mahayana path.

Even if all of the other ten qualities are lacking, at the very least a spiritual teacher must have trained in ethics, concentration, and wisdom, and have the thought of loving concern for the disciple. Besides these inner qualities, a qualified spiritual teacher should also have listened extensively to the oral transmissions.

In degenerate times such as these, it is very rare that a spiritual teacher who obviously embodies all of the ten qualities appears to us. Of course it's not impossible; those with the karma and the incredible merit will come across such teachers in their lives.

Advice on How to Find a Qualified Teacher

The very best of spiritual teachers is someone who embodies these ten qualities. If we cannot find someone who embodies the ten qualities, we should follow the teacher who embodies at least five of the ten, who has trained in the three higher trainings, and has the thought of loving concern for the disciple. If we cannot find someone like that, at the very least we should find someone who thinks that the future life is more important than this life and who thinks that others are more important than him- or herself.

Since it is said that it is impossible to know someone else's inner realizations, how can we verify these qualities in a spiritual teacher? Although we cannot see the inner qualities directly, it is possible for us to come to know a teacher's speech, personality, and attitude, and from these we can infer the teacher's internal qualities. In addition, there are often external signs that indicate whether someone embodies certain qualities. For example, if someone has generated the realization of the great value and rarity of perfect human rebirth, this person will feel an extreme sense of loss in wasting any time or opportunity. In the same way, when someone has generated a realization of impermanence, there is a certain manner in which a person conducts him- or herself as a result of having had that realization. When someone has generated a particular kind of realization, a particular kind of attitude results.

In order to encounter pure and holy beings in our lives, for our part we need to accumulate merit and purify our negative karma. When we want to examine a material thing, we clean our glasses well, or look under a microscope or through binoculars in order to be able to see it more clearly. In the same way, from our own side we need to accumulate merit and purify the obscurations caused by our negative karma in order to clearly see the pure and holy beings in our lives. It is important that we have a Mahayana spiritual teacher, that we have such a force of guidance in our lives, but these Mahayana spiritual teachers do not come ready-made. As our own understanding of the teachings increases, we can come to see ten of those qualities in the teacher, or five of those qualities in the teacher. And as long as we can see those qualities in the teacher, it doesn't matter whether this particular spiritual teacher is highly regarded by others and well known or not.

If we have not yet met with virtuous friends, or pure and holy beings, we should pray to be able to meet with them. And if we have met the virtuous friend that we are seeking, if such a guiding force is already present in our lives, then we should pray never to be separated from that being for all of our lifetimes to come.

Most of us are very fortunate to have taken teachings from His Holiness the Dalai Lama, who perfectly embodies these ten qualities.

Sometimes when there have been many positive prayers from both sides, a spiritual teacher who embodies the qualities of experiential knowledge, is extremely persevering in virtue, and has great goodness and kindness of heart will meet with a disciple who fulfills all of the basic qualities of a suitable student. If there is such a relationship, free of all nonharmonious things, fully endowed with all harmonious conditions, then, when study takes place with regard to emptiness, liberation, and renunciation, it will not be so hard to achieve the results of spiritual practice.

Qualities of the Disciple

The first quality that you must possess as a disciple is honesty. This means possessing a state of mind that is totally unbiased. A biased mind means that, from your perspective, your own side takes precedence over others'. In this case, honesty in the disciple means honesty in your viewpoint: the way you think, the way you see, the way you feel. The greater the sense of honesty that you are able to cultivate in yourself as a disciple, the more your mind will be free from seeing mistakes in others.

If you truly wish to meet a great Mahayana teacher, it is really important that you give up too much attachment to your own point of view, too much belief in the way that things appear to you. Right now, you rely far too heavily on what appears to your sense consciousness. In fact, the sense consciousness is the grossest level of consciousness. Of course you shouldn't take this too far either—although you should be able to let go of the failings or mistakes in your spiritual teachers that appear to you, you should not go to the extreme of totally disregarding this level of information. You have a very good sense of equanimity toward your own faults, so you should try to apply that same sense of equanimity toward any faults that you may see in your spiritual teachers.

The second quality you should have is the intelligence to be able to differentiate what is right from what is wrong. If you do not have a sense of discriminating wisdom accompanying your sense of honesty, people will take you for a ride. The wisdom that is able to discriminate means, for example, that when you come across an explanation about the disadvantages of cherishing self and the advantages of cherishing others, you have the wisdom to see that this kind of practice is worthwhile. If you were not protected by your own inner discriminating wisdom, it would be possible for someone to come along and say, "Forget about this kind of altruism; you are better off working for your own individual liberation." Then, being convinced of that, you might give up the higher goals of altruism for lesser attainments.

The third quality that you must have is faith and interest in achieving your goals. Although the qualities of the disciple are stated in order as honesty, discriminating wisdom, and an aspiration to achieve your goals, in actual practice you must first cultivate the aspiring interest in your mind. On that basis comes discriminating wisdom. And as a result of that, you will be able to cultivate the unbiased mind of total honesty.

If, as a disciple, you are rich in these three qualities—honesty, discriminating wisdom, and interest—it is profitable for you to rely upon as many spiritual teachers as possible. If, however, you are not rich in the qualities of the disciple, it is better to rely upon fewer teachers, because of the lack of potential within your mind.

Regardless of whether you have taken on a particular spiritual teacher as your personal teacher or not, if you receive teachings from someone, on the path to enlightenment, you should restrain yourself from criticizing whatever mistakes you may see in that teacher. That is the least that you should do. Particularly in the West, people have the habit of immediately expressing whatever comes to their minds. At times this is a very good thing, but when you take this habit to an extreme, it becomes harmful. When you make Dharma connections, regardless of whether you have made the mental commitment to that particular spiritual teacher, out of respect for that connection, it is important to not be critical of whatever failings or mistakes that you may see.

Then again, although in the practice of guru devotion there is a lot of emphasis put on the practice of pure devotion to the spiritual teacher, this doesn't mean that you have to do everything that the spiritual teacher tells you to do, totally disregarding karma or ethics or logical reasoning. Devotion doesn't mean disregarding everything.

When spiritual teachers and disciples come together due to previous karmic connections and by the force of the power of their prayers, the disciple will experience an intuitive sense of faith, which arises in his or her mind upon merely seeing or hearing the name of the spiritual teacher. On the part of the teacher, when seeing a disciple to whom he or she is connected through the power of past prayers, right away there is an intuitive inclination to take care of this disciple. That is how the powerful result of karmic connection and prayer is experienced when suitable disciples meet with suitable teachers.

In degenerate times such as these, sometimes people seek out spiritual teachers, go to teachings, follow advice, and then, in due course of time, when a particular spiritual teacher decides that this is a suitable disciple and goes out of his or her way to take care of that person, the disciple backs out of the situation. There is a story to illustrate this. Once there were two monks returning home, and as they were walking, they noticed a puppy following along behind them. The two monks realized that the puppy must be in desperate need of someone to look after it, but when they stopped to take care of it, it ran away. Yet when they began to walk ahead, the puppy followed them again.

As disciples on the spiritual path, you should make the effort to cultivate the qualifications as stated by Lama Tsongkhapa: an unbiased, honest mind, discriminating wisdom, and the aspiration to seek out your spiritual interests. Once you have met a qualified spiritual teacher, you should cultivate pure devotion through action and through thought.

The Manner of Relying on the Spiritual Teacher

Relying through Thought
Relying On the Spiritual Teacher in General
From the general advice on the kind of attitude with which to rely upon the spiritual teacher according to the *Lamrim Chenmo,* there are nine points, or nine ways in which to devote yourself to the spiritual teacher.

The first of these nine points is the instruction to abandon your sense of independence and develop a sense of reliance or devotion toward your spiritual teacher that is like an obedient son or daughter. You should have the mental attitude that allows your spiritual teacher to guide you without resistance. Being obedient here means making sure that the way in which you think and the way in which you act are harmonious with the wish of the spiritual teacher. Sometimes the teacher will give you certain advice as to what to do or what not to do. Even if from your point of view that particular advice does not appear appropriate or does not seem to fulfill the necessity of the situation, for the sake of being able to train your mind in the practice of pure devotion, you should be able to give up your own interest and follow that advice.

Many of those who serve Lama Zopa Rinpoche can be considered examples of disciples who give up independence and freedom like an obedient child. When you serve Rinpoche, you give up your interest in sleep. You give up your interest in food. And you give up your interest in time for yourself. If you want to serve Rinpoche, you have to be able to give up all of these things.

Upon encountering a pure, virtuous friend, you should think: "What can I do to fulfill the wishes of my spiritual teacher?" You should think like this, rather than being concerned with what you want or what you need. Although at first it may feel like you are giving up a lot—your freedom, your independence, your own interests, and so forth—indirectly, this is the very best way of taking care of yourself. This kind of attitude parallels that of the bodhisattvas, whose only thought is to benefit others, whose attitude embodies the altruism of having totally renounced self to cherish others. By thinking only of others, they have taken care of themselves completely.

The second point from the general advice on devoting yourself to your spiritual teacher is that your mind of devotion to your teacher should be unshakable like a vajra. When you practice devotion, it shouldn't be only for a week, or a month, or at the most a year. Your devotion shouldn't be subject to limitations of time and circumstance. It should be as stable and unchanging as a vajra. If you do not have that vajra-like quality in your devotion, then if someone comes along and tells you that you are just wasting your time, you may be swayed.

The third point is that your mind of devotion to the spiritual teacher should be like the earth. Just as the ground carries all existence, and all things are born and grow on it, in the same way, you should develop the strength of mind willing to shoulder the responsibility of fulfilling the wishes and advice of the spiritual teacher. You should aspire to develop the mind that is never tired of the advice of the spiritual teacher, or tired of the next thing to do. But please understand that having earth-like devotion doesn't mean that you have to actually be able to carry out everything that the spiritual teacher wishes. What it means is that mentally, from your side, you should be determined to fulfill as much of the advice of the spiritual teacher as you possibly can. This means that when the spiritual teacher asks you to do something, you do not think, "Why do I have to do that? My teacher could do it himself." Regardless of how great or small the task, you should maintain a mind like the earth, fully prepared to bear the complete responsibility for fulfilling the advice of your spiritual teacher.

The fourth general point of advice is that your devotion be stable like a mountain. In trying to fulfill the wishes or advice of the spiritual teacher, you are certain to incur both physical and mental hardships. Rather than allowing your sense of devotion to decline under this strain, you should maintain it with the endurance of a mountain. Sometimes in Tibetan we say that when our stomachs are full and the sun is shining, we have the complete appearance of being a very good practitioner. But, when hardships come, we show the aspect of being a totally worldly person. Instead of a type of devotion that is subject to the conditions of a particular situation, you must aspire to cultivate devotion that is stable like a mountain, regardless of the difficulties you may experience.

The fifth point of advice is to cultivate an attitude of devotion that is like the devotion of a servant to the world. This advice counteracts the attitude whereby one wants to do selective service—only wanting to serve in the immediate circle of the spiritual teacher, not wanting to do distant jobs, and only wanting to do those jobs that are high-profile. In the expression of your devotion to your spiritual teacher, you should be able to follow every piece of advice regardless of whether you think it's good or bad, or whether it's near or distant. Your service should be without limitations and conditions. When you are very new to the spiritual path, you may experience the pitfall of wishing only to offer service in the immediate area of the spiritual teacher, where you will be recognized by others. This act of service, however, is completely warped by the eight worldly dharmas.

The sixth point of advice is to develop devotion that is like a sweeper. This means that you should offer service to the spiritual teacher free of the mind of superior complexes. For example, if your spiritual teacher doesn't know anything about computers, and you offer service with an attitude of pride in your own superior knowledge of computers, you are not fulfilling this advice. When you offer service, you must offer service with a mind that is totally free of thoughts of feeling superior and so forth. You must hold your spiritual teacher as the most supreme in every respect, and offer your service with that kind of attitude.

The seventh point of advice is to express your devotion with a mind that is like a vehicle that carries every load, no matter how great. In fulfilling the wishes of the spiritual teacher or in undertaking the advice of the spiritual teacher, you must aspire to be able to take on the most difficult, the most undesirable tasks.

The eighth point is having devotion toward the spiritual teacher that is like a dog's. Whether you treat a dog badly or whether you treat it well, this animal will remain totally devoted to you. In the same way, in the course of your relationship with your spiritual teacher, even if that spiritual teacher totally ignores you, doesn't give you any particular attention, doesn't hold you in any particular regard, and so forth, rather than feeling unhappy or disturbed by this, you must not lose your sense of faith and respect. Above all you must not feel unhappy or negative about the situation. Sometimes you may feel, "I have offered so much time, so much service in fulfilling the wishes of this spiritual teacher; I've made many offerings, and yet this lama didn't even dedicate prayers for me or bless me or greet me." Should such thoughts occur in your mind, they are a transgression of this particular point.

The last point is cultivating a sense of devotion that is like a ship, ready to come and go at any time. For example, if your spiritual teacher told you to leave McLeod Ganj in one of those terrible buses to Delhi right that very moment just to pick something up and come right back on the next bus, you must be willing to go, feeling no sense of difficulty, no sense of hesitation or resistance. Even if you end up in the very last seat on the bus, you should feel that it's no problem at all.

It is a great fortune to have the opportunity to practice these nine points of advice in relation to a spiritual teacher who embodies all of the ten qualities. Training our mind in these ways involves a lot of letting go of ourselves, and brings about enormous benefit.

These are the general instructions on how to express devotion to the spiritual teacher.

Relying through Faith

The next topic is the root of devotion: cultivating faith in the spiritual teacher.

There is considerable significance in saying that the root of devotion is faith, for faith is not only the basis of the entire spiritual path, but also the basis for every virtue. Faith causes our positive potentials to develop and reach fulfillment. The more we can enhance our faith in the spiritual path and the spiritual teacher, the better chance we will have to cut through the root of cyclic existence, to attain the enlightened body, speech, and mind and the four bodies of a buddha.

Faith also has the effect of uplifting our entire mentality. Often, when we feel depressed or when we feel a sense of great loneliness, we are lacking the presence of faith in our lives. Of course, the immediate causes of our depression or loneliness might be anger or attachment, but if we can only generate faith, we will be able to cut through all of these negative states of mind and lift our spirits. The more we are able to express our faith physically and mentally, the more we will be able to counteract our deluded sense of pride and thereby naturally cultivate respect for all beings in our thoughts and actions. An individual lacking faith may have a mind of great pride and total lack of respect and consideration for others. In this kind of person there is no chance for any positive development.

Faith is really the greatest form of internal wealth that we could ever have. Just as we say that extensive listening is like a treasure that cannot be stolen away, in the same way, the faith that arises from listening is also precious. It is a great storehouse for generating virtue, generating positive potentials, and enabling us to attain liberation and enlightenment. Faith is like the limbs that carry us forth to enlightenment, like the hand that is able to gather things together—like this, the mind of faith gathers virtue. Faith is regarded as the most supreme of all vehicles, as it leads us from the very beginning of the path all the way to the attainment of enlightenment. It is faith that introduces us to the spiritual path; it is faith that helps us develop on the spiritual path; and it is faith that completes the fruits of the path. Of all of our listening, understanding, and meditation, faith is what empowers the teachings to become an antidote. Without faith, the teachings are totally ineffective. As a seed that has been burned cannot become a flower, a mind without faith will not bear fruit.

Generally, we categorize faith into three types. The first is the faith of conviction, arising through a sense of belief, as we experience when we take refuge in the Buddha, Dharma, and Sangha. The second is pure faith, such as the faith that we cultivate in relation to our spiritual teachers. The third is aspiring faith, such as the faith in enlightenment and liberation. This is the faith that arises due to wishing to attain these results.

None of these types of faith are what we call *blind faith*. They are all grounded in sound reasoning or logic.

Take, for example, our faith in the Dharma jewel. Which kind of logic should our faith in the Dharma jewel be based in? In the ultimate logic that establishes conventional and ultimate truth. By establishing these two truths, we can then go on to establish the four noble truths. There is suffering. There is a cause of suffering. There is also a method to liberate oneself from that suffering, which is the true path, and there is the defeat of the cause of suffering, which is true cessation. True path and true cessation are the actual Dharma jewel, and all the teachings about true path and true cessation are the conventional Dharma jewel.

Of the three types of faith, the faith that we are trying to cultivate in the section on guru devotion is pure faith, the faith of the pure view that sees the spiritual teacher as an enlightened being. Even pure faith must be cultivated through analysis of scripture and through logic.

In Tibetan the word for buddha is *sang gye (sangs rgyas). Sang* means purified, cleansed of all mistakes and failings, and *gye* means complete, having fully developed all qualities. That is how we should see the spiritual teacher—free of mistakes, failings, and shortcomings, and having fully developed all positive potentials. The practice of this kind of pure guru devotion is best suited for those individuals who have had a lot of familiarity with spiritual practice in past lifetimes and who have encountered a spiritual teacher in this lifetime through the force of karma and prayer. Of course, even if we meet all of these conditions, we will still be unable to truly develop the capacity to be able to see the spiritual teacher as a buddha without some basic training of the mind, such as the reasoning that establishes why it is essential to do so. It is also important that we should recognize our own limitations, and understand that the reason that we are not capable of seeing this right now may be because, due to habituation and ignorance, mistakes appear so easily to our deluded minds.

Seeing the Spiritual Teacher as Buddha

If we wish to profit from spiritual practice, if we do not wish to take any loss, it is essential that we train in the practice of seeing the spiritual teacher as a buddha. If the spiritual teacher is in reality an enlightened being and we lack devotion, faith, and respect, there is no way for us to receive the blessings of the guru-buddha. However, even if the spiritual teacher is not a buddha, as long as we practice seeing the spiritual teacher in this way, we will still receive the blessings of the guru-buddha. The blessings that we receive are completely dependent on our own faith and devotion.

Generally we say that we must receive this blessing in order to bring forth positive transformations within our mind. So how does this happen? Actually, the explanation of how this works is very difficult to communicate through words. Just do it. If you practice, you will see how it is possible to receive these benefits.

Once you establish that it is necessary to see the qualified spiritual teacher as totally free of all mistakes and possessing all good qualities, you may then think: "It may be necessary but I can't do it!" thus allowing doubt to arise. The solution to this is to meditate on the fact that it is not only *necessary* to see the spiritual teacher as a buddha, but also, you have the *potential* to see the qualified spiritual teacher as free from all mistakes and possessing all good qualities. How is this possible? You must train yourself. You must make your mind familiar with doing it. In the morning, in the daytime, or in the evening, try to remember the spiritual teacher's kindness, the spiritual teacher's good qualities. If you see a mistake, try to ignore it. Of course, a qualified spiritual teacher generally won't make too many mistakes. Even if training yourself in this point of view does not eliminate your lack of faith, it will surely lessen it.

Once you are accustomed to this practice, even if something appears wrong to your sense consciousnesses, you faith will not be shaken. You can check to see how this would be so by taking yourself as an example. In terms of yourself, you are very familiar with noticing your own good qualities. In fact, you are so familiar with them that most of the time you focus entirely on your own good qualities and never see your faults. Even when you do see your faults, it does not shake your faith in yourself. You still trust yourself. So all that remains to be done is to change the object from yourself to the qualified spiritual teacher.

How do we deal with a mistake, should we see one in our spiritual teachers? First, we should reason that it is not a truly existing mistake. Second, we should reason that the mistake is merely an imputed phenomenon. Third, we should remember that our minds are polluted by negative imprints accumulated since beginningless time. On the basis of all of these reasons, we will be able to conclude that the consciousness that perceives mistakes in the spiritual teacher is not reliable.

For my own practice, I find it very useful to recall the story of the spiritual teacher Marpa. To the ordinary mind, Marpa appeared as a violent alcoholic who was constantly fighting with his neighbors. Even when Marpa's consort, Dagme-ma, was set to marry Marpa, she was cautioned— she was told that Marpa was very unstable, and was given jewelry so that she would have something just in case the marriage didn't work out. When we reflect on stories like this, the mistakes of our spiritual teachers today appear very, very miniscule. Thinking like this can help us to counteract the mind that sees faults in them. We say that even if a particular medicine is made from a toxic flower, as long as it cures our illness, we should take that medicine. In this case the spiritual teacher is analogous to the medicine that cures, and the poison is the erroneous appearance of mistakes.

The authority of the practice of seeing the spiritual teacher as a buddha is established within the tantras as well as within the sutras. In the tantras, Buddha Vajradhara points out that we see the historical buddha, Shakyamuni Buddha, as an enlightened being completely free of all mistakes and possessing all positive qualities due to the power of his teachings, the Dharma. The tantric commentaries advise us to see our spiritual teachers in the same light, reasoning that it is our spiritual teachers who enable us to enter the spiritual path and guide us up until the attainment of our own enlightenment. Just as Shakyamuni Buddha gave teachings from the beginning of the path to the end, our own teachers do the same. Since we see the historical Shakyamuni Buddha as an enlightened being on this basis, by the same reasoning it is completely valid that we should see our own spiritual teacher in the same way.

According to the tantric texts, the reason for encouraging our mind to see more of the qualities in the spiritual teacher is because that kind of viewpoint becomes a blessing in our mindstream, whereas the mind that focuses on the failings or the mistakes of the spiritual teacher becomes an obstacle.

Another way to reflect on this subject is to contemplate how kind the spiritual teacher is to manifest in an ordinary form for us. What does it mean to manifest in an ordinary form? Ordinary form means that a spiritual teacher manifests showing mistakes, showing all the poisonous states of mind. It is extremely kind of the spiritual teacher to manifest for us in this aspect, because due to our own karma and delusions we simply do not have the merit to be able to interact with a faultless spiritual teacher. Manifesting in an ordinary aspect, our spiritual teachers make themselves accessible to us, whereas in their perfect form they are totally inaccessible because we do not have the propensities to see perfect forms. Thinking from this angle is another way to counter the mind that sees mistakes. We are extremely fortunate that our spiritual teachers should manifest for us in the ordinary aspect of human beings with human mistakes and delusions, as opposed to manifesting for us as dogs and donkeys.

When Lama Atisha came to Tibet, many people came to him claiming that in Tibet there were a lot of meditators but very few who were able to generate realizations of the path. Lama Atisha said that this was due to making the mistake of seeing the spiritual teacher as an ordinary person.

On the one hand, the more obscured our sense perceptions and our minds are, the harder it is for us to be able to view the positive qualities of the spiritual teacher. On the other hand, the more we are able to purify our obscurations, the more we will be able to see the perfection of the spiritual teacher. When we interact with our spiritual teachers, we use our five sense perceptions, which are in turn dependent upon our mental perception. The more we are able to eliminate the obscurations of delusions and negative karma from our mental perception, the more we will be able to perceive the spiritual teacher as free of mistakes through our five sense consciousnesses. For some practitioners, a deep sense of faith arises within the mind just by hearing of or seeing a particular spiritual teacher. We too can achieve this result through the power of purifying our obscurations.

If you yourself embody the three qualities of a suitable disciple, in your meditation you can visualize the presence of a fully qualified spiritual teacher entering your life. At the same time, visualize this spiritual teacher with the ten qualities manifesting in an ordinary form, thereby showing the aspect of having faults. In meditation, you can practice by trying to counteract the mind that sees mistakes, trying to see the spiritual teacher as embodying all qualities, and remembering that the spiritual teacher is merely manifesting in this ordinary aspect to benefit you. In this way you can prepare your mind for the practice of pure guru devotion ahead of the actual encounter with the guru, so that should this issue arise when you actually meet your teacher, you will already know what to do.

When Lama Atisha was with his teacher Serlingpa, his mind was completely focused on the qualities in his teacher's mind, so that Lama Serlingpa's having a lesser philosophical viewpoint did not matter. It was not an issue in Lama Atisha's mind at all. That is how it should be. In fact, although Lama Atisha had many, many teachers, he regarded Lama Serlingpa the most highly of all of them.

Training our mind to see more qualities and fewer mistakes in others is not only relevant to our relationship with our spiritual teacher. This practice can also be carried forth in every aspect of our lives, with everyone that we encounter. Training our minds to see the positive qualities as opposed to seeing the mistakes and failings of others is a basis for developing ourselves into holistic human beings. This is essential advice to enable us to become better people within our community or within our society.

Spiritual teachers can be ordained people as well as lay people. Regardless, the way in which one practices devotion, seeing qualities, not seeing mistakes, is the same.

Developing Respect by Remembering the Kindness

The next topic in this section is cultivating respect by recollecting the kindness of the spiritual teacher.

We can begin by thinking that since beginningless lifetimes we have been bound by karma and delusions to cyclic existence, totally confused about how we exist. Then we can think about the spiritual teacher's kindness in showing us how we exist in samsara, or cyclic existence, and pointing out the reality of what we need to abandon and what we need to cultivate. We should generate a sense of appreciation toward the teacher whose knowledge inspires us, not only ensuring the benefits of this lifetime, but also the benefits of infinite future lifetimes.

Our spiritual teachers awaken us from the deep sleep of our delusional minds of attachment, anger, and ignorance. In recognition of that, we cultivate respect. In addition, we can reflect that our spiritual teachers free us from engaging in totally wrong ways of thinking or living. They show us a path that leads to liberation, a way of life that will bring about our own enlightenment. In this way, they guide us to great fortune, not only for ourselves but also for the benefit of others. Think about the kindness of our spiritual teachers in protecting us from mistaken and distorted paths, and in guiding us on the path to liberation and enlightenment.

When the delusions rage like fire within our minds, it is our spiritual teachers who shower us with the Dharma rain that stifles the flame of our negative thoughts. It is our spiritual teachers who treat us with the ultimate medicine of the Dharma teachings to cure the chronic disease of our negative minds. And it is our spiritual teachers who show us the paths of profound method and wisdom, and the unified practice that enables us to attain enlightenment.

We can also reflect upon the kindness of our spiritual teachers in accordance with the *Array of Stalks Sutra.* In the context of this text, we reflect upon the kindness of the spiritual teacher in terms of the four noble truths—considering the kindness of the spiritual teacher in introducing us to the reality of true suffering and true cause, as well as showing us the means by which to become free of these, true path and true cessation.

Moreover, we can think of the spiritual teacher as a mother, nurturing the perfection of our thoughts and actions. And we can also think of the spiritual teacher as a father, eliminating our obscurations and enabling the full completion of all of our positive potential. As well, the spiritual teacher is like a support, protecting us from all downfalls and from the harm of our self-cherishing mind. The spiritual teacher is also like the full moon, complete in all qualities, and like the sun, illuminating the path to liberation and enlightenment.

These are some of the points on which to reflect in order to recollect the kindness of our spiritual teachers.

The kindness of our spiritual teachers is different from the kindness that we remember in our daily life, such as that of a friend helping us in some small way. The latter is a very limited kindness, and its benefit is restricted to this one brief lifetime alone, while the kindness of our spiritual teachers is the most pervasive, most extensive, most profound kindness there is. It is an incomparable kindness; it is wonderful in every respect.

As our experience of the path deepens, so will our recognition of that kindness. When the antidote of the teachings begins to reduce the three poisons in our minds, and when we feel a sense of conviction in the attainment of enlightenment, when we realize that all of our delusions really are extinguishable, and when on the basis of such faith we apply the antidote of the teachings—when we experience all of these results, we will fully come to appreciate the kindness of our teachers.

The essence of all guru yoga practice is cultivating pure faith and respect for the spiritual teacher by clearly recognizing his or her kindness. This respect should arise from the very depth of our hearts. Practicing guru devotion through thought is basically cultivating faith and respect, and practicing it through action is doing everything that pleases our spiritual teachers the most and abandoning everything that would incur the teacher's displeasure.

This is the most general advice. In the specific forms of advice, it is said that if, however, in order to please the spiritual teacher, we are asked to undertake inappropriate actions, actions that go against the instructions of the Dharma, or actions that are contradictory to the three higher trainings, then we need not undertake them. If this situation should occur, we can politely decline, and offer our reasons for not complying. And even that experience should never become an obstacle to our pure faith.

Relying through Practice

We please our spiritual teacher in actual practice by making offerings of respect and through service of our body and speech. When we make an offering of material things to our spiritual teachers, we should offer the very best of what we have. We should not offer things because we don't need them. Making offerings to the spiritual teacher is considered an indirect channel to making offerings to all of the buddhas and bodhisattvas, and therefore it is considered very, very meritorious. The benefits of making offerings to our spiritual teachers is that not only do we receive the merit of offering, but we can also receive the merit of seeing the offering accepted with great pleasure, which is something we cannot usually experience when we make offerings to the buddhas and bodhisattvas in general.

On the part of the disciple, being able to make the best of offerings without any sense of miserliness and with the mind of faith is the very best. On the side of the teacher, being free of the mind that discriminates among students based on the quality of their offerings is the very best. The way the spiritual teacher cares for the disciple should not depend on the quality of the offerings. The spiritual teacher's mind should be free of that kind of concern.

The other activities by which you can please the spiritual teacher are offering words of praise and admiration and offering physical service.

Of course, pleasing the spiritual teachers by offering material gifts, verbal forms of praise or admiration, and physical service are the very ordinary modes of causing the spiritual teacher to be pleased with you. The most extraordinary way in which to please the spiritual teacher is through the offering of your practice, and by being able to live in accordance with the instructions of the spiritual teacher. Jetsun Milarepa says in one of his songs: "I do not have the offering of material wealth, but I do have the offering of my practice."

The Benefits of Relying on a Spiritual Teacher

Next, we should reflect upon the advantages of relying and the disadvantages of not relying upon a spiritual teacher, as well as the disadvantages of breaching that reliance after taking on a spiritual teacher. Then, we must examine whether we have the capacity to devote ourselves to such a practice or not.

What are the benefits of cultivating the practice of guru devotion in our minds, and of expressing our devotion through our thoughts and practice? The first and foremost benefit is that it brings us closer to our own enlightenment. Also, expressing pure devotion pleases all the buddhas. As the parents of an obedient child become happy, the enlightened beings are most pleased with the expression of our pure devotion to our spiritual teacher. The third benefit is that for all of the lifetimes to come we will never be separated from our Mahayana spiritual teachers.

Additionally, through the practice of pure guru devotion, we will be able to purify our heaviest negative karma and its subsequent results. And the more we are able to express pure devotion in thought and action to our spiritual teacher, the less our minds will come under the control of the delusions.

Sometimes in the monasteries we see teachers who are highly influential in the education of a particular disciple, not just in terms of their studies, but also in the mode of conduct of that student. So strong is the influence of the teacher that even if the student is in the company of many negative friends, the student is not easily swayed.

Another benefit is that in this life and in the lifetimes to come, we will encounter pure Mahayana spiritual teachers who embody the ten qualities. Not only will we encounter them, but they will care for us, teach us the paths of method and wisdom, and we will be able to undertake the practices of these paths. Should we experience this result one day, we should be certain to dedicate our merits so that other sentient beings may also encounter Mahayana spiritual teachers and accomplish these practices.

The disadvantages of not being able to rely upon a spiritual teacher are the exact opposite of what has been stated, especially that we place ourselves further away from liberation and enlightenment. Also, in all the expressions of our thoughts and actions, there is nothing that pleases the enlightened beings, and all of our delusions increase.

This completes the topic of how to rely on a spiritual teacher according to Je Tsongkhapa's *Lamrim Chenmo*.

THE MEDITATION PRACTICE

THE NEXT SECTION OF THE TEXT explains the actual practice of the lam-rim: the way to train the mind in meditation and the way to practice after meditation. Within the section on actual practice, the topics are the preparatory practice, the actual practice, and the completion of the practice.

PREPARATORY PRACTICES

Preparation for Meditation

Generally speaking, the preparatory practices are the basis upon which we create an environment conducive to meditation. Included within them are the activities of cleaning the meditation area, arranging objects, pictures, or statues of the objects of refuge, making offerings, arranging ourselves in the correct physical posture, and cultivating our motivation. Once we have cultivated our motivation, we then take refuge, generate the mind of enlightenment, and practice the seven limbs in order to accumulate merit and purify our negative karma.

We begin with cleaning the meditation area. As we clean, we can imagine that our external actions represent the internal practice of clearing away our delusions and negative karma. The advantage to maintaining the cleanliness of the meditation room is that it invites the presence of gods who are appreciative of virtue. If the meditation area is dirty, they don't come. Of course, the best form of cleanliness is that of the mind cleansed of the eight worldly dharmas. The eight worldly dharmas are:

1. Wanting wealth
2. Not wanting poverty
3. Wanting happiness
4. Not wanting suffering
5. Wanting a good reputation
6. Not wanting a bad reputation
7. Wanting praise
8. Not wanting criticism

If we keep our meditation room clean thinking that this will prove to others how well we are practicing, even if our physical space is spotless, our mind is polluted by the eight worldly dharmas. The very best of all offerings of cleanliness is the cleanliness of mind.

Another advantage to keeping our meditation area clean is that it becomes a very inviting place for our own minds, and we will want to spend time there. This condition can become a cause to further enhance our virtue. Our place of meditation and Dharma study should be as inviting as possible.

In accordance with the tradition of the lineage lamas of the Kadampas, we should have four main objects of refuge on the altar. The first is a statue or an image of Shakyamuni Buddha, the founder of the teachings. In addition, we should have images of Arya Chenrezig, the deity who embodies compassion, Arya Tara, the deity who embodies virtuous activity, and Miyowa Buddha, the Immovable Buddha, the deity who embodies the elimination of obstacles. Images of these four deities represent the holy body of Buddha. The holy speech of Buddha should be represented by scripture—traditionally we place a collection of sutras or a lamrim text upon our altar. The holy mind of Buddha should be represented by a stupa or a *tsa-tsa* of a stupa.

We should not set up our altar according to the material value of the objects. Putting holy objects around the house solely for decoration is also a mistake, as is placing holy objects in irrelevant areas, like hallways or passageways, or near the door. We should place holy objects in the best, most prominent part of the room, the part that we would consider the most respectful. Also, we should not ignore the objects on our altars because we feel that we are already familiar with them. This attitude is wrong. In fact, if we are doing four sessions a day, at the beginning of each session we should make a point of looking at each one of our holy objects. If we are able to view them on a daily basis as if we were seeing them for the first time, we receive great benefit.

Our offerings should be free of material contamination and free of the pollution of negative motivation. We should make the very best offering that we can manage and not be miserly. In general, the offerings must be materially and physically clean. For example, when we offer meals as a service to our spiritual teachers, it is very important that we do so with a great sense of cleanliness. If we taste part of the food and then put it back, this is very, very disrespectful, and we are also polluting the offering with our own lesser state of mind.

In America, Lama Zopa Rinpoche once decided to offer a meal to Geshe Sopa Rinpoche. Lama Zopa Rinpoche washed his hands thoroughly, and washed everything that he was going to use as part of the cooking. Rinpoche also wore a face mask to prevent breathing on the food as he was preparing it. It was very inspiring to see the purity with which he made that offering. Usually, when we talk of perfect examples of demonstrating pure guru devotion, we talk of Milarepa, Marpa, Tilopa, and Naropa. But in our generation, the quality of Lama Zopa Rinpoche's guru devotion is a perfect example. When we reflect on the kindness of spiritual teachers, in addition to reflecting upon the historical teachers and their great activities, we can also think of the great teachers of today, whose lives are totally dedicated to the service of the Dharma.

The next preparatory practice is arranging our meditation seat. The back of our cushion should be raised slightly higher than the front, and we should adopt the seven-point posture of Vairocana Buddha, who represents the purified form of the aggregates. In this posture, the back is straight like an arrow, the shoulders even and relaxed. The legs are in the vajra position with the hands in the posture of meditative equipoise. The head is tilted slightly forward, one's gaze directed at the level of the tip of the nose, and the back of the tongue rests lightly against the back of the upper row of teeth. This seven-point posture is said to be the most conducive to maintaining a long meditation. Sitting upright straightens the channels within the body so that the energy winds flow more freely and the mind is clear, creating conducive external and internal conditions for meditation. Among the seven points, the most important is the arrow-straight back.

Once you are seated, visualize the merit field in the space in front of you, with Guru Shakyamuni Buddha in the center. To his left and right are the lineage lamas of the profound path of wisdom, the extensive path of method, and the entourage of the direct and indirect lineage gurus. They are further surrounded by buddhas, bodhisattvas, meditation deities, and so forth. This field of merit is unlike ordinary fields, where you can harvest crops just once or twice, at limited times of the year. In this field you can harvest the fruit of merit at all times and in every direction.

For something to be considered an assembled field of merit, it needn't necessarily be composed of holy objects alone. In general, as long as there are sentient beings, it can qualify as a field of merit. In the *Guide to the Bodhisattva's Way of Life*, Shantideva states that both the buddhas and sentient beings are equally kind in helping us to assemble the accumulation of merit enabling the attainment of enlightenment. In this case, however, we create the specially visualized merit field composed of holy objects for the specific purpose of receiving the blessings of the lineage masters.

The Seven-Limb Practice

Next is the actual method to accumulate merit and purify nonvirtue, the seven-limb practice.

PROSTRATION

The first of the seven limbs is the limb of prostration. Prostrations purify the obstacles of our negative karma, and thereby enable us to accumulate merit. Prostrations can be physical, verbal, or mental. We can do elaborate or very short forms of prostration. Actually, any physical gesture that we make as a demonstration of respect is a form of physical prostration. In the various prayers of prostration, such as the *King of Prayers* dedication, we offer prostrations to all the buddhas of the ten directions, and to all the buddhas of the three times. In accordance with this prayer, we visualize replicas of our own body equaling the number of the atoms of this world emanating from us, and imagine a complete field of merit before each one of them, to which they prostrate. This is the mental form of prostration, and reciting the prayers of praise and admiration is the verbal form of prostration.

When we do prostrations, we should put our hands together leaving a space inside, with the two thumbs folded into the hollow. The shape of the outside of the hands symbolizes the form body of a buddha, and the shape of the inside represents the truth body of a buddha. In its entirety, this hand gesture symbolizes that our ultimate goal is to achieve the two bodies of a buddha. With the hands in prostration mudra, we can touch our crown, forehead, throat, and heart. Some people prefer to touch just three places: the forehead, the throat, and the heart. Others touch five: the crown, the forehead, the throat, the heart, and the navel.

Sometimes at teachings in Dharamsala when there is very little sitting space, and everyone wants to sit down as quickly as possible so as not to lose their places, they do prostrations in a great hurry without touching the ground with the five limbs. This is not correct. In a proper prostration, the two hands, two knees, and the forehead must touch the ground.

When you are doing many prostrations, you should not use the part of the prostration when you are flat on the ground to take a break if you get tired. This is very improper. After your forehead touches the ground, you must get up quickly, and if you want to take a break, take a break apart from the prostrations.

Offering

For the second limb, the limb of offering, we visualize limitless offerings of limitless kinds. I have already discussed the way to make offerings.

Confession

Next is the limb of confession, or purification, which is very important. The best way to purify our negative karma is by the method of the four opponent powers. We should begin with the power of the basis, which means taking refuge and generating bodhichitta. To counteract the negative actions that we have done in relation to holy objects, we take refuge. To counteract the negative actions that we have done in relation to other sentient beings, we generate bodhichitta. All of our negative actions are done in relation to either or both of these two objects.

Next, we should generate the power of regret. If by mistake we were to drink poison, right away we would want to take the antidote to that poison to counteract the pain. Our regret should follow the same pattern. It should be as sincere and as quick as if we had taken poison by mistake. Imagine that there are three people who have eaten the same poison. The first person has died from it, the next is violently ill, and the last person has yet to experience any effect at all. Having seen the effects of that poison, the last individual will do everything he can to remove it from his or her system, so as not to have to suffer like the others. In the same way, we all have great stores of negative karma. Others who have also accumulated negative karma are already experiencing the results of the lower realms, or are on their deathbeds, waiting for their karma to ripen. But we ourselves have yet to die; our karma is yet to ripen. Like the person who has been poisoned, in order not to experience the resultant suffering, we should do everything we can to apply the antidote while we are able. Therefore, we should sincerely regret all of our negative actions.

On the basis of the power of regret we apply the antidote. The antidote purifies the effects of negative karmic actions. The very best antidotes are meditating on emptiness, meditating on bodhichitta, and meditating on compassion. Other antidotes include recitation of the names of the thirty-five Buddhas, offering prostrations, reciting the Vajrasattva mantra, and so forth.

The fourth opponent power is the power of the resolution, which means making the commitment that in the future we will not do that action again, even at the cost of our life. The strength of the resolution or commitment we make is dependent upon the strength of our regret. And how well we are able to keep the commitment of the resolution is, again, very much dependent on the quality of our regret.

In case you are wondering, one sign that you have accumulated heavy negative karma is that you are not easily able to engage in positive actions and Dharma activities. Or, though you may not find it difficult to begin such activities, you may experience great resistance and exhaustion while actually doing them. If you have experienced something like this, you should persevere in the practices of purification as set forth in the preliminaries of this text. The signs that you have successfully purified your negative karma are that your understanding of what you are studying improves, and you experience positive changes in your thoughts and actions.

Throughout all of the preparatory practices you should also maintain the visualization of the merit field. As a note, in the Sutrayana tradition the practitioner visualizes and makes offerings to only one merit field at a time, but in accordance with the Vajrayana we visualize additional merit fields related to the practice that we are doing.

According to lamrim, in the extensive version of the visualized field of merit there are five main groups. Shakyamuni Buddha sits in the center, and he is surrounded by the lineage masters of the extensive conduct, the lineage masters of the profound method, the lineage masters of the blessed practices, and the spiritual teachers from whom you have taken teachings directly and indirectly. All of these beings are then surrounded by other buddhas, bodhisattvas, dakas, dakinis, and Dharma protectors.

REJOICING

The fourth limb of the seven-limb practice is the limb of rejoicing. Lama Tsongkhapa has praised the limb of rejoicing as a practice by which we can accumulate great stores of merit without a great deal of effort. When we rejoice, we should rejoice for all other beings regardless of whether they are friends, enemies, or strangers. Sometimes when we think about the virtuous activities of our friends and loved ones, we are able to rejoice very easily. But if we consider the virtuous activity of a person that we do not care for, we are often unable to rejoice, and instead we feel a sense of competition.

If we are ordained as monks or nuns and rejoice in the merits of a layperson, the merit that we receive is double what they have accumulated. If the realizations in our own minds equal those in the mind of the other person—whether a layperson or a fully ordained or novice monk or nun—by rejoicing we accumulate an equal amount of merit. And if the person whose virtue we are rejoicing in is more realized than we are, then we receive at least half of that merit. There are five types of beings in relation to whom we should cultivate the mind of rejoicing: the buddhas of the ten directions, the bodhisattvas of the ten directions, beings on the hearer's path, beings on the solitary realizer's path, and all sentient beings.

It is commonly said that the best way to create a connection to virtuous actions that we cannot do ourselves is to rejoice in them. Even if we dedicate our entire life to the practices of accumulation of merit, purification, and study and meditation, all the merit from these activities cannot equal the merit that is generated by a bodhisattva in just one session of meditation. Therefore, if we rejoice and receive even a part of that merit, the benefit is really extraordinary.

For example, if we think about Lama Zopa Rinpoche's project, the five-hundred-foot Maitreya statue, and we rejoice in it, we will get part of that merit too. But if we think, "That's such a big project, so unbelievable; I wonder if it will ever come to fruition"—even to doubt that it will happen is a great obstacle for our mind. Bodhisattvas with great bodhichitta think in a very, very extensive, profound, and noble way. The prayers of dedication that have been written by bodhisattvas of the past are so immense, so deep, so extensive—it is quite beyond our own ordinary conception to think that anyone could ever hope that such prayers be fulfilled. But the magnificence of the mind of bodhichitta is the very fact that it embodies such extensive hope. It is that kind of mind that sees the possibility for all of these things. A project such as the Maitreya Buddha statue influences sentient beings like us toward the goodness of the teachings of the Maitreya, the Fifth Buddha. It creates the cause for us to be among the foremost circle of disciples, holding the teachings of Maitreya Buddha. In preparation for that, we should offer every service of our body, speech, and mind for such projects, even in the form of prayers, in order to make a connection with them.

We should also remember to rejoice in our own virtuous activities. When we do this, we should think that this "I" of today has come into being as a result of many lifetimes of existence, and the fact that we are experiencing the fruits of such an existence today means that we have definitely created the merit arising from ethics, the merit arising from generosity, and the merit arising from stainless prayers in the past. Just as we understand that there is fire in a certain area because we can see the smoke, in the same way, by looking at the positive result of our present-day conditions, we should understand that in the past we have done the positive actions that led to this result. Therefore, our present activities of listening to the Dharma, our meditations, and all of the positive activities of body, speech, and mind that we engage in should be cause for us to rejoice.

However, when we rejoice in our own virtue, it is very important to keep our minds free from pride. When we feel a sense of pride in practices such as holding the eight Mahayana precepts, the individual vows of liberation, or ordination, the virtue that we create is lessened.

In relation to that, some of you here have taken vows of ordination with great determination and courage. After taking vows, you must try not to feel that now that you are ordained you get to sit in front, that you have achieved something, and so forth. Instead you should try to understand that being a monk or nun is like volunteering to respect other sentient beings and your Dharma friends. You must try to be very humble, without any pride at all, and with wisdom. This is very important. If you are able to accomplish this hour by hour, day by day, then you can really rejoice.

As ordinary beings, we practice rejoicing by merely admiring and feeling happy about the virtuous activities of others. But if we were bodhisattvas, we would also feel an incredible sense of joy when we rejoiced for sentient beings. This is because a bodhisattva's main purpose is to seek the well-being of others, and when sentient beings create positive karma, their well-being is ensured. If we are able to rejoice in this way now, even before we have become a bodhisattva, it will become easier for us to rejoice in the virtuous activities of our enemies or the people we do not like.

REQUESTING THE BUDDHAS TO TEACH

The next limb is the limb of requesting the buddhas to turn the wheel of Dharma. In accordance with the life story of Buddha, once Buddha attained enlightenment, Brahma and his entourage requested that Buddha teach the Dharma according to his experience and knowledge. The limb of requesting follows in this tradition. Our request should be made to the buddhas of the past, present, and future. Of course, since many requests have already been made to the buddhas of the past and the present, it is especially important to dedicate strong prayers to all the buddhas of the future and to those who are attaining enlightenment right now. As we make our requests, we should not visualize ourselves in an ordinary aspect as we are today, but rather in the aspect of Brahma in accordance with the history. It is best if we can visualize many replicas of ourself in the aspect of Brahma, and request not only the founding Buddha, but also the limitless numbers of holy beings and holy objects to turn the wheel of Dharma.

REQUESTING THE BUDDHAS TO REMAIN IN THE WORLD

The sixth limb is the limb of requesting the buddhas not to pass into *parinirvana,* but to remain in the world. What does it mean to request a buddha to remain in the world? When a being attains enlightenment, he or she attains the holy bodies of a buddha—the *dharmakaya,* or truth body, the *sambhogakaya,* or enjoyment body, and the *nirmanakaya,* or emanation body. The truth body is a continuum that rests in the state of uninterrupted meditative equipoise, and, because the truth body is a continuum, the forms that emanate from it also function in a continuum. This means that the form aspects are born and pass away in this world. A buddha will manifest the great parinirvana, or passing away, for many reasons. The main reason is to destroy sentient beings' grasping at permanent existence, as the passing of a great being exemplifies the reality of impermanence. Another reason may be to prevent the beings of that time from losing faith and accumulating the karma of abandoning Dharma.

You should never think that because the buddhas have attained enlightenment, it is not necessary to request them to remain. Buddha's attendant Ananda never made a single request to Buddha to remain in the world, and as a result Buddha manifested passing away into parinirvana comparatively soon. In order to create the causes from your side for the buddhas to remain, you should constantly request them to do so.

When you have finished requesting the buddhas to turn the wheel of Dharma and asking the merit field to not pass away into parinirvana, it is important to think that the merit field has accepted your request completely.

DEDICATION

The seventh limb is the limb of dedication. We should begin every activity that we do with the proper motivation, and complete it by dedicating the virtue that we have created. The reason that we dedicate our virtue is to secure it and ensure that it cannot be destroyed. The purpose to which we make our dedication is the attainment of enlightenment. The objects for whom we dedicate are all sentient beings. And the way we should dedicate is with the thought of compassion, with the thought of bodhichitta, and with the thought reflecting on the emptiness of the three spheres—the emptiness of the person who is dedicating, the emptiness of the merit that is dedicated, and the emptiness of the enlightened state. We could say that the merit we accumulate is like a car, and that our prayers and dedications are like the driver who determines in which direction the car is going to go. The results of our prayers and dedications are completely dependent upon the way in which we pray and make dedications.

When people make very strong prayers or wishes with negative objectives, like, for example, Mao Tse-Tung or Hitler, they often experience the results within one lifetime. Conversely, very strong positive prayers such as those made by His Holiness the Dalai Lama or Mahatma Gandhi are able to bring about positive results over a long period of time.

In ancient times in Tibet it was customary for pilgrims to visit the Jokhang Temple in Lhasa and make prayers and wishes there. The people from Lhasa were very well trained to make long, extensive prayers—for the Dharma, for the buddhas, for sentient beings. They were able to list a lot of objectives in their prayers, expressing many things through the words of the prayer with great eloquence. One day a poor nomad pilgrim who didn't know any prayers stood in this temple beside a lady from Lhasa. As he was unable to recite anything himself, he looked at the lady beside him and prayed, "Whatever she says, I say one hundred percent."

If we lose our opportunity to dedicate our merit, we run the risk of destroying great amounts of virtue with our powerful negative emotions. Our negative emotions are like monkeys, and our virtue is like oranges and bananas inside the house. If we are not very careful to close the door, our negative emotions jump inside and grab everything for themselves. Our dedication is like closing the door.

The main thing, as it says in the sixth chapter of Shantideva's *Guide to the Bodhisattva's Way of Life,* is that we have thousands of eons of virtue that we have accumulated through practicing generosity, making offerings, and so forth. To destroy it we don't need many powerful thoughts. We only need one. One single moment of anger will destroy huge amounts of virtue. Therefore, as soon as possible, we need to put our virtue in the bank. Dedication ensures that we are able to enjoy the results of our merit for a long time. Dedicating our merit toward the attainment of enlightenment in particular is like putting a few drops of water into a great ocean—as long as the ocean remains, so do your drops of water.

Dedication also has the effect of purifying all the wrong views that we have generated in the past, and ensuring that we do not generate wrong views in the future. When we dedicate our merit to protect it from being destroyed by future negativity, we are simultaneously reconfirming our belief in the laws of cause and effect. A person who has wrong views of karmic cause and effect has no basis for the practice of dedicating merit.

When we dedicate our merit, we should dedicate all the merit of all beings, as well as our own merit, and put it all together toward the cause of enlightenment. We should dedicate for the long existence of the teachings, which are the one medicine for the sufferings of all sentient beings, and for ourselves and all sentient beings to be guided by pure Mahayana gurus embodying the ten qualities in all of our lifetimes.

Generally speaking, prayers of altruistic motivation are not considered dedications. But dedications can be prayers. The difference between a prayer and a dedication is that a prayer is usually just our wishes, our thoughts, or an expression of our altruistic aspiration. In order for a prayer to be a dedication, it must involve the dedication of merit, either in the form of internal virtue or external substances. Our prayers of altruistic motivation, or our prayers generally, do not have such merit.

SUMMARY OF THE SEVEN LIMBS

To conclude this section, I will give a brief summary of the seven-limb practice. The first limb of prostration—paying homage with our body, speech, and mind—is an antidote to our sense of self-importance and pride. The limb of offering is an antidote to our tendency toward miserliness. The limb of confession or purification is an antidote to all of our delusions. The limb of rejoicing is an antidote to jealousy. The limb of requesting the buddhas to turn the wheel of Dharma purifies negative karma that we have accumulated in relation to the Dharma, such as that of abandoning Dharma. The limb of requesting the long life of our spiritual teachers purifies all of our negative karmic actions in relation to these beings. And the limb of dedication protects our merit from being destroyed by anger and other nonvirtuous states of mind.

The seven limbs are a very common form of practice on the spiritual path, both in the Mahayana and the Hinayana vehicles. In the context of the *Lamrim Chenmo*, however, the seven limbs are to be practiced on the basis of Mahayana refuge and a Mahayana motivation. This means that we practice in this way only for the benefit of others.

At the end of the seven limbs, we should dedicate with the prayer of three great purposes as follows.

> I take refuge in the three precious gems and my spiritual teacher and I make this request: send forth to me waves of inspiring strength. Inspire me and all mother beings to bring to an end all distorted states of mind—from showing precious gurus the slightest disrespect through insisting that we ourselves are truly different from all others. Send forth to us waves of inspiring strength to develop most quickly all true states of mind that especially include showing gurus respect. Send forth to us waves of inspiring strength to clear away outer and inner hindrances to our practice of Dharma.

To summarize the three great purposes, the first great purpose is the removal of all obstacles and obscurations from the mind, from the initial lack of guru devotion up to the subtle dualistic view. The second great purpose is to be able to generate all the realizations of the path—from the pure mind of guru devotion up to realizing the unmistaken view of selflessness. And the third is to be free of all hindrances, to accomplish the total pacification of all obstacles.

This prayer is also known as the request of the four noble truths. Lacking guru devotion at the beginning of the path up to and including all mistaken views shows the first two truths—the true cause of suffering directly, and the resultant suffering, indirectly. The first request is for the pacification of true suffering and the true cause of suffering. The second request—that we may be able to practice pure guru devotion and generate every realization up to the unmistaken view of selflessness—is the request for the realization of the true path. The truth of cessation is shown indirectly.

The prayer for the three purposes also encompasses the two truths— conventional truth and ultimate truth. The request to be able to generate all realizations beginning from pure guru devotion represents conventional truth. Ultimate truth is represented by the realization of the unmistaken view of selflessness.

Up to this point, we have discussed the foundations of practicing the lamrim in terms of the proper way to rely on the spiritual teacher and the preparatory rites. These practices help us to purify our obscurations and to create the basis of merit in our minds. Having completed the seven limbs and offered the mandala, we can then begin our actual meditation practice.

HOW TO DEVELOP A MEDITATION PRACTICE

The word for meditation in Tibetan, *gom (sgoms)*, means "to become familiar." Familiarity is accomplished either through analytical meditation or by concentrating single-pointedly on a particular subject. Of the two methods, establishing familiarity through analysis is more effective.

If we think about it, we are not strangers to analytical meditation at all. If we are angry with someone, for example, we contemplate an entire list of reasons for our anger—one reason supports the next reason, and that supports the next, and so forth, and before we know it, we have completely justified our anger with this person. On occasions such as these, we analyze the situation from every possible angle in order to validate our anger. We use the analytical process to examine our objects of desire from every angle in a similar way, building up support for the mind of attachment.

It works the same way in meditation on the lamrim. We can engage in an analytical process in support of virtue, examining it from every angle to completely validate it, or we can engage in an analytical process to counteract nonvirtue, examining it from all sides to defeat it. If we then engage in single-pointed meditation on the result of such analysis, our meditation will be extremely effective.

Furthermore, the imprints that we create in our minds during conceptual analysis are far more powerful than the imprints we create with single-pointed concentration alone, without analysis. The stronger the imprints within our mind, the greater the influence our understanding will have on our behavior, on the way we think or act. If we are able to make strong imprints in our minds, we will experience their influence even in our sleep and at the time of death. Positive imprints activated at the time of death ensure that positive karma will ripen for the future lifetime.

From the perspective of long-term meditation, we should maintain our object of meditation until we notice some positive effect on our mind. If we constantly change our object—one day meditating on guru devotion, another day on precious human rebirth, another day on impermanence and death, for example—it will be very difficult for us to generate the realizations of that particular subject. Especially if we are in extended retreat, we should persevere with meditation on one topic until we have gained an experience of it.

Also, while we are focusing on a particular topic, for example, on impermanence and death, we should try to see everything that happens to us in the course of the day in the context of that subject matter. When we walk, we should reflect on impermanence and death; when we sit, we should focus on impermanence and death; when we sleep, the same—we should reflect on impermanence and death with every activity of body, speech, and mind. If we focus in such a concentrated way, we should be able to bring about change in our minds and move closer to enlightenment.

Of course, in reality, we should remember that without realizing emptiness, there is no way to attain liberation or enlightenment. The wisdom that realizes emptiness is the antidote to the ignorance that is the root of cyclic existence. If we engage in all of these practices while grasping strongly at true existence, we are only creating a difficult situation for ourselves. This may not be easy to understand, because ordinarily our minds grasp with such force at the inherent existence of "I" and phenomena.

In fact, this "I" that we hold to be so important does not exist from its own side, does not inherently exist, or truly exist. It is *existent,* however, and the way in which it exists is as a mere imputation. The basis of imputation is the mind and body. When the mind imputes the label "I," the "I" does not exist from the side of the basis of the imputation. Nor does it exist from the side of the imputing mind. But again, it does exist as a mere imputation.

For example, a center director does not exist from her own side, nor does she truly exist. She exists as a valid mind imputing a valid label "director" on a valid basis of imputation. That is all there is to existence. The director does not exist on the basis of imputation alone without the imputation of a valid mind, because if she existed without a valid mind imputing the label "director," from the very beginning she should have been that.

Perhaps you are thinking, "This lama should teach lamrim without so much explanation of the view." But what is the purpose of doing the preparatory practices? Not just to pass time. The purpose is to prepare our minds to realize the three principal paths. Of course we have the long-term goal of enlightenment in mind, but along the way we do preparatory practices, mandala offerings, and so on. If we do all of these things without some idea of the ultimate view, then the merit field itself will appear to us as truly existent, and we will grasp it as being so. In that case, even if we have very strong faith as we meditate upon it, our practice will be polluted.

Perhaps some of you are new to Buddha's teachings. Perhaps some of you already have some understanding. Perhaps some of you are bodhisattvas here. Perhaps some of you are already enlightened. Who knows? If any of you feel more interest in researching the topic of the way that phenomena exist, and have a little bit of courage, there are many books available to help you. For example, Geshe Sopa Rinpoche has written *Cutting Through Appearances,* which includes a detailed explanation of the philosophical schools and the view of emptiness, especially in its second part.

Within a single session, we should try to combine the practice of analytical meditation with single-pointed meditation. The understanding of the subject that we come to through analysis should be the basis upon which we cultivate single-pointed concentration. For example, if we are working on the topic of seeing the spiritual teacher as Buddha, we should examine the reasons it is necessary to do this, the benefits of doing this, and how it is possible to do this. Having undergone this analysis, we come to the certainty that the guru could not be anything but Buddha himself. On the basis of that, pure faith arises, and we apply single-pointed concentration using that state of mind as our object.

HOW TO PRACTICE BETWEEN SESSIONS

We should also make an effort to carry forth the spirit of our meditation into the post-meditation periods. Our post-meditation periods should enhance upon the subject matter of our meditations. If we are meditating on the view of emptiness, for example, then in our post-meditation periods we should try to maintain that view, dedicating all of our practices of purification and accumulation of merit toward realizing it. In this way, every aspect of our life will be complementary to our objective of gaining meditative realizations. Also, we can assess how effective our meditation has been by the off-session time. If we are in a great hurry to finish the session and get outside, that is not a good sign. If, however, after finishing the session, we find that we are still experiencing an effect from whatever we have been meditating upon, it is a sign that our meditation is improving.

We need to apply an extra sense of mindfulness and remembrance in the post-meditation periods in order to be able to maintain the taste of our meditation practices. The mental function of introspection should be like a sentry, watching with vigilance. And the mental function of mindfulness should be like a guard, ensuring that our thoughts and actions accord with the spirit of our meditation practice, and that we do not come under the influence of the delusions. This is the way to ensure success in our practices.

Of course, all of these practices should be founded on ethical discipline. We should close the doors of our body, speech, and mind against nonvirtue. We should ensure that we do not engage in negative activities, and we should also ensure that we do not overindulge in basic necessities such as food and sleep. Very serious practitioners sometimes abandon onions and garlic, and of course meat, which can dull our mental state.

REFUTING THE WRONG THOUGHT

Within the general category of meditation, there is a difference between objective meditation and subjective meditation. When we meditate on selflessness, the four noble truths, or subtle impermanence, we are meditating on an object. In contrast, compassion, loving-kindness, and faith are topics that we meditate on from a subjective point of view. This means that we generate our mind in the nature of that particular subject. Meditating on ultimate truth in the aspect of consciousness and the aspect of form is considered an aspiring meditation, and is a different type of meditation altogether. This type of meditation is cultivated primarily in tantric practice.

There are those who believe that the discriminating wisdom of analytical meditation is an obstacle to meditation. We find the refutation of this view in Maitreya's *Ornament for the Mahayana Sutras*. In this text it is said that the generation of the transcendental wisdom of the pure view develops from the graduated process of cultivating the wisdom that arises from listening. On the basis of that, the wisdom that arises from correct understanding develops, and on the basis of that, the wisdom that arises from meditation is born. As a result we are able to generate the transcendental wisdom of the pure view. This statement in itself shows the importance of the analytical process in meditation.

According to the view of the Hashang school, analytical meditation is an obstacle to liberation. However, according to our own view, when analytical meditation is refuted, the other option is to meditate on nothingness, the absence of all thought processes. If we meditate in this way, it is not possible for us to generate the realization of the experience of Buddha's teachings. And when there are no practitioners cultivating the realization of the teachings, the scriptural tradition will degenerate.

When we meditate, we are seeking to achieve strength of mind and to bring forth transformations in our way of thinking. In order to bring about these results, analytical meditation is essential. Through analysis we are able to enhance our wisdom, make it greater, clearer, more profound, and quicker, and rapidly attain the objective of our meditation. If we come to hold the view that analytical meditation is an obstacle to our meditation, and if we only want to do single-pointed meditation, we will completely undermine our wisdom. Our meditation will become a way of harboring ignorance. The more we can apply the analytical process, the more we will be able to make clearer positive imprints in our minds, and thus develop wisdom.

This completes the point refuting the wrong views of the methods of meditation.

Precious Human Rebirth

ENCOURAGEMENT TO TAKE THE ESSENCE
FROM OUR PRECIOUS HUMAN REBIRTH

Recognizing Our Good Fortune

THE NEXT TOPIC is how to train in taking the essence of our perfect human rebirth. Within this topic there are two main parts: recognizing the perfect human rebirth and understanding its great value and rarity.

Generally speaking, we waste away our lives because we fail to recognize the opportunity, the value, and the rarity of our human rebirth. The more we reflect on the great value of our perfect human rebirth, the less we will be inclined to squander the occasion, and the more we will be inclined to take our spiritual practice to heart.

A perfect human rebirth is endowed with two unique sets of privileges: the leisures and the opportunities. *Leisures* refers to the eight states of freedom from being unable to develop our minds through Dharma practice, and *opportunities* refers to the good conditions that we have to do so.

THE EIGHT LEISURES

The eight leisures are characterized by being born free from certain kinds of existence that lack the conditions to be able to practice Dharma. There are four human states and four nonhuman states that lack the leisure to be able to practice Dharma.

Of the four nonhuman states, the first is that of a hell realm being. A hell realm being experiences the suffering of extreme heat or extreme cold, depending on the hell in which it resides. This being's mind is completely consumed by its experience of suffering, and thus it is deprived of the leisure to study and practice Dharma. We should think about this, and rejoice that we are not bound to such a torturous state of existence.

The second nonhuman state is rebirth in the realm of the *pretas* or hungry ghosts. The mind of a hungry ghost is entirely consumed by the suffering of unbearable hunger and thirst, and thus it is also deprived of the leisure to study and practice Dharma. Even if we ourselves are not experiencing this kind of rebirth at the moment, if we think about it we can understand how difficult it would be for us to practice even when suffering from ordinary hunger and thirst. In comparison, the suffering of a hungry ghost is thousands of times worse. We should think about this, and rejoice that we are free from this kind of suffering.

The third nonhuman state is rebirth as an animal. Beings born as animals suffer as a result of their extreme ignorance and stupidity, and thus are deprived of the opportunity to study and practice Dharma. If we tell a dog or a donkey to repeat one mantra, such as *Om mani peme hung,* it is almost certain that they will not be able to do it. An animal could, perhaps, engage in a physical activity to accumulate merit such as circumambulating, but that animal could not do it with intent, with mental awareness, or with a wish to create virtue. Being aware of all this, when we see animals, we should generate great compassion for them with sincerity. However, we should also take their example to heart, and be reminded that if we ourselves were to take such a rebirth, all of the opportunities that we have now would be gone. With this awareness, we can then rejoice that in our previous lives we accumulated the causes and conditions for our present human rebirth.

The fourth nonhuman state lacking the leisure to practice Dharma is rebirth as a long-life god. In between the awareness of birth and the awareness of death, the long-life gods remain in a state of meditative concentration in which they accomplish nothing at all.

Up to this point we have discussed the nonhuman states that afford no opportunity to study and practice the Dharma. But according to the lamrim, it is also possible to be born with a human body, and still be lacking these opportunities. The examples of how this is so make up the second part of this explanation.

The first of the four human states that lack the leisure to be able to study and practice the Dharma is being born a human in a place where there is no Dharma. This is often translated as "being born a barbarian," but essentially it means taking rebirth in a place where one cannot hear a single word of Dharma.

The second state is being born in a place where a buddha has not descended, meaning a place where a buddha has not come and taught.

The third is being born with extreme mental or physical defects, being born extremely stupid, or being born with severe handicaps that make Dharma practice impossible. In these situations, even if we have been born in a place where the teachings are available, due to our own mental or physical limitations we are unable to study or practice the teachings.

The fourth is being born with strong wrong views, particularly in relation to cause and effect, past and future lives, or the three objects of refuge. Being born with strong wrong views means that we must actively and adamantly *disbelieve* in these concepts. In this situation, even if we are intelligent and born in a place where the teachings are available, if we have strong wrong views, we will be unable to study and practice Dharma. Having wrong views is considered the worst of all of the eight states lacking the leisure to study and practice Dharma. Because of this, wrong view is actually named first in the list from Nagarjuna's *Friendly Letter.*

Generally, there are two kinds of wrong view: the wrong view holding that which exists to be nonexistent, and the wrong view holding that which doesn't exist to be existent. The wrong view of the eight leisures explained above is the wrong view holding that which exists to be nonexistent. This is the more serious of the two. For example, believing that future lives or cause and effect, which do exist, are nonexistent is a more serious fault than believing in a creator god, which according to Buddhism, simply does not exist.

In our own practice, we should make a strong effort to overcome doubts as to whether or not cause and effect or emptiness exist. In the *Treasury of Knowledge,* Vasubhandu instructs us to cut off the view of nonexistence because this view severs the roots of virtue in our minds. As long as we hold this view, we have no basis for the practices of compassion and loving-kindness. Compared to the wrong view of total nonexistence, having a mind of doubt in terms of cause and effect is better. There are three types of doubt: doubt inclining toward fact, doubt that is evenly balanced, and doubt inclined away from fact. Of the three types of doubt,

doubt inclining away from fact is the worst, and of course doubt inclining toward fact is the best.

Having considered all of these points, we should look at our own situation and feel a great sense of joy and gratification in having attained the eight leisures in this life. If in a day's time we had to fulfill eight different jobs, at the end of the day, having completed all of them perfectly, we would experience a great sense of fulfillment in having done so. Rejoicing in our present situation is the same.

THE TEN OPPORTUNITIES

The second set of privileges that we experience having gained a perfect human rebirth are the ten opportunities, five of which pertain to ourselves, and five of which pertain to external conditions. The first of the five pertaining to oneself is being born as a human being, which there is no doubt that we are experiencing.

The second privilege is being born in a central place, which can be understood from the point of view of geography, which means being born in a physically central location, or from the point of view of Dharma, which means being born in a place where the four types of ordained people live.[6]

The third is having perfect and complete senses and sense organs.

The fourth opportunity pertaining to oneself means not having committed one of the five heinous crimes,[7] and thus having the potential to change one's karma.

And the fifth and final opportunity pertaining to oneself is having faith in the lamrim, and in the three vast collections of Buddha's teachings.

The first and second of the five external conditions are having been born in a time when a buddha has descended into the world and in a time when a buddha has taught. Although there are occasions when enlightened beings appear in the world without necessarily giving teachings, a buddha must have descended *and* given teachings in order to fulfill this condition. But what about us, in this day and age? According to this explanation, do we really have precious human rebirths? After all, Shakyamuni Buddha came to our world more than two thousand years ago and passed away soon after, so how can we say that we are truly experiencing the benefit of these opportunities? There is a point here. However, if we consider this issue in the context of the explanation on guru devotion, although we have not encountered the supreme emanation body of Buddha himself, if we recognize our spiritual teachers as enlightened beings and receive teachings from them, we do indeed possess these two opportunities.

The third external condition is that the teachings of Buddha still remain in the world. This refers not only to the scriptural teachings, but also to the realized or experiential teachings. The realized teachings remain in the experience of the beings living in this world who practice the three higher trainings, especially the training in higher ethics and in particular Vinaya, the rules of ethical discipline.

The fourth external condition is that there are still people practicing the teachings.

And the fifth of the five external opportunities is that through the kindness and compassion of others it is possible that practitioners—those who live in hermitages, those who study in the great monastic centers, and those who live in centers as ordained and lay people—have the opportunity to receive material support that enables them the freedom to practice.

If we find ourselves with a human rebirth endowed with these eighteen attributes—eight leisures and ten opportunities—we should remember that such fortune is the result of our positive actions and prayers from past lives. Understanding this, we should rejoice in our fortune again and again and again.

Recognizing Its Value and Rarity

The next point is reflecting on the great value of this human rebirth.

We can contemplate the value of our human rebirth in general through several angles. From a temporary standpoint, our human rebirth affords us the opportunity to practice ethics in this lifetime, on the basis of which we can prevent a future rebirth in the lower realms. Also, on the same basis, we can actually accumulate the causes to take a higher rebirth in the human realm, and to attain liberation from cyclic existence altogether. Ultimately, our human rebirth is the basis upon which we can attain enlightenment for the sake of sentient beings.

From yet another point of view, we can consider that in order to attain enlightenment it is imperative that we practice the three higher trainings, the foundation of which is the training in ethics and living in the vows of individual liberation. In order to take these vows, we must have the basis of a human rebirth. On the basis of a human rebirth we can generate the mind of renunciation most quickly and most forcefully. Also, with a human rebirth we can cultivate the mind of bodhichitta in the most effective way, and we can realize emptiness and enter the path of seeing for the first time. Likewise, according to Vajrayana, there is no basis more conducive than a human rebirth for cultivating the realizations of the tantric path.

Once we have contemplated these points for a while, we can move to the next topic: reflecting on the rarity of our perfect human rebirth by way of its causes, by way of example, and by way of its nature.

RARE FROM THE POINT OF VIEW OF CAUSE

If it were easy to attain a human rebirth, then even if we were to waste our opportunity this time, it wouldn't matter a great deal. However, this is not the case. A perfect human rebirth endowed with such great potential is not something that we will easily encounter over and over again. In order to obtain this kind of rebirth, we must practice pure ethics, and in addition to that we must practice the six perfections. We must support all of this by making pure and fervent prayers. If we practice only generosity, without ethics, we create the cause to be reborn as a *naga*.[8] If we practice perfect ethics but do not practice generosity, we will be reborn as a human living in poverty.

Since it is clear that in our previous lives we invested a great deal of energy in positive thoughts and actions that has led to the perfect human rebirth that we have today, we should not waste it. If we disregard our present human rebirth, thinking that in the future when we attain another, we will make better use of it, we are like the ignorant beggar who finds a lump of gold, but keeps it aside thinking he will use it when he finds another.

In the *Guide to the Bodhisattva's Way of Life* by Shantideva it is said:

If even one moment of negativity
Causes me to be born in the hells for eons,
Then consider the results of the nonvirtues I have accumulated
    from beginningless time.
How could I ever be reborn anywhere but the lower realms?

By some great fortune all of us here today have found a human rebirth, and have the incredible opportunity to be able to train in the practices of the three paths. It is far easier to attain enlightenment from our present state than it is to reach a higher rebirth from the hell realms. If we were to imagine that our path to enlightenment is like a mountain, our present human rebirth alone would place us more than halfway up. From here, even though we may not be able to reach the peak tomorrow, at least we can prevent ourselves from falling all the way down.

Of course, if we try to think about the rarity of our perfect human rebirth in terms of its causes without a firm belief in the existence of past and future lives, the reasoning will be difficult to apply. So, to begin, we need to understand early on how the five aggregates are established as the basis for imputing the "I." When we talk about the five aggregates, we are not just referring to the form aggregate, but also to the aggregate of consciousness. The cause and effect relationship—whereby virtue brings its corresponding result and nonvirtue brings its corresponding result—is established on the basis of consciousness. If we have faith or belief in this, or even if we don't totally believe in it but we think that it's possible, we thus have the basis for applying the reasoning of creating the causes to generate the result of perfect human rebirth. If we have complete wrong view, meaning that we are totally certain that cause and effect don't exist, we have absolutely no basis for the application of this kind of logic and reasoning.

When we are unable to appreciate the opportunities our perfect human rebirth affords us, it is almost like we have not been born with those leisures at all. When we spend our human lives obsessed with attachment and desire, chasing after objects that we wish to possess and consume, our mental state is no different than that of a being born as a hungry ghost. When we pass our human lives burning with hatred and anger toward those whom we perceive as our enemies, our mind places us in a state no different than that of a hell realm being. In the same way, when our entire human lifetime is characterized by dullness, confusion, and ignorance, our human rebirth is really no different than a rebirth in the animal realm. Likewise, if we pass our lifetimes as a human selfishly enjoying the extreme bliss of meditative concentration, completely lacking in wisdom, our mental experience is no different than that of a long-life god.

Therefore, although on the surface it may appear that we enjoy the freedom from the states of rebirth that do not allow us the opportunity to practice Dharma, if we are not able to utilize these leisures in this lifetime, then in reality, we lack them.

As I have mentioned, the teachings of Shakyamuni Buddha are generally categorized into two groups: the scriptural teachings and the experiential, or realized, teachings. In the current time period, which is considered an age of degeneration, the teachings that exist in the experience of practitioners are declining, and as a result we rely more heavily upon the scriptural teachings. However, even though *in general* we say that the realized teachings are declining, if an individual perseveres in the training of ethics, concentration, and wisdom, it may not prove to be so in that individual's case. I want to make this distinction clear. In this way you see that the responsibility is really in your own hands—you are your own best friend, you are your own protector. As Buddha said: "I will show you the path to liberation, but understand that whether you are liberated or not is dependent upon you." We should persevere in generating the realized teachings in our minds, and we should pray to be able to enhance whatever experiences we are able to generate.

If you think about it, you will realize that there is really a great deal of work involved in trying to maintain this human body. When it wakes up, you have to give it breakfast, lunch, and dinner, and many things to drink in between. If your body is not feeling well, you have to give it all kinds of medication. If it's feeling cold, you have to find it heat. If it's feeling hot, you have to find it cool conditions. So much maintenance! If you pass your lifetime stagnating in the unhappiness of the self-cherishing mind, you are squandering a great opportunity. If you cannot use your human rebirth to accomplish the ultimate benefit for yourself and others, then all of this maintenance is a total waste. This was stated by Shantideva.

RARE FROM THE POINT OF VIEW OF EXAMPLE

In general, when we think about the great value of our precious human rebirth, we should focus on ourselves. But when we think about its rarity, we should make the comparison in terms of external conditions.

An example to illustrate the rarity of our precious human rebirth is thinking that those born in the lower realms are as plentiful as the grass that grows in the rich valleys, and those born in the higher realms are as rare as the grass that grows on the peaks of mountains. In the same way, among those who have attained higher rebirth, those who have the eight leisures and the ten opportunities in the human realm are even more rare than that. Furthermore, in one of the direct teachings of Shakyamuni Buddha himself, it is stated that beings who migrate from the higher realms to the lower realms are as many as the number of atoms of the earth. And those who migrate from the lower realms to the higher realms are as few as the number of the atoms of the earth that you can hold between your thumb and index finger.

Another analogy utilized in the *Guide to the Bodhisattva's Way of Life* is that of the great turbulent ocean in which a blind turtle swims. On the surface of the ocean, riding on the turbulent waves, is a golden yoke. This blind turtle makes it to the surface every one hundred years. Although there is of course the possibility that the turtle could one day put its neck through that yoke as it surfaces, it would be a very rare event. That occurrence is compared to the rarity of gaining a precious human rebirth. The ocean represents cyclic existence, the turbulence is the force of our own delusions and karma, and the blind turtle is symbolic of our mind of ignorance. The turtle putting its head through the yoke represents the times we can attain a precious human rebirth. We can't say it's impossible, so we say "almost impossible." But how could it be done?

Even after we have considered the rarity and great fortune of our precious human rebirth, we might still wonder how this implies that we need to practice Dharma. The answer is that as long as we wish happiness in this or future lifetimes, we have no other choice than to rely upon the spiritual path. The Dharma is the ultimate method to eliminate the disturbing, unsubdued negative minds that cause all of our suffering. When we think about the rarity of our precious human rebirth by way of these examples, we should be inspired to make use of this opportunity. As a result of all of these contemplations, the conclusion that we should draw is that it is very necessary to take advantage of this perfect human rebirth, right away, in this very lifetime.

RARE FROM THE POINT OF VIEW OF NATURE

When considering how difficult it is to obtain the result of a perfect human rebirth, we should remember that among all the realms of existence, the greatest number of beings exist in the hell realms. A fewer number are born in the hungry ghost realm, and fewer than that in the animal realm. Even fewer than the number of beings born in the animal realm are the beings who have the opportunity to be reborn in the human realm. And among those, those who are born with the eight leisures and the ten opportunities are fewer still. Among those, the ones who have the eight leisures and the ten opportunities and are able to make such fortune worthwhile are even more rare. We should contemplate in this way.

The fact that you are involved in Dharma practice at all at this moment has been your choice. It has not been forced upon you, but rather you have chosen to follow this path based on an understanding of cyclic existence, and an understanding of the essenceless nature of the temporary pleasures of this life. Consider the fact that there are so many others born in human form, from your own country, your own background—and yet there are so few who do not focus all of their energy on the material attainments of this life. Those who emphasize the importance of infinite future lifetimes are fewer. Even among those who have been exposed to the teachings, those who really make an effort to understand the Dharma are even fewer. Those who cultivate this understanding into an antidote to negativity—even fewer still. Those who are able to cultivate the spiritual path and the realizations of the path from liberation to enlightenment are far fewer than that. And those beings who have realized bodhichitta and so forth are even more uncommon.

Even among those who are interested in a spiritual path, those who have the opportunity to listen to the teachings of the profound path of wisdom and the extensive path of method and to cultivate the understanding of them are very, very rare. There are some who come to Dharma centers and feel that it is a very relaxing and comfortable environment, and are satisfied with that. Then there are others who have a strong wish to learn and make great effort to excel in their studies, and are satisfied so long as they are able gain more knowledge. Among those, the people who gain real knowledge of the Dharma *and* are able to realize the teachings and use them to subdue their negative minds are far, far fewer.

We should rejoice in our great fortune in having met the teachings of Lama Atisha and Lama Tsongkhapa, these teachings that are the essential heart teachings, and we should rejoice that we have the fortune to be able to hear, understand, and contemplate them. We should not be satisfied with this alone, but should also work toward being able to utilize these teachings as the antidote to our delusions, and further develop our minds in order to obtain liberation and enlightenment for the benefit of all mother sentient beings.

Abandon Clinging to This Life

Lama Tsongkhapa's *Three Principal Paths* says:

> Leisure and opportunity are difficult to find,
> This life is impermanent.
> Familiarizing your mind in this way,
> Reverse clinging to the appearances of this life.

Clinging to the appearances of this life means focusing on the benefits of this one brief lifetime alone—seeking our happiness in terms of a better reputation, better food, better clothing, better shelter, and the temporary pleasures of this existence. Essentially, this mentality is obsessed by the eight worldly dharmas. The best method to free ourselves from this kind of thought is to reflect on the great value of our perfect human rebirth and to think about impermanence and death.

Often, even though we seek to subdue our minds through Dharma practice, we do not succeed because we are still caught up in the eight worldly dharmas. In fact, we are so habituated to this kind of thinking that even what we consider our Dharma practice—our daily prayers and commitments, our prostrations and circumambulations—is usually affected by it. If, however, we are able to completely abandon our fixation with the appearances of this life, our minds will truly become free.

Lama Atisha had one disciple who made great effort in all of his daily practices. Yet somehow, despite this student's great perseverance, Lama Atisha told him repeatedly that he would still be better off practicing Dharma. The student became understandably frustrated, and one day he finally came to Lama Atisha and asked what exactly he had meant by this, since he felt that he was doing everything that was required of him. Lama Atisha answered that he needed to give up the thought of this life, to give up the thought of the eight worldly dharmas. After hearing this particular advice, that disciple became a very pure, highly accomplished practitioner.

The essence of abandoning the eight worldly dharmas is abandoning the thought of concern for reputation, better food, better clothing, and better shelter. Of these, the most difficult to give up is the wish for a good reputation. Even great meditators who live in seclusion without attachment to material things may still hold onto the thought that seeks reputation, hoping to be praised or admired for their meditation practice.

The Ten Innermost Jewels of the Kadampas

One of the most profound methods to eliminate the thought that is consumed only with the concerns of this life—which is the cause of so much suffering—is the practice of the ten innermost jewels. This practice originated with the Kadampa geshes, whose tradition is rooted in the works of the great Atisha and his disciple Dromtonpa. The practice of the ten innermost jewels is made up of four entrustments, three vajras, and three types of expulsion.

The first of the ten innermost jewels is entrusting your deepest thoughts to the Dharma. This means realizing the opportunity of your perfect human rebirth, its great value, and its fragility. It means thinking of the uncertainty of the time of death, and that when death does come, the only thing of value will be the extent to which you have developed your mind in the Dharma. The worldly pursuits that you have so emphasized up until this point will be of absolutely no benefit. This is how to entrust your innermost thoughts to the Dharma.

The second jewel is to entrust yourself to the state of a beggar. This means that you cultivate the attitude that is prepared to dedicate your life entirely to Dharma practice, even if it means you will be unable to provide for your livelihood and become a beggar to do so. This is the attitude that is willing to surrender to the most minimal kind of existence in order to be able to practice.

The third jewel is entrusting yourself even to death. This means that even if survival itself becomes difficult—if you are lacking food and shelter, and even if you die—you will persevere in your Dharma practice. We have died again and again in many past lifetimes, but to die with this sense of commitment to our practice is really worthwhile.

The fourth jewel is the entrustment to the thought of having to die alone in a cave. By giving up the thought that seeks the benefits of this one brief lifetime, perhaps you will end up in a very pitiful physical condition: old, sick, with nobody to care for you. This entrustment means giving up all aversion to this possibility, as long as you are able to fulfill the objective of developing your mind in Dharma.

The four jewels of entrustment are followed by the cultivation of the three vajras. A vajra is used as a symbol here because it is unchangeable and immutable, and very strong. Among the three vajras, the first is the vajra of determination. For example, imagine that you decide to dedicate your life completely to spiritual practice and live humbly in a cave or hermitage, causing all of your friends and loved ones to become extremely concerned. As a result, they try very hard to convince you to give up this type of existence and return to worldly life. If you have cultivated the vajra of unshakable determination, you will persevere in your practice regardless.

This issue is a very big one for Western Dharma practitioners, and particularly for those who become ordained. Generally speaking, Westerners who take on the appearance of monks and nuns need to cultivate a very strong, unshakeable mind in conjunction with changing their outer appearance. If you just rush into things without thinking carefully about what you are doing or considering the consequences, making this kind of decision will only bring confusion in the long run. In order to really make this change not only externally, but internally as well, the first step you should take is to completely abandon the thought, "What will people think of me?" As long as that thought remains, there will be instability in your mind. Instead, from the depth of your heart you should feel that you have willingly and freely chosen your own path, and you should keep all the reasons why you have done so very fresh in your mind.

The second of the three vajras is the vajra of total disregard. This means not being concerned about what people might think of you, or how they might criticize you. In the face of all kinds of criticism and praise, you must be unshakeable, unchangeable, and unmoved. You should consider the feeling that you must fulfill the hopes or expectations of your friends and loved ones or that you must live your life in accordance with the views or expectations of others an obstacle to your decision to live your life in Dharma practice.

The third vajra is to keep the vajra of transcendental wisdom with you always. The vajra of transcendental wisdom is the wisdom that arises out of extensive listening, analyzing, and understanding. When you apply this understanding as an antidote to the delusions within your mind, you will be able to free yourself from the thought of the eight worldly dharmas, cut through all of the meaningless affairs of this life, and focus on spiritual practice.

The last three of the ten innermost jewels are the three types of expulsions. It may happen that by undertaking the practice of abandoning the eight worldly dharmas, you become a total outcast from the world. Worldly life revolves around the eight worldly concerns—you are considered abnormal if you don't have a sense of competition toward your equals, a feeling of jealousy toward those who have more qualities than you do, or a disparaging attitude toward those who are lesser than yourself. If a person doesn't have these types of attitudes, it is almost like being crazy. Thus, as a result of practicing the thought of abandoning the eight worldly dharmas, you experience a sense of exile from society, which is the first expulsion.

From this separation from society you then attain the rank of the dogs, having given up emphasis on better food, better clothing, better shelter, and better reputation in this life, and become a total misfit.

On the heels of this you attain the third expulsion, the rank of the gods, because in dedicating your life to the practice of subduing the mind and freeing the mind from the delusions, eventually you will attain liberation and enlightenment, and attain the state of the celestial beings.

Generally speaking, you almost never hear of practitioners who have died of starvation or due to lack of other basic necessities. However, in the case of those who still cling to the appearances of this life, there are many who have died due to not having the basic necessities. The more the mind is caught up in clinging to the appearances of this life—seeking better food, better clothing, better shelter, better reputation—the less the mind can experience any sense of contentment. No matter how much we have, it never is quite enough, and no matter how rich we are, we still remain in a mental state of poverty.

Historically, there are many examples of highly accomplished spiritual beings and masters who were born into affluence but left it behind to benefit sentient beings through their practice and teachings. Shakyamuni

Buddha, who was born into a royal family, gave up his entire kingdom and the luxury of a princely life in order to engage in spiritual practice. Shantideva and Lama Atisha have similar stories. Lama Tsongkhapa too, following the advice of Manjushri, gave up his retinue of hundreds and thousands of disciples in order to undertake purification retreat and meditate on the pure view.

The great yogi Milarepa said:

Material gifts and respect do not support my happiness; hateful enemies do not cause my suffering. It is through my life in this hermitage that my wishes as a yogi are completely fulfilled.

He also said:

Nobody knows that I am getting old; nobody knows when I fall sick in this hermitage; nobody knows that I am dying in this cave; but in this hermitage all my wishes are fulfilled. If even upon death my bones are left where the vultures can pick at them, it makes no difference to me, so long as my life in the hermitage has been fulfilled.

As a yogi it makes no difference if your dead body is surrounded by people crying over you or not, so long as your aspirations for practice are fulfilled.

If we wish to practice the ten innermost jewels of the Kadampas as outlined above, it is important that we begin with the first of the ten and move on from there. It is necessary to have the foundation of the first jewel in order to practice the second, and the second for the third, and so forth. The reason for this is that, right now, we do not have the strength to complete the practices of the latter jewels right away. We need to begin slowly, and increase our capacity from there.

In the time of Milarepa, a businessman inspired by the great yogi's life decided to try to emulate him. Acting upon the advice of Milarepa's teachings that say to abandon clinging to appearances, the businessman immediately gave up all of his material belongings. Unfortunately, although he physically parted with everything, he was mentally unable to do so. Soon enough he became very unhappy, claiming that Milarepa was nothing more than a beggar who had caused his ruin. By this example we see the importance of practicing these steps in the proper order.

In order to be able to practice according to the ten innermost jewels, it is first necessary that we recognize the great value of our own perfect human rebirth, and that such an opportunity does not last forever. It is as rare for us to attain a perfect human rebirth with the eight leisures and ten opportunities as it is for an enlightened being to descend into our world. We should try to see how using this rebirth merely for survival is a very limited use of our potential. This priceless, incredibly valuable, highly meaningful perfect human rebirth with its eight leisures and ten opportunities is a most rare and precious opportunity.

THE MANNER OF TAKING THE ESSENCE FROM OUR PRECIOUS HUMAN REBIRTH

The Three Scopes

In order to be able to take the essence from our human rebirth, we need to have a clear understanding of the spiritual path. In particular, we need a clear understanding of the three principal paths as taught by Manjushri, as they have been applied to the framework of the three scopes by Lama Tsongkhapa in the *Lamrim Chenmo.*

Upon attaining enlightenment, Buddha Shakyamuni turned the wheel of Dharma three times, giving the 84,000 teachings for the temporary and ultimate benefit of sentient beings. The teachings of temporary benefit for sentient beings are the path and practice of the small scope, which create the causes to be reborn in the higher realms. Practitioners of the small scope are categorized into two: those who are mere small scope beings, and those who are extraordinary small scope beings. The mere small scope beings practice the ethics of living in the ten virtues and abandoning the ten nonvirtuous actions for the benefit of this lifetime alone. The extraordinary small scope beings live in the ethics of the ten virtues with the thought of seeking to benefit future lifetimes. To be considered a small scope being who is actually on the spiritual path, the practitioner must be an extraordinary small scope being, placing a greater sense of importance on the attainments of future lives.

The teachings of ultimate benefit are divided into those that bring the benefit of liberation and those that bring the benefit of full enlightenment. The teachings that bring the benefit of liberation are the path and practices of the medium scope. Lama Atisha's *Lamp for the Path to Enlightenment* states that the path of the medium scope is the practice of those who turn their back on the pleasures of cyclic existence in order to cease the delusions and the karmic actions that perpetuate cyclic existence, and thereby attain an individual state of peace and happiness.

To summarize, practitioners of the small scope turn their back on the temporary pleasures of the present lifetime and place greater emphasis on the attainment of a higher rebirth in the future. Their entire practice is based on that motivation. Practitioners of the medium scope have a more advanced motivation, in the sense that they consider any birth within cyclic existence to be a birth under the control of delusions and karma. For them, attaining higher rebirth alone is not sufficient because they feel that even if they attain a higher rebirth, it is still a birth bound by delusions and karma and therefore subject to the cycle of aging, sickness, and death. A practitioner of the medium scope seeks to terminate the entire cycle of rebirth brought on by delusions and karma, and to attain the state of liberation.[9]

The goal of a practitioner of the great scope is to attain complete enlightenment, free of mistakes, and complete in all positive qualities and knowledge. This attainment is rooted in the motivation of compassion. The practitioner generates the mind of bodhichitta, renouncing self and cherishing others, and undertakes a unified practice of method and wisdom to attain this goal. Through this practice, the great scope practitioner is able to eliminate the affliction obscurations and the obscurations to omniscience, and thereby actualize the result of enlightenment.

The division of the three scopes can also be understood by examining the various levels of ethics that are practiced in each. In accordance with Vinaya, small scope practitioners take the abandonment of the ten non-virtuous actions as their main objective on the path. These practitioners do not necessarily take vows, but they live in the ethics of abandoning those actions. Medium scope practitioners take the vows of individual liberation, the *pratimoksha* vows, based on the determination to definitely emerge from cyclic existence and attain liberation. For practitioners of the great scope, the practice of ethics is incorporated into the practice of bodhichitta.

Beings of the three scopes can also be categorized in terms of the three different types of results. The lowest result is a higher rebirth, which is the result of the practice of a small scope practitioner. This is followed by liberation, which is the result of the practice of a medium scope practitioner. The most supreme result is enlightenment, which is the result of the practice of a great scope practitioner. Alternatively, the three scopes can also be categorized in terms of the kind of path the practitioner focuses upon. In the small scope, the path is living in the ethics of abandoning the ten nonvirtues. In the medium scope, the path is the profound path of wisdom. In the great scope, the path is the unified practice of both method and wisdom.

The Need to Train in All Three Scopes

Taking the essence of our precious human rebirth means developing our mind in the path and practices set forth in the three scopes. It is not anything different than this. The attainment of enlightenment by way of the graduated path is the best way to fulfill the opportunity of our perfect human rebirth. And yet you may wonder, if the objective is to lead a sentient being to complete enlightenment, which can only be attained through the practice of the great scope, what need is there to train in the paths of the small and medium scopes at all?

Actually, in the context of the lamrim, the trainees in the small or medium scope are not training in the paths of the small and medium scope alone, but rather in the path and practice that are *common* to the small and medium scopes. The two lower scopes are considered to be the foundation of the cultivation of the path and practices of the great scope. We train in the path and practices common to the small and medium scopes because in order to enter the Mahayana we must develop the mind of bodhichitta. The practice of bodhichitta is rooted in love and compassion. Compassion in turn is rooted in the understanding of suffering. In the small and medium scopes, there are extensive explanations of the general and particular types of suffering of the realms of cyclic existence. Before we can generate compassion, we need to identify these types of suffering in terms of the suffering that we ourselves experience. Once we have cultivated a sense of renunciation based on our own suffering, we will then be able to comprehend the mind of compassion, which perceives the suffering of others, and wishes them to be free from it.

As Shantideva says:

Before conceiving of that for sentient beings,
If one has not dreamed, even in a dream,
That thought for one's own purpose,
How can one ever imagine producing it for the purpose of others?

Also, in the small scope we come to understand the cause and effect of our karmic actions, and by this method we are inspired to abandon non-virtue and to cultivate virtue, accumulate merit, and purify our negative karma. The practice of refuge then creates the foundation to be able to cultivate the path and practices of the medium scope. In the medium scope, we practice the three higher trainings, which act as the basis to cultivate the path and practices of the great scope, the Mahayana path. In this way, the path of the small scope becomes a means to establish ourselves on the path of the medium scope, and the path of the medium scope becomes a means to actualize the path and practice of the great scope.

The entry into the graduated path to enlightenment is the practice of guru devotion, but the entry into the Dharma is the recognition of our own perfect human rebirth. If the training in the small and medium scopes becomes disconnected to the training in the great scope, it will be impossible for our efforts in the lower scopes to support our development of bodhichitta. Therefore, we must take care to ensure that this does not happen.

The graduated path of method is the means to accumulate the extensive collection of the merit of virtue. It is also known as the conventional graduated path to enlightenment. The profound path of wisdom is the means to accumulate the merit of wisdom. It is also known as the ultimate graduated path to enlightenment. Complete enlightenment is accomplished through the unified practice of method and wisdom, through the inseparable practice of the conventional graduated path to enlightenment and the ultimate graduated path to enlightenment. The paths of the profound and the extensive are like the wings of the bird which enable it to fly.

After training in the graduated path to enlightenment, when we attain the Mahayana path of preparation, we enter the Vajrayana vehicle, the path of mantra. In order to develop our capacity to train in the Vajrayana vehicle, we need to establish the foundation of the causal vehicle of the Paramitayana first. In order to create this basis, we first need to train in the medium scope path and practice, and in order to create this basis, we need to train in the small scope path and practice. It should be clear by this explanation that in order to secure the foundations for the later parts of the path it is essential that we first establish the basis of the earlier parts.

Finally, an individual should be guided through the three scopes based on explanations using logic and reasoning, and through the blessings of the oral transmission. The instructions that one receives should be in accordance with the explanations of the teachings of Nagarjuna, Asanga, Aryadeva, Atisha, Lama Tsongkhapa, and so forth, and not merely an individual teacher's composition of the path.

This completes the section on precious human rebirth according to the *Lamrim Chenmo.*

PART 3

The Small Scope

REMEMBERING DEATH
AND IMPERMANENCE

B UDDHA HIMSELF said that all sentient beings down to the tiniest crawl-
ing insects have the potential to become enlightened. In his *Guide to
the Bodhisattva's Way of Life,* Shantideva writes that if even beings such as
flies and mosquitoes have the potential to become enlightened, what need
is there to mention human beings, with perfect human rebirths? If we
accept that flies are endowed with this great potential, then we must accept
that it is even more so in our own case. As human beings we are able to
express ourselves and understand others; we possess the wisdom that is
able to discriminate right from wrong; and we have been born with the
eight leisures and the ten opportunities. Thus we find ourselves in an
extremely good position to complete the path to enlightenment.

Understanding this, we should strive to take the essence of our good
fortune by applying ourselves in the practices common to the small,
medium, and great scopes, and learning the graduated steps of the path so
that we do not make mistakes. As we discussed, in order to develop the
basis to train in the great scope, we must create the foundation of the
medium scope path, and in order to develop the basis to train in the path
and practices of the medium scope, we must have the basis of the path
and practices of the small scope. The path and practices of the small scope
are based on the practices that seek to eliminate the mentality that grasps
at the appearances of this lifetime and cultivate the mentality that seeks the
benefits of future lifetimes.

THE FOUR MISCONCEPTIONS
AND THE FOUR WHITE SEALS

Why is it that our minds are occupied by the fact of our present existence, unable to generate the thought of the importance of the future lifetimes? What is the obstacle hindering us? We are bound to concern for this lifetime alone by the thought grasping at true existence, by the innate sense that we are going to live forever. In order to eliminate this innate grasping at a permanent mode of existence, we need to focus on the awareness of the fact that we ourselves are in fact subject to impermanence and death.

Buddha summarized our misconceptions of the world we live in, and of ourselves, into what is called the four wrong views. They are as follows.

1. Holding what in reality is impermanent to be permanent
2. Holding what in reality is impure to be pure
3. Holding what in reality is in the nature of suffering to be true happiness
4. Holding what in reality is essenceless to have essence

These wrong perceptions ensure that we focus primarily on the activities of this one brief lifetime, and create obstacles to developing the thought that seeks the benefit of the infinite future lifetimes.

Seeing these four misconceptions in the minds of sentient beings, Buddha taught their antidote, the four white seals. The four seals are:

1. All compounded phenomena are impermanent.
2. All contaminated phenomena are suffering.
3. All phenomena are selfless.
4. Nirvana is peace.

Of the four misconceptions, perceiving what is impermanent to be permanent is the most harmful. This view blocks the awareness of impermanence and death from our minds entirely. Although intellectually we know that we will in fact die eventually, because we are so habituated to our misconceptions about impermanence and death, generally in our day-to-day lives we have the feeling that we will not die *today*. As a result we make absolutely no effort to develop the thought that seeks the benefit of future lifetimes. We are fooled by our innate grasping at permanence. Therefore, the first of the four white seals is establishing impermanence.

There are two types of impermanence, gross and subtle. The awareness that we will not live forever and that we are definitely going to die is the awareness of gross impermanence. Without this awareness, all of the activities of our body, speech, and mind will serve this one brief lifetime alone. All of the activities of our body, speech, and mind will function only to accomplish our own well-being. However, in actual fact, without depending on others, no happiness can come about in our lives at all. Our grasping at permanence encourages a very narrow way of thinking that becomes the basis for much unhappiness and suffering.

No matter how much you talk about liberation to an individual who believes that he or she will live forever, no matter how much you talk about enlightenment, you are uttering empty words. Furthermore, this person will be much more easily inclined to engage in nonvirtuous activities, and much less inclined to engage in virtue. In contrast, someone who has some basic awareness of impermanence and death and some concern for his or her future lives, but lacks the full understanding of the reality of these things, will undertake virtuous actions with laziness. For example, at the end of his or her life, after having been totally distracted by worldly affairs, this kind of person may then recall what is coming next and try to engage in virtue from that point forward.

What are the shortcomings of not thinking about impermanence and death? What are the shortcomings of not considering the fact that we are not going to live forever? If we do not train our minds in these topics, we will not be inspired to engage in virtuous activities benefiting future lifetimes, and even if we do engage in virtuous activities, they will be comparatively weak. Even if we make an attempt to practice Dharma, we will be unable to persevere. And without recalling impermanence and death, all of our delusional ways of thinking and the actions that result from them will increase.

The benefit of generating the realization that we will not live forever, and particularly realizing that we could die this very day, is that it inspires a sense of urgency in our Dharma practice. We will not fall under the control of the eight worldly dharmas. We will be able to direct our thoughts and actions toward the benefit of future lifetimes by way of the practices of refuge and cause and effect. Not only will we be able to secure the benefit of higher rebirth in this way for ourselves, but we will also become a guiding force for others. Also, although generally when we are trying to eliminate our delusions, we attempt to apply a different antidote to each delusion individually, the awareness of death in conjunction with the recognition of the leisures and opportunities of our perfect human rebirth is like a hammer, pounding out all of our afflictions with one blow.

Even if we have a field that did not produce a good harvest last year, regardless of our doubt about this year's harvest, we still make the effort to plow and plant the seeds. In the same way, even if we do not have the total realization of the recognition of perfect human rebirth, or the total realization of impermanence and death, it says in the text that as long as we have positive forms of doubts with regard to these topics, as long as we have a feeling for them, we still have the basis to accomplish both the temporary and ultimate benefits.

Even if we are fortunate enough to find a perfect human rebirth blessed with the eighteen attributes (the eight leisures and the ten opportunities), it is still possible that we will not be able to persevere in Dharma practice. Why is this so? It is mostly because of the feeling of *I won't die*. This very strong sense of grasping at *I won't die* is our greatest downfall. Its only antidote is cultivating the realization of impermanence and death, and understanding that this is the entry point to the path of virtue.

To think that meditation on impermanence and death and perfect human rebirth are only for beginners and needn't be emphasized in our daily contemplations is completely wrong. Constant reflection on these two topics is an important form of meditation at the beginning of the spiritual path, in the middle of the spiritual path, and even at the very end of the spiritual path. In the beginning, this meditation enables us to enter the path of virtue and the path of Dharma practice. In the middle, these points of contemplation free us from the traps of our own laziness and encourage us to persevere in our practice. In the end, these points ensure that we reap the fruits of all our efforts. For these reasons we should contemplate these topics on a daily basis.

An ordinary individual who has not been exposed to a spiritual path fears death because of having to part with friends and loved ones, material possessions, and so forth. Death for this individual will be an experience under the control of the eight worldly dharmas, and at the time of death, this person will probably develop a nonvirtuous mind. But as Dharma practitioners, we should not fear death for such reasons. We should realize that creating karma is like planting seeds, that delusions fuel the accumulation of these karmic seeds, and that as long as we have taken a rebirth induced by delusions and karma, death is inevitable. If we must fear death, we should fear it because of the loss of the opportunity to make our lives worthwhile, because of the loss of opportunity to subdue our minds. We should fear death because we have not been able to purify the negative karma that will bring a lower rebirth and because we have not been able to accumulate the positive karma that will secure a higher rebirth. This is the kind of fear of death generated by practitioners of the small scope.

If, while we are alive, we reflect daily on the subtle impermanence of all of the things that we are connected to and on the changes that take place in everything from moment to moment, this, too, can counteract our obsessions with material belongings or with our friends and loved ones. If, also, due to familiarity with death and impermanence as they are taught in the lamrim, we are motivated to engage in spiritual practices while we are still alive, then at the time of death we will have no reason to fear it. It is said that for the very best spiritual practitioners death is a joyful experience. Those of medium ability have no fear of death when it happens. And even the least of practitioners die without any sense of regret. If we fear death while we are alive and, as a result, do our best to make our time positive and meaningful, when death suddenly descends upon us, we will certainly have one of these three experiences.

MEDITATING ON DEATH

In addition to thinking in a very general way as outlined above, in order to develop and maintain the awareness that we are not going to live forever, we can meditate on the three roots, the nine reasonings, and the three conclusions.

The three roots are that death is certain, the time of death is uncertain, and nothing can help you at the time of death except your Dharma practice.

Death Is Certain

There are three reasons supporting the fact that death is certain. The first is that when death does happen, there is no condition that can reverse it. It doesn't matter what kind of body we are reborn into, there is no aggregate or form anywhere that is not subject to death. Even the holy supreme emanation body of Buddha was no exception: at the age of eighty Buddha manifested the activity of passing away in order to benefit sentient beings who habitually grasp at permanence. Likewise, all the great spiritual practitioners of the past have had bodies that were eventually subject to death. If this is so, it is needless to mention our own case.

Thus, no matter how many realizations a person may have, or how many long-life initiations he or she has taken, or how many long-life retreats he or she has done—despite all of that, he or she will not survive death. Even the greatest doctors are helpless when the body succumbs to death. Even if we take care of our bodies in the best possible way, treating them with medications prescribed by the very king of physicians, eventually our bodies are going to die. When the process of death takes place, there is no condition that can reverse it. Whether we travel to the depths of the ocean or to the heights of outer space, or even to the moon, there is no place where we can go where we will not die. Whether we are a sentient being living in the past, present, or future, when death happens, it cannot be reversed. Regardless of what kind of body we are born into, regardless of what kind of place, and regardless of where in time we exist, we cannot escape the fact that we will die one day.

In sutra, there is an example cited of four mountains from four directions that close in upon the center. As these four mountains roll in from the four directions, they destroy everything in their path. If we were trapped in the center when such a thing occurred, we would be helpless, without anything to protect us—no medicine, no tools, no power of mantra. In the same way, our perfect human rebirth is overtaken by the four great mountains of aging, sickness, death, and downfall. Aging takes away our youth, sickness takes away our health, death takes away our life, and downfall takes away our glory or magnificence. Just as we would have no method to stop the four great mountains, so we have no method to stop the experience of death from occurring.

In the advice of the Kadampa masters, it is said that while you are living, you should fear death. But at the actual time of death, you should not be afraid. In our own case, as ordinary human beings, we have this completely reversed. While we are alive, we have no fear of death. We can't even remember the fact that we will die. But when death arrives, we suddenly experience great fear, grasping, and desperation.

The second reason supporting the fact that death is definite is that our karmic lifespan cannot be extended. Not only that, but as the weeks, days, hours, and minutes pass, our lifespan is constantly diminishing. Even if we take care of our health, and even if we have the fortune to live a very long time—say one hundred and ten years—that time will eventually come to an end. When twelve months have gone by that is one year less. When four weeks have passed, that's one month less. Those weeks in turn are finished as days go by, and those days are passed in hours. Shantideva says in the *Guide to the Bodhisattva's Way of Life*:

Day and night unceasingly
My lifespan is constantly diminishing.
There is no increase.
For one like me, why won't death arrive?

If we wish to contemplate this topic by way of example, we can consider a waterfall with descending rapids that never cease. In the same way, our lifespan continues to decrease without rest. We can also take the illustration from sutra in which impermanence and death are exemplified by the image of a constantly shifting cloud formation. Like that, so are the continual changes of birth and death in the experience of the sentient beings of the three realms. Or we can consider the example of performers in a play, whose roles shift from scene to scene. In the same way, the lives of sentient beings pass away.[10]

The third reason that we should contemplate to support our understanding of the fact that death is definite is that even while we are alive, there is so little time for Dharma practice. Therefore, we will surely die before we are able to complete anything of value in this life. In short, this is the fear of dying without having done anything meaningful for our own or for others' ultimate happiness.

We might think that perhaps if we live to an old age, we will have the time to make our lives useful, the time to practice Dharma. But even so, much of our life gets wasted—in eating, drinking, and in various distractions, and so forth. Before long it becomes too late. Even if, after all of this, we then wish to practice Dharma, our sense perceptions and our bodies can become too incapacitated to support it.[11]

The great Tibetan teacher Kuntang Jampelyang says that the first twenty years of our lives are spent without any thought of the spiritual path. Early on, we have far too many distractions to focus on the objectives of a spiritual practice. In the next twenty years, we try very hard to get all the right conditions together to practice, but really don't end up doing much at all. Finally, we spend the last twenty years of our lives realizing that it is just too late.

Whatever has happened in the past in relation to today is just like the dream of last night—when we awaken, it is only a memory of a dream. In terms of today, all that is left of the past is our experience of its consequences in the future. If we reflect upon the activities of our body, speech, and mind thus far in this context, we will be left with the feeling of a blazing fire of regret.

Having ascertained that death is definite through these reasons and examples, we should come to the resolution that we must make our life meaningful through Dharma practice. As a result of repeated contemplation on the first root and the first three reasons, we should develop the strong aspiration to apply ourselves to the spiritual path. When this occurs, it means that our contemplation has been fruitful.

The Kadampa masters say that if we don't think about impermanence and death in the morning, the whole morning is lost in nonvirtue. If we don't think about it in the afternoon, the whole afternoon is lost, and if we don't think about it in the evening, the whole evening is lost in nonvirtue. So we can see the importance of the recollection of impermanence and death according to these great practitioners. It is equally important in our own case, especially when we practice four daily sessions.[12] Sometimes by the time we do the second session, we find that we have become completely disconnected from the first. In order to ensure the continuity of our practice and to avoid coming under the control of laziness and so forth, meditation on impermanence and death is essential.

The Time of Death Is Uncertain

The second root is thinking that the time of death is uncertain.

Beings such as ourselves do not have the luxury of a predetermined life-span,[13] such as a hundred years exactly—our death is not scheduled to occur in a specific year, month, or on a particular day. Despite this, we have such a strong intuitive sense of grasping at the permanence of our existence that in our daily lives we feel certain that we are not going to die. The objectives of our day-to-day activities serve this lifetime alone. Since it does not occur to us that we may die today, or that we will die soon, we do not prepare for death. Because we feel so strongly that *I won't die now,* none of our activities are directed toward benefiting our future lives. And then when death does come upon us, it happens most suddenly, most unexpectedly.

Since the time of death is uncertain, since we can die anytime, it is to our advantage to train ourselves to think that, in fact, we *could* die today. With this thought, it is to our advantage to abandon nonvirtue in order to prevent rebirth in the lower realms, and to engage in positive actions in order to secure a higher rebirth. If we have the feeling that we could die anytime, we will be completely prepared for death if it does occur, and we lose nothing even if it doesn't.

Think of it like this: imagine that you are expecting a guest, and it is definite that this guest is going to arrive, but you do not know when. In this situation, you make general preparations for this guest regardless of the fact that you are not certain of the date or the time of arrival. That way if the guest arrives, you are prepared, and if the guest doesn't arrive, there is no loss. In the same way you can prepare yourselves for your future lives by thinking that you could die today. Without this thought in your minds, you become totally focused on this one brief lifetime alone, and thereby seek out only the objectives of the eight worldly dharmas. Of course, in order to engage in Dharma practice you need the basic means of survival such as food, clothing, and so forth, but not to the extreme degree that we tend to focus on these things.

The first of the three reasons supporting the reality that you could die anytime is that your lifespan is indefinite.

An Indian professor who lives in the United States told me the following story. Before he came to America he checked his prospects for a long life with an astrologer, and the astrologer mentioned a certain date that was dangerous. On the evening preceding that day the professor was quite nervous. The next morning when he got up, he thought, "I haven't died!" He woke up with the perfect awareness of the uncertainty of death. In fact, everything he experienced throughout the entire day—riding in the elevator, crossing the street, driving his car—brought the uncertainty of the time of death to his mind. That day this professor had an excellent meditation on death and impermanence.

As I mentioned earlier, all of existence is subject to death. You may have the experience of seeing someone in the morning and then hearing that afternoon that this person has died. And you may meet people in the evening and learn the next morning that they have passed away. This is how suddenly death descends upon us. One day that person is there, and the next day that person is not around anymore. Sometimes you feel that because people are young, they might live longer, and you feel that death is something more likely to happen to older people. But this way of thinking is not correct. People die after a long fruitful life, and people die very suddenly. Once you are born, death can come in the very next moment. It is a great loss to die without having made your life meaningful by purifying your negative karma to prevent lower rebirth, and accumulating the merit of virtue in order to secure higher rebirth.

Sometimes it is also beneficial to think about this topic in terms of our spiritual teachers, in whom we take refuge, in whom we seek protection, who guide and support us on the spiritual path. When our teachers pass away, it is the greatest lesson for us to counteract our strong view of permanence. Some great teachers have even passed away in the midst of composing something, such as the great master Kuntang Lama Rinpoche, who died without completing a commentary on Lama Tsongkhapa's *Essence of Eloquence: Distinguishing the Interpretable and the Definitive Meanings of All the Scriptures of the Buddha.*

We should think about death in relation to great spiritual masters and in relation to our friends and our relatives, in relation to people who are equal to ourselves, people who are younger, less fortunate, and those with greater fortune. Utilizing the entire scope of all of these examples, we should reflect on the uncertainty of the time of death in every possible way.

Making your life meaningful right away by your practice of Dharma doesn't necessarily mean that you should begin retreat immediately, and persevere in generating realizations. It does mean, however, that you should not come under the control of laziness, and that you should apply your body, speech, and mind in virtuous activities that are not influenced by the eight worldly dharmas as much as possible. Also, the objective of this contemplation is not to incapacitate you in a state of terror. That is not the point. You should be afraid when you realize that you are not going to last forever, that death could happen anytime, but that fear should not become an obstacle. Rather, it should encourage you to work for the benefit of future lifetimes.

The second of the three reasons supporting the reality that the time of death is uncertain is that there are many more conditions for death than there are conditions for survival. Our lives are subject to harm from many sources, sources we cannot even perceive directly—animate and inanimate, human and nonhuman forces. There are countless diseases that could become a cause of death, including diseases that are brought on by the force of our own karma, which are usually incurable. Even the imbalance of elements within our own body can bring on sickness. Imbalances of the outer elements such as earthquakes, floods, and so forth can also become conditions for our death. Actually, all of the conditions that exist now in our environment can easily cause our death. There are certainly many more conditions in the world that could contribute to our death than there are conditions that support our lives.

One of the meditation practices taught by Buddha for the purpose of habituating the mind to the thought of death is to visualize all of your enemies surrounding you, threatening your life. Alternatively, you can meditate on Nagarjuna's example of the image of a candleflame flickering in the wind and elements. The chance that the flame will survive in a storm is very small. Our perfect human rebirth is like that candle flame, surrounded by overwhelming conditions for its demise. You can also consider the example of a water bubble, which bursts at the slightest touch. Your existence is exactly that fragile.

In fact, considering the many conditions for our deaths, it is quite amazing that we have even survived this long, especially when we think about the fact that we have been born in the time of the five great degenerations.[14] Due to the degeneration of this era, even the food that we eat lacks basic nutrients. Even medicines become ineffective. And year after year, we discover different illnesses that cannot be cured. Due to the degeneration of delusions, our afflictions are serious and pervasive, and whatever virtuous undertakings we engage in are, in contrast, a very weak form of virtue. In addition, even the things that are meant to support us—such as our food, shelter, and so forth—can end up causing harm. A perfect example of this in the West is our cars, which are meant to make our lives easier but often become the foremost condition for our deaths.

The third reasoning supporting the fact that the time of the death is uncertain is that our own body is very fragile. The smallest thing—a needle prick, for example—can become a condition for our death. Although this is in fact the reality of our existence, by the force of our mistaken view grasping at permanence we simply do not perceive the delicate nature of our existence. We see our body as being solid and concrete, quite indestructible. Yet even our own world will be destroyed at the end of the eon by fire and water—mere elements.[15] If our own world will be reduced to nothing but ashes at the end, what need is there to wonder about our own bodies?

I don't know if this is true or not, but I heard a story about a Tibetan astrologer who mapped his own chart, curious to see when his own death was going to come. The chart showed that his death was going to occur that very day. From every angle the chart insisted his death was going to happen that very day. Naturally, the astrologer thought, "I don't see how that can happen." He was sitting in his room alone, quite safe. So he kept thinking, thinking, and in his hand he had a bamboo pencil. As he thought, his ear began to itch, and he stuck the pencil in, and at that very moment the window next to him blew open due to the force of the wind, and—

The conclusion that we should come to at the end of this contemplation is to practice Dharma, immediately, right away, without laziness or procrastination.

When Death Comes, Nothing Will Help You Except Your Spiritual Practice

The third root is thinking that when death does happen, nothing will be of any help to us except our Dharma practice.

If we consider this point, we will realize that even the body that we are born with will be of no help at all to us when we die. While we are alive, we can use our physical bodies to accumulate virtue, but when we are dying, it is useless. Also, when we are alive we have the support of many friends and relatives. But we have to experience death by ourselves alone. And we cannot take an atom of the material wealth that we have accumulated during our lifetimes with us into the next life. All that we can take is the negative karma that we have accumulated by greedily collecting material things, and the rare positive karma that we were able to generate in acts of generosity. Therefore, all of our friends and loved ones cannot help us, all of our wealth and material possessions cannot help us, and even our own body cannot help us when death occurs. The only thing that will be of any value or benefit at the time of death will be our Dharma practice through which we have been able to rid our minds of their delusions.

If, while we are alive, we have the opportunity to make positive imprints in our minds through practice and prayer, at the time of death these virtuous states of mind can be drawn upon. Since, according to the laws of cause and effect, a result must accord with the cause, if we manifest a positive state of mind at the time of death it will bring the result of a positive future rebirth. Thus we can understand how nothing benefits us at the time of death except our spiritual practice.

By reflecting on the fact that death is definite, we will come to the resolution to practice Dharma. This resolution will help us to discriminate clearly between worldly and spiritual activities. By reflecting on the fact that the time of death is uncertain, we will come to the resolution to apply ourselves to Dharma practice right away. This eliminates the wrong view of laziness or procrastination. And by reflecting on the third root that when death happens, nothing is of any benefit except our Dharma practice, and the reasoning behind that, we will come to the resolution only to practice pure Dharma.

Shantideva says:

Having found this opportunity,
If I do not meditate on virtue,
There is no greater deception,
There is no greater ignorance.

The realizations of impermanence and death are not easy to evoke, but they are essential. We often pray: may our minds become the Dharma, and may the Dharma become the path, and may that path be free of obstacles. The reason our minds cannot become the Dharma, and the reason that whatever Dharma we do understand does not become a path for spiritual development is because we are hindered by obstacles. The reason we are hindered by obstacles is that we do not have the basic realizations of impermanence and death. Although initially these realizations may be difficult to cultivate, as we familiarize our minds with each of the points of the path, we will find that it will become easier. Of course, we will not be able to realize impermanence and death by contemplating these examples only once. If we really wish to generate the experience of these topics, we will have to reflect on them repeatedly, applying examples to reinforce our understanding.

In addition to meditating in order to realize impermanence and death, we must also accomplish the supporting practices of purification and accumulation of merit, making prayers and requests to the guru-deity, and so forth. It is necessary that we fulfill all of these positive conditions to be able to fully realize these points of the path. Also, we should not think that these topics are too minor to deal with because we have gotten higher practices or better practices through initiations and so forth. Generating the realization of impermanence and death is an essential point at the very beginning of our spiritual practice, in the middle of our spiritual practice, and even at the end of our spiritual practice. It is a point of contemplation that we should cultivate throughout the entire spiritual path.

This completes the discussion on impermanence and death according to the *Lamrim Chenmo.*

CONTEMPLATING THE SUFFERING AND HAPPINESS OF FUTURE LIVES

THE NEXT POINT is the contemplation on the suffering and happiness of future lifetimes.

The "I" that is imputed on the basis of the five aggregates is what will experience the suffering or happiness of future lifetimes. Among the five aggregates, though the aggregate of form ceases at the end of this lifetime, the aggregate of consciousness proceeds into future lives. The aggregate of consciousness, or the merely imputed "I," does not have the liberty of choosing its rebirth independently. It takes rebirth without choice. The type of rebirth it will experience is determined by the power of delusions and karma. Powerful nonvirtuous karma will lead to the ripening result of rebirth in the hell realm. Moderate nonvirtuous karma will ripen in a rebirth in the realm of the hungry ghosts. Light nonvirtuous karma will ripen in a rebirth in the animal world.

A nonvirtuous karmic action is made powerful by the fulfillment of the motivation, the course of action, and the completion of the action. When the beginning, the middle, and the end of a negative action are complete, that karma becomes very powerfully negative, thereby causing a hell realm rebirth. When there is the motivation and the course of the action, but no completion, that karma is classified as a karma of moderate strength. When there is just one part of the three, it is a light nonvirtuous action.

At this point, we should stop for a moment and try to think about all of the actions that we have done in our lives with the fulfillment of the three parts. We should realize that every time we have done a nonvirtuous action with these three parts, we have accumulated the full force of that nonvirtuous activity. Therefore, we have definitely accumulated the karmic potential to be reborn in the realms of the hell beings, hungry ghosts, or animals. As we continue through this section of the *Lamrim Chenmo,* we should think of the extreme sufferings of the beings of these realms as they are described here, and imagine how unbearable it would be for us if we were actually to be born in one of these places. This will help us to cultivate a sense of concern for the suffering that results from our negative actions, and inspire us to resolve to abandon these actions in the present and refrain from doing them in the future.

Should you think: "I am already suffering too much to have to think about all of this anymore," you should remember the advantages of thinking about suffering. First and foremost, thinking about suffering eliminates your sense of self-importance or pride. Also, the more you think about your own karmic potentials and their ripening results, as well as the respective forms of suffering that are in store for you, the more you will become aware of the consequences of your negative actions, and thus will not engage in them so lightly.

THE HOT HELLS

The contemplation on the hell realms begins with the description of the eight hot hells.

The first of the eight is the Hell of Continual Resurrection, where the native beings are surrounded by weapons, continually attacked, and then die. Soon after, they are revived from death by the force of a very loud, unpleasant sound, and their suffering begins all over again. Among the eight hells, the suffering in the Hell of Continual Resurrection is the lightest.

The next hell is the Black Line Hell. The bodies of the beings in this hell are marked with black lines by ropes of burning iron. They are then sawed and hacked to pieces along the lines.

The third hell is the Assemble and Destroy Hell, where all the beings are killed at once. For example, a huge group of beings may be crushed together between two mountains until they die. This process is repeated again and again, endlessly. When I was a child, my aunt would advise us not to kill lice between our fingernails to avoid being born in this kind of hell.

The next is the Hell of Lamentation, in which beings suffer excruciating pain due to the fact that their bodies are constantly engulfed in flames, and they express their experience of intense suffering through great wailing and howling.

The fifth is the Hell of Great Lamentation, where the fire is even greater, like an incinerator, and the burning beings are trapped inside a double-walled iron building.

Then there is the Hotter Hell, where beings with even heavier negative karma are reborn. The beings in this realm are boiled alive repeatedly by the fire of the heat.

Then there is the Even Hotter Hell, where the beings are not only cooked in molten iron, but simultaneously impaled by spears and so forth.

Finally there is the Hell Without Respite, also known as the Vajra Hell, or the Avici Hell, where the heat is hundreds and thousands of times more intense than the heat in the others and there is not even a moment's opportunity for rest. The beings born in this particular realm have very sensitive bodies, like an infant's. They are totally engulfed in flames to the point where their bodies cannot be distinguished from the fire, and they experience extreme suffering.

The purpose of thinking about the hell realms in this detail is to heighten our awareness of the fact that all of our negative actions have consequences. Because they are negative actions, their consequences can be nothing but suffering. Following this logic, it is only reasonable to assume that extremely powerful negative actions can bring tremendous suffering as a result. Thinking about all of this should bring forth the wish to purify them.

Besides the manifest suffering that they experience, beings born in the hell realms also have an incredibly long lifespan. Just to give you an idea: fifty human years is one day for the four directional protectors. Thirty of their days make one month. Twelve months make a year. Five hundred years of their life make up just one day in the Hell of Continual Resurrection. Thirty days in this hell become a month. And twelve months of that become a year. Five hundred of those years is the measure of the lifespan you would have were you to be born in the Hell of Continual Resurrection. The lifespan in the hells below this hell become comparatively longer and longer.

Generally speaking, on the Buddhist path we believe that the practices of developing loving-kindness, compassion, and wisdom while accumulating the two types of merit will bring forth the result of enlightenment. We believe that the collection of these causes will bring forth the result of the incredible qualities of the body, speech, and mind of an enlightened being. We examine our positive potentials and look forward to the attainment of the result of positive things. If we are going to think in this way, then logically, to be consistent, we must also try to see the possibility that all the negativity that we have created with our body, speech, and mind over countless lifetimes could result in sufferings that we cannot measure, or even imagine, such as the suffering of a hell realm rebirth. This awareness should lead us to make two resolutions: to purify past negative karma and to abandon accumulating negative karma in the future. We should also cultivate compassion for sentient beings who are in a similar situation.

In our own case, if we waste our perfect human rebirth with its eight leisures and ten opportunities, we may indeed have to experience the consequences of these lower states of rebirth in the future. For example, if you have a child who has never gone to school, when the child grows up he will be unable to find a proper job and have difficulty making his way in the world. In order to avoid these kinds of problems, from youth we prepare ourselves with the skills we will need when we grow up and become independent. In the same way, in order to benefit our future lives, in the present we need to observe thoughts and actions very carefully. We need to be aware of what we should abandon, and what we should cultivate. And finally, we should remember that our karmic seeds are ripened by our own mental states. Positive mental states ripen positive karmic imprints, and negative mental states ripen negative karmic imprints. Since a hell realm rebirth is a ripening result brought on by negative mental states, we should strive to create virtue in order to avoid this outcome.

THE COLD HELLS

The next topic is the explanation of the cold hells. In general, the cold hells lack all the features of warmth and light such as the sun and the moon, and even extra clothing to keep one warm. Due to the power of karma none of these things are there at all. There are eight cold hells, each one being successively colder, and the beings who reside in them experience greater and greater suffering.

The first of the eight cold hells is the Blistering Hell, so named because it is so cold that the bodies of the beings who reside there break open in blisters. In the second of the cold hells, the Broken Blister Hell, the blisters crack open and ooze. The suffering in the Broken Blister Hell is a hundred thousand times worse than that of the Blistering Hell. The next hell is the Chattering Teeth Hell, where the teeth of the beings born there bang together incessantly as a result of the extreme cold. Then there are the Wailing and the Sneezing Hells, which are self-explanatory. In the sixth hell, the Hell of Utpala-Like Splits, the entire body of the hell being splits open into deep cracks like an *utpala* flower as a result of the extreme cold. In the seventh hell, the Hell of Lotus-Like Splits, the cracks deepen, and in the eighth, the Hell of Great Lotus-Like Splits, the body splinters into pieces like a hundred-petalled lotus.

Rebirth in a cold hell can be caused by holding wrong views with regard to the nonexistence of karma. Stealing warm clothing and causing sentient beings to freeze also bring this type of rebirth, as does the destruction of holy objects. Prior to rebirth in a cold hell, at the time of death an individual feels very hot, and develops the craving to be cool. Even in the intermediate state, that person will experience a very strong craving for coolness, similar to a sensation we might have in a dream.

Considering the fact that we have had countless lifetimes, it is not possible that we have not generated the wrong views that cause this kind of rebirth at some point. It is not possible that we have not accumulated these kinds of karmic potentials. If we take this opportunity to think about our own potential to experience the cold hells, and if we try to imagine ourselves enduring this suffering, it will be very easy for us to generate the incentive in our minds to purify our negative karma. Simultaneously, we can strengthen our resolution not to engage in the actions that bring about this kind of result. If we fear suffering, we should fear the negative actions that bring the results of suffering.

Vasubandhu uses the analogy of a mustard seed to give an idea of the lifespan in the lightest of the cold hells, which is the Blistering Hell. Vasubandhu says if you fill a bag with one hundred kilograms of tiny mustard seeds, and every one hundred human years you take one mustard seed out of one bag, the time it takes to empty one hundred of those bags is the lifespan of a being born in the Blistering Hell. The beings in the subsequent cold hells have lifespans twenty times longer than that.

THE REALM OF THE HUNGRY GHOSTS

The next topic is the discussion of the realm of the hungry ghosts, or *preta* beings. The intensity of the suffering of the beings born in the realm of the hungry ghosts is less intense than that of those born in the hell realms, but far more intense than that of those born in the animal realm. However, it is also true that the beings born in the hungry ghost realm are generally endowed with greater intelligence than animals. In fact, there is a story in sutra about a practitioner named Arya Jigten Wangchuk who actually gave Dharma teachings to the pretas and thus enabled them to accumulate enough merit to be able to have the direct realization of emptiness.

Generally, the beings born in the preta realm suffer from heat and cold, hunger and thirst, extreme hardship, and a constant state of fear. Although we have not now been born there, because we have the karmic propensities in our minds for this kind of rebirth, we can meditate as if we were experiencing these things ourselves and in this way cultivate the awareness of how unbearable it would be to be born as a hungry ghost.

The specific sufferings of the hungry ghosts are the internal and external obscurations with regard to food and drink and the hunger and thirst obscurations in relation to food and drink. The internal obscurations are the suffering of extreme hunger and thirst. Even when these beings do by chance happen upon food and drink, the food becomes flames, and thus becomes a cause for them to experience even further pain. The external obscurations cause food and drink to appear as a mirage. For example, under the power of external obscurations, preta beings may see trees and fruits and delicious things, but when they approach, everything disappears. The hunger and thirst obscurations in relation to food and drink manifest in such a way that when a hungry ghost discovers food by chance, the food immediately takes on the appearance of blood and pus, and will taste like molten iron.

Even if the obscurations with regard to food and drink do not occur, due to the physical makeup of the body it is very difficult for a preta to eat. A preta's neck is thin and knotted, so the food is very difficult to swallow, and as a result these beings continually suffer extreme hunger and thirst but are unable to satisfy it. Further descriptions written by His Holiness Kelsang Gyatso, the Seventh Dalai Lama, say that hungry ghosts have stomachs that are huge like a mountain, necks that are thin strands, knotted in places, and extremely fragile limbs. When they see water, rather than being able to quench their thirst, their craving increases even more. When they see food, they are not only unable to eat it, but it becomes a cause of even greater suffering.

The karmic causes that result in a preta realm rebirth are the inability to rejoice in the generosity of others, obstructing generous acts, and being strongly bound by the mind of miserliness. Having an extremely covetous way of thinking is also a cause of rebirth in the realm of the hungry ghosts, as is not sharing the Dharma with others due to miserliness or jealousy, and not wanting others to know what you know about the spiritual path. All of these powerful negative actions, accumulated with strong motivation, actual action, and the completion of the action, will cause rebirth in the hungry ghost realm.

THE ANIMAL REALM

The last topic within the discussion of the suffering of lower rebirths is the discussion of the animal realm. Among the sufferings of animals, there are general types of suffering and specific types of suffering in relation to particular animals. In general, animals experience the suffering of the fear of being eaten by one another, the suffering of ignorance and stupidity, hunger and thirst, heat and cold, and the suffering of being used as a beast of burden.

Due to our proximity to the animal realm, most of us probably have a better understanding of the suffering of animals than we do of the suffering of those in the realms that we cannot see. In fact, we may see that much of the suffering that animals experience comes as a result of our own actions. We know that many animals are used as food for humans. Many are also used for medical experiments. Of course, all of the harm that we do toward animals arises from our own ignorance. And much of it comes as a result of the eight worldly dharmas, particularly from the point of view of wanting happiness and not wanting suffering. In support of that mentality many innocent animals lose their lives.

In our world, there are animals that we use for our own benefit, and then there is a whole class of animals that we cannot see, such as the animals in the depths of the ocean, and so forth. There are also animals in our universe that are not directly known to us but are still life forms. The general suffering is the same for all of the beings born in the animal realm. You should imagine these sufferings as if you were experiencing them, and realize how unbearable it would be to be caught in this kind of existence.

The kinds of actions that result in an animal rebirth are actions that are strongly motivated by confusion and ignorance. Calling people by animal names and showing disrespect and lack of faith toward those who are living in pure ethics is also a cause for rebirth in the animal realm.

As Pabongka Rinpoche says, once we are born in the lower realms, even if we were to encounter the good fortune of meeting with the Dharma and spiritual teachers, we would be unable to take advantage of them in order to benefit our future lifetimes. Thinking like this, we can rejoice in the good fortune of our present rebirth, and bring forth the wish to purify all of our negative karma, without procrastination and laziness. We can apply ourselves to the practices of purification and accumulation of merit, and remembering to continually recall impermanence and death, persevere in these practices.

Shantideva says:

If I do not engage in virtuous actions now
Although at this time I have the opportunity to do so,
What will I do once I am
Confused by the suffering of the lower realms?

THE METHOD TO ATTAIN
HAPPINESS IN FUTURE LIVES

HAVING CONSIDERED THE EXPERIENCES that may be in store for us as a result of our negative karmic accumulations, the next point is the explanation of the method to attain happiness in our future lives. Within this section, the first topic is training in going for refuge, the holy gateway to the teachings.

THE CAUSES OF REFUGE

The basis of your practice of refuge at this stage is the awareness of impermanence and death, the fact that you are not going to last forever, and the realization that your entire existence is completely controlled by karma and delusions. Also, at this point you should begin to think about the fact that you have accumulated negative karma in great abundance, but have accumulated comparatively little positive karma.

The mind of refuge arises as the result of two causes: fear of the future suffering that you will certainly experience due to your own negative karmic propensities, and faith that the objects of refuge have the power to protect you from the fear of suffering and the consequences of your negative karmic actions. Merely folding your hands together or reciting the refuge prayer does not qualify as taking refuge. If you do not have the fear of suffering and faith in the objects of refuge present in your mind, you do not have refuge. You do not enter the path of the Buddhadharma. If you find at the beginning that it is difficult for you to generate an effortless, intuitive sense of refuge, you should at least try to effortfully create the mind of refuge, and progress from there.

Cultivating the mind of refuge is what distinguishes the Buddhist spiritual path from other spiritual paths, just as cultivating the mind of bodhichitta differentiates the Mahayana path from the path of the individual vehicle. On the basis of having a sense of refuge arising out of fear and faith—which is the refuge in the mind of a small scope practitioner—you will eventually be able to develop the refuge of the medium scope, and on that basis you will then be able to develop the refuge of the great scope.

How is refuge a method to ensure the happiness of future lifetimes? In order to create the causes of happiness, we need to accumulate virtue. Virtue is rooted in the mind of faith, and faith is the root of refuge practice. Of course, to think that we can actualize refuge on the basis of faith alone is not correct, and faith alone is also not sufficient to enable the happiness of our future lifetimes. However, from the basis of faith we will be able to cultivate all the good qualities of the path.

THE OBJECTS OF REFUGE

The ultimate object of refuge is Buddha, who has shown us the path that is the means to abandoning the two types of obscurations—the affliction obscurations and the obscurations to omniscience. The actual refuge is the Dharma, and the Sangha is the means of support on the spiritual path. According to the Mahayana, each object of refuge possesses a conventional and ultimate aspect.

The conventional Buddha refuge is the two aspects of the form body or *rupakaya* of a buddha: the enjoyment body or *sambhogakaya* and the emanation body or *nirmanakaya*. According to the *Sublime Continuum,* sambhogakaya emanations possess a definite field of residence, which is a pure land. They also possess a definite entourage, which means the entourage is composed only of arya bodhisattvas, and engage in a definite form of teaching, which means that they teach only the Mahayana path of the profound and extensive conduct. Sambhogakaya emanations are also endowed with a definite timespan, which means that they will remain until the end of cyclic existence, and a definite holy body, which means a physical form beautified by the glory of all of the major and minor marks of a buddha.

While sambhogakaya emanations are forms that only appear to and interact with arya bodhisattvas who have the direct realization of ultimate truth, nirmanakaya emanations manifest for beings with impure karma as well. A buddha's supreme emanation body is called the nirmanakaya, and possesses the thirty-two major and eighty minor marks. Practitioners who have generated the concentration arising out of calm abiding and attained the state known as the "continuum of the Dharma" are able to access all supreme nirmanakaya emanations wherever they reside and continuously enjoy the Dharma from them. The term supreme emanation body refers specifically to buddhas who manifest themselves in our world—for example, to the historical Buddha Shakyamuni, who manifested enlightenment in the aspect of a monk. When a teaching has been given by a supreme emanation, it is classified as part of the Sutra Pitaka. The explanatory commentaries, however, such as the five treatises of Maitreya, are rooted in the teachings of the Buddha but are not considered sutras because they were not specifically taught by the supreme emanation body.

The ultimate Buddha refuge is the true path generated in the mental continuum of an arya buddha. Among the bodies of a buddha, this is considered to be the truth body or dharmakaya.

The conventional Dharma refuge is the entire collection of scriptures that contain the teachings of the three higher trainings.

The ultimate Dharma refuge is the wisdom that directly realizes emptiness in the mind of an arya being. Ultimate bodhichitta, the extraordinary pure bodhichitta generated on the path of seeing, the state of total abandonment of all the delusions, and the cessation of the delusions are also part of the ultimate Dharma refuge. As well, when an arya being trains in higher ethics, higher concentration, and higher wisdom with the unification of pure bodhichitta and wisdom that directly realizes emptiness, this is also considered to be the ultimate Dharma refuge.

The conventional Sangha refuge is a group of four fully ordained practitioners.

The ultimate Sangha refuge is a Mahayana practitioner who has realized emptiness directly.

These are the three objects of refuge according to the Mahayana system. However, you should keep in mind that there are variances within these explanations among the other schools of Buddhist philosophy. Proponents of the Vaibashika system, for example, do not accept the conventional Buddha refuge or the conventional Sangha refuge at all.

Some practitioners may take refuge without necessarily having the complete understanding of the objects of refuge, their qualities, or the difference between them. Despite this, these practitioners may have an intuitive feeling of trust in the objects of refuge. In contrast, others may have the complete understanding of the three objects of refuge, their specific qualities, and the differences between them. If this latter type of practitioner is able to cultivate a sense of faith in conjunction with this understanding, he or she will develop the natural aspiration to attain all of these qualities. Between the two, the latter practitioner possesses a much more stable type of refuge. Of course, to develop the most excellent, perfect mind of refuge, we need to understand the ultimate mode of existence of phenomena in accordance with the profound path of wisdom. But even if, at the moment, we do not have this kind of realization, our refuge should be accompanied by the understanding of, correct assumption of, or, at the very least, the belief in this path.

There are two distinctive forms of refuge: causal and resultant refuge. Causal refuge means taking refuge in an object other than ourselves—in a being who has generated the realization of true cessation, such as the founder Shakyamuni Buddha. Resultant refuge means taking refuge in our own future attainment of enlightenment. Resultant refuge arises from the understanding of the innate nature of our own mind, which is clear, luminous, and knowing, and from the understanding that our delusions are only temporary. However, in order to develop the foundation for resultant refuge, it is first necessary to establish causal refuge firmly in our minds.

To develop causal refuge, we need to understand why the objects of refuge are worthy of our faith. To accomplish this, we begin by establishing Buddha as an infallible object of refuge. On this basis, we can thus infer that his teachings and the beings who have realized those teachings are likewise infallible objects of refuge. The source of this logic is Dharmakirti's *Commentary on the "Compendium on Valid Cognition."*

The first reason listed in the text is that Buddha is free from fear. As a result of purifying and overcoming all his faults, abandoning everything that is to be abandoned, and developing every positive quality in his mind, Buddha has attained the nature body or *svabhavakaya,* and attained the state of fearlessness.

The second reason is that Buddha is skilled in liberating other sentient beings from their states of fear. This is because Buddha has completed the extensive accumulation of the merit of virtue, and as a result has attained the form body for the benefit of others.

The third reason is that Buddha has compassion that does not discriminate. As a result of having nurtured the mind of loving concern to its fullest extent, Buddha has attained the fearlessness of committing himself to revealing the path of the antidotes to all other beings.

The fourth reason is that Buddha is completely free of bias toward sentient beings because of his faultless compassion and bodhichitta, and thus is able to perfectly benefit all sentient beings regardless of whether they have helped or harmed him in the past. This is the fearlessness of fully committing himself to revealing the objects of abandonment to others.

Once we have examined these points, checked their validity, and thus established Buddha, the teacher, as an infallible object of refuge, we implicitly substantiate that his teachings and the community of Sangha that lives in the realizations of the teachings are also valid.

HOW TO TAKE REFUGE

Again, let us recall the stanza from the very beginning of the *Lamrim Chenmo:*

> Your body is produced from millions of excellent virtues,
> Your speech fulfills the wishes of countless sentient beings,
> Your mind sees all objects of knowledge as they exist—
> I prostrate to Buddha Shakyamuni.

Buddha's holy body, holy speech, and holy mind are all the results of his auspicious accumulation of extensive virtues, which in turn is the result of having completely abandoned the wish for personal attainment alone and the result of having completely developed the wish to attain liberation and enlightenment with compassion, only for the benefit of others.

According to the *Lamrim Chenmo,* the way we should go for refuge is by recognizing the qualities of the objects of refuge, understanding the differences between the three objects of refuge, accepting the objects of refuge as the ultimate objects of refuge, and going for refuge to the Three Jewels without seeking any other refuge.

Recognizing the Good Qualities of the Three Jewels

If we can remember what has been abandoned and what has been attained by the objects of refuge when we go for refuge to the Buddha, Dharma, and Sangha, our faith in them will be far more stable. Although all of the explanations that follow are not explicitly presented in the *Lamrim Chenmo,* I thought it might help you to have information from many different angles when you try to meditate, so that you will be able to generate a deeper, more stable sense of faith in the Three Jewels.

QUALITIES OF THE BUDDHA

Although Buddhists do not accept an external god who creates our happiness and suffering, we should remember that this does not imply that our spiritual path is not dependent on any kind of refuge, or that a practitioner on this path must depend completely upon him- or herself.

In Maitreya's *Sublime Continuum,* it is taught that the Buddha object of refuge must possess eight qualities in order to be considered an object of refuge. First, the Buddha object of refuge must experience death and rebirth that are free from the two obscurations. The Buddha object of refuge must possess spontaneous activity and be endowed with omniscient mind that knows phenomena beyond words and beyond conception. The Buddha object of refuge must also know both conventional and ultimate phenomena, possess limitless loving compassion, and possess ability or power. Finally, the Buddha object of refuge must also fulfill the ultimate benefit for oneself and others.

A Buddha's Body

When we reflect on the holy body of a buddha, in general we can consider the eighty marks and thirty-two signs that adorn the body of an enlightened one, such as the crown protrusion, the forehead curl, and so forth. The complete list of these marks and signs can be found in the eighth chapter of the *Ornament of Clear Realization* by Maitreya.

Although we lack the karmic fortune to actually see a buddha's holy body in person, when we look at representations of a buddha's body in art and statues, it will behoove us to try to recall each of the positive qualities that the statue or painting or picture represents. We can reflect that the holy body of a buddha is completely free of faults or mistakes in the view of anyone who beholds it. And furthermore we can reflect on the four fearlessnesses in particular: that this holy body is the result of having become completely free of fear, that this holy body is perfectly skillful and can guide us into a state of fearlessness, that this holy body represents compassion without discrimination, and that this holy body benefits all sentient beings regardless of past experiences of help or harm.

A Buddha's Speech

The holy speech of a buddha arises from the auspicious accumulation of a hundred billion excellent virtues and fulfills the wishes of all sentient beings. A buddha's holy voice is extremely mellifluent and beautiful to hear. When a buddha speaks, each disciple hears exactly what is relevant to him or her according to karma. For example, when Shakyamuni Buddha said that form is empty at Vulture's Peak in Rajgir, some of the disciples assembled there heard teachings on selflessness, some heard teachings on emptiness, and some heard teachings on suffering. Each disciple understood the instructions that were most suitable for him or her according to karma.

From *Praise of Dependent Arising,* by Lama Tsongkhapa:

Homage to the One who by seeing and speech
Became the unsurpassable Wise One and Teacher,
The Victor who saw dependent arising
And taught it.

Although we do not have the karmic fortune to actually hear the speech of a buddha directly, the representation of a buddha's speech still exists today in the form of the scriptural collections.

A Buddha's Mind

As I mentioned, refuge is what differentiates our own spiritual path from other spiritual paths, and is what enables us to enter the path of the Buddhadharma. As we take refuge, whether the objects of refuge are actually present or not does not depend upon whether we have done the invocation, or whether we have done the visualization properly. Generally, we say that there is no existence that is not pervaded by Buddha's omniscient mind. Since this is the case, wherever the holy mind is, the holy body is there as well. Wherever the holy body is, the holy speech is there as well. Therefore, whether the objects of refuge are present or not is not dependent upon our faith in them. However, to create the auspiciousness of our practice, to make it complete, and to strengthen our faith, we recite the prayers of invocation and so forth. If we practice with the strong awareness that Buddha's omniscient mind pervades all existence, recalling that wherever there is omniscient mind, there is the holy body and speech, we will be able to maintain our faith without interruption, feeling the presence of the enlightened ones wherever we are. This way, our faith will not be limited to the times when we artificially create the visualization of the deities or the merit field.

The general characteristic of the holy mind of Buddha is omniscience. The specific qualities are the ability to perceive existence exactly as it is, the ability to perceive the two truths simultaneously and directly with one consciousness, and the ability to effortlessly understand the subtle details of cause and effect. Also, just as we are bound by karma and delusions, Buddha's holy mind is bound by the thought of loving concern and compassion for all sentient beings. This compassion is based on seeing the suffering of beings in the form of the three types of suffering, which we will discuss later.

A Buddha's Activity

The activities of the buddhas manifest in the world through the dharmakaya, which acts as the condition activating the virtuous imprints in the minds of sentient beings. Sentient beings, from their side, are able to experience the positive results of this activity because they are endowed with buddha-nature. This can be understood further by examining the *Sublime Continuum,* in which the author outlines six points and three examples to illustrate how the blessings of the divine activities flow without interruption.

The first two are the ten grounds and the two accumulations. This means that because they have completed the path of the ten grounds and the two accumulations of merit, the enlightened beings are able to benefit others without interruption. The ten grounds are compared to the ocean, and the two accumulations are compared to the sun. The more water, the greater the ocean becomes. In the same way, the trainee on the ten grounds and five paths increases in qualities, enabling the result of enlightenment. Also, as the sun nurtures the growth of the plants and flowers on earth, in the same way the two accumulations of merit nourish sentient beings in general, and particularly those sentient beings on the path to enlightenment.

The next two points are the enlightened mind and the nature of sentient beings. This means that because the ultimate mode of existence of the enlightened beings and ordinary sentient beings is the same, we have the potential to be the recipients of their divine activities. The enlightened mind is compared to space, and the nature of sentient beings is compared to a treasury. Just as space is infinite and limitless, likewise the qualities of enlightenment cannot be measured, and just as a treasury of jewels is a source of great material wealth, so the buddha-nature in the minds of all beings is a great source of positive qualities.

The last two points are the two obscurations—the affliction obscurations and the obscurations to omniscience—and great compassion. Although sentient beings are obscured by the two great obstacles to enlightenment, due to the power of great compassion the enlightened activity of the buddhas flourishes unceasingly to benefit them. The two obscurations are like clouds, and the buddha's compassion is like the wind. Sentient beings' buddha-nature is temporarily clouded by the delusions, but these delusions do not exist in the nature of their minds, as clouds do not exist in the nature of the sky. The compassion of the buddhas drives away every obstacle in the minds of sentient beings as the wind, when it blows, clears the clouds from the sky completely.

By these six points and three examples, we should understand that we have the basis for liberation, the means to be liberated, that there is a path by which we can be liberated, and that the result of liberation exists. All of our obscurations are temporary, and therefore we possess an appropriate basis for liberation. The compassion of the buddhas extends equally to all sentient beings; therefore, we have the means to attain liberation. By these examples we should also understand clearly how we, as sentient beings, are suitable to be recipients of the blessings of the pure activity of the buddhas.

When we receive the blessings of the activity of the buddhas, our virtuous thoughts and actions increase and our nonvirtuous activities decrease. Specifically, the blessing of the activities of the holy body is such that upon seeing the form of a buddha, even with a gross consciousness, the delusions in the minds of sentient beings will be pacified or lessened. The blessing of the activities of the holy speech is all the teachings of method and wisdom. The blessing of the activities of the holy mind is the compassion that extends to all sentient beings.

The divine activity of the buddhas is completely spontaneous. In contrast, the activities of the bodhisattvas on the first seven grounds, for example, are dependent upon a gross level of motivation. Their activities on the eighth, ninth, and tenth grounds, which are regarded as the pure grounds, depend upon a subtle motivation. Once a bodhisattva has attained full enlightenment, however, his or her activities are completely spontaneous.

Although this is the case, whether sentient beings actually receive the blessings of the enlightened beings or not is dependent on them. This can be illustrated by the following example. In a lake filled with very clear, still water, you will be able to see the reflection of the moon perfectly, without any effort on the part of the water. However, in a lake filled with muddy water you will not see the reflection of anything. In the same way, sentient beings must have some basis—like the clear water—to be suitable recipients of the blessings of the divine activities of the buddhas. The blessings are only a condition for your virtue to flourish—they are not its cause. The cause of your virtue must arise completely from your own side. You cannot expect success if you rely solely upon the blessings of the pure activity of the buddhas without making any effort yourself. It won't work. You have to create the actual cause yourself.

This phenomenon can be further understood by taking the example of the sun. If you want your body to be warmed by the sun, you must go outside where the sun is shining and expose your body to the rays. There is no discrimination, no motivation, and no effort on the part of the sun. But in order for you to experience its warmth, you must make an effort from your side. The sun itself is not the main cause: it is merely a condition for the warmth that you will experience. The main cause is putting yourself in its rays.

The benefits of the blessings of the divine activity of the buddhas are not like the fruit that you eat when you're hungry, or like worldly happiness, which will satisfy the needs of this one brief lifetime alone. Rather, the benefit of these blessings lies in the fact that they are the condition for you to create virtuous karma, which will help you in future lives. Better than that, they can help you to attain liberation from cyclic existence. At the very best, the blessings of the divine activity of the buddhas can enable you to attain enlightenment for the sake of other sentient beings. That is the kind of benefit you should seek from the blessings of the buddhas' pure activity.

Perhaps it would be useful to clarify what we mean when we say "blessing." A blessing is a positive transformation within your mind. Viewing it as an external event that happens to you with no effort on your part is a misunderstanding. The primary cause of receiving a blessing comes from you, and the main cause that is needed from your own side is faith.

For example, when we have faith in our spiritual teacher, we automatically develop respect, as well as a great sense of appreciation for his or her kindness. If we then approach this teacher and ask, "Will you bless my rosary?" the blessing will actually occur due to the combination of the conditions of the teacher's mantra and our own mind of faith. If, however, we have no faith in our minds at all, and we say, "Bless this, bless that," we receive very little benefit. A rosary is blessed in dependence upon two conditions: the qualities of the person giving the blessing and our own recognition of and faith in those qualities. If these two conditions are present, then, after that rosary has been blessed, we will consider it to be very special. We will not observe it with the same kind of ordinary view that we have toward our other belongings. When we lose the ordinary view of the rosary and perceive it as something special or sacred, the blessing of that rosary has taken place. The conventional appearance of the rosary is eliminated in this process, and the extraordinary view of the rosary replaces it.

Qualities of the Dharma

The Dharma object of refuge also possesses eight qualities, as taught in the *Sublime Continuum.*

The first quality is the inconceivable quality, meaning that an ordinary mind cannot conceive of what appears to the mind of an arya being directly perceiving emptiness.

The second quality is when an individual on the hearer's path attains the true path, if that individual has not specifically abandoned a particular delusion or karma before, attaining the true path will be the cause for eliminating this delusion or karma.

The third quality is that even if the practitioner has not abandoned the incorrectly assuming mental consciousness up to this point, by attaining the true path alone this mind is completely eliminated.

The fourth is that the nature of the path is totally pure, free of pollution, and not tainted by obscurations.

The fifth is the quality of being able to see things exactly as they are.

The sixth is that the mind becomes totally empowered to act as an antidote to the nonharmoniuous states.

The seventh is the quality of cessation, which comes forth as the mind's potential to act as an antidote is enhanced.

The eighth is the quality of the true path, which in general means that an arya being, whether in equipoise or in the post-meditation period, has attained the true path in all respects.

Qualities of the Sangha

There are also eight qualities of the Sangha object of refuge.

The first three qualities that the Sangha object of refuge must possess are the wisdom knowing existence as it is, the wisdom knowing all existent things, and inner wisdom.

The fourth, fifth, and sixth are the qualities of having freed oneself from any of the three obscurations: the affliction obscurations, the obscurations to knowing, and the obscuration of lower aspiration, meaning the wish for one's own liberation according to the individual vehicle.

The seventh quality is knowing the truth directly, and the eighth is possessing the liberation that comes as a result of knowing the truth directly.

A Sangha object of refuge can be an arhat who has attained liberation by way of the path of the individual vehicle, because such a being has accomplished the wisdom accumulations of the path. For a solitary realizer to be recognized as a conventional Sangha object of refuge, he or she must accumulate the first third of one hundred eons of merit. For a bodhisattva to qualify as a Sangha object of refuge, he or she must have completed the first of the three countless eons of accumulation of merit in accordance with the five paths. An ultimate Sangha object of refuge on the first of the ten Mahayana grounds is able to emanate a hundred bodies, see existence over a hundred eons, engage in a hundred concentrations, see a hundred buddhas, receive a hundred blessings, and so forth.

Understanding the Differences between the Three Jewels

The next topic is the explanation of the differences between the three objects of refuge. The differences between the Three Jewels can be presented in terms of the distinctive characteristics of each of the Three Jewels and the differences between them in terms of activity, aspiration, lineage, recollection, and merit.

The three distinctive characteristics attributed to Buddha are that the holy mind sees existence clearly and directly, is purified of the two obscurations, and is adorned with all qualities. The distinctive characteristics of the Dharma are that it embodies the truth of cessation or the truth of the path that leads to cessation. The distinctive characteristic of the Sangha object of refuge is that a person who qualifies as such should be one who has realized ultimate reality, entered the path of seeing, or or one who possesses cessation.

The differences in terms of activity is that the Buddha is the founder of the refuge of true cessation, the Dharma is the actual path of true cessation, and the Sangha is the support that encourages the practitioner to actualize the refuge of true cessation.

The differences in terms of aspiration between the three objects of refuge are as follows. The Buddha becomes an object of offering, an object of faith, and an object of respect for us, and subsequently becomes the representation of our faith in what we aspire to attain. The Dharma is what we aspire to generate within our own continuum. And the Sangha is what we rely on as our support in actualizing the spiritual path.

In accordance with Maitreya, another way to organize the Three Jewels is to assert the Buddha as the Mahayana practitioner, the Dharma as the solitary realizer, and the Sangha as the hearer. The Buddha jewel is represented by the Mahayana practitioner because Mahayana practitioners wish to totally eliminate all mental faults and attain all qualities, and their actual practice is the unified practice of method and wisdom, which is the means to attaining this state. The Dharma jewel is represented by solitary realizers because these practitioners have the strong aspiration to achieve nirvana, true path, and true cessation, and their actual practice is the path that leads to this goal. Hearers practice the path not only by listening, but also through the active engagement of enabling others to hear as well.

Therefore, hearers are given as examples for the Sangha jewel, the support in actualizing refuge.

In relation to the Buddha object of refuge, we accomplish the merit of virtue through making offerings and doing other practices. In relation to the Dharma object of refuge, as we become familiar with the Dharma, our awareness and introspection increases, so that our mind is less under the control of deluded ways of thinking. In relation to the Sangha object of refuge, the Sangha can clarify the points of the practice that we do not understand.

Establishing the differences by recollection means remembering the Buddha, Dharma, and Sangha for their qualities as they were explained in accordance with the *Sublime Continuum* by Maitreya.

Establishing the differences by merit refers to the merit that we accumulate in our interactions with each of the Three Jewels. In terms of the Buddha object of refuge, we accumulate merit by seeing that the Buddha has eliminated everything that is to be eliminated and realized everything that is to be realized, and generating pure faith on this basis. In relation to the Dharma, particularly the experiential or realized form of Dharma, we accumulate the merit of faith that wishes to attain those realizations. In relation to the Sangha, who have the direct realization of the truth, we accumulate the merit of cultivating the faith that inspires us to attain those qualities.

Accepting the Three Jewels and Not Asserting Another Refuge

The next topic is the advice for taking the Buddha, Dharma, and Sangha as our ultimate and only objects of refuge. In order to have refuge, we need the cause of refuge, which is the fear of suffering and faith in the objects of refuge. It is also useful to understand the result of refuge, which means understanding the qualities of the objects of refuge. In the case of the Buddha refuge, this means understanding the qualities of the holy body, holy speech, and holy mind. Also, when we take refuge, we should do so with the thought that we go for refuge throughout all of our lifetimes up until our enlightenment, as opposed to merely thinking, "I will take refuge until I die."

The mind that accepts the Buddha, Dharma, and Sangha as the ultimate objects of refuge arises from the causes of developing fear of the suffering of the lower realms and faith in the potential of the qualities of the objects of refuge to protect us from our fear. Our faith should not be blind faith, but faith enriched with wisdom and based on logic and reasoning. It should arise on the basis of understanding what we are taking refuge in, not just because Buddha is described as having the major and minor marks, and so forth.

In general, it is very important that we have a clear understanding of and appreciation for the qualities of the Buddha, Dharma, and Sangha. This is particularly significant if we are doing preliminary practices such as the one hundred thousand repetitions of the refuge prayers and so on. If this understanding accompanies our recitation, rather than just fulfilling a recitation quota, we will be able to enhance our faith and our aspiration to attain the qualities of the objects of refuge.

Moreover, in the post-meditation periods, we should try to improve our understanding of the two truths and direct yogic perception, especially seeking to understand the way that it arises for the first time on the basis of a generic image and how, as the practitioner familiarizes him- or herself with that conceptual mind over and over again, he or she can eventually cultivate the ultimate view. We should also strive to understand the two truths, the paths of method and wisdom, and the result of the two bodies of a buddha. All of this can be understood in the context of the preliminary practice of the refuge recitation. If done properly, within the practice of refuge it should be possible to include the roots of the practice of the four noble truths, the generation of the mind of bodhichitta, the two truths, and so forth.

Of course, in the beginning, when we are unfamiliar with all of the qualities and so forth, this kind of practice is not possible. But as we become more familiar with them through constant listening, reflection, and contemplation, gradually we will find that every time we say, "I go for refuge in the Buddha," the qualities of the Buddha appear clearly in our minds. This works in the same way for the Dharma and Sangha jewels. For example, although we are unfamiliar with all the details of everything that His Holiness the Dalai Lama does for the benefit of sentient beings and for the Dharma, in general we have the understanding that His Holiness brings about incredible benefit for the sake of both. Therefore when we see

His Holiness, we are instantly overcome by a feeling of pure faith and admiration, despite lacking the details. In the same way, in the beginning, although we do not have the details of all of the qualities of the Buddha, Dharma, and Sangha, we have the overall general idea. Therefore when we say, "I go for refuge to the Buddha," at the very least we should be able to generate some sort of positive feeling. This can become the foundation for our mind of faith.

If you have accepted the three objects of refuge, you should practice in the following way. You should make an effort to recognize the myriad forms of the three poisons in your own mind and see the way they manifest in your actions. In particular, you should recognize the negative states of mind that are the strongest in your experience. You should recognize the Buddha as the supreme physician, the Dharma as the medicine, and the Sangha as the support enabling your recovery. Having understood the Three Jewels as ultimate, infallible, and valid objects of refuge through logic and reasoning, you should not take refuge in anything other than the Buddha, Dharma, and Sangha. Most of all you should keep the following advice of Chandrakirti in mind:

Refuge in the Buddha, Dharma, and Sangha
Is for those who seek liberation.

The Three Doors of Thorough Liberation

If we examine our lives, we can see that although we constantly make great effort to arrange things so that we can be happy, somehow we only succeed in creating further unhappiness. Even though happiness is what we wish for and what we strive to attain, somehow, no matter what we do, we only end up experiencing suffering. If we think about this, we will surely understand that there is something wrong. Looking closely, we can become fairly certain that what is wrong is not external, so therefore we must consider the possibility that it may be internal. It is not the heart, or the lungs—it is not form, and it has no color, or shape, and yet somehow it plays such an important role in our lives.

The subject matter of the *Sutra Requested by Arya Yulkhor Kyong* is the absolute nature of phenomena, the selfless nature of phenomena, and the reasons that sentient beings must realize ultimate truth in order to be free from cyclic existence. According to this text, the reason that sentient beings wander endlessly in cyclic existence is because of not understanding the three doors of signlessness, wishlessness, and emptiness. Although this subject matter does not appear explicitly in the root text at this point, I wish to discuss it a bit at this stage for a very important reason. We will find that if we try to take refuge as we have discussed here while deep down we are simultaneously strongly grasping at an independently existing self, our practice of refuge will not be able to provide us a firm foundation for training our minds. If we try to subdue our minds on this basis, we will definitely not be successful.

The first door of thorough liberation is the pacification of inherently existent causes and conditions. Any compounded phenomenon is the result of causes and conditions, and without depending on these causes and conditions, phenomena cannot come into existence. Yet the causes and conditions that produce phenomena are themselves merely imputed and do not exist from their own side.

For example, as sentient beings we have the sense of an "I" or a "self" or a "me" that exists continually as we go from lifetime to lifetime. This kind of existence is brought on by karma and delusions. When we reflect on the causes that generate the cycle of rebirth, we see that the first cause is the first link of the twelve links of dependent origination, namely ignorance. Due to ignorance we create karma, which is imprinted upon the third link, consciousness. Looking at this process, which we will discuss in greater detail in the medium scope section, we will notice a dependent cause and effect relationship: each of the latter causes depends on the previous cause. Even though the causes themselves do not exist independently or from their own side, due to our grasping at inherent existence, the cycle of karmic accumulations is established.

The level of dependent arising that I have just outlined here is the grossest level of dependent arising. To understand dependent arising at a more subtle level we should examine it in a more detailed manner. For example, in the case of the link of consciousness, we should consider that it is the interdependence of three things—the basis of imputation, the imputed label "consciousness," and the imputing mind that labels it—that brings about the existence of consciousness.

It is not possible for causes that are dependent and do not truly exist to bring results that are independent and inherently existent. Therefore, if the three causes that are the first three links—ignorance, karma, and consciousness—existed independently or truly, then the cyclic existence that arises as a result of these should also exist in that way. If that were the case, we would have no choice but to accept that it would not be possible to be liberated from cyclic existence, because cyclic existence would be truly existent, and thus unchangeable. But because the causes do not truly, inherently exist, and because they are dependent and exist due to causes and conditions, we understand the first door of liberation, which is the door pacifying all signs of true existence of causes and conditions. Because the causes are not truly or inherently existent, we can understand that it is possible for us to attain liberation.

When we grasp at inherent or independent existence with strong attachment or aversion, we experience happiness or suffering. We feel as if we are never going to be separated from the happiness or suffering that we are experiencing. We feel as if that happiness or suffering exists in the very nature of our minds. This kind of solid, concrete idea arises as a result of our ignorance. In the beginning, we may find it difficult to differentiate the subtle ways in which we grasp at our experiences, but in time we can come to recognize and extinguish these mental states.

The second door of liberation is the fact that there is no truly existent resultant rebirth. Going back to the twelve links, the first three throwing links bring the result of the links of name and form, the six senses, contact, feeling, attachment, grasping, existence, birth, and aging and death. These links are the results of the first three links, and are also empty, lacking true, inherent existence. If there were such thing as a truly existent result, it would be logical to posit that, from the basis of our present human rebirth, from lifetime to lifetime we could only continue to take more human rebirths. And yet we know that this is not the case.

The third door of thorough liberation is the emptiness of the truly existent nature of a particular phenomenon. This comes as a result of understanding the emptiness of truly existent causes and conditions.

The way we apply the understanding of the three doors of thorough liberation to our own case is in terms of the "I" that takes constant rebirth in cyclic existence. First we apply the understanding that the causes inducing this rebirth do not truly, inherently exist, and the understanding that this rebirth itself is also not truly existent. Then we apply the understanding that the self, the "I" that has taken rebirth, is also empty of being truly or inherently existent.

To clarify, the explanation of the three doors of liberation does not refer to three different doors that one must enter through to reach liberation. Buddha himself taught that there is no second door to liberation. There is only one door, which is the door of realizing the ultimate nature of reality. The three doors of liberation are simply another means to help us to do this.

HOW TO TRAIN AFTER TAKING REFUGE

Returning to the main outline, the next topic is the way to train after having taken refuge in the Three Jewels. In the root text Lama Tsongkhapa cites two sources of advice for those who have taken refuge. The first is Asanga's *Compendium of Ascertainments* and the second is personal advice from the lineage gurus.

The Training According to Compendium of Ascertainments

There are eight pieces of advice from *Compendium of Ascertainments,* divided into two sets of four.

According to this text, the first piece of advice is that once we take refuge, we should rely on a spiritual teacher who embodies the ten qualities. If this is not possible, we should rely upon a spiritual teacher who embodies at least six of these qualities. Also, we should regard that spiritual teacher like a buddha.

Second, we should listen to the Dharma with the six discriminating attitudes and free of the three faults of container, as we discussed earlier. Also, while listening to teachings we should maintain a pure motivation, free of the eight worldly concerns. We should also be free of the motivation of wishing to engage in the spiritual path or in the study of Dharma in order to acquire intellectual knowledge or merely to gather extra information. We should have the wish to benefit ourselves as well as others.

Third, we should cultivate faith, wishing to attain what is taught in the scriptural and experiential teachings.

And finally, having taken refuge in the Dharma, we should train in ethics, concentration, and wisdom, and seek the support of the friendship of people who live in these practices.

The next set of four pieces of advice is as follows.

First, once we have taken refuge, we should train in keeping our five sense perceptions from being distracted by objects that may cause negative states of mind to arise. By applying the forces of mindfulness and awareness, we should think about the shortcomings of engaging with these objects and not allow our five senses to interact with them. As we are beginners on the spiritual path, we do not yet have the power of mind to be able to apply the antidotes to our delusions right away, and therefore it is important that we focus on avoiding the objects that give rise to our delusions—such as things that inspire our obsessive attachment and things that make us feel angry and hateful. Taking the vows of monks and nuns or taking the eight Mahayana precepts is one method to train in incapacitating the delusions.

The experience of a delusional state of mind is usually preceded by two conditions: the observed object condition and the immediately preceding condition. The object of our attachment or anger itself is the observed object condition and our five sense perceptions are the immediately preceding condition. The five sense powers precede the negative state of mind that is generated by our mental consciousness. Our five sense perceptions themselves are not responsible for inducing the negative mind, but act as the immediate preceding condition to the mental consciousness that generates the anger or the attachment. However, since our five senses are not able to realize ultimate reality on their own, once our mental consciousness is habituated to understanding emptiness, even if our senses bring in the information of the observed object condition, although the object of the delusions will still appear, the mental consciousness will not be overtaken by afflictive emotions. However, as long as we have yet to cultivate this kind of antidote within our minds, it is better to stay away from the objects of our delusions altogether.

The second piece of advice is to practice Buddha's teachings to the best of our ability. We should not engage in actions that are considered to be "negative by nature," and we should learn and follow the advice set forth for the actions that are considered "negative because of being prohibited." The ten nonvirtues of body, speech, and mind, for example, are activities that are considered negative by nature, and therefore, we should not engage in them under any circumstances. Precepts such as not eating in the evenings, however, are not negative by nature, and even if we have taken a vow not to engage in this action, allowances can be made with special permission. In general, we should take and train in as many of the vows and commitments of practice that we possibly can. All of these activities are the training in higher ethics and will help us to accumulate the collection of virtuous merit that will result in our liberation.

The third piece of advice is to cultivate compassion in your attitude. The teachings of Buddha are rooted in compassion, and it is for this reason that we say that the Dharma is the one medicine that extinguishes all suffering. Having taken refuge in the Dharma, you should work to develop your compassion for the pain and suffering of others. If you cannot genuinely feel for the pain and suffering of others, at the very least you must ensure that you yourself do not become a cause of their suffering.

The result of following the advice and commitments of refuge is that you will be able to embody or generate qualities similar to those of the objects of refuge. For example, if a student has a spiritual teacher in his or her life who is extremely knowledgeable, kind, and compassionate, due to the influence of the teacher, the student will develop habits that are similar.

When I was studying at Sera, my philosophy teacher had a very beautiful manner of clapping his hands during debate. A classmate of mine who was also one of his students tried very hard to imitate our teacher when he debated. But this student was not very tall, and his attempts didn't come out so well. Then, just one month later he began imitating someone else! We teased him a lot, but generally I think he was right.

The fourth piece of advice is to make a special effort to express your faith and devotion toward the objects of refuge. We can do this by making offerings, remembering the qualities of the objects of refuge, making prayers, and so forth. Even if we are unable to do these things on a daily basis, there are special days on which it is particularly auspicious to engage in such activities.[16] In the monasteries in Tibet and India, from the very first moment of the day, the senior practitioners take refuge, generate bodhichitta, and begin their daily prayers. If it is possible, we too should try to develop this habit, as it will be very beneficial for our minds.

The Training According to the Personal Instructions

SPECIFIC ADVICE

The next topic is the specific forms of personal advice on what to abandon and what to practice once we have taken refuge. Within this list, there are three to abandon and three to practice. The three to abandon are as follows.

Once we have taken refuge in Buddha, we should abandon taking refuge in anything less than an enlightened being, such as worldly gods, *nagas,* or spirits. Although these beings may have the power to bring us benefit in the short term, since they are not completely enlightened yet we should not trust our welfare to them entirely. We cannot even consider arhats, who still have imprints of the delusions in their minds, ultimate objects of refuge, although we can regard them as temporary objects of refuge.

Second, because the Dharma is rooted in compassion, when we take refuge in the Dharma, we must abandon harming others directly or indirectly. For example, sometimes when traveling in India we may hire a porter to carry our luggage. Thinking that we are paying him and that therefore it is okay to overload him with our bags is inappropriate. Supporting activities involving intoxicants, alcohol, tobacco, drugs, or weapons—things that are in general harmful by nature—is also against the refuge advice. And then of course it is really wonderful if it is possible for one to give up eating meat. I myself am not vegetarian, but I deeply respect and rejoice for those who are. Even if you are not vegetarian, if you find yourself in a situation where meat is difficult to obtain it is better to abstain entirely.

In these degenerate times, when negative thoughts are so prevalent, we are witness to a great deal of abuse of other sentient beings, abuse of the environment, and so forth. As the essence of the Dharma is the practice of nonharmfulness, abusing other sentient beings and abusing the environment are transgressions of your refuge in the Dharma. The smallest of harmful actions, such as harming the life of a tiny insect, all the way up to something like working to create weapons of mass destruction should be abandoned once you have taken refuge in the Dharma. Having taken refuge in the Dharma, you should abandon every single kind of harm toward other beings in your thoughts and actions.

Third, having taken refuge in the Sangha, you should no longer interact with people who inspire you to do negative things or give you ideas that could lead to nonvirtue. This is not to say that you should abandon all your friends who are not in the category of the Sangha, but rather, that you should not be influenced by their negative thoughts and actions. Having taken refuge in the Sangha jewel, if it is possible, you should try to keep the company of others who have the same code of ethics, or at least who aspire to the same code of ethics, and whose thoughts and actions accord with what they aspire to attain.

Of course, it is true that what is considered appropriate and inappropriate in the world, to a large degree, are the forms of thought and action that society has decided are appropriate and inappropriate. However, a better measure to use may be to consider whether that mode of conduct brings positive or negative results—whether it harms or benefits others. This is how we should decide whether an action is virtuous or nonvirtuous, and this is how we should decide whether our conduct is appropriate or inappropriate. If we find that we are easily swayed into acting or thinking in inappropriate ways by others, since we are beginners, it is better to keep a distance from these people. However, if we have reached a stage where we are not influenced by such negativity, it is not necessary to take such precautions. The point is to protect our own minds.

Next are the three things to practice.

Having taken refuge in Buddha, you should show physical and mental respect for every single symbolic representation of enlightenment that you see—such as statues, drawings, paintings, and so forth. Through your respect and devotion, you should give the objects that represent enlightened beings the same recognition that you would give an actual buddha. It is inappropriate to regard the symbolic representations of Buddha as ordinary material objects, and to leave them lying around on the floor where you sit with callous disregard. You should also treat books that have pictures of buddhas with more respect than you treat your ordinary books.

Additionally, you should not put material value on the symbolic representations of the buddhas. You should not value these items according to how much you paid for them. Also, you should not consider them valuable because of the quality of the artwork. Every single symbolic representation of the buddhas—even a simple line-drawing of Manjushri —represents the embodiment of all buddhas, their infinite wisdom, and our aspiration to attain their qualities. You should consider all images of buddhas to be your personal objects of refuge.

Seeing a person selling statues or paintings of buddhas, you may say to yourself that you are not going to purchase anything because that money will become a form of wrong livelihood for this person. It is correct to make this decision in order to prevent this person from accumulating negative karma. On the other hand, you may instead decide to buy the statue or the painting, feeling that it is better off on your altar where you can make offerings to it and accumulate merit than it is sitting in a shop gathering dust. This is also fine. As I mentioned earlier, as long as you have a positive motivation, whatever you decide turns out right, and as long as your motivation is corrupted by negativity or nonvirtue, then whatever you decide will be wrong. Everything is dependent on the quality of your motivation.

Having taken refuge in the Dharma, we should treat every sentence, every page, every text that contains the teachings with the highest respect and devotion. The texts are the material representation of the Dharma refuge. Also, we should abandon all disregard for these objects, such as leaving books lying the floor, stepping over them, or using them as collateral on a loan.

Having taken refuge in the Sangha, we should cultivate the attitude of respect for anyone who has the signs of being in the Sangha. If you yourself have the robes of the Sangha, for your own part you should practice humility. The attitude whereby one thinks "I am part of the Sangha and therefore I have the right to be respected by others" is completely inappropriate. If you are humble in your attitude, these things will happen of their own accord. If you cultivate positive qualities within yourself, one day you will really become a part of the field for others to accumulate merit. You should try to become an object of the admiring faith of others, and in this way become a service to both Dharma and sentient beings.

GENERAL ADVICE

There are six additional points of refuge advice from the *Lamrim Chenmo.*

The first of the six is to take refuge again and again, knowing the qualities and the special characteristics of each one of the objects of refuge.

The second is that you should reflect on the kindness of the Buddha, Dharma, and Sangha, and make continuous offerings. Offering whatever you are planning to enjoy before you enjoy it is a fulfillment of the practice of refuge.

The third is to introduce others to the Dharma with the motivation of compassion, taking into consideration the factors of the appropriateness of the time, the occasion, and the mental predisposition of that person. This does not mean forcing the Dharma on others when they do not want to hear it or when they are not particularly interested. This instruction means that you must first see the correct accumulation of all the factors, and then act if it is appropriate.

The fourth piece of advice is to begin all activities—whether a Dharma activity or a secular activity—with the practice of taking refuge.

The fifth is to take refuge three times in the day and three times at night.

The sixth is never forsake the Three Jewels of refuge, even as a joke. You should not give them up even at the cost of your life.

It goes without saying that without understanding the characteristics of your objects of refuge, their qualities, and so forth, you will not be able to develop the kind of joyful enthusiasm in your mind that you will need to practice these forms of advice.

Understanding the Benefits

The base of your joyful enthusiasm for the practice of refuge is understanding its benefits. According to the *Lamrim Chenmo,* there are two sources from which we derive eight benefits each, making sixteen altogether. The first set is in accordance with Asanga's *Compendium of Ascertainments,* and the second is in accordance with the personal instructions.

The Benefits According to Asanga

The first benefit according to Asanga is that cultivating a proper form of motivation and generating the mind of refuge enable you to accumulate the extensive merit of virtue. As it is stated in sutra:

> The qualities of Buddha are inconceivable.
> The qualities of the Dharma are inconceivable.
> The qualities of the Arya Sangha are also inconceivable.
> By cultivating faith in these inconceivable [objects],
> The ripening result is also inconceivable.

It is said that if one was able to imagine the inconceivable merit that is generated from taking pure refuge in the Three Jewels as form, even the three realms of samsara would be too small to contain it. This analogy is given in case you are wondering how exactly to imagine this merit. When you accumulate money, for example, you deposit it into the bank and are then able to gauge the amount as it increases. It is difficult to measure merit in the same way, but roughly it can be said that when you have the basis or the support of an extensive accumulation of merit, you will not experience difficulty engaging in virtue. You will not need a lot of effort to subdue your mind. You will be able to put whatever teachings you listen to into practice and you will experience positive results from your meditations easily.

In the monasteries, there are some monks who are able to engage in their studies very easily without many obstacles. Then there are those who, when they make an effort to engage in their studies, experience many obstacles such as health problems and difficulty remembering things. The support of merit is what makes this kind of distinction. You may also have heard of people who get sick, and regardless of having the very best physician, treatment, and medicines, are unable to get better. This is also due to lack of merit. Also, sometimes you may encounter people in your lives whom you immediately like or dislike, without having any previous relationship with them at all. This is also determined by an individual's merit. When someone has the support of great merit of virtue, everyone who looks at that person will have a pleasant feeling.

The second benefit is that when you practice pure refuge, uncontaminated by the eight worldly dharmas, even if you are completely alone, you will naturally experience joy and supreme joy.

The third benefit is that you will be able to cultivate pure concentration.

The fourth benefit is that as a result of engaging in the practices of the path with a strong basis of pure concentration you will be completely liberated.

For the second set of benefits there are also four.

The first is that, having taken refuge, you will be blessed with great protection. If you are an American citizen, for example, you receive all the benefits of the protection of the American government. In the same way, as long as you generate the pure mind of refuge from your own side, from the side of the objects of refuge you will receive unfailing care and protection—protection from cyclic existence, protection from wrong paths, and protection from being overcome by your delusions. The protection that you receive is completely dependent upon the quality of your refuge. If your refuge is one hundred percent genuine, then so also is the benefit of the protection.

The second benefit is that, having taken refuge, the negative karma that you have accumulated by having followed mistaken paths in this life or in past lives will be reduced.

The third benefit is that you become a valid person. In this case a valid person means a trustworthy person.

The fourth benefit is that by practicing pure refuge, you become an individual inspiring faith and joy to all who appreciate virtue.

The Benefits According to the Personal Instructions

The first benefit of taking refuge according to the personal instructions is that once you have done so, you will enter the inner path of the Buddhadharma.[17] Calm abiding, superior insight, and the resulting states of clairvoyance are not practices unique to the Buddhist path. Generating the mind of refuge makes the difference between the Buddhist and non-Buddhist paths. If you attain high states of meditation without refuge, you will be able to abandon all the gross delusions of the desire realm, the form realm, and the first three levels of the formless realms. However, you will not be able to abandon the delusions of the fourth level of the formless realm, which is called the peak of samsara.

You can cultivate the mind of refuge through listening to the instructions and through study. Some people are also able to spontaneously generate the mind of refuge. This usually only occurs in the case of practitioners who have strongly familiarized their minds with the practice of refuge in past lifetimes and as a result feel a sense of faith, belief, and trust upon encountering the objects of refuge in the present lifetime. For example, in ancient India there was an individual who had very strong faith in Shiva, did many practices, and attained magical powers by which he was able to control other beings. But one day he found that there was one little boy who was not overtaken by his power. Surprised, he asked the child why this was so, and the child replied that he was protected by his intuitive, spontaneous refuge in the Buddha, Dharma, and Sangha.

The second benefit is that refuge acts as the foundation for all of the other vows and precepts that you take. This refers specifically to Buddhist vows and precepts, such as the vows of individual liberation, bodhisattva vows, and tantric vows. Even if your refuge is not spontaneous, it creates the basis for you to generate vows or precepts in your mind. Also, the vows and precepts that you hold will enhance your mind of refuge. The mind of refuge also allows you to accomplish the practices in accordance with your vows.

The third benefit is that with the mind of refuge you will be able to purify all of your past negative karma, or at the very least reduce it. In the time of Buddha, a particular person took rebirth as a human being with an extremely ugly appearance. Buddha, from his mind of great compassion, advised him to take up the practice of refuge in order to help purify the causes of this karma. As a result, the individual subsequently took rebirth in the god realms.

The fourth benefit is that you will be able to accomplish extensive accumulations of the merit of virtue. As it says in sutra, all the wishes of individuals who are rich in the accumulations of merit become fulfilled, and whatever they contemplate becomes a reality. This is the case for anyone who has this basis of the extensive accumulation of merit.

There was a very unsuccessful potter who lived in the time of Buddha. Every pot he tried to complete was beset by some accident, or wouldn't come together at all. The potter requested Buddha's help, and Buddha suggested that he travel to the local monastery and accumulate merit with the mind of faith and refuge. The potter did so, and as a result his practice of making pottery became very successful, and with gratitude he was able to make extensive offerings to Buddha.

The fifth benefit is that you will not fall to the lower realms.

The sixth benefit is that you will be protected from harm by humans and nonhuman beings.

Once, an arya being came to visit the house of a layperson, where he ran into some trouble. The father of the house came back unexpectedly early so the mother hid her visitor very quickly in the storeroom in a basket. Unfortunately, that night there was a robbery, and because the basket that the arya being was hidden in was the heaviest, it was carried away as part of the loot. When the robbers were far enough away, they opened the basket, and the arya being came out. Naturally, the robbers were all terribly upset, and they decided to kill him. This arya being was a very strong practitioner of refuge, so at the moment when the robbers were going to kill him the worldly gods called down from the sky to protect him, and he was spared.

The seventh benefit is that all your wishes will be fulfilled.

And the eighth benefit is that by cultivating the mind of faith in causal refuge, you will be able to attain enlightenment very quickly.

If refuge has ever failed us, it has failed us from our own side. If refuge has ever failed us, it has failed us because we were lacking the fundamental attitudes of fearing suffering and having faith in the objects of refuge. The external objects of refuge—the Buddha, Dharma, and Sangha—are endowed with countless qualities and will never let us down.

The loss of the mind of refuge occurs when you have the thought that you are no longer going to take refuge in these objects. Incurring transgressions in your practice does not in itself cause you to lose refuge. However, if you incur transgressions, you should be sure to engage in purification practices with the thought of regret.

In order to deepen your comprehension of the subject of refuge, it is best to study texts such as the *Sublime Continuum,* entire sections of which are dedicated to explaining the pure activities of the objects of refuge and the basic nature of the mind in detail. Likewise, the first chapter of Maitreya's *Ornament of Clear Realization* discusses the three objects of refuge, and the eighth chapter discusses the result of the four bodies of a buddha.

This completes the section explaining refuge, the gateway or the entrance into the path of Dharma.

THE LAW OF CAUSE AND EFFECT

Where could I find leather enough
To cover all the earth?
With merely the leather of my shoes
It is as if the entire earth were covered.
　　—Shantideva

SINCE WE ARE BEGINNERS, it is difficult for us to identify the ignorance that grasps at true existence as the root cause of all of our suffering. We do realize to some degree that we have self-cherishing and selfishness, but nonetheless we tend to blame our unhappiness on other people and on external events. As a result, we experience anger and hatred toward what we perceive to be the sources of our harm. In accordance with Shantideva's thought, if we were to try to destroy our external enemies, our battles would never end. However, if we are able to eliminate anger and hatred from our minds, our external enemies can no longer harm us. If we think about it, we will see that this second method is much more practical. Disengaging from the analytical process that puts the blame for our suffering on external causes is the best way to begin to detach ourselves from our mental afflictions. It may also be useful to spend time reflecting on the shortcomings of anger—how the immediate results of anger are unpleasant, and how anger ultimately destroys our own happiness as well as the happiness of other beings.

　Removing anger and hatred from our minds will not cause us any injury. In fact the opposite is true—allowing anger and hatred to remain in our minds can cause us great harm. Even if we are completely justified in our actions or words, the things that we do under the control of anger are generally very ineffective. However, if we are able to communicate without the motivation of anger, and especially if we are able to do so with the motivation to help others, whatever we say or do will be effective. Our Dharma practice is not composed of our prayers, commitments, and meditations alone. The main target of our practice is to subdue the mind. If in the course of a day we do not pay attention to how many times negativity arises in our minds, or how many times we engage in a negative physical or verbal act, but at the same time insist that we are focusing all of our energy on trying to understand the path to enlightenment, we are being hypocritical.

Also, we should remember that no matter how much it seems that our minds are completely under the control of the three poisons, even this state is impermanent. As some negative states of mind cease, others arise, and as those cease, still others arise—in this way, our minds are in constant fluctuation from moment to moment. It is most important that we try to ensure that our negative thoughts do not gain strength, but rather become weaker over time.

In considering these points, we come to the next topic of the text, which is generating faith in the law of cause and effect, the mind that is the root of all excellence.

THE GENERAL EXPLANATION OF KARMA

As the text mentions, the root of happiness and excellence in our lives is faith and belief in karma, the cause and effect of our actions. Although refuge protects us from the lower realms temporarily, it doesn't ensure total freedom from rebirth in the lower realms. The practices of abandoning the ten nonvirtuous actions and respecting the laws of karma, however, do ensure this freedom. The root of all happiness and excellence is faith in karmic cause and effect, and when we have this kind of faith we will find it possible to abandon the smallest of our nonvirtues and engage in positive activities.

Perseverance in the practice of purely observing karma is essential for everyone. Whether you are a holder of the three vast collections of the teachings or a holder of Vinaya, no one is above the workings of cause and effect: karma is applicable to us all. There are many stories of great practitioners, such as Ra Lotsawa, who, despite their attainments, have had to spend lifetimes in the hell realms due to not having purified a certain karmic result. In the same way that we begin a meditation with the cultivation of the proper motivation of virtue, when we apply ourselves on the spiritual path, we should begin with cultivating awareness of the cause and effect of our actions.

In general, awareness of karma means knowing which thoughts and actions we should abandon and which thoughts and actions we should cultivate. We can think of this awareness as the ultimate pure view of worldly existence, just as we say that the view of emptiness is the ultimate pure view of absolute reality.

Understanding karma is dependent upon understanding the relationship between cause and result. In order for us to understand this, we need to have some comprehension of what a cause is, what a result is, and what a condition is with respect to the four Buddhist schools. Generally, all of the Buddhist philosophical schools assert that every cause has two aspects: a direct cause and an indirect cause. Every result also has two aspects: a direct result and an indirect result.

In terms of a more detailed explanation of causes, we can speak of the substantial cause, the cooperative cause, and the ripening cause. The *substantial cause* is defined as the cause that transforms into the nature of the result. An example of this is the clay that becomes the pot. A *cooperative cause* does not transform into the nature of the result, but helps in effecting the result. An example of this is the potter who makes the pot. A *ripening cause* is the cause that most directly affects the final result and is most often applied to cause and effect in terms of rebirth. For example, the throwing karma that ripens at the moment of death and determines a sentient being's next rebirth is a ripening cause.

In terms of the aspects of the result, in general we say that there are three, the result that is similar to the cause, the fundamental or environmental result, and the ripening result. The *result that is similar to the cause* is exactly what it sounds like—an action done in one lifetime brings a result that is similar to that action in the next. There are two types of results that are similar to the cause. The first is related to experience and the second is related to action. An example of a result that is similar to the cause related to experience is when a person who kills a lot in a particular lifetime takes a rebirth in which he, himself, is killed. An example of a result that is similar to the cause related to action is when a person who kills a lot in this lifetime takes rebirth as a being whose mind enjoys killing. The *fundamental or environmental result* is a result that ripens in a person's immediate physical surroundings. For example, if a person has a bad temper in one lifetime it leads to rebirth in a very ugly, unpleasant place in a future lifetime. The *ripening result* is the result of the conduct that we practice in a particular lifetime. A ripening result must always manifest in an animate form, having a consciousness. For example, practicing ethics in one lifetime brings rebirth as a human being in the future.

Let us take another example, such as the result of our present perfect human rebirth with the eight freedoms and the ten endowments. The substantial cause of this result is the virtuous karma of a previous lifetime in which we accumulated the merits of living in ethics, generosity, pure prayers, and so forth. These virtuous actions are also categorized as the ripening cause for this present perfect human rebirth, as they resulted in the throwing karma that brought it about. Therefore, in this example, the ripening cause and the substantial cause are the same. The parents who brought us forth into this world are the cooperative causes.

Our strong habits of virtue and our strong habits of cherishing others are all results that are similar to the cause. Being born and living in a world where there is Dharma is the fundamental result. And the present aggregates of the mind and body of this precious human rebirth are the ripening result of our precious human rebirth.

There are three characteristics of karma that are set forth within the topic of the general explanation of karma. These are: karma is definite, karma increases, and one never experiences a karmic result for which one has not created the cause—thus, whatever karma is created is never lost.

Karma Is Definite

When we say that karma is definite, we mean that everything we experience arises as a concordant result of past actions.[18] Even the feelings in the minds of arhats and bodhisattvas on the tenth ground arise as a result of the virtues of past karma. The experience of happiness cannot come as a result of a nonvirtuous cause, and the experience of pain or suffering or unhappiness can *only* come as a result of a nonvirtuous cause. Since karma is definite, all negative actions, no matter how small, bring suffering, and all positive actions bring happiness. Whatever we sow, we will reap. Whatever the cause is, so is the result. This applies to any kind of karma—positive karma, negative karma, virtuous karma, nonvirtuous karma, throwing karma, completing karma, and so forth. All of it is definite.

There was a man named Nyenpa Sangden who lived a long time ago. He was involved in an extremely big project commissioned by a king to build a huge *stupa,* similar in scope to today's Maitreya Project. At some point along the way, Nyenpa Sangden got discouraged, felt that the project would be impossible to finish, and became very irritated with the king for starting it to begin with. However, the *stupa* was actually completed in his lifetime, and at the completion Nyenpa Sangden regretted having generated such a negative mind, so to make up for it he offered a bell with a very beautiful sound as an adornment to the *stupa.* The karmic result of this was that in his next life Nyenpa Sangden was born with a very melodious voice and an extremely ugly appearance.

Generally, the workings of karma are classified as slightly hidden and extremely hidden phenomena. We can understand the grosser levels of karma, which are considered slightly hidden, through the use of logic and reasoning, but we can only gain understanding of the subtle levels of karma, which are considered extremely hidden, by relying on faith and the authority of the scriptures. However, please remember that this does not imply that we accept that something is true *merely* by the power of the authority of being the teachings of Buddha. Also, we must ensure that if the subject—karma, in this case—is presented in an extremely hidden way, it should not be faulted by a correctly assuming valid cognition. For example, in sutra Buddha says that material wealth results from the practice of generosity, and that higher rebirth results from the practice of morality. Although it is impossible for us to point to the specific act of generosity that leads to the specific result of wealth, it is possible for us to apply a correctly assuming consciousness that infers that one arises from the other. To understand the workings of karma at the level of extremely hidden phenomena, which would be, in this case, pinpointing the particular act of generosity that brings the particular result of wealth, we need to apply the resources of other teachings, such as the teachings on the four noble truths and the teachings establishing Buddha as a valid or infallible person.

Karma Increases

The increasing nature of karma means that even a very small negative action can bring forth a tremendous negative effect. In the same way, even a very small virtuous action can bring forth a very powerful positive effect. As an entire ocean can arise from the accumulation of a few tiny drops of water, so even small actions of body, speech, and mind can bring forth enormous results. For this reason, we should work very hard to purify even our most minor negative actions, and rejoice in and cherish even our most minor virtuous acts.

At one time Maudgalyana, who was one of Buddha's main disciples, renowned for his psychic powers, visited the hell realms and there he found a man who had been a spiritual teacher in his previous life and had enjoyed a large following. Yet this man himself was reborn to great suffering, and as more and more people engaged in the practices that he had taught, his karma in the hells became heavier and heavier. Maudgalyana saw this clearly, and with compassion he went to this man's followers and ordered them to stop their practice, explaining that the more they followed his instructions, the heavier their teacher's karma became. The followers were so upset with him for insisting that their leader had gone to hell that they attacked Maudgalyana and beat him up. This experience was the result of some unpurified karma that Maudgalyana had with his mother, and because he failed to purify it, even with all of his psychic powers and so forth, he still experienced this unfortunate ripening result.

We can also look at the story of the disciple named Pakpa Lamchungpa, who had a lot of difficulty studying, but was blessed with a good heart. One day he found a dead mouse and offered it to one of Buddha's benefactors. He did not mean anything offensive, but offered it from the heart, and thus the benefactor took no offense. In return, the benefactor gave Pakpa Lamchungpa some grain. Wherever Pakpa Lamchungpa planted that grain, an abundant harvest grew. Eventually, Pakpa Lamchungpa collected a great deal of wealth from his sales of the grain, and from this wealth he had a golden mouse made, and offered it back to the benefactor to repay his kindness.

You Will Never Experience a Result
for Which You Have Not Created the Cause

It is commonly said among Tibetans that lack of knowledge is like an open gateway for the downfalls. Therefore, it is important to be as informed as possible about actions and their results in order to avoid creating unnecessary bad karma. Then, once we really understand the workings of karma, it becomes necessary for us to take a great deal of responsibility for ourselves and our actions. Without exception, there is always a direct cause and many conditions that bring about the results of every single thing that we experience. And it is impossible to experience a result for which we ourselves have not created the cause.

For example, imagine you are traveling with a group of people in a car together, and you all get into an accident, and everyone escapes without injury except you. This means that although the entire group has created the karma to have an accident, only you created the karma to be injured at that particular time and under those particular circumstances. Since they did not create the cause for injury at that time and under those circumstances, the others did not experience injury as a result, regardless of the fact that all the external conditions were present.

We can also consider karmic cause and effect in terms of our own minds. Right now, our minds are filled with expectations and hopes for our spiritual practice. We want to attain enlightenment, we want to attain liberation, we want to complete the path and practices of the medium and great scopes. But in order to actually accomplish these things, it is not enough to wish for them. We must create their causes or it will not be possible for us to experience the respective results.

As Buddha states in sutra:

The ripening result of an action
Does not occur to the earth,
To the water,
To the wind, or
To the elements.
It only occurs to the one who created the cause.

Once we engage in an action, in the very next moment the karmic seed or the imprint of that action is established within our consciousness. For example, if in this lifetime we practice ethics, generosity, and so forth, the imprints of these actions are pressed into our consciousness, creating the throwing karma to be reborn as a human being. Even though after we die we may not experience a human rebirth for many, many lifetimes, the karmic imprint is still carried in our consciousness until the conditions arise for it to ripen. Since we have lived countless, beginningless lifetimes, there is no doubt that we all have the karma in our minds to be reborn in a pure land, to take a higher rebirth, or to be reborn in the form and form-less realms. We also have the karmic potential to be reborn in the animal realm, the realm of the hungry ghosts, or the hell realms. We should not forget that we have the karmic potential to experience all of these results.

DETAILED EXPLANATION OF KARMA

Abandoning the Ten Nonvirtues

In general, both virtuous and nonvirtuous actions are limitless in number. However, as Vasubandhu discusses in *Treasury of Knowledge,* we can summarize the different types of karma in terms of body, speech, and mind and categorize them into ten nonvirtuous actions and ten virtuous actions. Abandoning the ten nonvirtuous activities of body, speech, and mind and cultivating the thought of refuge is the practice of the small scope, which is the means to ensure a higher rebirth. This practice is also the basis for cultivating the realizations of the medium scope, and the foundation for cultivating the path and practices of the great scope.

THREE OF BODY
Killing
The first of the ten nonvirtuous actions is killing. To accumulate the complete karma of killing, you must complete the four parts of the action: the basis, the intention, the course of action, and the completion of the action.

For the action of killing, the basis must be a sentient being.

The intention can be further divided into two: the motivation and the determination of the object. The motivation should be any one of the three poisonous minds. Motivations can be general or specific. An example of someone with a general motivation is a person who randomly, but intentionally, sets fire to a forest, or someone who goes to war and kills. This person does not have the motivation to kill any specific person, but does have the motivation to kill in general. On the other hand, someone with a specific motivation intends to kill a particular being. If, for example, you thought of killing a person named Devadatta, you would have generated the specific motivation to kill Devadatta. If you intended to kill Devadatta but by mistake killed somebody else, you would incur the karma of killing, but not the full negative karma. This is for two reasons: because the basis, the intention, the course of action, and the completion of the action would not follow one track, and because by mistakenly killing someone else, it would be easier for you to generate regret. In the case of a general motivation, you would incur the full karma for every being that you kill.

There are four types of determination that can be made. The first of these is determining the base that is a sentient being to be a sentient being. The second is determining the base that is a sentient being not to be a sentient being. The third is determining that which is actually not a sentient being not to be a sentient being. And the fourth is determining that which is not a sentient being to be a sentient being.

If you have a specific motivation to kill a particular being, but have the second or the fourth determinations, you make a mistake in what you kill. When you make this mistake, you do not accumulate the full karma of killing. However, when you have a general motivation to kill any living being at all, even if you have a mistaken determination—number two or four—this same rule doesn't apply because the motivation to kill is pervasive, and you incur the full karma.

In order to create the full karma of killing in the case of generating a specific motivation to kill a particular being, you must have the first or the third forms of determination. When the first or third are applied, if you then have the course of action and the completion of that action, you incur the full karma. This is a karma that needs to be purified by generating the mind of regret. If, in cultivating a specific motivation to kill someone, there is a mistake in the determination, the complete karma of killing is not accumulated.

Again, these four aspects of determination do not apply in the case of actions done with the general motivation to kill.

In terms of motivation, killing with the motivation of attachment means, for example, that you are attached to eating meat, so you kill for it. An example of killing with the motivation of anger is killing in times of war, or for revenge. An example of killing with the motivation of ignorance is when people make sacrificial offerings.

When we kill sentient beings as we go about our daily lives—driving, walking, and so forth—we do not receive the full karmic effect of killing because we are lacking the motivation to kill. Yet, since a sentient being has died, there is karma involved. For that reason, during the summer when there is a lot of moisture and hence many life forms outside, it is traditional for ordained people to do a rains retreat in order to restrict the area of their movement to lessen the accumulation of negative karma.

Killing yourself is also regarded as an extremely negative action. Aborting a fetus is the same as killing, and if the father is involved and encourages and supports it, the father accumulates the same karma. Euthanasia is also killing. In the case where, for whatever reasons, you assist in the death of a person who has been chronically ill for a very long time, you fulfill almost all of the four parts of the complete action of killing except possibly that of motivation, if you act solely out of compassion for this person's sickness. Even so, although the causal motivation may be compassion, the immediate motivation would certainly be the intention to kill. Thus the action would be complete. If there were some basis of compassion, the karmic effect would be slightly lighter, but of course it would be difficult to say whether there was really pure compassion, because the compassion in the mind of an ordinary sentient being is usually polluted with thoughts of attachment.

The course of action for the karma of killing is that yourself undertake the action, make someone else undertake the action, or kill through black magic and so forth.

To complete the act of killing, it is not necessary that you yourself do the action. As long as you have completed the base and the motivation and you have set up the course of action, even if someone else takes over for you from that point forward, you still incur the full karma. A karmic cause cannot be split up into parts, so if you are an army general sending a lot of soldiers out to kill, and they each kill one person, you yourself accumulate all of that karma. This means that when you receive a medal of honor for that kind of thing, you are receiving a heavy-duty negative karma kind of medal.

The completion of the act of killing comes when the other being dies, and you feel satisfaction that that being has been killed. You do not receive the full effect of the karma of killing if you die first.

Stealing

The second of the three nonvirtues of body is the act of stealing, which also has four parts: the basis, the intention, the course of action, and the completion of the action.

The basis of stealing is things that are owned by others—either by an individual or a community. Objects do not need to be of a particular value in order to qualify as a base for stealing. According to Vinaya, however, a person holding the vows of a monk or nun must steal something of a certain value in order to incur the defeat[19] of stealing. However, even though an ordained person must steal something of a particular value in order to incur the *defeat* of the vow of stealing, even if he or she steals something worthless, the karma of stealing is still accumulated.

As before, the intention is divided into two parts: the determination and the motivation. The four aspects of determination are the same as for killing, listed above. A specific motivation would be the intention to steal a particular thing, and a general motivation would be the wish to separate someone else from an object that has not been given to you.

The course of action for the karma of stealing is the act of stealing itself, which also includes making others steal. Stealing can be accomplished by taking something away from another person forcefully, or taking it away through use of deceit. Taking a loan with the intention not to repay it is stealing. Borrowing things without the clear intention to return them is also stealing. Taking a loan from a bank and then declaring bankruptcy and thinking that you no longer have to repay it, or adjusting the boundaries of your property and feeling that you have acquired more land by having done this alone are also stealing.

The karma of stealing is complete when you obtain the object and feel satisfaction.

Sexual Misconduct

The third of the three nonvirtues of body is sexual misconduct.

The basis of sexual misconduct can be a male or female. Usually, the basis is considered in dependence upon four categories: inappropriate person, inappropriate organ, inappropriate place, or inappropriate time.

Inappropriate person means someone who is the wife or husband of someone else, someone who has a relationship with someone else, an ordained monk or nun, or someone who is engaged to be married.

Inappropriate organs are the mouth and the anus.

Inappropriate places are places where one's spiritual teachers reside, where there are holy objects, or public places.

Inappropriate times are during the daylight hours, or during pregnancy or menstruation.

Inappropriate organs, places, and times apply even if the person you engage with is your partner, and these things also apply to homosexual relationships. In order to incur the full karma of sexual misconduct, you must not make a mistake in your determination of the object.

Sexual misconduct can be motivated by attachment, anger, or ignorance. Sexual misconduct motivated by ignorance was rampant, for example, in the time before Lama Atisha came to Tibet, when people engaged in sexual activity in order to further their spiritual experiences while seriously misunderstanding the role of this type of conduct on the path.

The course of action for sexual misconduct is the sexual act itself.

The action is complete when contact takes place and bliss is experienced.

FOUR OF SPEECH

Lying

The first of the four nonvirtues of speech is lying.

The basis for lying is another person who can hear.

The intention, again, has two parts: discrimination and motivation. The discrimination is intending to tell a lie to a specific person or about a specific subject matter. The motivation is the wish to deceive.

The course of action can be verbal or it can be more subtle, such as a implying a "yes" or a "no" through your physical conduct.

The completion of the action is when the other person understands the lie that you have told.

Divisive Speech

The basis of divisive speech is two or more people who are friendly toward one another, or who are not friendly toward one another.

In order to collect the full karma of divisive speech, you must have an unmistaken determination.

The motivation can be any one of the three poisons.

The course of action is speech that divides those who are harmonious, or those who are about to be harmonious. It also includes intensifying divisions among those who are disharmonious, ensuring that there is no chance of reconciliation. In the course of action, the words you say may be true or false—it doesn't matter as long as it engenders a split. Whether what you say is something pleasant or unpleasant also doesn't matter.

The completion of the action is when the parties involved have heard and understood what you have said. If the basis, intention, cause of action, and completion are all present, the full negative karma is accumulated whether or not the split actually takes place.

Harsh Speech

The basis of harsh speech is anyone toward whom you wish ill will.

The discrimination is the mind clearly deciding to speak harsh words. The motivation can be any one of the three poisonous minds.

The course of action is speaking the harsh words. In this context, it makes no difference whether what you say is true or false.

The completion of the action is when the person you are talking about comprehends what you have said.

Gossip

The fourth nonvirtue of speech is baseless gossip. This nonvirtue actually encompasses a much wider range of activities than what we normally think of as gossip. Here, any kind of speech that serves no constructive purpose is considered gossip. According to some scriptures, reciting mantras in order to fulfill the purposes of this lifetime is also considered to be a part of the nonvirtuous activity of baseless gossip.

The basis of gossip need not necessarily be another sentient being. For example, even if you are by yourself singing a song or something like that, and hence there is no audience, it is still considered part of the activity of gossip.

The determination for gossip is the intent to engage in that action. The motivation can be any one of the three poisonous minds.

The course of action is the useless activity of speech in whatever form.

The completion of the action is when you have finished engaging in it.

THREE OF MIND
Covetous Mind
The first of three nonvirtues of mind is covetous mind.

The basis of covetous mind is animate or inanimate objects that belong to others.

The discrimination is the wish to possess that object. The motivation can be any one of the three poisonous minds.

The course of action is when your mind becomes completely overcome by the wish to possess those objects.

In order to accumulate the full karma of covetousness, the object need not end up in your possession. Rather, once the craving mind solidifies, becoming very firm and set, the action of covetous mind is complete.

To elaborate, covetous mind is generated in five stages, beginning with a sense of attachment to your own possessions. This foundational delusion sets off the second part, the mind wanting the possessions of others. This leads to the mind becoming focused on the qualities, benefits, or the mental taste of someone else's object, which is the third part. In the fourth part that thought gains strength, wanting the object to become "mine." The fifth part is full-blown covetousness. In this stage, you may display a boldness or audacity in your attitude of coveting. You may have no feeling of shame, or any sense of consideration. All the fences of the mind are completely down, and the nonvirtue is complete.

Some texts say that when we aggressively engage in the practices of pacifying and increasing[20] with the thought of seeking the eight worldly dharmas or the benefits of this lifetime, these activities become part of the actions of covetous mind.

Ill Will
The basis of ill will is the person whom you are unhappy with.

The motivation is the intention to cause harm physically, mentally, or verbally based on any one of the three poisons.

The course of action is when the mind is overcome by that harmful intention.

The action of ill will is complete when the mind has definitely decided to harm. It is not necessary that physical harm is actually done.

The first stage of the nonvirtue of ill will is a sense of aversion toward the person whom you perceive has harmed you. The second part is feeling that whatever way this person has harmed you is unbearable, and feeling unable to let it go. The third part is thinking over and over again about how this person has wronged you until strong anger arises. The fourth part is the thought wishing to retaliate. The fifth part is the full-blown mind of ill will.

Engaging in mantra practices of wrathful deities with the wish to fulfill the eight worldly dharmas can also be considered constituting ill will.

Wrong View

There are two kinds of wrong view. The first is the wrong view in which you superimpose or fabricate more onto a basis than it actually possesses. The second is believing that things that do exist in reality do not exist at all.

The basis of wrong view in terms of the ten nonvirtues must be something that exists, something that can be established by valid cognition. When explained in the context of the ten nonvirtues, the base of wrong view is usually cause and effect, the existence of past and future lives, and so forth.

The motivation for wrong view can be any of the three poisonous minds.

The course of action is any action that you engage in under the influence of the wrong view—with the belief that karma or past and future lives do not exist and so on.

The action is complete when you become certain that your wrong view is correct.

There are also five stages of progression for wrong view. The mind that is ignorant of ultimate reality is the foundation. The second stage is the development of the strong thought that totally disregards cause and effect or past and future lives. The third stage is continuously reinforcing this idea to yourself, and in this way becoming habituated to it. The fourth stage is when you decide with certainty that your wrong view is correct. The fifth stage is when you become influenced by that wrong view to the point that you develop complete disregard for cause and effect and behave accordingly.

Of the two wrong views, believing that something that does exist is non-existent is the more serious wrong view. The philosophical systems of the lower schools incur this fault. For example, the Chittamatra system asserts that phenomena exist by way of their own characteristics. Thus, they believe in a form of existence that in reality does not exist. However, although they fall into that category of wrong view, holding a view of the lower schools is not considered one of the ten nonvirtues.

The Way in Which Karma Is Categorized as Heavy and Light

The nonvirtues of body and speech progress from heaviest to lightest in accordance with the order in which they are set forth in the explanations of the lamrim—killing is the heaviest physical nonvirtue, and those that follow are lighter. Killing is considered the heaviest physical nonvirtue because it results in the greatest harm. The nonvirtues of speech—lying, divisive speech, harsh speech, and baseless gossip—follow the same order, from heaviest to lightest. The three nonvirtues of mind, however, are listed in the opposite order. That is, the first in the list—covetousness—is comparatively light, while the last in the list—wrong view—is a comparatively heavy nonvirtue.

Karma can also be categorized as heavy according to the way in which one undertakes the action. For example, taking pleasure in killing or killing in a way that inflicts the greatest amount of pain and suffering upon the victim is extremely heavy karma. Praising or rejoicing when others kill also makes the negative karma much heavier, as does killing many beings at one time.

An action can also be considered heavy if there is no antidote, which means that when we do it, we do not have any sense of regret in our minds at all. Karma without an antidote can also refer to a nonvirtue done on the special days of the month or year, such as the eighth of the Tibetan calendar, the new moon, and the full moon days.

An action can also become heavy is if it is done by someone who simultaneously holds wrong or perverted views. An example of this is killing in order to make a sacrificial offering in the name of your spiritual path or religion. Another example is killing with the idea that it is a glorious, heroic, virtuous act.

The act of stealing is made more powerful when we take many things or when we take something very valuable. Stealing from the Three Jewels also accumulates a very heavy karma, especially stealing from the Sangha jewel. If we steal offerings made to the Buddha or the Dharma jewel, our karma can be purified if we later generate regret and reimburse what we have stolen. But if we steal from the Sangha, even if we later regret that action and return what we have stolen, we will still experience the result of that negative action.

The nonvirtue of sexual misconduct is considered heavy when it involves people who have taken precepts or ordination vows, utilizing inappropriate parts of the body, or engaging in the action at inappropriate times or in inappropriate places such as places containing holy objects, *stupas,* one's spiritual teachers, or in monasteries.

The nonvirtue of lying is considered heavy when you lie to your parents, your spiritual teachers, or to friends who have placed a lot of trust in you. One of the heaviest nonvirtues is lying in order to create disharmony within the spiritual community.

Divisive speech is considered heavy when it is intended to separate people who have been living in harmony for a long time, or when it causes a split between spiritual teachers and disciples or between parents and children, whether or not what is being said is true.

Harsh speech is considered heavy when it is directed at or is about one's parents or spiritual teachers.

Baseless gossip also becomes heavy when the subject is your parents or your spiritual teachers. Reading or studying explanations that hold wrong practices such as animal sacrifice to be superior kinds of conduct is also considered a heavy nonvirtue.

Covetous mind is heavy when you covet the belongings of the Sangha or offerings made to the Buddha and Dharma.

Ill will directed toward your spiritual teacher is much heavier than general forms of ill will, because your spiritual teacher shows you and others the path to virtue.

Wrong views are considered heavier when you have knowledge of the path and of the three higher trainings, yet despite this you bear the wrong view that thinks that there is no liberation.

In general, negative actions are made more powerful by the influence of one of several factors: the motivation, the course of action, or the person in relation to whom we complete the action. Actually, since we are ordinary sentient beings, it is difficult for us to generate an action that is *not* made powerful by one of these factors. However, we should keep in mind that whatever negative karma we have accumulated can be purified by the antidote of the four opponent powers and by purification practices such as Vajrasattva.

Throwing and Completing Karma

Generally speaking, there are four kinds of karmic results that an action can produce: the ripening result, the result that is similar to the cause, the habitual result, and the environmental result.

The ripening result is caused by the maturation of two particular kinds of karma: throwing karma or completing karma. Throwing karma, which is activated at the time of death, is responsible for determining where we will take rebirth. It propels us to the lower realms, the higher realms, the form and formless realms, and so forth. All nonvirtuous throwing karma brings rebirth in the three lower realms. Karma that brings rebirth in the human, *asura* or jealous god, and god realms is contaminated, virtuous throwing karma. The throwing karma that brings rebirth in the form and formless realms is a kind of virtuous karma called invariable throwing karma.

The root motivation of throwing karma is ignorance, which drives the positive or negative actions of body, speech, or mind. The second moment of that action is transferred into a karmic imprint in the consciousness. This karmic imprint is then matured by the links of craving, grasping, and existence, which are the eighth, ninth, and the tenth links. That brings forth the ripening of that particular karmic imprint. Since we have a lot of karmic imprints, the question of which karmic imprint will be ripened is determined by whichever is the heaviest karma in the mind—negative or positive. If the negative and positive are equal, then whichever was created first will be the one to ripen. If they were created at the same time, then the one that we are most familiar with will ripen.

Completing karma is the cause that determines the characteristics of that rebirth—our personalities, our experiences, and our environment. The eighth, ninth, and tenth links in the twelve links of dependent arising are all completing karma. Completing karma is generally considered to fall under the categories of virtuous and nonvirtuous.

It is possible for a virtuous throwing karma to be accompanied by a nonvirtuous completing karma. An example of this would be taking rebirth as a human being (contaminated virtuous throwing karma) with major mental and physical defects and living in terrible poverty (nonvirtuous completing karma). It can also work the other way around: a nonvirtuous throwing karma might be accompanied by a contaminated virtuous completing karma. This would result in a rebirth such as that of a pet in America. The rebirth into the animal realm is the result of a nonvirtuous throwing karma, but the virtuous completing karma ensures that they have everything taken care of—medical care, food, affection, and so forth.

An extremely heavy nonvirtue becomes a throwing karma that will bring a hell realm rebirth. A heavy to moderate negative action becomes a throwing karma that will bring rebirth in the realm of the hungry ghosts. Light negative actions will result in an animal realm rebirth.

A question that often comes up is whether a particular throwing karma affects one or many lifetimes. In Vasubhandu's *Treasury of Knowledge,* it is stated that one particular throwing karma affects one lifetime alone, and not other lifetimes. However, Asanga argues in the *Compendium of Ascertainments* that a particular throwing karma can affect one lifetime *or* many lifetimes, provided it was created by a very strong action. For example, in sutra there is the story of a monk who used very harsh speech with a strong base, motivation, course of action, and completion of action. As a result, he accumulated a very, very heavy karma with only one action. This one action caused him to take a lower rebirth five hundred times.

The Specific Results of the Ten Nonvirtues

In terms of the nonvirtue of killing, the result that is similar to the cause is a short life, or a life that is constantly endangered. The habitual result is that you are born possessing an intuitive sense to kill. The environmental result can be one of several: medicines may be ineffective in curing any illnesses you may have, food and drink may be unable to nourish your body, and you may experience untimely death.

For stealing, the result that is similar to the cause is that you experience great difficulty amassing wealth despite your efforts, and you are unable to protect or preserve what belongs to you. The habitual result is having a natural inclination to steal.

For sexual misconduct, the result that is similar to the cause is that you will have relationships with people who will constantly betray you. The habitual result is having a strong tendency to engage in sexual misconduct.

The result that is similar to the cause of lying is that you will be continually deceived or lied to, or others will not believe what you say. The habitual result will be a strong tendency to lie.

For divisive speech, the result that is similar to the cause is that you will constantly be separated from those whom you like or love by some dispute. The habitual result is that you will naturally be inclined toward speaking divisively about others.

Harsh speech and baseless gossip follow the same patterns. The result that is similar to the cause is that you will become the object of harsh speech or baseless gossip. The habitual result is that you will have a habit of speaking in these ways.

The results similar to the cause and habitual results of the three nonvirtues of mind are as follows. Craving brings a rebirth in which you will not achieve your aims, harmful intent brings a rebirth in which you are terrified of your surroundings, and wrong view brings a rebirth in which you are blind to the correct view.

The environment in which you are born and live is also a result of karma. Being born in a place where you cannot practice virtue, an environment that is very rough and unpleasant, being born in a war-torn, life-threatening place or a place where there is no physical or mental nourishment— these things are also the result of engaging in specific nonvirtuous actions. Specifically, the environmental result of stealing is that you will be reborn in a place with sparse crops and little fruit and that is plagued by frost and hail. The environmental result of sexual misconduct is that you will be reborn in muddy, filthy places. Lying brings rebirth in a place where you are surrounded by people trying to cheat you, and divisive speech brings rebirth in a place with uneven ground. Harsh speech brings rebirth in a place overrun with tree stumps and prickly bushes. Gossip brings rebirth in a place with crops that fail and with rain at the wrong times. Craving brings a rebirth in which, even when you experience pleasant things, you don't enjoy them, and harmful intent brings rebirth in a place where there is war, sickness, and famine. Wrong view brings rebirth in a place where water and precious things are sparse.

All of the suffering that we experience in our own lives, today, has arisen from specific causes. As I have just explained, an early death is the result of taking another's life in a previous lifetime, poverty is the result of stealing, and so on. However, in a more general sense, we can also say that the suffering that we experience in our lives comes as a result of cherishing ourselves alone, and seeking only our own personal happiness. Although the self-cherishing mind has the appearance of protecting us or looking after our own interests, in reality it only causes destruction, for ourselves as well as for others. For example, self-cherishing causes us to disregard our parents, our spiritual teachers, our friends, and our relatives, and causes us to act negatively toward them. It also causes us to have high expectations and minds full of doubt and suspicion. It induces jealousy toward those who are better than us, competitive feelings toward those who are equal to us, and disparaging attitudes toward those who are less fortunate than we are. It causes our minds to swing back and forth between feelings of great happiness when we receive small compliments or praise and intense feelings of agony at the slightest criticism. All of this is brought on by the self-cherishing mind.

Once there was a king who fell ill—he became so sick that no doctor or medicine or prayers were able to help him. At that time, the king sought the help of a great mahasiddha who was a very accomplished practitioner. The mahasiddha examined the situation and decided that a special torma ritual should be done to drive away the interference. Generally, this kind of ritual is done outside, as it involves the use of fire. However, this time, before beginning the ritual, the mahasiddha went into the palace, saying the obstacle was not outside, but inside. He carried his things around everywhere inside, looking for the obstacle, and finally he approached the king himself. As he stood right in front of the king, the great mahasiddha said, "Aha! I have found the obstacle," and he made the fire right there.

Also, at the beginning of empowerments you may see the initiating lama offer a ritual cake to appease interferences. What are these interferences?

They are ignorance, ego-grasping, and the self-cherishing mind. They are the obstacles that are the manifestations of our own ignorance and self-cherishing.

Shantideva says:

Oh mind, countless eons have passed
As you wished to accomplish your own benefit—
Yet that great hardship
Has resulted only in suffering.

From the basis of self-cherishing we have sought only our own selfish interests. We have applied ourselves with great force to achieve our goals, making effort with our body, speech, and mind. But all that has resulted from this has been suffering! Understanding this, we should excuse ourselves from the service of the self-cherishing mind. In the same way that all of our suffering can be blamed on the mind that cherishes ourselves alone, all of our happiness can be attributed to the mind that wishes happiness for others. As a result, if we truly want happiness, even should sentient beings rise up as our enemies, we should vow to cherish them forever, no matter if it should cost us our lives.

Although the practice of abandoning the ten nonvirtues is not a practice exclusive to the path of the great scope, it is certainly possible for us train in this way—with the motivation of cherishing others. For example, instead of abandoning a negative action—killing, for example—in order to avoid accumulating negative karma and experiencing suffering, we can abandon killing because we cherish the lives of other beings, and wish to benefit them, not harm them. In this way we are practicing the path of the small scope with the motivation of a Mahayana practitioner.

Virtuous Actions and Their Results

We have already spoken of the ten nonvirtuous karmic actions in terms of how they are created, what their results are, what makes them powerful, and so forth. Now we will consider the other side of the coin: virtuous karmic actions.

In order to create virtue, it is not sufficient merely to happen not to create any nonvirtue. If this were the case, we would be creating virtue all the time, and we might already be enlightened! Rather, virtuous karma is created when we engage in a positive action with intent, or when we consciously refrain from creating nonvirtue even when all the conditions are present to do so. This is the reason that vows are such an important part of Buddhist practice.

There is a great difference between someone who does not engage in the ten nonvirtuous actions kind of "by the way," and someone who actually makes a commitment—takes a vow—to abandon them. An individual who has not taken vows to abandon the ten nonvirtuous actions must meet with all of the conditions to engage in that action and consciously refrain from doing so in order to accumulate the merit of not engaging in those actions. He or she will not accumulate any merit simply by not having the occasion to kill.

However, those who have taken a vow not to kill accumulate the merit of not killing from the moment they take that vow, for whatever duration they hold that vow, at all times whether they are sleeping or awake. This is the case regardless of whether they meet with the situation or all the conditions or not. If you hold the full lay precepts, or just four, or just three, or just two, or even just one, you are generating continual merit from the moment you take that precept until death. The situation is the same for those who have taken the ordination of the thirty-six precepts, or the two-hundred and fifty-three precepts, or the bodhisattva vows, or the tantric vows—you accumulate continual merit accordingly.

For a person who has not taken a vow, in order to create the virtue of abandoning killing, for example, the basis, the intention, the course of action, and the completion of the action are required.

The basis, as in the nonvirtue of killing, is another sentient being.

The motivation is feeling compassion for the suffering of others.

The course of action is completely abandoning the nonvirtuous action. Additionally, enabling the survival of that particular sentient being or saving the life of that particular sentient being can also become a course of action.

The completion of the action is when one makes the complete resolution not to kill.

The completion of nonvirtuous actions is usually marked by external actions. However, the completion of virtuous actions usually occurs within one's mind.

If one abandons killing—complete with the basis, intention, course of action, and completion of the action—all with great strength of mind, the ripening result is a rebirth in the higher god realms. If one abandons killing with moderate strength of mind, the result will be a rebirth in the lower god realms. If one abandons killing with less strength of mind, the result will bring a rebirth in the human realms.

The result that is similar to the cause of abandoning killing is a long life without sickness, disease, and so forth. The habitual result is that one will be born with an intuitive sense of compassion and appreciation for life from a very young age.

To complete the action of abandoning stealing, the basis, the intention, the course of action, and the completion of the action are also necessary. The result will be material wealth that comes very easily.

The result of abandoning sexual misconduct or adultery is very harmonious relationships with your partners that endure a long time, and harmonious relationships with the friends and relatives who surround you.

The result of abandoning lying is that people naturally have a sense of trust in you.

The result of abandoning divisive speech is that you are never lacking friends. Due to the merit of abandoning divisive speech, you develop pleasant characteristics that naturally attract the company of others.

The result of abandoning harsh speech is that people always speak well of you, and you have a good reputation.

The result of abandoning gossip is that you develop powerful speech, and people will listen to whatever you have to say and value it.

The result of abandoning covetous mind is that you will easily be able to accomplish whatever you wish for.

The result of abandoning ill-will is that you will be born with fearlessness and great confidence.

The result of abandoning wrong views is that whatever you study will only help to expand your mind to encompass a wider understanding of the world.

Other Divisions of Karma

There are two more divisions of karmic action that we have not yet discussed: those actions whose result will definitely be experienced and those actions for which the experience of the result is uncertain.

In order to ensure that one is definitely going to experience the ripening result of a particular action, one first has to accumulate the karma. As taught by Asanga, there are four possible relationships between the action and accumulation of karma.

The first is doing an action, but not accumulating its karma. This can only occur with regard to actions of body or speech but not with regard to actions of the mind. Lama Tsongkhapa gives ten examples that illustrate how this is possible.

The first situation takes the example of a dream. If you kill someone in a dream, you do not accumulate the karma of killing. However, because it would be untenable to consider the act of dreaming of killing someone to be neutral or virtuous, we must say that there is negative karma accumulated. However, it is not the particular karma of killing. The reverse is also true. If you do something virtuous in a dream, such as the action of abandoning killing, even though it can be said that you have the basis, motivation, course of action, and completion of action, you will not accumulate that particular positive karma of abandoning killing, although you will accumulate some virtuous karma. Of course this also means that people who have taken the vow not to kill are continually accumulating positive karma, even in their sleep.

The second situation in which an action is done but the karma is not accumulated is when you do something virtuous or nonvirtuous without knowing that it is virtuous or nonvirtuous, respectively.

The third situation is when you do something without intention, such as killing insects without knowing it.

The fourth is doing an action without aggression, and where the continuum ceases. For example, you might recite a short prayer, but your mind is roaming the Internet. In this situation, you lack the continuum and strength of the virtuous activity, and that virtuous karma is not accumulated.

The fifth situation is when you do an action by mistake.

The sixth is when you do an action out of forgetfulness, for example, if you take the eight Mahayana precepts and then forget for a slight moment and bite into something.[21]

The seventh situation is when you are forced to do something against your will.

The eighth is when you engage in neutral karmic actions (actions that are neither virtuous nor nonvirtuous).

The ninth is doing a negative action with a strong thought of regret.

The tenth situation is when you accumulate a karma and subsequently purify it with an antidote.

The second of four possible relationships between the action and accumulation of karma is not doing the action, but accumulating its karma. An example of this is thinking about killing someone—fantasizing about the process extensively and in detail. Even if the action is not actually completed, due to the power of this kind of mental activity, you accumulate the negative karma of killing.

The third possibility is both doing the action and accumulating its karma.

The fourth possibility is neither doing an action nor accumulating its karma.

The third and fourth possibilities are of course the most common.

A mental nonvirtue cannot be accumulated if it hasn't been done, nor can it be done but not accumulated. It is for this reason that we are warned, "When you are with others, look after your mouth. When you are alone, look after your mind." It is possible that one can appear very holy, in the physical posture of meditation, while one's mind is simultaneously marching along indulging in covetousness, ill will, and wrong views.

There are three time frames in which karmic results ripen. Some actions can be accumulated and the results experienced during the course of one lifetime. Some of the results will ripen in the immediately following lifetime. And some of the results will ripen in any other lifetime.

There are eight situations in which the accumulation of the karma and the experience of the result occur within one lifetime.

The first of the eight situations is when the karma is very, very powerful. An example is when you have an obsessive mind of attachment toward your own or another person's physical body, or strong attachment to material possessions.

The second is in the case of extremely powerful virtuous actions that are free of the eight worldly dharmas.

The third is negative actions done with very strong anger and hatred.

The fourth is its opposite—positive activities done with the wholehearted wish to benefit others or with the extraordinary mind of compassion based on understanding the suffering of pervasive conditioning.

The fifth is when our minds lack faith in the Buddha, Dharma, and Sangha.

The sixth is the opposite of that—when we generate extraordinary faith for the objects of refuge.

The seventh is when we do negative actions in relation to our parents, to whom we owe our existence, and our spiritual teachers, who nurture our spiritual growth.

The eighth is its opposite—when we do virtuous actions in relation to our parents and spiritual teachers.

There is no such thing as a throwing karma whose result will be experienced in this lifetime. If it is a throwing karma, its result must be experienced in a subsequent lifetime.

The Eight Fruitions

The next topic in the outline is the discussion of the eight fruitions of karmic actions. According to the *Lamrim Chenmo,* the eight fruitions are the qualities that one would be endowed with having taken a rebirth that is very conducive to practicing the spiritual path. These qualities are thus considered to be the result of good karma, and are intended to encourage us to practice positive actions and abandon negative actions in order to attain similar results.

The first fruition is a long lifespan. The result of this is that having a long life allows you the time to be able to accomplish your practices.

The second fruition is having a glorious appearance or shape. In other words, having nothing unpleasant about your appearance. This is often the result of having abandoned ill will, or having practiced patience. The result of this is that when such an individual talks about Dharma, he or she is able to attract followers by a beautiful appearance.

The third fruition is being born into a respectable family. On the path to enlightenment itself, there is no differentiation between the classes of society into which one is born. However, among societies these kinds of divisions exist. The result of this is that, due to your rank in society, you are placed at an advantage to more easily accomplish the benefit of others. Also, having affluence, you can materially benefit sentient beings with ease.

The fourth fruition is having a very dynamic, charismatic personality, so that whatever you say, people listen. The result of this is that you will be able to guide others on the path to enlightenment more easily because they will listen to you.

The fifth fruition is having authority of speech, which is the result of abandoning the vices of speech, particularly gossip. The result of the power of speech is that people will feel an intuitive sense of trust in whatever you say.

The sixth fruition is being endowed with the power of reputation, which has come about as a result of your learning, compassion, and the virtue of your pure actions of benefit toward others. The result of this is that whatever you tell others to do, they are able to do it very easily, which allows you to have influence in the lives of those you are seeking to benefit. For example, if Lama Zopa Rinpoche tells one of his students to do 100,000 of this and 100,000 of that, they very happily accept this commitment, and they try to do it quickly.

Being born as a male is the seventh fruition. According to the text, a male rebirth is a conducive basis to practice the spiritual path. However, this does not mean that a female rebirth is not also a conducive basis to practice the spiritual path. There have been many, many great female practitioners of the Buddhadharma, and in the future there will be many more. According to the text, the result of being born as a male is that you will feel less fear in large gatherings and less fear when seeking the life of a solitary retreatant in a hermitage. Please keep in mind that this text was written in accordance with the social conditions that existed at the time of Lama Tsongkhapa, and that conditions have certainly changed in the world since the fifteenth century.

The eighth fruition is having the power of strength and endurance, in the sense that when you engage in virtuous activities, you are not easily discouraged by negative conditions. The result of this is a great sense of endurance and a great sense of joy in being able to undertake activities to benefit others, physically as well as mentally.

The causes of experiencing the fruitions and their effects are as follows.

The causes of an auspicious long life are abandoning harm against other sentient beings, saving lives, and liberating animals. Also, giving blood, saving lives with your own body or material wealth, donating parts of your body—an extra kidney, bone marrow, and so forth—and looking after sick people. In order to bring this result, all of these activities must be done from kindness and compassion and from your heart, not because you are forced into that situation.

Causes for a beautiful appearance are offering light or clothing to holy objects. The practice of tolerance and patience in daily life, and maintaining an attitude in which negativity and jealousy do not easily arise are also causes for a beautiful appearance.

The causes of birth in a respectable family that places you at a great advantage to accomplish acts of benefit is abandoning pride and holding ourselves as the lowest of all.

The practice of the four types of giving—giving of Dharma, giving of fearlessness, giving of love, and giving of material wealth—brings the fourth benefit, that of having a dynamic, charismatic personality.

Gaining the authority of speech comes as a result of having totally abandoned the nonvirtues of speech: lying, harsh speech, divisive speech, and gossip. Some scriptures say that if you undertake Dharma practice with the thought that seeks the eight worldly dharmas, it becomes part of the action of gossip.

A powerful reputation is the result of making offerings and showing respect to those individuals who benefit sentient beings and the Dharma.

The cause to be reborn as a male is having the wish to be reborn male, and making prayers to take such a rebirth.

The result of having physical and mental endurance and strength arises from spontaneously undertaking actions benefiting others. It also arises as a result of encouraging and empowering others on the virtuous path, and not discouraging them.

The three causes that make these eight causes very pure are practicing pure ethics, engaging in the practices of the perfection of generosity and so forth, and making pure prayers that you will experience these ripening results in the future.

Purification through the Four Opponent Powers

SEEDS AND IMPRINTS

All of the negative karma that we accumulate as beginners on the path arises as a result of the actions that we engage in under the power of the two types of obscurations. Though we will be unable to cease the accumulation of negative karma completely as long as we have delusions, through the application of the practice of the four opponent powers we can purify the resultant suffering that would otherwise arise from them. If we apply the four opponent powers perfectly, we can even purify the fruit of actions whose results are certain to be experienced.

Now perhaps you are confused. On the one hand, I am saying that through the practice of purification you can purify all of your negative karma, and on the other hand, we have already discussed that there are actions whose karmic results must definitely be experienced. These two appear to be contradictory. But actually, they are not. Those karmic results that are certain to be experienced are those actions to which the four opponent powers have not been applied at all. Karma that is *not* certain to be experienced is so regardless of whether it has been purified by the four opponent powers or not.

Although the practice of the four opponent powers can purify the experience of suffering that results from our negative actions, it cannot eliminate their seeds or imprints. In the same way, when it is taught that a single moment of anger can destroy the thousands of eons of merit accumulated through practicing generosity and so forth,[22] what is destroyed is the ripening result of that virtue, not its seeds or imprints. This is an important distinction.

At this point, perhaps it would be helpful to give a brief explanation of what we mean when we discuss *karmic seeds* and *karmic imprints*. The difference between a seed and an imprint is primarily a matter of subtlety—a karmic imprint is more subtle than a karmic seed, and thus it is more difficult to eliminate the imprint of an action from the mind than it is to eliminate the seed. The two also function differently within the mind. According to the philosophical texts, the karmic imprint of ignorance is what causes the appearance of inherent existence, and the karmic seed is what ripens to cause the grasping at that appearance.

The process of creating an imprint works as follows. When we do a virtuous physical action, the physical sense consciousness plants an imprint of that virtuous action in our mental consciousness. Roughly, this can be compared to making a copy on a Xerox machine. Because the action is virtuous, when the substantial continuum of that positive imprint of this physical virtue ripens as a sensory consciousness, it will ripen in a similar experience.

Imprints are not considered consciousness or form, yet they are composite phenomena. Also, the imprints of virtuous and nonvirtuous karma themselves are not considered to be either virtuous or nonvirtuous; rather they are neutral by nature. However, although the imprint itself is neutral, its *substantial continuum* may be either positive or negative. This is determined by the status of the action that created the imprint—if the action was positive, the substantial continuum of the imprint will be positive, and if the action was negative, the substantial continuum of the imprint will be negative as well.

A substantial continuum is one type of continuum of consciousness, and the continuum of a similar type is another. There are also two types of continuums of imprints: the substantial continuum and the continuum of the similar type. The continuum of the similar type of an imprint must always remain of the same nature—meaning that it cannot be altered by the four opponent powers. In fact, the continuum of the similar type can only be altered by the direct realization of emptiness. The substantial continuum, however, can be affected by the four opponent powers. The negative karmic imprints of the substantial continuum cannot be eliminated by this method, but they can be blocked.

When the karmic action has been purified by the method of the four opponent powers, then the conditions for the karmic seed to ripen are completely removed, although the seed itself remains. For example, when one generates calm abiding, it is no longer possible for the gross delusions of the desire realm to manifest. The seeds of the delusions remain in the mind, but they cannot meet with the internal conditions to ripen them, so there is no gross manifestation of the delusions. The converse is also true. One moment of anger is said to destroy a thousand eons of merit arising from generosity and making offerings. Again, this anger cannot destroy the seed of virtue, but it removes the internal conditions that will ripen that seed and bring forth happiness.

THE ACTUAL PRACTICE OF THE FOUR OPPONENT POWERS

All of the four Buddhist philosophical schools accept the practice of the four opponent powers as a method to purify negative karma. The four opponent powers are the power of regret, the power of the antidote, the power of the resolution, and the power of the basis.

Within the four points of this practice, applying the first power, the power of regret, is the most important. Your application of the power of regret should be supported by your understanding of karma, your understanding of the consequences of your actions, and, in particular, your understanding of karmic results. When you understand these things clearly and think about a negative action that you have done—today, yesterday, in this lifetime, or in other lifetimes—regret will arise without effort. However, in order to develop this heightened awareness of actions and their consequences, you must be mindful and aware of your physical, verbal, and mental actions. If you do not have any sense of mindfulness of your thoughts and actions, then it will not matter how much you know about karma—you will not be able to generate regret. And as long as you do not feel regret for your nonvirtuous actions, no matter how well you apply the other three powers, it will be impossible to purify your negative karma. The power of regret empowers the other three.

For example, when you recite one mantra, such as *tayatha gate gate paragate parasamgate bodhi soha,* three times, seven times, or twenty-one times, it can only become the power of the antidote if you recite it in conjunction with the power of regret. Without the mind of regret, it is still a virtuous activity, but it is not the power of the antidote. Likewise, even if you spend an hour meditating on emptiness, without cultivating the mind of strong regret this meditation cannot become the power of the antidote.

The power of the antidote is the second power of the four. In the *Lamrim Chenmo,* Lama Tsongkhapa cites six specific practices that function as the power of the antidote.

The first antidote is reciting sutras. This usually refers to the recitation of the *Sutra on the Perfection of Wisdom,* of which there are the long, medium, and short versions. The first antidote also includes memorizing, reading, and reflecting on the meaning of these texts.

The second antidote is meditation on emptiness. This refers primarily to meditation on the selflessness of persons and the selflessness of phenomena.

In addition to this, we can also reflect on the emptiness of the "I" that has accumulated the negative karma, the emptiness of the negative karma itself, and the emptiness of the action that was done to accumulate it. We can reflect that ultimately these do not exist inherently, and that the basic innate nature of the conventional mind is luminous, clear, and knowing. We can also think that our nonvirtuous karmic imprints are temporary pollutions obscuring the mind, and that they do not exist innately in the nature of mind itself.

It is said that merely generating a single thought of the positive form of doubt with regard to the philosophy of emptiness has the effect of setting a crack in one's cyclic existence. Because of this, even if you do not have a clear ascertainment of emptiness, as long as you apply the emptiness of the three spheres based in the mind of regret as an antidote to your nonvirtue, you can be assured that it will definitely affect the ripening result of your karma.

The third antidote is the recitation of mantras, particularly the hundred-syllable Vajrasattva mantra. In general, the recitation of mantras can be thought of as fierce flames that burn away the seeds of negative karma. However, in order for a mantra to have this effect, you must have the basis of pure ethics in your mind, having kept the pledges, vows, and commitments of your practices purely. And again, this power of the antidote must be rooted in the power of regret—merely reciting a mantra is not sufficient. Also, when you use mantra recitation as the power of the antidote, you should always do so with the intent to continue the recitation until you definitely feel the signs of purification. Doing a required quota of mantras can become merely a form of taxation, and once it becomes so it will probably not fulfill the objectives of the practice. Of course, as we are living in degenerate times, sometimes imposing the supreme form of recitation might deter us from making any attempt to practice at all. In order to prevent this situation, certain quotas are given to encourage us to fulfill a minimal number of recitations. However, the very best way to practice is to continue our recitation until the signs of purification arise, regardless of the number.

General signs of purification that may arise during the course of doing intensive purification practices include dreaming of eating yogurt or drinking milk, flying in space, or vomiting terrible substances. Dreams of seeing flames—particularly seeing one's body in flames—and wearing new clothing, seeing Sangha members, listening to teachings, sitting on high thrones, and entering beautiful palaces are also signs of purification. If you dream of these things in times of retreat or intensive periods of practice, you can understand them to be external signs of successful purification. More importantly, the internal signs should include fewer delusional minds arising, a strong, extraordinary sense of a new understanding, and powerful faith in karmic cause and effect. Also, you may experience the arising of the extraordinary pure mind of refuge, more faith in your spiritual teachers, and a clearer understanding of the paths of method and wisdom.

The fourth of the six antidotes is making statues, or making anything that symbolizes the enlightened holy body, holy speech, and holy mind of the buddhas. We shouldn't buy statues or *tangkas* or *stupas* with a wish to make our rooms look more grand, but rather with a wish to purify our negative karma. When we make *tsa-tsas,* we shouldn't do so for the purpose of fulfilling the required number, but for the purpose of purification.

The fifth of the six antidotes is making offerings, which we have already discussed briefly. When we make offerings, they should be free of the pollution of the material and free of the pollution of the motivation. Free of the pollution of the material means that they should not have been acquired through means of wrong livelihood. Free of the pollution of the motivation means free of the motivation of the eight worldly dharmas, free of the thought that seeks the happiness of this life alone, and free of the thought that seeks the reputation of someone who makes extensive offerings. The minds of pure faith and devotion are the most essential part of the offering. Even if you make a priceless offering, if your mind lacks faith and devotion and is totally ensnared in worldly dharmas, then your offering becomes very small. And even if you only offer seven simple bowls of water, if your mind is rich in faith and devotion, your offering becomes very great. Also, in the context of the four opponent powers, we should remember to root our minds in the strong thought of regret when we make offerings.

The sixth of the six antidotes is reciting a name mantra, such as that of Shakyamuni Buddha, a bodhisattva, or one's spiritual teacher.

Tsongkhapa cites these examples from Shantideva's *Compendium of Trainings.* But in summary we can say that any virtuous activities we undertake physically, verbally, or mentally can be dedicated as a means of the power of the antidote purifying negative karma.

The third power within the four opponent powers is the power of the resolution not to engage in nonvirtuous actions again. As long as you have faith in karma, and as long as you understand the ripening results of your karmic actions, this kind of resolution should be naturally forthcoming. One hundred percent of the power of the resolution is dependent upon the power of regret. If you have a very strong sense of regret, you will be like a person who has eaten poison by mistake—you will do everything possible to get the poison out and neutralize its effects as quickly as possible.

To complete the purification, the powers of regret and resolution are essential. Sometimes we get all wrapped up in the power of the antidote because we find it very exciting to have many things to do. Yet the first and the third of the four opponent powers are really the most important. As beginners, practices such as using meditation on emptiness as our antidote are quite beyond us. Before we can tackle the roots of our suffering, we need to try to tackle the suffering itself. We do this by cultivating the pure mind of refuge, cultivating the pure mind of bodhichitta, and focusing on regret and resolution. This is within our capacity and most important at our level.

The fourth power is the power of the basis, which is refuge and generating bodhichitta. Refuge and bodhichitta are regarded as the power of the basis because we usually accumulate negative karma on the basis of sentient beings and on the basis of holy objects. Just as we take the support of the ground itself to help us stand up again when we have fallen down, in the same way, the negative karma that we accumulate in relation to sentient beings must be purified in relation to sentient beings. To fulfill this requirement, we generate bodhichitta. Also, the negative karma we accumulate in relation to holy objects must be purified in relation to those holy objects. To fulfill this requirement we generate refuge.

As we mentioned, the four opponent powers do not purify negative karma down to its very roots, but they can lessen or eliminate the resultant suffering. For example, having applied the four opponent powers to a particularly powerful karmic action, you could still experience the result of being reborn in the lower realms, but you may not suffer there. Alternatively, you may be reborn in the lower realms for a very short time, or you may even experience the result of that powerful negative karma as a very small amount of suffering in the human realm. And, if you are able to apply the four opponent powers with great strength and over a very long period of time, very powerful karma can ripen with almost no suffering at all.

We should remember that even the smallest amount of purification practice is never meaningless—if we didn't make any attempts at purification at all, our suffering would be even more extensive and continuous. However, we shouldn't think that since the four opponent powers exist as a remedy, it gives us license to do anything that we want and then purify it. This is like breaking your legs on purpose, thinking that they can be fixed later on. Between a leg that's fixed and a leg that was never broken, it's better to have an unbroken leg from the very beginning. Although bodhisattvas who incur a root downfall can purify that particular action, once they have created that downfall, there is no possibility that they can realize the truth directly in that particular lifetime. Thus we should understand that all negative actions always have consequences on some level, even if they are purified.

The Measure of the Small Scope Practitioner

Everything that we will learn as we progress on the path—including the practices to generate bodhichitta and the understanding of the pure view of emptiness—will rest upon the support of our careful understanding and regard for karma, the cause and effect of our actions. Although at our level there are not a great many arguments using logic and reason to prove that doing virtuous things leads to happiness and doing nonvirtuous things leads to suffering, this understanding is the basis of the path. Traditionally, karma is taught in the sutras mainly through the use of narrative that describes the lives of certain individuals, and tells how certain actions led to corresponding experiences in their lifetimes. These stories, coupled with the explanations from the lamrim, can give us a general idea of how karma works in our lives.

As I mentioned, a perfect human rebirth can be compared to getting halfway up a mountain with a huge boulder. Even if we can't push the boulder all the way up to the peak, we don't want to lose it by letting it fall

all the way down, because to bring it up again will take a huge effort. Observing the laws of karma and engaging in the practices of purification and so forth are what ensures that the boulder doesn't fall down. At the moment, we place a lot of emphasis on this lifetime, because this is where we are right now, and what is going on in this life is very obvious to us. Our next life seems secondary in importance—because we have doubts about its existence to begin with, and even if we don't doubt it, it's not affecting us right now. Training seriously in the path and practices of the small scope—perfect human rebirth, impermanence and death, and the laws of cause and effect—will cause us to change our perspective on this completely. The next life and the infinite future lifetimes become far more important than this lifetime. When this happens, we have attained the measure of the realization of the path and practices of the small scope.

You might wonder: if we place such emphasis on attaining a higher rebirth within cyclic existence, isn't this just aspiring for more cyclic existence, and therefore isn't it contradictory to the training? Although it's just a temporary benefit, as it says in Shantideva's *Guide to the Bodhisattva's Way of Life,* you rely on the ship of this human rebirth with the eight leisures and ten endowments to cross the ocean of cyclic existence. Even if you have the aspirations of the medium scope or the great scope, you should not abandon the path and practices common to the small scope. In the same way, if you are a fully ordained monk, although you have taken two hundred and fifty-three vows, you are not released from keeping the thirty-six vows of a novice purely.

With the topics of refuge, perfect human rebirth, impermanence and death, and the explanations on cause and effect, we complete the section on the small scope of the *Lamrim Chenmo.*

PART 4

The Medium Scope

RECOGNIZING AND GENERATING THE WISH FOR LIBERATION

Every accumulation ends in dispersion,
The high end up falling,
Meeting ends in separation,
Living ends in death.

—the Vinaya

AS WE DISCUSSED in the preceding sections, observing the laws of cause and effect and purifying our mistakes by the practice of the four opponent powers are the means to ensure the happiness of future lifetimes. If we do these things perfectly, we will create the causes for a higher rebirth within cyclic existence. If we are fortunate, we will be reborn as an intelligent human being in a comfortable environment, or perhaps even into great luxury in the realm of the gods. As appealing as this may sound to us, the next step on the graduated path to enlightenment is to consider the fact that according to the *Lamrim Chenmo,* a good rebirth in cyclic existence is not the ultimate goal. In fact, as long as we are reborn in samsara, our lives will remain entirely under the control of delusions and karma. Hence, no matter how wonderful the conditions of our next rebirth may be, we are certain to experience suffering again eventually. Therefore, according to the text, we must strive to free ourselves from cyclic existence completely. This is the subject matter of the next sections, which cover the aspiration of the practitioner of the medium scope.

In order to develop the incentive to train in the path of the medium scope, we must first gain an understanding of the way that we are controlled by delusions and karma. Thinking that the only result of being under the control of delusions and karma is future rebirth in cyclic existence reflects a very limited understanding. In fact, delusions and karma control us at all times. We are totally in their service.

Also, at this point, we need to develop an understanding of the true nature of samsaric pleasure and happiness. When we examine what we perceive as the wonderful things in our lives, we will find that in reality, they cannot be trusted at all. Just as it is impossible for a person who is falling from a very high peak to experience happiness before hitting the ground, in the same way, as long as we are in samsara, between the moment of birth until we hit the rock bottom of our death, we have no opportunity to experience true joy. Of course, due to our delusions, we often hold what in fact is the suffering nature of existence to be happiness. But in reality, our experience in cyclic existence from birth until death is exactly the same as the experience of the unfortunate person who falls from a cliff to the ground below. Thinking that there is happiness in between is proof of our ignorance.

This does not apply to the human realm alone. In fact, the pleasures of any kind of rebirth—including the god realms and the form and formless realms—are completely unreliable. Aryadeva says in *Four Hundred Stanzas:*

Rebirth in the higher realms
Frightens the wise as much as the hells.

We should examine why this is so, and try to convince ourselves of the reality of our situation.

If we are to discuss cyclic existence, it is first essential that we have a clear idea of what cyclic existence means. And if we are to discuss liberation, it is first essential that we have a clear idea of what liberation means. The three realms—the desire, form, and formless realms—are the realms of cyclic existence, but they are not cyclic existence itself. Liberation from cyclic existence does not merely mean liberation from these places. Nor does liberation merely mean liberation from delusions and karma. This is part of it, but not the totality. Liberation from cyclic existence means liberation from the bondage of the continuum of our aggregates, which are created by delusions and karma.

If we cling and grasp and seek out the pleasures of cyclic existence, our confused, ignorant minds become even more confused and ignorant.

However, if instead we slowly begin to gain understanding of the reality of the fact that the pleasures of cyclic existence are in the nature of suffering, our confusion will gradually disappear. When we realize that the feelings of happiness or pleasure that we experience in samsara are contaminated because they only lead to the inevitable result of suffering, our obsessive thoughts of attachment and the suffering that arises from it will lessen. On the contrary, when we believe the glory and magnificence and comforts of cyclic existence to be true happiness, our attachment will increase, and so will our suffering.

In Aryadeva's *Four Hundred Stanzas* it is stated:

How can one who has no weariness
For cyclic existence aspire for peace?
Like their households,
It will be difficult to leave.

What we all wish for is ultimate happiness, eternal happiness, happiness that we can trust. However, as long as our existence is under the control of delusions and karma, this kind of happiness is not possible. Anything that is worthy of total trust cannot come about as a result of delusions and karma.

To attain liberation from delusions and karma, we must first recognize the kind of thought that aspires to attain this goal, and we must then strive to understand how to cultivate it. In order to recognize the thought that aspires to attain liberation, we need to understand what we are to be liberated from. Therefore, we have to understand what it is that binds us. It is not sufficient merely to understand that we are bound by karma and delusions in a very general way. Rather, we should know *how* these things bind us—in what realms, in what transmigratory states, in what sort of birth and rebirth.

Karma and delusions bind us in the three realms: the desire, form, and formless realms. Karma and delusions also bind us in the six transmigratory states of rebirth, and in the four types of birth: birth from a womb, spontaneous birth, birth from an egg, and birth from heat and moisture. Birth occurs due to karma or action, and karma brings about this result because we accumulate it. We accumulate karma due to our delusions, and among the delusions it is ignorance that initiates the entire cycle. This is how we should begin to understand the process.

The wish to attain liberation is characterized by the desire to be free from every one of these types of bondage. When we don't think well, or clearly, we think that liberation is somewhere out there ahead of us and that someday we will get there and attain it. However, this is not the case. Liberation is not somewhere outside of us. Liberation must be attained within our very own minds, as what binds us to cyclic existence also exists within our very own minds.

We may have doubt as to how we can be liberated from the bondage of karma and delusions, as, upon examination, we see that we are so deeply ensnared. However, if this kind of doubt should arise, we should meditate on the fact that all phenomena are impermanent, including the bondage of karma and delusions. Cyclic existence itself is also impermanent. It is brought on by delusions and karma, and although it is without beginning, cyclic existence does have an end.[23] Cyclic existence ends when we cut the continuum of the bondage of delusions and karma by the direct realization of emptiness. This is the only antidote powerful enough to achieve this result.

There are two methods discussed in the *Lamrim Chenmo* by which one can generate the wish for liberation. The first is contemplating true suffering and the true cause of suffering in accordance with the four noble truths. The second method is meditating on the twelve links of dependent origination.

CONTEMPLATING TRUE SUFFERING
AND TRUE CAUSE

In general, if we experience the unpleasantness of a bad result, we are more easily moved to abandon its causes. As we are inclined in this way, Buddha arranged the four noble truths to reflect this tendency. The four noble truths are:

1. True Suffering
2. True Cause
3. True Cessation
4. True Path

Although the discussion in this section traditionally revolves around the first two truths, I will also give a brief explanation of the third and fourth noble truths here as well, as an understanding of the four noble truths in their entirety is very important to facilitate the complete understanding of the path to liberation. In fact, as Buddhists, there is no point of meditation on the path that is outside of the circle of the four noble truths.

Usually, when explanations of the mechanics of cause and effect are given, the cause is explained first followed by the explanation of the result. In the context of the four noble truths, however, the explanation of the result is given first, and is followed by the explanation of the cause. According to this order, we must begin on the path to liberation by recognizing the state of suffering that is our existence. Once we understand this result, we can begin to work toward understanding and eliminating its causes, which are ignorance, karma, and delusions.

Similarly, in the actual attainment of the path, we train in the path first, and then achieve the resultant cessation. However in the explanation of the third and fourth noble truths, true cessation is explained first, and the true path to that cessation is explained later. This is the order in which the four noble truths are arranged in order to guide disciples on the path.

The four noble truths are called *pag pai den pa shi (phags pa'i bden pa bzhi)* in Tibetan, and can also be translated as the "four truths for arya beings." An arya being is someone who has attained the direct realization of emptiness. To these beings, these four points appear as reality or truth. In contrast, the reality of these truths are obscured to beginning practitioners such as ourselves by a very gross form of ignorance. In order to help us remove this veil of ignorance, Buddha taught true suffering first.

From *Four Hundred Stanzas:*

As there is no end
To this ocean of suffering,
Why are you, who are bound by this,
Not afraid?

The reason we are not afraid is because, clouded in ignorance, we perceive what is in the nature of suffering to be in the nature of happiness. Because we have no fear, there is no thought of liberation, and as long as there is no thought of liberation, there is no attainment of liberation. However, if we are able to understand the suffering nature of existence, we will be able to develop the wish to be free from it.

True suffering refers to anything that is the result of delusions and karma, especially the form aggregate, which means our bodies. However, the environment and the sentient beings within it, the world and the sentient beings within it, and the universe and the sentient beings within it all embody true suffering as well. The four characteristics of true suffering are impermanence, suffering, emptiness, and selflessness. Although these characteristics in fact define the suffering nature of existence, in everyday life our minds apprehend them as existing in exactly the opposite way. In our ordinary view, we hold that which is impermanent, such as the aggregates, to be pure, we hold that which is suffering to be happiness, that which is empty of permanence, unitary status, and autonomy to be permanent, and that which is selfless to be self-existent.

Suffering cannot exist without causes and conditions. It is not produced by a creator. As suffering itself is impermanent, is it not logical to assert that its causes are some permanent phenomena. The result of suffering must be in accord with its cause—it is not logical to have a nonharmoniuous cause and result. By examining all of these points, we will come to the conclusion that karma and delusions are the causes of suffering.

If we analyze further, we will also realize that karma and delusions themselves cannot arise without causes. And like before, the cause and result must accord. Ultimately, the causes of karma and delusions are the self-cherishing mind and the ignorance that grasps at true existence.

Please keep in mind that all karma needn't necessarily be categorized as the true cause of suffering. For example, arya bodhisattvas on the first ground have karma but they do not have karma in the context of the true cause of suffering. In the same way, arhats on the hearer's path have karma but they don't have karma as categorized as the true cause of suffering. In fact, all activities of body, speech, and mind of those beings who have abandoned ignorance and delusions are uncontaminated karmic actions.

However, for ordinary beings such as ourselves, even virtuous actions arise out of ignorance. Therefore, all of our virtuous actions except for those done in relation to holy objects fall under the category of the true cause of suffering. Virtuous actions done in relation to holy objects are not categorized as the true cause of suffering because these activities do not depend upon our motivation to be virtuous. They are virtuous by the power of the object itself. Throwing karma, completing karma, and all the general explanations of the characteristics of karma—such as how it is definite and how it increases—are also categorized as part of the true cause of suffering.

The term *delusions* usually refers to consciousnesses that are secondary mental factors, such as the three poisons, and so forth. According to most of the philosophical schools, these are all states of consciousness that need to be abandoned. According to the Chittamatra or Mind-Only school, which posits eight consciousnesses,[24] the deluded mental consciousness holds its object, the fundamental consciousness or *kunshi (kun bzhi),* to be self-sufficient and substantially existent. According to the Chittamatra system, the deluded mental consciousness is actually a mind of ignorance that proceeds from lifetime to lifetime. Thus, the Chittamatra philosophical system is unique among the four schools in positing the deluded mental consciousness as the true cause of suffering.

According to this school, as long as an individual cycles in samsara, the fundamental consciousness and the deluded mental consciousness are uninterrupted continuums. In contrast, the continuum of the five sensory consciousnesses can be interrupted. The mental consciousness, however, takes on the uncontaminated nature of the path when the practitioner attains the path of seeing, and therefore its continuum is not always present in cyclic existence. Because of that, the Chittamatras instead present the seventh and eighth consciousnesses as the unbroken continuum that proceeds throughout cyclic existence. According to them, the fundamental consciousness is not categorized as karma or as delusions. They say that this consciousness does not belong to any category of the four noble truths. Again, this view is unique to the Chittamatra school.

Since, according to our own system, we have posited ignorance, or the view that all things are inherently existent, as the root cause of karma and delusions, the next logical step would be to investigate whether this is a mistaken view or not. We will discuss specific methods for determining this later on in the great scope section, but for the moment, let us assume that if we analyze, we will eventually come to the understanding that this view is indeed mistaken. Once we understand that the ignorance that grasps at true existence is mistaken, we can begin to understand that it may be possible to bring forth its cessation. This brings us to the third of the four truths, the truth of cessation.

What is the difference between cessation and liberation? When we say *cessation*, we can be referring to one of two things: cessation abandoning the gross manifestations of the delusions or ultimate cessation. The former can be attained even by those who have not entered the path. This is known as symbolic cessation, and although we label it *cessation*, it is not a true state of cessation. A true cessation is when, through the antidote of an uncontaminated path, we abandon the delusions in such a way that they never arise again. According to the philosophical system of the Prasangika, the antidote must be a path that realizes emptiness.

If one has attained liberation, that means that one has attained cessation. If one has attained a cessation, however, it doesn't necessarily mean that one has attained liberation. The reason that we differentiate between relative cessation and ultimate cessation is because there are some spiritual paths by which practitioners attain a cessation of all of the gross manifestations of the delusions, and mistake that for liberation. This is terrible, because those practitioners may think that they have attained liberation, when in reality they have not yet abandoned the root of the delusions. As a result, when that particular karma is finished, those practitioners realize that they are going to be reborn in cyclic existence, and lose faith in the idea of liberation entirely.

The suffering nature of existence itself is the mind, and the cause of the suffering nature of existence is also the mind. Liberation and cessation are also the mind. And the path to attaining liberation and cessation is also the mind. Therefore, to think that the path to cessation is somewhere outside, or to think that liberation is somewhere outside, is completely mistaken. Both cessation and the true path to cessation must be attained on the basis of your own mind.

So what is your own mind? What is this "I" that wanders in cyclic existence, that is brought into existence by karma and delusions, that practices the path, and that eventually attains liberation? Most of the Buddhist philosophical systems say that the "I" that wanders in cyclic existence is some kind of a mental consciousness. The Svatantrika-Madhyamikas, or Middle-Way Autonomists, say that it is the continuum of the mental consciousness. The Chittamatras say that it is the consciousness that is the basis of all imprints. According to our system, however, the "I" that wanders in cyclic existence is the merely labeled "I."

All of the Buddhist schools except the Prasangika designate an "I" that is substantially existent. According to the Prasangika system, however, because it is a mere "I," it is not substantially existent, but exists by mere imputation. The Prasangika system does not accept existence by way of its own characteristics, or even an atom of inherent existence. Therefore, everything is just imputedly existent. According to the Prasangikas, when we say that "I am suffering," "I was under the control of the delusions and accumulated negative karma," "I trained in the path," or "I attained cessation"—when we speak like this on the basis of a substantially existent "I," we do not have a pure form of the practice of the four noble truths.

Maitreya's *Sublime Continuum* states:

Recognize that you are sick,
And then eliminate the cause of the sickness.
Obtain that state,
Thereby rely upon the medicine.

The same philosophy should be applied to the four noble truths. The four noble truths explain, "this is the sickness, this is the cause of the sickness, there is a cure for this sickness, and this is the means to that cure." Whether we are training in the individual vehicle or training in the Mahayana path, a clear understanding of the points of practice of the four noble truths is very important. When we reflect on the four noble truths in terms of our own suffering, it becomes the practice of the four noble truths of the individual vehicle. When we contemplate the four noble truths in terms of other sentient beings, it becomes the practice of the universal vehicle. Since they are such an important framework of practice, I think it is good to go through them as much as possible, from different angles.

Aside from the general explanation of the four noble truths that I have just completed, it might also interest you to know that according to the Prasangika-Madhyamaka system, which is the system that Lama Tsongkhapa is following, the liberation that the Svatantrika-Madhyamaka system and all the philosophical schools below it aspire to achieve is not true liberation. The Prasangikas say that these systems fail to recognize the root of the bondage to cyclic existence. If the root cause of bondage is not ascertained, one cannot be liberated from it.

In the Prasangika system, each of the four noble truths has further divisions of gross and subtle. Accordingly, the gross form of true suffering is the suffering produced by the ignorance that apprehends the self as independent and substantially existent. The gross level of the true cause of suffering is that ignorance itself and the karma that is cultivated on that basis. The gross level of true cessation according to the Prasangika system is the abandonment of the ignorance that grasps at a person's independent, substantial existence. The gross level of the true path is the direct realization of the emptiness of a person's independent, substantial self-existence. According to the Prasangika system, through the achievement of this type of cessation alone, the practitioner cannot attain the state of an arhat on the hearer's path, the solitary realizer's path, or the Mahayana path.

Because each of the philosophical systems explains a slightly different presentation of the path, and a slightly different definition of and means to attaining the view of ultimate reality, cessation also has varying levels according to each school. In order to practice the four noble truths well, it is best to understand the basis, path, and fruits as explained in accordance with each one of the four Buddhist schools. It is also important to understand their explanations in relation to the obscurations. To think that philosophy is merely an intellectual game is totally mistaken. By understanding how these four schools view the practice of the four noble truths, we understand how they view what is to be abandoned on the Buddhist path.

According to the Prasangika system, the mind of liberation is the mind that wishes to be liberated from the root cause of cyclic existence, which is the grasping at true existence. In this case, in order to generate the spontaneous mind that seeks liberation, it is necessary to generate the realization of emptiness. We can understand that we have the potential to attain liberation because the root, which is ignorance grasping at true existence, is removable and extinguishable since it is a completely mistaken consciousness. It is a completely mistaken consciousness because the object that it grasps does not exist at all.

The Eight Types of Suffering

To further increase our awareness of true suffering, and thus develop the incentive to strive for liberation, in the *Lamrim Chenmo* Lama Tsongkhapa presents a discussion of the general sufferings of cyclic existence in three sets: the eight types, the six types, and the three types of suffering. We will begin with the discussion of the contemplation of the eight types of suffering.

Generally speaking, there are two methods of meditation that are commonly taught in Buddhism: the first is to focus with single-pointed concentration on a single object of meditation, and the second is to first identify the subject of single-pointed concentration through extensive analysis, and then meditate on it. When we meditate on suffering, we should use the second technique, free of the faults of mental excitement and sluggishness.

In the *Guide to the Bodhisattva's Way of Life* Shantideva says:

Although we have accumulated merits,
Ravished by the thief of nonintrospection,
Which follows the degeneration of mindfulness
We will go to the lower realms.

Of the eight sufferings, the first is the suffering of birth, which has five aspects.

Birth itself is the first aspect of the suffering of birth. Birth here refers to birth from the womb or birth from an egg. The other two types of birth, spontaneous birth and birth from heat and moisture, are not considered birth whose nature is suffering.

The second aspect of the suffering of birth is the fact that we are born without any choice, completely under the control of delusions and karma, and that birth itself becomes a basis on which to further accumulate delusions and karma. Because our aggregates are controlled by delusions and karma it becomes difficult to engage our minds and bodies in virtue.

The third aspect of the suffering of birth is that birth becomes the basis of suffering, meaning that once we are born, we are bound to experience aging, sickness, and death. In tantric philosophy it is said that in the very first moment of birth the seventy-two thousand channels of the body begin to disintegrate. At birth, the process of aging has already begun.

The fourth aspect is that birth is the basis of delusions, causing one to experience the manifold sufferings of the body and mind brought on by the afflictions.

And the fifth aspect is that the inevitable result of birth is death.

Another way to reflect upon the suffering of birth is to think of yourself as you were in your mother's womb. Think about the discomfort of being enclosed in such a small area, and all the suffering you experienced as your mother moved here and there. Also, consider the suffering of having to live among impure substances, and the suffering of experiencing extreme sensitivity to whatever your mother ingested, hot or cold.

Your main objective in thinking this way should be to develop awareness of what it means to be born under the control of delusions and karma. As this awareness increases, so will your incentive to seek liberation from this state. If we do not put our minds through this kind of analysis, we may simply dismiss the suffering of birth as a natural course of existence, and come to disregard it. However, when we understand that the suffering of birth—and, indeed, all of the sufferings that we experience—is the result of delusions and karma, and that it is possible to be released from ever having to experience it again, we can then begin to cultivate the thought of seeking liberation.

Sometimes, when we experience the suffering of being separated from an object of attachment, we may generate a feeling of renunciation as a result. However, this is rare, and, regardless, is based on a very limited scope of thinking. Usually this renunciation is momentary, and not concerned with the greater problems of our existence. And, in these circumstances, when we search for the causes of the suffering that we are experiencing, we find only a very gross level of cause—usually we blame our situation on an external thing or person, and not on the delusions that exist within our minds. Thinking in this way, eliminating the causes of our suffering becomes an eternal task, as even if we are successful in removing one cause of the problem, another will soon appear to take its place. As a result, there is no end to dealing with the causes of problems in our lives.

The second of the eight types of suffering is the degeneration of one's life, meaning that our lives get shorter and shorter as each moment passes. Just as attachment creeps into our minds very slowly, like oil seeping into a cloth, in the same way the suffering of aging sneaks up upon us. Our aging is determined by the fact that we take birth into the five aggregates that are created by karma and delusions. If we are born, we age and die. There is no other option.

The suffering of sickness, the third of the eight types of suffering, is also explained in five parts.

The first aspect of the suffering of sickness is the suffering involved in the change that takes place in the elements of the body. When we are healthy, there is a balance within the elements of our body, and we have a sort of vitality. But when our elements are out of balance, sickness comes, there is change in the appearance of our skin and flesh, and our vitality dissipates. As a result, we experience the unhappiness of the mind, which increases as our sickness progresses. The unhappiness of the mind is the second aspect. As this occurs, the things that we normally regard as pleasant—such as cool weather—become unbearable. This is the third aspect. The fourth aspect is having to use many undesirable things, such as powerful medications and treatments, and being completely alone in our experience of sickness. The fifth aspect is losing our life to sickness in the end. Disease chases the aggregates like the hunter chases its kill. It eventually destroys us in the same way that the winter consumes the glory and magnificence of the trees, flowers, and fruits.

When we try to meditate on these topics, it is important that we do not distance ourselves from them by thinking of the experiences of other people. Instead, we should apply these experiences to ourselves. On this basis, we should think that as long as we are reborn into cyclic existence with contaminated aggregates, these experiences are inevitable. In this way we can begin to cultivate the mind that wishes to be free from the cycle of rebirth.

We can also contemplate the suffering of death, the fourth type of suffering, in five aspects. Death is also something that we do not desire—it is not pleasant or happy, yet it is certain that we will have to experience it. As a great flood clears away everything that lies in its path, death clears away our entire existence, leaving nothing.

The first aspect of the suffering of death is that when we die, we have to part with our material possessions. Second, when we die, we are also separated from our environment. In addition, when we die, we are separated from all of our friends and relatives and even our spiritual teachers—from every aspect of every relationship that we have established in this life, without exception. The fourth aspect is that we are forced to part with our body, which has been with us throughout our entire life, and the fifth is that we will experience great unhappiness due to the fact that we are dying.

The fifth suffering is the suffering of encountering what we do not want. This happens when we are under the control of the three poisonous minds, and we then meet with an outer condition that we impute as an enemy. If we have imputed the label "enemy" onto an individual, for example, we feel unhappiness even upon hearing this person's name. If the person is equal in status to ourselves, we feel competitiveness or jealousy. If the person is in a position of power and influence, we may feel fear, and unhappiness that we are forced to listen to all the unpleasant things that they have to say. Our lives pass in this misery, and then we die. Meanwhile, we accumulate a great deal of negative karma in relation to these undesired people in our lives, and then become terrified when we consider the result of the suffering we will experience.

The sixth suffering, having to part with what we want, also has five parts to it.

The first is the mental aspect of having to be separated from an object of desire. For example, we may encounter someone from whom we cannot bear to be separated, even for a moment. Then this person goes away, and we feel unhappy, even though it is totally impossible to be together all the time. Due to the three poisons, we superimpose additional qualities onto our image of this person, fabricating a projection of this person as being totally extraordinary. This person then becomes an object of obsession from which we cannot bear to be separated.

The second is the verbal aspect of having to part with what we want, which refers to the wailing noise that we make in our expression of our sorrow upon being separated.

The third is the physical aspect, which refers to the harm we do to our physical bodies when, due to the torment of this separation, we become unaware of what we eat or drink.

The fourth is the mental aspect, which refers to the way that we miserably obsess about all of the good qualities of the object from which we have been separated. Of course, in our ignorance we are unaware that all of these qualities have been merely imputed or projected onto the object by an incorrect consciousness.

The fifth suffering is the suffering of being troubled by the thought that all of our expectations were not fulfilled and that we lost many good opportunities. This is the torment of the mind of dissatisfaction.

The seventh of the eight types of suffering is seeking out what we want, but not being able to attain it. For example, we may wish for a bountiful harvest, but no matter how much we exert ourselves to ensure it, the harvest fails. In the same way, we may venture into some kind of business with expectations of profit and so forth, only to end up with an enormous loss.

These last three types of suffering—encountering what we do not want, having to separate from what we do want, and seeking out what we want but being unable to attain it—are the most evident aspects of suffering in our lives, because from birth until death we are tormented by them. We deal with them on a daily basis, so we should be able to identify with them most easily.

The eighth type of suffering is a summary. In short, it states that we experience all of this suffering because we possess the contaminated aggregates of the mind and body, which arise as a result of our delusions and karma.

In his *Friendly Letter,* the great master Nagarjuna exhorts the king to reflect upon the suffering nature of existence in terms of these eight points. In the *Lamrim Chenmo,* Lama Tsongkhapa discusses the eight general sufferings of cyclic existence with reference to the fact that their authority derives from Nagarjuna's presentation in *Friendly Letter,* and Buddha's presentation of them in the sutras.

A few days ago I met a friend of mine, and we went to have dinner in an Indian restaurant. Afterward I had stomach problems, and when I came home, I complained that the restaurant wasn't very clean. A few days later, I went to eat in a restaurant that I know for a fact is very clean. But when I came home, I had stomach problems again. This is an example of suffering due to the aggregates, which are a receptacle of pain and misery.

When we cultivate the wish for liberation in accordance with the path and practice of the medium scope, we should reflect on suffering in a very, very detailed manner as I have just explained. This kind of contemplation should not seem excessive at all. When we meditate on these points, the renunciation that we cultivate as a result will be renunciation in accordance with the path and practices of the medium scope. If we do not contemplate in such a detailed way, but rather rely only upon our limited experiences of our immediate problems to generate renunciation, the state of mind that we will develop as a result will be very unstable and temporary.

The Six Types of Suffering

The next topic within the contemplation on true suffering is the discussion of the suffering of cyclic existence as divided into six types.

The first of the six is the suffering of uncertainty. We should all be very familiar with this type of suffering. The suffering of uncertainty is present in almost every aspect of our lives in cyclic existence. It can be applied to our relationships with people in the sense that our family, friends, and enemies change from lifetime to lifetime. Even within a single lifetime, someone who has been very dear to us can become our worst enemy overnight. The suffering of uncertainty is also present in our environment—from rebirth to rebirth, our country, our society, and the language that is spoken around us change. Even our gender is not stable from lifetime to lifetime.

The suffering of uncertainty is present in our internal experiences as well. For example, we may complete a powerful virtuous action and then rejoice that we have done so, and feel that the merit that we have accumulated is quite solid and concrete. However, in the very next moment we may become mad with rage, and completely destroy our merit by the force of anger.

The second of the six is the suffering of dissatisfaction, which we can also contemplate in terms of this and previous lifetimes. There are eight examples presented in the *Lamrim Chenmo* to illustrate the way that we suffer as a result of dissatisfaction.

The first is that we have drunk oceans of mother's milk in numberless rebirths and still it has not been enough. Second, within our numberless lifetimes, we have experienced everything that exists within the three realms of existence—from the bliss of meditative concentration to the torture of the lower realms—and still it has not been enough. Third, we have experienced every form of pleasure, and yet we have not had enough. We have also experienced incurable sicknesses, diseases of the worst kind, and immeasurable suffering, but still our minds are not tired. Still it has not been enough. Fifth, there is not a single pleasure or a single type of suffering in cyclic existence that we have not experienced. Yet despite that, our minds are not fed up, and we still cycle under the power of clinging and grasping. Sixth, we have been born in the hells and swallowed countless gallons of molten iron, and still our minds are not satisfied. Seventh, we have attained aggregates that are good and aggregates that are bad countless times, yet nothing meaningful has been accomplished at all. The eighth is the summarized meaning, which is that despite all of these experiences, we still cycle in samsara, unsatisfied.

Thinking about these examples in detail, we should consider that, despite all we have done, our existence has been meaningless up until now. Realizing that, we should make a conscious effort to emerge from cyclic existence.

The third type of suffering within the classification of the six is the suffering of having to lose this body in death over and over again.

The fourth is the suffering of having to take rebirth over and over again.

The fifth is the continual experience of rising and falling—which refers to our endless cycle between the peaks of high rebirth in the formless realms and the depths of low rebirth in the hell realms.

The sixth type of suffering is the suffering of being completely alone, without any support. This can refer to the physical experience of loneliness that we all know to some degree in our lives, and also to the fact that as we move from life to life we lack the comfort of the support of the light of virtue.

The contemplation on suffering in the context of the categorization of the six types is primarily concerned with the analysis of mental suffering. This kind of contemplation is much more psychologically oriented than merely reflecting on the unpleasantness of the physical sufferings of samsara. Therefore, when you meditate on the six types of suffering, you should bring to mind the experiences of all of the mental torment that you yourself have experienced in this lifetime. Then, identify the causes of your suffering as being the fact that you are bound by karma and delusions, and burdened by the contaminated aggregates of mind and body, and from that point begin to cultivate the thought of renunciation.

The Three Types of Suffering

We now move on to the final category within the explanation of true suffering and true cause, which is the contemplation on the three types of suffering.

Please remember that when we reflect on suffering, we should try to understand that it does not arise inherently by way of its own nature. Every single type of suffering arises and exists due to causes and conditions, due to interdependence. Since it does not exist inherently, it is definitely possible to eliminate its causes and thus eradicate suffering from our lives forever.

The first of the three types of suffering is the suffering of suffering. This is the most common, gross form of suffering, and is easily recognizable. It refers to the ordinary suffering that we experience in our everyday lives.

The second of the three types of suffering is the suffering of change. The suffering of change operates in the context of all of those things in our lives that we ordinarily consider to constitute happiness. In fact, all of the feelings of happiness and pleasure that we experience in cyclic existence are, in reality, the suffering of change. We call them "happiness" because they bring us a sensation of pleasure. However, according to Buddhist philosophy, what we label "happiness" is actually only the moment of relief that arises between the previous experience of suffering and the next. If we have a sore on our body that itches terribly, at first, when we begin to scratch it, it feels extremely pleasant. But if we scratch long enough, we will only cause ourselves more pain.

The third type of suffering is the suffering of pervasive conditioning. This kind of suffering is always with us—it is a continual underlying factor of our existence. The suffering of change, in contrast, is there at times, and not there at other times. Although the suffering of pervasive conditioning in its natural state feels like a neutral kind of existence, when we encounter adverse circumstances, it causes contaminated feelings of suffering. When we encounter positive or conducive outer conditions, it causes contaminated feelings of pleasure or happiness. It is on the basis of the suffering of pervasive conditioning that we accumulate karma.

The experiences of the first two types of suffering revolve primarily around our feelings—the objectives of our feelings, the aspects of our feelings, and the objects of our feelings. When we try to develop the wish to be free of the suffering of suffering and the suffering of change, we should renounce not only the resultant suffering itself, but also the causes and conditions that contribute to that result. It is important to look at the bigger picture. While we are in samsara, we are constantly craving the experience of feeling. We should try to understand that any feeling that we experience in cyclic existence is contaminated, bound by the nature of suffering. When we experience feelings of pleasure, we will develop obsessive thoughts of attachment. When we experience feelings of unhappiness, we will develop thoughts of anger and hatred. Neutral feelings will cause us to develop confusion or ignorance. As a result of all these delusions, we will accumulate negative karma, and eventually experience negative ripening results. The feelings that produce the mind of anger bring rebirth in the hell realms; those that produce attachment bring rebirth in the hungry ghost realms; and those that produce ignorance bring rebirth in the animal realm.

The suffering of pervasive conditioning is like being tied to the load of karma and delusions. As long as we are bound to this load, we will experience suffering. The term "pervasive" can be understood in two contexts. First, suffering is pervasive in the sense that it extends throughout all samsara, from Avici Hell to the peak of samsara. Second, suffering is pervasive because we are entirely under its control.

When we train our minds in renunciation based on the contemplation of the three types of suffering, we should begin with the contemplation of the suffering of suffering, followed by the contemplation of the suffering of change, and then the contemplation of the suffering of pervasive conditioning. Contemplating the grosser levels of suffering first will inspire us to develop aversion to them, and reflect on their causes. In this way, our minds will be led toward the contemplation of the more subtle causes of karma and delusions.

These groupings of the eight, six, and three compose the general explanation of the shortcomings of cyclic existence.

Advice on How to Practice

Among the groupings of the eight, six, and three types of suffering, it is most appropriate that you use whatever type of contemplation you find most effective to generate the mind of renunciation. It is not necessary to think about every single type of suffering listed here. For some, reflecting on the grouping of eight alone is effective. For others, the grouping of six is more useful. The presentation of suffering that has the greatest impact on your mind is the one that you should focus on.

Since the contemplation on suffering in accordance with the four noble truths is a practice of the medium scope, you should try to reflect on each of these types of suffering in terms of what you experience. However, if you do this while holding the "I" that experiences the suffering to be truly existent, you will not affect the root of suffering, which is ignorance that grasps at true existence. Generally when we meditate on the eight types of suffering, we do so with the feeling of this "I" that truly exists, independently exists, and exists inherently without any kind of dependence, and hence we experience a strong sense of aversion to all of these experiences of suffering. However, the main point of meditating on the eight types of suffering is to generate renunciation and the wish for liberation. Since this meditation is ultimately directed toward attaining liberation, we must seek to understand how the "I" functions—how it does not truly exist, how it exists through interdependence. In the same way, just as we apply the understanding of the merely imputed existence of the "I" to our own case, when we reflect on compassion for the sufferings of others, we can think that they also exist only by mere imputation. If we do this, whatever renunciation or compassion we generate will be of an extraordinary kind.

Therefore, when you train in the path and practices of the medium scope, when you contemplate suffering, you should begin with a short examination of the "I." Focus on the mode of the existence of the "I" that experiences these types of suffering. Try to see how a truly existing "I" cannot be found anywhere in your body or mind. Try to see how it exists merely in dependence upon the imputing mind, the label, and the basis of imputation. Then try to see how although it exists merely in this way, it is able to perform all of the functions of the "I."

If you do not take time to reflect on the "I" in this way, there is a danger that your contemplation on suffering will only become a cause for more cyclic existence, and thus more suffering. Therefore it is best that you try to determine the mode of existence of the "I" from the outset. Then you may proceed with the traditional meditation.

In sutra it is stated that the tathagatas cannot wash away negative karma with water. Nor can the ripening results of karma be removed by their hands. Nor can the omniscience, great compassion, and the perfect power of the buddhas be transferred to sentient beings. The only way that the buddhas can enable the liberation of sentient beings is by showing the path to ultimate reality. Enlightened beings are not self-arisen, permanently existent enlightened beings from the very beginning. They attained this state by training and developing their minds in accordance with the path. As the buddhas themselves are not self-arisen, as they themselves trained in the path to attain that result, in the same way, they benefit sentient beings by explaining their experiences of the path.

When we consider enlightened beings such as Shakyamuni Buddha, we feel faith and admiration for their perfect qualities. Yet it is also important for us to remember that beings such as Shakyamuni also trained in the path to enlightenment, and that they, too, once upon a time, were completely controlled by delusions and karma as we are today. The difference between these beings and ourselves is that they applied themselves on the path to enlightenment, and by persevering in the extensive accumulations of the merit of method and wisdom over three countless eons, they freed themselves completely from samsara. These beings applied themselves with great diligence on the path for the benefit of sentient beings, and attained the result of enlightenment, and we have not. That is the difference. Considering things in this way, we will become more aware of our own potential for enlightenment, and strive to fulfill it.

The Specific Suffering of the Realms of Cyclic Existence

The next section discusses the particular types of suffering of each realm of cyclic existence. As we have already discussed the types of suffering that one experiences in the hell realm, the hungry ghost realm, and the animal realm, in this section I will primarily address the suffering of the higher realms.

In the human realm we experience both physical and mental suffering, and of the two, mental suffering is much worse. Much of our mental suffering comes as a result of our unfulfilled hopes and expectations—which are completely in the interest of the eight worldly dharmas—and also from the mind of doubt. Our uncontrolled minds also direct our bodies and speech to engage in nonvirtue, which brings further suffering as our negative karma bears fruit.

The primary form of suffering in the realm of the jealous gods is also mental suffering. Although beings born in the realm of the jealous gods are generally very intelligent, upon seeing the glory and magnificence of the higher god realm, they experience the suffering of aggressive competitiveness and bitter jealousy. Because of this and in spite of their intelligence, it is almost impossible for them to understand the meaning of emptiness, much less to realize it. As a result of constantly waging war with the beings of the higher god realm, the jealous gods also experience physical suffering.

The suffering of the beings born in the higher god realm is also predominantly mental. The gods enjoy glorious material comfort and divine sensual pleasures during their life, and are completely absorbed in their blissful existence. When the time of death approaches, they are able to perceive the place of their next rebirth, and they experience extreme anguish when they realize that they are on their way to the lower realms, having exhausted so much positive karma in their present rebirth. As the time of death approaches, they begin to perspire and lose their physical beauty. The flower garlands that adorn them wither and dry up, and their fine celestial garments become dirty and start to smell bad. Never having experienced any of these things before, they become distraught.

Although beings in the form and formless realms do not experience the gross manifestation of the delusions, or any kind of gross suffering, their existence is nonetheless bound by karma and delusions. Therefore, the beings in these realms are subject to uncontrolled birth and rebirth. During their lifespans, by the power of meditative concentration they abide in a state of continual bliss. Since they no longer experience the gross manifestations of suffering, they feel that they have attained liberation. However, when their karmic lifespan comes to an end, through the strength of their clairvoyance they are able to see that they will die and take rebirth. When they realize that they still bound to cyclic existence, they decide that liberation must not exist after all and give up on the idea completely, and as a result of this wrong view they accumulate very powerful negative karma.

We might wonder how applicable these meditations on the shortcomings of the experiences of the form and formless realms or the hell realms are for our minds right now, since we are not directly experiencing these states. If this doubt occurs to us, we should recall that the thought of renunciation is the wish to be released from *all* of cyclic existence. From the peak of samsara to the depths of the Avici Hells, every experience of happiness in cyclic existence is contaminated happiness, and every experience of suffering is brought on by karma and delusions. In cultivating the thought of renunciation, we should take all of these states of existence as objects to be abandoned. In order to accomplish this, it is necessary to familiarize our minds with each of these experiences.

The Stages of Entering Samsara

The Ten Root Delusions

As we have discussed, cyclic existence is perpetuated by our continual rebirth as a result of karma and delusions. Of the two, the delusions are the greater danger. If we are able to eliminate the delusions from our minds, our karmic seeds and imprints will not have the conditions to ripen, and thus will never bear fruit. Karmic seeds and imprints cannot ripen into a result without the condition of the delusions. Hence, we should make an effort to understand the nature of the delusions, the way that they manifest in our lives, and the antidotes that can eradicate them.

The general nature of the delusions is that they interrupt our peaceful states of mind and create disturbance. According to the lamrim, there are ten principal delusions: six root delusions and four that are divisions of the sixth.

The first of the six root delusions is the deluded mind of attachment. The mind of attachment superimposes qualities onto its object and then generates clinging and grasping toward that object based on its projection. Attachment is like the lasso that binds us to cyclic existence. Conventionally, it is of course true that there are things that can be said to be relatively beautiful, unattractive, pleasant, unpleasant, good, or bad. But the mind of attachment sees a solid, concrete beautiful object that exists in this way *from the side of the object itself.* This is its main mistake.

The second delusion, the mind of anger, arises in relation to those whom we have labeled the enemy, in relation to that which we have labeled bad, or in relation to that which we consider unpleasant. The mind of anger is aggressive and violent. The mind that wishes ill will or harm on others is suffused with anger, but the mind of anger is not necessarily pervaded by the wish to harm. The mind of vengeance and the mind that holds a grudge are also permeated by anger. Anger can arise as a result of incorrect logic and reasoning, and anger can arise out of ignorance, without any logical reason.

The third delusion is the mind of pride, which arises based on wrong view in association with the collection of the aggregates. The mind of pride relies upon an outer or inner condition that inspires an inflated sense of self-importance. Pride is a great obstacle to cultivating positive qualities, especially the qualities of the Mahayana path such as bodhichitta and the thought that cherishes others.

The fourth delusion is ignorance. The type of ignorance that is referred to here is ignorance in relation to cause and effect, the four noble truths, the knowledge of the three objects of refuge, and so forth.

The fifth delusion is doubt, specifically doubt in relation to the roots of cyclic existence, the four noble truths, and the three objects of refuge.

The sixth, seventh, eighth, ninth, and tenth root delusions come under the heading of deluded views, and can be divided into five parts: the view of the transitory collection, extreme views, holding false views to be superior, holding false ethics and conduct to be superior, and wrong view.

The first of these, the view of the transitory collection, is the habitual perspective that grasps at the "I" or the "mine" on the basis of the aggregates. *Transitory collection* refers to the accumulation of the aggregates, which is impermanent. Although the aggregates are in reality merely a collection of impermanent things, our minds hold them to be a permanent, independent, single entity.

According to the Svatantrika-Madhyamaka system and all the schools below it, the view of the transitory collection is the consciousness that grasps at "I" or "mine" as existing independently or substantially. According to the Prasangika system, the view of the transitory collection is the consciousness that grasps at "I" or self as existing inherently.

The view of the transitory collection can be intellectually acquired or naturally present. When we speak of the view of the transitory collection as one of the six root delusions, we are usually referring to the innate form, which is the root of cyclic existence.

The second of the deluded views is extreme views, which refers to nihilism and eternalism. Nihilism means believing that an existent entity does not exist, and eternalism means believing that a nonexistent entity is existent.

The third of the deluded views is holding wrong views to be superior. This means holding extreme, deluded forms of wisdom to be correct, as opposed to the views that liberate us.

The fourth of the five wrong views is holding wrong ethics and conduct to be superior. *Conduct* refers to practices of extreme physical austerities and so forth. In the texts there are stories of people who saw that they were animals in their previous lives, and reasoned that in order to create the cause to be reborn as a human again they must practice the conduct of a dog or a pig. This kind of mistaken view also falls under this heading. An example of holding wrong ethics in contemporary times is those who commit mass suicide with the idea that taking their lives in a particular way at a particular time will lead them to liberation.

The fifth view is wrong view itself, which means believing that cause and effect do not exist, and that there are no past and future lives. From the Buddhist perspective, believing in an omnipotent being who created the world and its inhabitants is a category of wrong view.

These ten delusions are categorized as the five views and the five nonviews. The five views can be considered forms of wisdom, but they are all deluded.

How the Delusions Arise

In Buddhist philosophy, there are two ways to present the order in which the delusions arise. This is so because some Buddhist schools regard ignorance and the view of the transitory collection as being one and the same, while other schools regard them as two different things. There is a slight difference in the explanation of the way the delusions arise according to each of these points of view. The following explanation is based on the Prasangika view.

The Prasangika system asserts that ignorance and the view of the transitory collection are two distinct things. That being the case, one might ask, which arises first? According to the Prasangika system, ignorance arises first, followed by the view of the transitory collection. The Prasangika system illustrates this through the commonly cited example of mistaking a coiled rope for a snake at dusk. In order for the mistaken consciousness to arise, first of all the condition of it being dark—dawn or dusk—is established. This condition is compared to ignorance. Due to this condition, it is difficult to clearly ascertain the rope as a rope, and thus it is possible for the person who approaches it to instead generate the wrong consciousness that labels the rope a "snake." As the condition of dusk must precede the generation of the mistaken consciousness, in the same way, ignorance must precede the view of the transitory collection, according to the Prasangika system.

Again, the Prasangikas say that the primary factor for generating the mistaken consciousness that sees the rope as a snake is the poor lighting. Using this analogy, they say that the obscuration of ignorance provides the condition that makes the true nature of the aggregates difficult to ascertain, thus leading to the generation of the view of the transitory collection. Then, as a result of the concrete sense of "I" that arises from the view of the transitory collection, one makes a strong distinction between what is "I" and what is "others." This in turn gives rise to attachment to what is "mine" and aversion to what is "others'," thus creating the basis for the experience of the gross delusions.

There are six causes of delusions.

The first is the basis. This refers to the countless seeds and imprints of the delusions that exist in our minds, accumulated throughout numberless lifetimes in cyclic existence.

The second cause is the external object. When we see an external object that is pleasant, the mind of incorrect assumption superimposes good qualities upon it, and we generate attachment. Likewise, when we see an external object that is unpleasant, the mind of incorrect assumption superimposes negative qualities upon it, and we generate anger or aversion. As this is the case, as beginners we are advised to keep as far away as possible from the objects of our attachment and anger. Physically removing ourselves from these objects lessens the manifestation of our delusions.

The third cause of the delusions is mental distraction.

The fourth cause is taking impure advice, such as reading books that make you angry, or that increase wrong view, attachment, or negative thoughts.

The fifth cause is habit, which means being habituated to negative thoughts.

The sixth cause is called inappropriate attention, which refers to the negative analytical process by which we hold the object of our attachment or aversion in our minds and continually review the reasons we find this object attractive or unattractive. As a result, the qualities that we have ascribed to that object begin to appear very solid and permanent. Inappropriate attention is often the direct cause of our delusions.

THE DISADVANTAGES OF THE DELUSIONS

Because the innate nature of mind is pure and luminous, the control that the delusions have upon us in our present situation is only temporary. However, because we grasp so persistently at permanence, our delusions may feel quite concrete, and we may despair that we will never become free.

As I mentioned earlier, of karma and delusions, delusions are our greater enemy, as they have accompanied us from beginningless lifetimes and we have great familiarity with them. In the teachings on mindtraining we are advised not to hold the delusions as a good council, not to rely upon the delusions to guide us. The only result that comes from depending on our delusions is our own downfall. As is stated in the *Ornament for the Mahayana Sutras,* the gross manifestations of the delusions destroy us, destroy other sentient begins, and destroy any sense of ethics or morality we may have. The deluded mind sees its own way and that way alone.

As we become more and more familiar with the delusions, the imprints of a particular delusion become imbedded in our minds, and will affect us for lifetimes. Also, one particular delusion can induce other deluded states of mind. For example if we are most prone to anger, the mind of anger may induce other deluded states of mind that are similar, such as ill will or vengeance. One delusion can induce the manifestation of many different aspects of the same kind of mind. As a result of this upheaval, there will be no occasion for peace or happiness. In fact, if we do not put effort into restraining our delusions, we will become totally overwhelmed by the force of them. At the end of our lives, having become so addicted to these negative ways of thinking, even at death our negative minds will take precedence and we will pass away with strong regret and be forced to take rebirth in the lower realms.

As Shantideva states in the *Guide to the Bodhisattva's Way of Life:*

The enemies of hatred and craving
Do not have legs, arms, and so forth;
They are neither heroic nor wise
And yet they have enslaved me.

Reflecting upon the manifold shortcomings of our delusions is essential in order to develop the inspiration to try to overcome them. As it is true that if we do not think about suffering, we will not wish for liberation, in the same way, if we are not familiar with the shortcomings of our own delusions, we will not make any effort to conquer them. As the negative thought manifests, we must think, "Here comes this thought to destroy my peace and happiness." Even if we can't remember the benefits of liberation and enlightenment, at the very least we must try to recall the immediate harm that this mind can bring us—when a delusion arises, it destroys the peace and happiness of all of our daily activities. This alone should lead us to wish to avoid its manifestation.

Just as we say, "Before the water rises, we build the floodgates," before the delusions arise we must construct our own internal barriers. Since we do not have the defense of having realized emptiness or pure compassion, we have a very small island of protection, but it is protection nonetheless. Even if we can do nothing else, at the very least we can resolve not to allow our minds to indulge in inappropriate attention on an object. It takes very little time for our mind to turn something into a really big deal. Once the water starts to overflow, it is much too late to stop it.

Having become familiar with the ten delusions, the five views, and the five nonviews, as you go through the course of twenty-four hours, you should take note of the number of times these delusions manifest in your minds. Then you should try to counteract them to the best of your ability. This is the essence of Dharma practice. Or, when practicing in a meditation session, you should bring to mind the object of your delusions, then reflect on the way that your delusions arise in relation to this object. You should begin with whatever delusion is the strongest and most apparent in your experience. Bring to mind a time when you experienced this strong delusion. Examine the delusion—think about the causes that gave rise to it, how it apprehended its object, how your body, speech, and mind were affected by that delusion, and how things were a few days later. Then think of the shortcomings of that delusion, and the ways to overcome it. Again, this meditation will be most effective if you use your own experience of attachment or anger as your main focus.

To overcome anger, you can consider Shantideva's advice from the *Guide to the Bodhisattva's Way of Life:* there is no evil like anger, as a single moment of anger can destroy the merits that you have accumulated over thousands of eons. In the stupor of the mind of anger, we totally disregard people who have been most kind to us. The physical or verbal activities that we engage in having been motivated by anger are extremely destructive. Also, although we may sometimes ornament ourselves to become beautiful, once our minds are consumed with anger, it doesn't matter how much we decorate ourselves, we cannot hide the ugliness of anger.

If you think about these points for a little while, you will begin to get a feeling for how destructive anger is. But please keep in mind that the antidote to anger—which is the practice of patience—brings as much benefit as anger does harm. It is said in the texts that the mind of patience creates the basis of happiness in this and future lifetimes.

To overcome attachment, you should begin by considering how there are countless lifetimes' worth of the imprints of attachment in your minds, and that it is attachment and the delusions related to it—such as craving and grasping—that create the causes to perpetuate your existence in samsara. Attachment is like the tether that binds you to cyclic existence.

Along with your contemplations on anger and attachment, you should try to cultivate the antidote to the eight worldly dharmas in your mind. You can do this by thinking about the general shortcomings of cyclic existence, and about impermanence and death. To counteract pride, you can think about a particular weakness of yours or an area in which you have no knowledge, such as medicine, astronomy, or whatever.

In order to attain enlightenment, you must begin by freeing yourself from the control of your delusions. The Kadampa masters say that the best attainment is developing faith in cause and effect, living in pure ethics, and eliminating one's delusions and negative states of mind. By having faith in cause and effect, one is able to live in pure ethics, and by living in pure ethics, one is able to eliminate the delusions from one's mind.

How Karma Is Accumulated

We accumulate two kinds of karma in our mindstreams—mental and intentional karmic action. *Mental karmic action* refers to activities of the mind, while *intentional karmic action* refers to the activities of the body and speech. Every consciousness or thought that we experience is accompanied by intention. Therefore, it is valid to say that we accumulate karma all the time, constantly.

Mental karmic action can be virtuous, nonvirtuous, or neutral. All throwing karma and invariable karma are categorized as mental karmic action. Also, of the twelve links of dependent origination, the second link of karmic formations and the tenth link of existence are considered karma, and are categorized as mental karmic action.

Intentional karmic action is the action that arises out of intention. This kind of karma must necessarily be a physical activity. Making prostrations or offerings are virtuous intentional karmic actions. The ten nonvirtuous activities are negative intentional karmic actions.

Does karmic action have form or not? Again, the answer depends on the particular Buddhist school. The Vaibashika school categorizes karma into karma that can be known and karma that cannot be known. Karma that can be known is karmic action that can be seen. According to the Vaibashikas, vows and precepts become a form that can be known in their first moment, but from the second moment onward they become a form that cannot be known. According to our own system, however, vows and precepts are consciousness, and therefore do not have form.[25]

As we have discussed, when karma ripens, its results can be virtuous or nonvirtuous. Neutral karma, however, does not have a ripening result. If a virtuous action is undertaken with the motivation of ignorance, when it is accumulated, it becomes a contaminated virtuous karma. This kind of karma ripens in the experience of temporary happiness. Contaminated virtuous karma, accumulated in the case of ordinary sentient beings, is further subdivided into meritorious contaminated virtuous karma and invariable contaminated virtuous karma. Invariable karma is the karma accumulated by the beings of the form and formless realms, which we covered earlier. The direct realization of emptiness is necessary in order to accumulate uncontaminated virtuous karma.

Sentient beings can accumulate virtuous karma from the first ground up until the tenth ground, and negative karma up until the path of preparation, the second of the five Mahayana paths.[26] Once you enter the first ground, you can no longer accumulate nonvirtuous karma, because from first ground on you have realized emptiness, and hence your mind is no longer under the power of the delusions. Although you have not abandoned them entirely, they do not control your mind. It is as if you have been poisoned, and though the poison is still circling in your system, its effects have been rendered innocuous by the antidote that you have taken.

However, if a bodhisattva on the path of accumulation or the path of preparation generates anger in relation to another bodhisattva, that bodhisattva accumulates nonvirtuous karma.

We may wonder, do buddhas accumulate karma as well? The answer is that buddhas engage in activities of virtue through the power of the completion of the two accumulations of merit, the merit of wisdom and the merit of virtue. The activities they engage in through the power of these two accumulations of merit are not considered the accumulation of karma.

The karmic accumulations of beings who have renounced cyclic existence and have only the conceptual realization of emptiness are not categorized as part of the true cause of suffering. However, they are considered to be *similar* to the true cause of suffering. This is so because these actions cannot be considered uncontaminated until the practitioner has generated the direct realization of emptiness. Because they are not contaminated, these actions cannot fall into the category of true suffering.

In the same way, on the Mahayana paths of accumulation and preparation, the practitioner has renunciation and has the generic realization of emptiness. The paths of accumulation and preparation are included within the true cause of suffering because they have yet to become a direct antidote to suffering, but they are not the actual true cause of suffering.

Within the true cause of suffering are the actual true cause of suffering and the ordinary true cause of suffering. Everything categorized as an actual true cause of suffering becomes a cause of cyclic existence. Anything categorized as an ordinary true cause of suffering cannot become a cause of cyclic existence. Whether our own contaminated virtuous karmic actions become an actual true cause of suffering or an ordinary true cause of suffering is mostly determined by the strength of our renunciation and so forth. At our level most of our actions become part of the actual true cause of suffering since we do not have the realization of bodhichitta, the direct realization of emptiness, or even the generic realization of emptiness.

However, there are actions that will bring virtuous results regardless of our motivation. These are actions that rely upon powerful bases—such as the merit field, our spiritual teachers, and holy objects. Virtuous actions that are done in relation to these objects do not require the purity of our motivation to become virtuous karmic actions. They are part of the ordinary true cause of suffering, and will not become a cause of cyclic existence.

Generally speaking, the karma that we accumulate physically, verbally, and mentally is accumulated in order to actualize some feeling of happiness that is actually a contaminated feeling of happiness. Seeking out the feelings of happiness generated in dependence upon the pleasures of the five sense objects primarily for the purpose of future lifetimes is regarded as virtuous karmic action. Seeking them out for the purpose of this lifetime is regarded as nonvirtuous karmic action.

Some people, of course, also accumulate karma for the sake of neutral feelings. Those who accumulate karma in order to experience equanimity are usually those beings who have abandoned aspirations for the contaminated feelings of happiness dependent on the pleasures of the five senses. Instead, they seek the feeling of peace that can be generated through meditative concentration. The karma that they accumulate results in invariable karma, which is the accumulation of the form and formless realms.

The Manner of Migrating to the Next Life

The next topic is the manner of migrating to the next life: how death and the intermediate state are experienced, and how rebirth occurs.

Death occurs because our karmic lifespan has ended, or because we have no merit of virtue remaining to sustain us, or because we have obstacles to our lives. Dying due to lack of merit means that the conditions for death overtake the karmic lifespan and death occurs before the lifespan is finished. A sudden death is usually due to lack of merit. For example, in Western countries, people work extremely hard and go into debt in order to buy a nice sports car. Then they go out one night, have a drink, and kill themselves in an accident driving home. In contrast, people who die in a very relaxed, calm manner are usually experiencing the natural end of their karmic lifespan.

At the time of death, the gross mind can take on either a virtuous or nonvirtuous aspect. Usually it is said that whichever mental pattern you have been most habituated toward—virtue or nonvirtue—will characterize the mental state that will arise most powerfully at the time of death. If at the time of death you can bring forth a virtuous state of mind of your own accord, that is the very best situation. If you are unable to do it alone, then it is good to have the support of people around you who will remind you of the practice of cultivating faith and virtue.

If we can transform the gross mind at the time of death into a virtuous mental state, then whatever feelings of physical suffering we experience will not overtake the mind. However, due to our past imprints, a nonvirtuous mental state may arise without our control. On other occasions, the conditions at the time of death may trigger a negative mind. For example, if while dying you see the people around you crying, you may generate a strong sense of attachment and wish not to be separated from them. In this way, outer conditions can destroy the peace of mind at the time of death. This is important to keep in mind if you are around a dying person.

Once near Sera Monastery in India there lived a simple monk who practiced the deity yoga of Vajrayogini with great diligence. One day he invited his close friends to his house to practice together. My own teacher was there. They did the sadhana together, and then had lunch. After lunch this simple monk told everyone else to relax and then went inside to take the selfinitiation. For a long time the others didn't hear anything, and finally, when they went to check on him, they found that he had passed away.

The way in which the heat of the body is absorbed at the time of death is an outer sign by which we can determine whether the mind at the time of death was positive or negative, whether it was in a virtuous or nonvirtuous state. If the person dies with a nonvirtuous state of mind, the heat is absorbed from the head first down to the heart. This means the lower portion of the body is warm and the upper part of the body is cold.[27] If the body starts losing heat from the feet first, it is a sign that the person has died with a virtuous state of mind.

The life of the intermediate state, or *bardo,* being, begins the moment consciousness leaves the body and death occurs. There is always an intermediate state, or bardo, if beings are born from the desire realm into the desire realm, or from the desire realm to the form realm. However, a being passing from the desire realm into the formless realm will not experience the intermediate state.

According to Vasubandhu's *Treasury of Knowledge,* an intermediate state being possesses five aggregates, which are similar to the aggregates of the next rebirth. The intermediate state being appears in the general form of the next rebirth, without the details. Also, intermediate state beings possess a type of clairvoyance, and those beings of a similar type can know each other, interact, and see their immediate past and future lives.

If an intermediate state being has accumulated a great deal of negative karma in the previous lifetime, that being will experience the bardo as very dark and gloomy. If, however, the intermediate being has accumulated great virtue in the previous lifetime, the bardo will appear shining and radiant, like the luminous light of the full moon.

Intermediate beings who will take rebirth in the hell realms have bodies that look like charred tree trunks. Those who will take rebirth in the animal realm have smoke-colored forms. Those who will be reborn in the preta realm have bodies of a watery color. Those who will be reborn in the higher realms—as humans or gods—have golden bodies. Those who will be reborn in the form realm have white bodies. And again, those who will be reborn in the formless realm have no intermediate life.

Those beings who are going to take a higher rebirth enter a bardo that is on an upward incline. Those who are to be born in the human realm move on an even plane. And those who are to be reborn in the lower realms move on a downward incline.

There are two different explanations regarding the lifespan of a bardo being. Generally we say that the lifespan of an intermediate state being is seven days long, and can be experienced up to seven times, which altogether makes forty-nine days. Within that amount of time the bardo being will definitely take rebirth. Some people say that in the case of someone who was a human being in the previous life and will take rebirth as a human again, the seven days are the same as seven human days. In accordance with this view, in the case of a being from the human realm who will take rebirth in the form realm or the sura or asura realm, the seven days should accord with the system of time of the future rebirth. Others say that regardless of where the future rebirth will take place, the seven days are equal to seven days in the human realm. Although most people accept the first explanation, if we want to offer prayers for someone who has died, it is more practical to consider the time period to be seven days according to the human realm.

As each lifespan within the bardo is seven days long, it is possible for a bardo being to experience one intermediate state lifespan as a human-realm bardo being, then after seven days pass away without actually taking rebirth in the human realm, to return in the body of a god-realm bardo being. Each bardo being has up to seven rebirths in the intermediate state itself. During this time, it is actually possible to change the potential for your future rebirth and take on a different kind of intermediate state life. However, this is only true for the beings who are to be reborn in the desire realm, and particularly so for those who will take human and god-realm rebirth. Beings who are to be reborn in the form realms cannot experience this kind of change, as their form realm throwing karma is invariable.

Among other things, a particular rebirth is brought about by a strong sense of attachment to a particular realm. For example, you may experience an existence as a human intermediate state being, and as a result develop a strong sense of attachment for humans. This attachment causes your consciousness to seek out human parents, and fuse with the union of a human sperm and egg. That is the beginning of your birth. The intermediate being destined to take rebirth through the womb will see a couple having intercourse at the time of the fusion of the egg and the sperm. If that being is to be born as a female, there will be a strong sense of attachment toward the male, and a sense of distance from the female. Conversely, if the intermediate being is to be reborn as a male, that being will have strong attachment to the female, and a sense of distance from the male. I am not sure whether the intermediate beings have their own distinctive sexes as male or female or not.

The joining of the egg and sperm creates the condition for the consciousness to enter. The Chittamatras say that the fundamental consciousness enters the fusion of the sperm and the egg. Those who don't accept a fundamental consciousness assert that it is the mental consciousness that enters at this point.

At the time the consciousness enters the sperm and the egg, it is accompanied by a very subtle collection of elements that come into existence due to the power of the individual's karma. This collection of the elements is in the category of extremely hidden phenomena. The way this works is similar to the process of making yogurt: in order to make new yogurt, a little bit of the previous yogurt is needed as a starter. In the same way, the gross elements of our body result not only from the sperm and egg of our parents, but also from the subtle elements that are the result of our previous life's karma.

The being's experience at the time when the mental consciousness enters the fusion of the sperm and the egg depends upon the power of its virtuous karma. For those of lesser merit there is a tremendous gross sound as the mind enters the sperm and egg. For those with virtuous karma the experience is much more clear and peaceful.

This is the explanation of the manner of taking rebirth for those who experience birth through the womb.

Those who take spontaneous rebirth will experience a strong desire for the place of birth from the last life and the bardo that will propel them to be born there. Those who take rebirth due to heat and moisture will experience a strong desire for smell. Those who are to be born in the hot hells experience strong desire for and grasping at heat. Those who are to be born in the cold hells experience strong desire for and grasping at cold environments. Those who are to be born in the animal and the preta realms experience great attachment for and find joy in the mode of conduct of those types of beings.

This completes the discussion of the manner of migrating to the next life within the topic of contemplating true suffering and true cause as a method to generate the wish for liberation.

Buddha-Nature

From Dharmakirti's *Commentary on the "Compendium on Valid Cognition"*:

The nature of mind is clear,
And all the defilements are adventitious.

Sentient beings do not know the true natures of their own minds, and it is this not-knowing that causes so much of the suffering that we experience in cyclic existence. According to Buddhism, the mind of every sentient being is ultimately empty of inherent existence, and, on the conventional level, is luminous, clear, and knowing. In addition to that, all of the delusions in our minds that bind us to this existence in the ways that we have just discussed are temporary and adventitious. The luminous nature of the mind and the fact that the delusions are temporary corroborate the fact that as long as one is a sentient being, one has the potential to become enlightened.

The presentation of buddha-nature, or *tathagathagarba,* differs slightly in accordance with the philosophical views of the different Buddhist schools.

According to the Vaibashikas, for example, buddha-nature is also known as the naturally abiding nature. According to them, buddha-nature is illustrated by the four natures of superior beings. The first nature of a superior being is that one is content with one's clothing, free of the worldly dharmas, as long as one has just enough to wear. The second nature is that one is content with whatever food one has received, again free of the eight worldly dharmas. The third is that one is content with one's shelter or housing, free of the eight worldly dharmas. And the fourth is that one has single-pointed joy for the practices of abandoning nonvirtue and persevering in the levels of meditative concentration. In short, the Vaibashikas regard the mental states that turn away from nonvirtue and aspire to virtue as examples of buddha-nature. According to them, buddha-nature is the nature of mind, which can be transformed in a positive way.

The proponents of the Sautrantika, or the Great Exposition school, define buddha-nature as the potential within the mind to generate an uncontaminated mental state.

The proponents of the Chittamatra view accept two kinds of buddha-nature: a naturally abiding buddha-nature and a transforming buddha-nature. According to their view, naturally abiding buddha-nature has three characteristics: it is a continuum, it exists naturally in the minds of sentient beings (not having newly arisen as a result of causes and conditions), and it is the seed that will become the uncontaminated mind. According to the Chittamatra school, naturally abiding buddha-nature is a compounded phenomenon. As long as one is a sentient being, one possesses it.

However, according to the Chittamatras, being a sentient being does not necessarily mean that one possesses transforming buddha-nature. When practitioners enter the path and progress through the stages of study and practice in relation to the three vast collection of the teachings, the naturally abiding buddha-nature that is present in their minds becomes transforming buddha-nature.

All of the schools below the Chittamatra school classify buddha-nature as a compounded phenomenon. And all of the Buddhist philosophical schools accept the luminous nature of the mind and the fact that the defilements are merely temporary.

According to the Madhyamaka schools, the ultimate reality of the aggregate of consciousness is the naturally abiding buddha-nature. All sentient beings are endowed with the aggregate of consciousness.

The Madhyamaka schools assert that the ultimate nature of this consciousness, which does not truly exist, which does not inherently exist, and which does not exist by way of its own nature, is what allows transformation to take place within our minds. It gives us the ability to limitlessly enhance the qualities of our minds and bestows upon us the capacity to eliminate every defilement. This is the context in which buddha-nature should be understood to function.

The ultimate nature of our own consciousness, which is the result of our karma, and Buddha's consciousness, which is the result of the accumulations of the two types of merit, are the same. Neither our consciousness nor Buddha's consciousness inherently or truly exists. The conventional mode of existence of both of these consciousnesses is also the same—a state of mere experience that is luminous and clear.

So if the ultimate nature of consciousness is buddha-nature, does it follow that the ultimate nature of a *mistaken* consciousness—such as the consciousness that grasps at true existence—is also buddha-nature? The ultimate nature of this consciousness is not buddha-nature. This is so because the substantial continuum and the continuum that is similar to the previous cause of this mistaken consciousness have an end. The end is the attainment of enlightenment, at which point all mistaken consciousnesses will cease. A second reason is that the more our minds become habituated to the consciousness that grasps at true existence, the less they have the capacity for limitless enhancement. Also, mistaken states of consciousness are not stable, as they have no valid basis, being based on ignorance.

As an individual develops through the path and practices of method and wisdom and is able to extinguish all the defilements and develop every positive quality, that individual's contaminated mind transforms into the bodies of a buddha. Of the four, the conventional mind of the practitioner completing the path becomes the transcendental truth body, and the ultimate nature of the mind becomes the nature body of a buddha. Both of the Madhyamaka schools assert that our present minds, which are controlled by karma and delusions, can eventually be transformed into the bodies of a buddha because they do not inherently exist.

There are three reasons establishing that all sentient beings have the potential for enlightenment according to the Prasangika system. The first is that sentient beings are beneficiaries of the ultimate pure activities of the buddhas. The second is that there is no difference between the ultimate reality of a sentient being and the ultimate reality of a buddha. And the third is that sentient beings have the potential to transform as they familiarize themselves with the path. The causes that enable us to actualize our buddha-nature are developing the aspiration to attain buddhahood and actually engaging in the path.

In Maitreya's *Sublime Continuum,* there are ten points of explanation establishing that the basic nature of the mind is luminous.

Of the ten points establishing the luminous nature of the mind, the first is nature. This means that the nature of the mind itself is clear.

The second is cause. This refers to the bodhisattva's wisdom that realizes emptiness, single-pointed concentration, and great compassion. These are the causes that purify the mind and transform it into the dharmakaya.

The third is the result. As a result of the Mahayana aspiration, we achieve the result of pure completion; as a result of wisdom we achieve true identity; as a result of concentration we achieve divine bliss; and as a result of great compassion we achieve the dharmakaya.

The fourth is karmic action. This refers to the fact that because sentient beings have the seeds of uncontaminated mind, they can engage in the actions of the practice of renunciation and bodhichitta. This point shows how all causes and conditions can work together to bring the ultimate result.

The fifth is the quality of possessing. Because they possess buddha-nature, sentient beings possess the potential for all good qualities.

The sixth is abiding. This refers to the clear luminosity of the nature of the mind, which abides in ordinary beings, arya beings, and perfect enlightened beings.

The seventh is the quality of being temporary. This means that the three types of beings are not distinguished by permanent differences in nature, but rather are distinguished by temporary distinctions.

The eighth is omnipresence. This means that the nature of mind remains the same all the time, on every occasion.

The ninth is unchangeability. This means that the nature of mind is unchanging.

The tenth is indivisibility. This means that once the result of enlightenment is achieved, the qualities cannot be separated from the nature of mind.

These ten points establish that the nature of the mind is luminous. Within the ten, the first five stand on their own. The sixth is the object to be proven, and the seventh through the tenth prove the sixth.

These points may help us to keep in mind the fact that the entire path to enlightenment must be cultivated within our own minds. Whatever negativities need to be extinguished must be done so within our own minds. The main objective of Dharma practice is limitlessly developing the positive potential within our minds. The mind can be limitlessly developed because its mental continuum is beginningless and without end, and because it is endowed with buddha-nature.

CONTEMPLATING THE TWELVE LINKS OF DEPENDENT ARISING

The Twelve Links

The second method by which one can generate the wish for liberation is through contemplation of the twelve links of dependent origination. This method is usually considered to be the most effective for those practitioners with sharper intellect. Some individuals are even able to generate the thought of renunciation by contemplating the twelve links alone, without extensive consideration of the individual aspects of suffering and the delusions.

The explanation of the twelve links of dependent origination is often accompanied by a visual representation called the "Wheel of Life." To inspire the awareness of cyclic existence in today's practitioners, an illustration of the Wheel of Life is usually placed prominently at the entrance of the main monasteries and temples in Tibet and India. In the illustration, the twelve links are depicted in chronological order in the shape of a wheel.

The first of the twelve links is the link of ignorance, illustrated by a blind old woman holding a cane. Ignorance is a state of consciousness, and thereby requires an object. The observed object of the mind of ignorance is the conventional "I." The ignorance that apprehends the "I" to be inherently existent is called the ignorance of ultimate reality. As a result of the ignorance of ultimate reality, we also experience the ignorance of cause and effect, which means ignorance of karma. When both of these two types of ignorance are involved in an action, the action and its result are usually nonvirtuous. However, if the ignorance of ultimate reality is present *without* the ignorance of cause and effect, the action will likely be virtuous or neutral.

The second link is the link of karmic formation. This refers to the mental action that creates the ripening result. In most Buddhist schools, the second link is considered to be a state of consciousness. Of the five omnipresent mental factors—feeling, discrimination, intention, attention, and contact—this link is categorized as intention. Karmic formation is the direct result of the first link of ignorance. It is illustrated by a picture of a potter making pots.

The third link is the link of consciousness, which is illustrated by a monkey leaping about. Those who accept the concept of fundamental consciousness consider the link of consciousness to refer to this. Those who do not accept the concept of fundamental consciousness consider this link to refer to mental consciousness. The link of consciousness occurs in two parts: consciousness at the time of the cause and consciousness at the time of the result. When an action is done, the moment its imprint is pressed into the consciousness, it becomes the consciousness at the time of the cause. When the karma later matures into its ripening result, it becomes the consciousness at the time of the result.

The fourth link is the link of name and form, which is illustrated by a picture of a person rowing a boat. Among the five aggregates, *form* refers to the body, and *name* refers to feeling, discrimination, compositional factors, and consciousness. Beings born into the formless realms do not possess the link of form.

The fifth link is the link of the six sensory bases, which is illustrated by a picture of an empty house with six windows, representing the foundation of the six senses.

According to the chronology of this explanation, the fourth link of name and form is followed by the fifth link of the six sensory bases. In reality, however, sensations and the mental sense bases are established at the time of the fourth link. Once the physical form comes into being, the sensory bases for tactile sensations also exist, and once the consciousness comes into being, the sensory base for the mental sense perception is also present. Therefore, the nature of the body is actually established at the time of the fourth link of name and form. What develop at the time of the fifth link of the six sensory bases are the particular characteristics of the individual who will utilize that body.

The sixth link is the link of contact. The link of contact arises as a result of the object, the sensory power, and the sensory perception coming together. The picture illustrating the sixth link is a couple in sexual union.

The seventh link, feeling, comes as a direct result of contact. Feeling is illustrated by a person who has been shot in the eye with an arrow. This illustration is meant to depict the extravagance with which we experience feeling—when we feel happiness, we feel an extreme sense of happiness, and when we suffer, we feel an extreme sense of suffering.

The eighth link is the link of craving, which is illustrated by a man drinking excessive amounts of liquor. Feelings of pleasure and pain arise from contact, and in response to those feelings we experience craving—craving for more pleasure or craving for less pain.

The ninth is the link of grasping, which is illustrated by a person plucking fruit from a tree. When craving reaches its fullest potential, it transforms into grasping. Among the six root delusions, both craving and grasping fall under the category of attachment.

The tenth link is the link of existence, which is illustrated by a picture of a pregnant woman, representing the potential of the next state of existence. When the karmic imprint (from the second link) is nurtured by craving and grasping, it ripens and results in the link of existence.

The eleventh link is the link of birth, which is illustrated by a picture of a woman giving birth. When the potential of the tenth link is fully ripened, it results in the link of birth.

The twelfth link is the link of aging and death, which is illustrated by a person carrying a corpse on his back. The link of aging refers to the continuous degeneration of the physical body, and the link of death refers to the point when the continuum of the body ceases. Because some die without any opportunity to age, and some die after aging, these two links are combined in the twelfth link. They are not necessarily chronological.

How to Meditate on the Twelve Links

The twelve links can be examined from the perspective of several different sequences. You can contemplate them as I have just described them, in the order that they are presented in the Wheel of Life. You can also think about them in terms of the divisions of the four limbs: the throwing limb, the thrown limb, the accomplishing limb, and the accomplished limb. The throwing limb is composed of ignorance, followed by karmic formation and consciousness. The thrown limb, which is the result of these, is composed of name and form, the six sensory bases, contact, and feeling. The accomplishing limb is composed of the eighth, ninth, and tenth links: craving, grasping, and existence. And the accomplished limb is composed of the link of birth followed by the link of aging and death.

The contemplation of the twelve links according to the divisions of the four limbs is particularly effective when one is trying to understand the way that karma can be accumulated in one lifetime and experienced in another lifetime. For example, the throwing limb of ignorance, karmic formations, and consciousness take place in this lifetime. However, the karma created during this time does not necessarily have to ripen within the same lifetime—it can ripen in the next lifetime, or, for that matter, any of the other future lifetimes. This can be compared to buying an open airline ticket without choosing a destination until the last moment. The first three links are like the ticket, but the destination will not be determined for certain until the completing limbs of craving, grasping, and existence take place.

Among the twelve links, the links of ignorance, craving, and grasping are links of delusions. The links of karmic formations and existence are karma, and the remaining links are all suffering.

Of the ten delusions, the first link is ignorance itself, and the eighth and ninth are two different types of attachment.

Of the second and the tenth link, which are karma, the second link of karma is a throwing karma. The tenth is not a throwing karma but a completing karma.

How do we experience the twelve links in relation to a single karmic action that we accumulate? Let us take the example of the result of our present human life. In our previous lives, we accumulated the karmic imprint for a human rebirth through the first three links: ignorance, karmic formation, and consciousness. The ripening result was a human body, which is inclusive of the links of name and form, the six sensory bases, feeling, and contact. What brought it to fruition were the links of craving, grasping, and existence. We have experienced the birth of this body, but we have yet to experience the twelfth link of aging and death.

It could also be the case that the body we have now is the result of karma created many lifetimes ago. The complete experience of one set of twelve links can be completed over two lifetimes at minimum, or three lifetimes at maximum. However, there can be many other lifetimes in between. For example, you may complete the first three links and accumulate a partic-ular karma. If you do not meet with the conditions to ripen it, it may lie dormant in your mind for a long while. In between you may experience many other lifetimes until finally the craving, grasping, and the link of existence that nurture that particular karma bring it to fruition, at which point you experience the result.

The main objective in studying the twelve links is to understand how cyclic existence is caused and how it is sustained. You should try to under-stand how you create the causes to cycle in samsara, and how you make the conditions to experience the result. You should also see how even while you have not finished experiencing one complete set of karmic links, you are simultaneously creating the causes for other sets of links to continue.

You may also find it helpful to contemplate the twelve links in reverse order, understanding that in order to bring forth the cessation of the twelve links, it is necessary to eliminate death, and that in order to do that it is necessary to cease aging, birth, existence, contact, feeling, sensory bases, name and form. In order to cease all of these links, it is necessary to cease craving and grasping, which need to be eliminated in order to cease the root cause of cyclic existence, ignorance.

Whenever you contemplate the twelve links, it is very important that you do so in the context of your own life. You should think about the "I" that experiences suffering and happiness traveling backwards and forwards in the twelve links. You should also bear in mind that although this "I" is just a conventional, nominal "I," it nonetheless experiences all the happi-ness and suffering of this existence.

You can also think about a particular set of the twelve links specifically in relation to the path and practice of the small scope—in other words, how a set of the twelve links works in relation to a lower rebirth. For example, you might think that as a result of the first three links you accumulate a nonvirtuous karma, which is later brought to fruition by craving, grasping, and existence, and thereby brings forth a rebirth in one of the lower realms.

After you have gained some familiarity with this, you can then consider a particular set of the twelve links in accordance with the path and practice of the medium scope. To do so you might contemplate how you accumulate a virtuous karma with the first three links, which is later brought to fruition and brings forth rebirth in one of the higher realms.

The contemplation on the twelve links in terms of your own potential experiences in accordance with the small and the medium scopes can become the basis for generating the mind of renunciation. If, however, you contemplate the twelve links in terms of the experience of others—your friends and loved ones, or other sentient beings in general—it can also become a condition to generate the mind of great compassion, which becomes a practice in accordance with the great scope.

THE MEASURE OF THE
MEDIUM SCOPE PRACTITIONER

The first step to attaining liberation is to cultivate renunciation. The mind of renunciation has two aspects: the determination to be free of suffering down to its very roots and the wish to attain liberation. In order to bring forth this mind, as we have discussed, we can practice the contemplations on true suffering and true cause according to the four noble truths, or we can meditate on the twelve links of dependent origination.

Understanding the failings or the shortcomings of cyclic existence is fundamental to the practices of the hearer's path, the solitary realizer's path, the bodhisattva's path, and even the path of the tantric practitioner. According to Aryadeva, for the practitioner of the stage on the tantric path called *completely without elaboration*, it is imperative to understand the suffering nature of cyclic existence, to remember the shortcomings and failings of cyclic existence, and thereby to develop the kind of mind that is totally free of grasping at the pleasures of cyclic existence.

Nagarjuna states in *Friendly Letter:*

Samsara being so—birth in the god, human,
Hell, hungry ghost, or animal realm—
There is no good rebirth.
Understand that birth is a vessel of great harm.

Moreover, since we are bound to this kind of existence due to the force of delusions and karma, there is nothing great or wonderful about it at all.

In the advice of one of the Dalai Lamas it is said that the happiness of this lifetime is contaminated. Our activities whereby we seek the happiness of this lifetime are endless like ripples of water—when one ripple has vanished, another one appears, and when that has disappeared, another one rises to take its place. The works of this life are like that. We are in this kind of situation primarily because our minds lack satisfaction, and because we have endless desire and discontent. All of our experiences are like drinking salt water—no matter how much we drink, we only thirst for more. And in lifetime after lifetime we behave in exactly in the same way.

In order to accomplish liberation from cyclic existence, it is most important to cultivate renunciation. Cyclic existence is like the container, and the sentient beings whose aggregates have been brought on by karma and delusions are the contents. Of course, in reality, both the contents and the container—from the very bottom of cyclic existence to the very highest of the god realms—are without essence. When you look at the reflection of the moon in a still lake, no matter how beautiful that moon may appear, it is still without essence.

You have realized renunciation when you experience the spontaneous, uncontrived, effortless wish to be free from suffering and attain the state of liberation. Generation of the spontaneous mind of renunciation is considered the entrance to the path of liberation. It is only then that whatever merits of virtue you accumulate can become the cause of freedom from cyclic existence.

The Sixteen Aspects of the Four Noble Truths

A practitioner of the medium scope takes the goal of liberation as his or her primary focus. The methods to attain this goal, according to the medium scope practitioner, are the practices of the sixteen aspects of the four noble truths and the training in the thirty-seven limbs of enlightenment.[28] However, because we are not *actual* practitioners of the medium scope, but in reality great scope practitioners practicing the path *common* to the medium scope, it is not necessary for us to engage in all of these meditations. Regardless, although they may not be our main focus, meditation on some of these practices may be useful as we progress on the path. Therefore, within this section I am going to include a brief commentary on the way to meditate on the sixteen aspects of the four noble truths as it would be practiced by a medium scope practitioner.

According to this practice, each of the four noble truths is attributed four characteristics, making sixteen in total. The sixteen aspects counteract the sixteen mistaken modes of engaging with objects.

True Suffering

The four aspects of the first noble truth, the truth of suffering, are impermanence, suffering, emptiness, and selflessness. The four mistaken modes of grasping in relation to the first noble truth are the way we hold the aggregates to be pure, the way we hold them to be happiness, the way we hold them to be permanent, and the way we hold them to be self-existent.

The base for meditating on true suffering is our body and mind. To counteract the first mistaken mode of grasping in relation to the first aspect, we can consider how our body and mind are impermanent and impure because they are under the control of karma and delusions and are changing moment by moment. We should already be familiar with how and why this is so from our earlier contemplations.

The understanding of our impermanent nature leads us to the recognition of the second aspect, that our body and mind are in the nature of suffering. We should also be familiar with this kind of contemplation from our earlier discussions in this section. Establishing the base of our aggregates as existing in the nature of suffering counteracts the mistaken perception holding our aggregates as sources of happiness.

Emptiness, the third aspect, refers to the fact that the "I" is designated in dependence upon the aggregates. This is in contrast to the ordinary way we perceive the aggregates, which is as permanent, unitary, and autonomous entities.

The fourth refers to the fact that the "I" or the aggregates do not have independent existence and are therefore selfless. Understanding this counteracts the mistaken perception that holds the aggregates to be self-existent.

TRUE CAUSE

The four characteristics of the second noble truth, the true cause of suffering, are cause, origin, ever-enhancing, and condition. The basis upon which we establish these four characteristics is karma and delusions. The four mistaken modes of engagement in relation to true cause are perceiving suffering as not arising from causes and conditions, perceiving suffering as being caused by a creator, perceiving suffering as arising from one single cause, and thinking that although the nature of the cause is permanent, it is temporarily changeable.

We begin by thinking that karma and delusions are causes, which bring a result. And of course, if we think a bit further, we understand that the result that they bring is suffering. This kind of contemplation counteracts our mistaken perception that suffering just happens, without arising from specific causes and conditions.

The second point is that karma and delusions are the origin of all. This means that karma and delusions are the origin of every type of suffering—the suffering of suffering, the suffering of change, the suffering of pervasive conditioning—and that they cause it over and over and over again. This counteracts our mistaken perception that suffering is caused by a creator.

The third characteristic of karmic action and delusion is the attribute of being ever-enhancing. This means that whatever suffering result they generate is generated very powerfully and for a long time. This counteracts our mistaken perception that suffering arises from a single cause.

The fourth point is that karma and delusions are a condition for the suffering of all sentient beings. Because things are affected by conditions, we should understand that they cannot be permanent. This counteracts our mistaken perception that although the nature of the cause is permanent, it is temporarily changeable.

TRUE CESSATION

Next are the four attributes of true cessation. As ordinary beings we have yet to attain cessation, and therefore cannot establish these attributes on the basis of our own minds, so on what basis should we establish them? We can establish them either on the basis of our own future liberation, on the basis of the mind of a Hinayana arhat, or on the basis of the mind of a Mahayana arya bodhisattva. It is essential that they be established on the basis of a mind that has abandoned the truth of suffering and the truth of the cause of suffering. The four attributes are cessation, peace, being the abode of all benefit and happiness, and definite emergence. The four mistaken modes of grasping that they eliminate are thinking that there is no liberation, thinking that contaminated modes of existence are true states of peace, thinking that what is actually the suffering nature of existence is liberation, and thinking that there is temporary liberation but no ultimate liberation.

The first aspect is that a state of cessation is cessation itself. It is a cessation because it is totally free and entirely separate from the truth of suffering and the true cause of suffering. Once cessation is accepted as a reality, the mistaken view that there is no liberation is naturally eliminated.

The second characteristic is the attribute of peace. True cessation is a state in which everything that creates disturbance has been totally extinguished. Once peace is established as a characteristic of true cessation, it counteracts the mistaken perception that other, contaminated modes of existence are true states of peace.

The third attribute of true cessation is that it is the basis or the abode of all benefit and happiness. Once this is understood, it counteracts the mistaken perception that what is actually the suffering nature of existence is liberation.

The fourth attribute is that cessation is definite emergence in the sense that karma and delusions have been abandoned in such a way that they cannot ever arise again. Once this is understood, it counteracts the mistaken perception that temporary liberation is possible, but ultimate liberation does not exist.

In order to undertake analytical meditation on the four attributes of true cessation, you must have the basis of some understanding of the meaning of emptiness. With no idea of emptiness or the meaning of emptiness and with a mind strongly grasping at true existence, you will be unable to appreciate these four attributes. Some individuals are born with a natural inclination to feel faith for the four noble truths, cause and effect, and past and future lives. Because of this natural tendency within the mind, these people also have the wish for cessation, the wish to engage in the path to reach cessation, and the wish to abandon suffering and the cause of suffering. However, if we were not born with this kind of tendency, we should make an effort to study and contemplate the teachings on emptiness and the meaning of emptiness, and through the force of our understanding begin to appreciate the workings of the four noble truths.

True Path

In order to attain true cessation it is necessary to rely upon an uncontaminated path, which in this case refers to the uninterrupted path of seeing. We need to know the aspects and the objects of this path. And in order to do that, again, we need to realize emptiness directly.

The basis upon which we apply the four attributes of true path is the direct realization of selflessness—the direct realization of the truth in the mind of a yogic practitioner. The four attributes of true path are the path itself, accomplishment, being a knower, and being a definite bestower. The four misconceptions eliminated by these four attributes are thinking that there is no path to liberation, thinking that some of the benefits that we attain on certain levels of meditative concentration are a state of liberation, thinking that certain specifics of contaminated modes of existence are a path to liberation, and thinking that there is no path to liberation that enables a total cessation of suffering.

The first of the four attributes is the path itself, which refers to the wisdom that realizes emptiness, the means to liberation. Realizing emptiness eliminates the mistaken perception that there is no path to liberation.

The second characteristic is accomplishment. Once the practitioner has the direct realization of the truth, he or she understands that there is no determined object of the ignorance that grasps at true existence, that such an object of these two modes of grasping does not exist at all. This counteracts the mistaken perception that the peace that we can attain on certain levels of meditative concentration is a state of liberation.

The third characteristic is that the path is a knower. The wisdom that realizes selflessness in the mind of a yogi is the antidote to the root of ignorance, thus it becomes a knower. Understanding this eliminates the mistaken perception that certain specifics of contaminated modes of existence are a path to liberation.

The fourth characteristic is that the path is a definite bestower, in the sense that as the practitioner trains on the path, the power of meditation is enhanced to its limitless potential. Once this antidote is applied to the delusions, none of the delusions will ever arise again in the mind. Understanding this eliminates the mistaken perception that there is no path to liberation by which one can attain the total cessation of suffering.

True path exists only in the mind of a superior being. If it is an arya path, it is necessarily a true path. Now you may wonder: must a cognition be a direct valid perception in order to be a true path? Not necessarily, because within cognitions that are considered true paths, there are conceptual valid perceptions and there are also direct valid perceptions. For example, an arya bodhisattva's conventional bodhichitta, until enlightenment, is a conceptual state of mind. So the bodhichitta of a bodhisattva from the first to the tenth ground is still a conceptual state of mind, although it is considered a true path.

The Nature of
the Path to Liberation

THE KIND OF BASE FROM WHICH
ONE ATTAINS LIBERATION

THE KADAMPA MASTERS SAY that this perfect human rebirth is an extraordinary opportunity, and that therefore we should be discerning and make use of it. Having a precious human rebirth but merely working in the service of our own self-cherishing mind is like being very rich but not using our resources to help others. The Kadampa masters caution us to use our intelligence to understand the value of what we have attained, and not squander our lives on selfish purposes. Using our precious human rebirth to achieve only the temporary pleasures of this lifetime is the most meager use of our potential. One Kadampa master says that, until now, without wisdom, we have been circling endlessly in cyclic existence under the control of karma and delusions. If we continue on like this we will only make things worse for ourselves. But now, with our eight freedoms and ten endowments, we actually have the opportunity to free ourselves from the prison of samsara. We should not waste such a fortunate occasion.

Once we have attained a human rebirth and met the Dharma, there are many ways we can organize our lives in order to practice the path to the best of our ability. The most conducive basis for cultivating the foundation of the path, the mind of renunciation, is the life of an ordained monk or nun. Living as a householder or layperson, generally speaking, we will experience more obstacles to being able to cultivate the mind of renunciation. As householders, we create a cyclic existence within cyclic existence itself—with endless obligations, responsibilities, and so forth. If we have a family, we cannot live as simply as we could if we were alone, and we experience the problems of having to work continuously to secure and maintain our livelihood. If we are a layperson without a family, we find ourselves in a different mess, distracted by trying to find an appropriate partner and so forth. As a result of these circumstances, it is much more difficult to cultivate a mind that has less desire and more contentment.

Of course, this perspective on the life of a householder is very general, and there are exceptions. While it may be true that often there more obstacles to the spiritual path for a layperson or a householder, even as a layperson or a householder renunciation and liberation are still possible. One of the best examples of how this is so is the example of the great Marpa himself, who completed the entire spiritual path as a householder.

For those of you who have chosen to live your lives as ordained people, you should keep in mind that changing your physical appearance is a start, but that the ordination of the mind is the essence of practicing as a monk or nun. Ordination of the mind means cultivating a mind that has no desire, or at least less desire, and cultivating a sense of contentment in the richness of your own spiritual practice. Geshe Sopa Rinpoche has a particular way of describing how an ordained person should appear. Geshe Sopa-la says that ordained people should be like a beautiful jeweled ornament for the minds of the fortunate, faithful ones who behold them, and that as an ordained person you should be so rich in the accumulation of merit that you, yourself, become a field of merit for others.

A life in ordination is praised not only as an excellent foundation upon which to generate renunciation on the medium scope, but also as a perfect basis from which to practice the bodhisattva's conduct of the perfection vehicle. It is also praised as the most conducive basis from which to bring about the result of enlightenment by the practice of the tantric vehicle. In the *Kalachakra Tantra* it is said that the most superior form for the vajra master to take is that of a fully ordained person, the next best is the form of a novice, and the third best is the form of a layperson or householder.

The foundation of ordination is praised so highly because the vows that are taken by monks and nuns in the presence of the buddhas of the ten directions, bodhisattvas, abbots, and preceptors in themselves are able to distance practitioners from their delusions. On this basis, the practitioner is able to accumulate a great amount of virtue with few obstacles. However, we must also keep in mind that there is a much greater risk when one practices this way, for when a practitioner has the basis of these vows and makes mistakes, the accumulations of negative karma can also be much worse.

THE KIND OF MEDITATION PATH FROM WHICH ONE ATTAINS LIBERATION

From Nagarjuna's *Friendly Letter:*

Even if your head or clothing should catch on fire
Forsake extinguishing it
And make effort to end rebirth.
There is no purpose more supreme than that.

Some people believe that liberation is a special place—a place that has a shape, color, and so forth. Sometimes it is described as resembling a white upside-down umbrella, or the sun, or the moon. In reality, however, true liberation is the state that is attained on the basis of training the mind in the practices of the three higher trainings: the training in ethics, the training in concentration, and the training in wisdom.

The Three Higher Trainings

At the moment, we are bound to cyclic existence because we are under the control of our minds, and our minds are under the control of our delusions. As a result, we find ourselves in a state of complete distraction all the time, consistently unfocused, and unable to apply ourselves to the meaningful pursuit of the spiritual path. The method to overcome this unfortunate state is the practice of the first of the three higher trainings, the training in ethics. However, in order to completely subdue the mind, accomplishing the higher training in ethics alone is not sufficient—we must also develop our minds in meditative concentration. Without the basis of single-pointed placement and the strength of meditative equipoise, we will be unable to stabilize our realizations, and unable to focus our minds on virtue. And eventually, we will even find that developing the mind in the higher training in ethics and the higher training in concentration is not sufficient.

In order to free our minds completely from the control of the delusions and their seeds, we will also need to practice the training in higher wisdom.

On the basis of the three higher trainings, a yogic practitioner can accomplish every objective on the path of subduing the mind. According to the Chittamatra presentation, the practices of the three higher trainings will bring three distinct results. The higher training in ethics will bring the result of a perfect human rebirth, which is the best state of rebirth from which to accomplish our spiritual goals. The higher training in concentration will bring rebirth in the form and formless realms. And the higher training in wisdom, on the basis of these two, will bring liberation, or the true cessation of suffering.

The Madhyamaka school presents the three higher trainings from the perspective of the objects to be abandoned, which are the gross manifestation of the delusions and their seeds. According to this presentation, when we practice the higher training in ethics, although we have not yet abandoned the gross delusions and their seeds, we are restrained from engaging in negative actions on a physical level. Through the higher training in concentration we are able to actually cease the gross manifestation of the delusions entirely. And finally, through the higher training in wisdom we are able to accomplish the complete cessation of the delusions and their imprints.

We may wonder why the three higher trainings are arranged in this particular order. The answer is found in a sutra that was taught at the request of Brahma, which says that in order to establish the basis, we need roots that are very firm and stable. The higher training in ethics is like the ground or the foundation upon which we can build the rest of the structure, which are the trainings in concentration and wisdom. And, subsequently, wisdom can only arise on the basis of the strength of single-pointed concentration. We can think of the higher training in ethics as the body, the higher training in concentration as two very strong arms, and the higher training in wisdom as a very sharp ax. Our delusions and their seeds are the tree.

The Higher Training in Ethics
In accordance with the text, among the three higher trainings, the higher training in ethics is discussed most extensively in the section on the medium scope. We will begin with a short discussion of the benefits of living in pure ethics.

It is often said that living in ethics is the basis of Buddhist practice. Your refuge vows become the basis of your pratimoksha vows, for example, which in turn can become the basis of your bodhisattva vows. Your bodhisattva vows in turn become the basis of your tantric vows. Thus we can see that the practice of ethics pervades every type of practice in which we could wish to engage on the Buddhist path. This in itself should convince us that the benefits of the practice of ethics are immeasurable. In addition, in our everyday lives—whatever our lifestyle, whatever our work—whatever we undertake with a strong foundation in moral principles, anything is possible. In our studies, as well, whatever wisdom we are able to cultivate through listening, understanding, and meditating on the basis of the practice of ethics will never degenerate. And in trying to implement our studies into reality, ethics is like a medicinal tree that cures us of the sickness of every nonvirtue. As Nagarjuna has stated, ethics is the very foundation of all of the qualities that we develop within ourselves.

If a container is broken, how can it hold anything? In the same way, how can those with broken ethics ever develop positive qualities, since the basis itself is in pieces? As a lame person cannot walk for long distances, how can someone without morality ever make their way to liberation? Buddha himself taught that after his passing the essence of his teachings would remain in the practice of higher ethics. Therefore, living in Vinaya or in the ethics of moral discipline is living in the very heart of Buddha's teachings. In sutra, Buddha states that keeping pure ethics and understanding the benefits of living this way become happiness in itself. In contrast, of course, when one lives in ethics for the sake of reputation or respect or for some other sort of worldly gain, it becomes suffering.

If, due to the circumstances of our existence, we should happen to incur transgressions of our code of ethics, we should remember to purify them and correct our behavior at once. We should also remember that it is often said that compared to living in numberless forms of ethics in the time of Buddha when the teachings were so well established, living purely in just one form of ethics in the degenerate times of today is more meritorious.

How do we define ethics, or morality, exactly? Ethics is the quality of mind that wishes to protect and abstain from nonvirtue and negativity. Protect what? Protect the body, speech, and mind. Abstain how? Abstain with body, speech, and mind. There are various parts to any nonvirtuous action we engage in. The preliminary part is the motivation, which is followed by the actual course of action, which in turn is followed by the completion of the action. The quality of mind that wishes to protect our thoughts and actions from nonvirtue is an antidote to the motivation. It is also an antidote to the actual action.

How do we generate and strengthen the mental quality that wishes to protect and abstain? There are two methods to accomplish this. The first is to take vows or precepts from an abbot or a preceptor. The second is to seek to understand the shortcomings and failures of ignorance, attachment, and anger, and their antidotes.

For some, the practice of ethics brings happiness, and for others, it brings only suffering. For example, if one thinks, "I took these vows and precepts and if I break them or incur transgressions, it will cause me to take rebirth in the lower realms," one's practice of ethics will not become the cause of happiness. This is not the practice of living in ethics that brings joy. When you take on the practice of living in ethics, you should do so with the understanding that this practice is the antidote to your negative thoughts, such as attachment, anger, and ignorance. If you have the wisdom that understands the dependent arising of actions and their results, your practice of living in ethics will bring you great happiness.

In order to practice the higher training in ethics, we must have thoroughly examined the reasons for doing so. We must understand why it is necessary to protect our minds and abstain from nonvirtue and negativity. Also, we must understand what we need to protect our minds from. In addition to seeking protection from the three poisons, we should also consider that we need to protect our minds from the mistaken view of the way that things exist. This means that in order to practice the higher training in ethics perfectly, it is very important that we cultivate a little wisdom within our minds.

The obstacles that prevent us from living in pure ethics are the four gateways of downfall: not knowing, lack of conscientiousness, disrespect, and having many delusions.

The first gateway to downfall, not knowing, means not knowing the types of activities of the mind and body that are negative by nature, and not knowing the types of physical and mental activities that are negative because they contradict a particular discipline or a rule, or because by doing them you cause others to lose faith. The antidote to this downfall is to be familiar with whatever vows, precepts, and commitments you have taken.

The second gateway to downfall is lack of conscientiousness. Its antidote is not forgetting the teachings that you have had on what is to be abandoned and what is to be cultivated. If you remember these things, you will automatically develop awareness of whatever transgressions of body, speech, and mind you may commit. There are three ways to generate a sense of conscientiousness in your thoughts and actions: having a sense of humility in relation to yourself and Dharma, having consideration for others, and having fear of the future suffering that could result from whatever transgressions of ethics you incur.

The third gateway to downfall is lack of respect for others, particularly lack of respect for our teacher, Buddha. If you have no respect for Buddha, you will have no consideration for his advice and teachings. Also, you should be wary of lack of respect for those who live in pure ethics, as this can also become a gateway to incurring transgression. Disrespect, in this context, refers not only to physical manifestations of disrespect, but especially to the mental attitude of disregarding and disparaging Buddha's advice and teachings.

The fourth gateway to downfall is having many delusions. We should recognize the delusions that are strongest within our minds, and try our best to apply their antidotes.

As beginners on the path, we have not yet developed the antidote of the wisdom that realizes emptiness, which is able to cut through all of our delusions and liberate us entirely from suffering. However, the training of living in pure ethics is a practice that we should be able to manage, right now, today. It is not beyond our reach.

Many people in the Western world these days are afflicted with the mental sickness called depression. Depression happens when the mind is overcome by a very strong sense of craving—for a certain object, for a certain person, for a certain experience. As this craving grows and its wishes are not actualized, aggression arises in the mind. The combination of these two emotions then gives rise to a sense of hopelessness. In some cases the person may become suicidal, and in some cases the person may become deeply depressed. The root of this mental state is the combination of extreme attachment and anger.

When we are already caught up in these emotions, applying the ultimate antidote of wisdom that realizes selflessness is far beyond our ability. The best method to handle such an experience, therefore, is to prevent
it before it occurs. And the most extraordinary, supreme way we can
choose to prevent it is to live in the joy of pure ethics. In fact, living in the
joy of pure ethics is the best antidote for all of the gross delusions that arise
in our minds.

The mental sickness of depression can also arise from a deeply rooted
sense of discontent, combined with limitless desires and expectations for
what life will bring us. Living in ethics can help us to liberate ourselves
from unrealistic hopes and assumptions. It can enable us to appreciate our
lives without being trapped by desire.

Especially if you are a lay practitioner, you can familiarize your thoughts
and actions with the training in higher ethics through such virtuous activities as taking the eight Mahayana precepts. If you can wear the beautiful
cloak of the eight Mahayana precepts every so often in your life, it becomes
a path to prevent your mind from being overtaken by delusions, and also
another method by which to show respect and admiration for Buddha's
teachings.

The master Sharawa says that in order to discriminate between what is
good and bad in our life, we should utilize the guideline of Vinaya, the
code of moral ethics. If we make a decision according to the guidelines of
Vinaya, whatever decision we make will bring peace and happiness to our
minds. Whatever result comes from that decision, we can be assured that
it will be a very good or fortunate result. Even monks and nuns practicing
the tantric path should hold the practice of Vinaya in highest regard. In
fact, particularly if you are a tantric practitioner, there is absolutely no way
you can disregard the teachings on living in ethics. The attainments of the
tantric path have no basis without the training in higher ethics. In fact,
there is no tantra that disregards Vinaya. Vinaya itself is the basis of tantra.

Of course, sometimes what is permitted in tantric practice is not permitted in Vinaya. In the cases of those individuals who are able to perform
extraordinary acts of benefit for others, even if Vinaya does not allow a
particular action, if tantra allows it, it can be undertaken. For example,
some very highly realized practitioners of tantra utilize the enjoyments of
attachment on the path to enlightenment. Since they are able to engage in

these activities without incurring any of the negative karma that is usually associated with the mind of attachment, this kind of conduct is considered permissible for these individuals. The restrictions in Vinaya are made only to prevent the practitioner from accumulating certain kinds of heavy negative karma that are ordinarily associated with certain actions. If a being with exceptionally high realizations is able to engage in that kind of action without accumulating the negative karma, and indeed instead accumulates great stores of positive karma, the action itself is permitted.

However, for those beings without realizations, as most of us are, whatever is not permitted in Vinaya is understood not to be permitted in tantra as well.

Generally, there are the rules of discipline that were set forth by Buddha and there are rules of discipline that are set forth within the Sangha. Of the two, the rules and regulations set forth within the community are considered more important. This is because whatever is set forth in the community includes the rules of discipline set forth by Buddha. And, in comparison to Buddha's rules of moral discipline, which are set forth in a very general context, the details of the rules of discipline created within the Sangha community are very specific—dependent on the time and the specific circumstances of those particular individuals.

There are many, many benefits discussed in the texts that describe how important it is to observe the internal rules of a Sangha community. The harmony within a Sangha community is the basis for happiness. Yet of all the hardships that we could ever encounter, the hardship of maintaining harmony within a community is the greatest, and the most admirable.

A Brief Explanation of the
Higher Training in Concentration

In the *Lamrim Chenmo,* the extensive instructions on the trainings in concentration and wisdom are set forth in the later sections on calm abiding and superior insight, within the context of the bodhisattva's practice of the six perfections. As the instructions for cultivating meditative concentration and the wisdom that realizes emptiness are exactly the same according to the three higher trainings and the training of the six perfections, I will present only a general explanation of each here, and leave the detailed explanations for later.

From *Thirty-Seven Practices of Bodhisattvas* by Togmay Sangpo:

By abandoning the objects of our delusions, we decrease the
    afflictions.
By abandoning mental wandering, we increase our practice of
    virtue.

In order to decrease the occasions when our mind gives rise to the afflictions, we should keep away from the six causes of the delusions, as we discussed before. According to Vasubandhu, it is most important that we
maintain a distance from the objects of our delusions. If we abandon the
circumstances that give rise to our negative states of mind, we will naturally experience a decline in those delusions. It will eventually become natural for us to place ourselves in a conducive environment, where our minds
are distant from the delusions, and where we have space to apply the antidotes to our negative thoughts should they arise.

Also, as this quote mentions, by abandoning mental wandering we are
able to increase our virtuous activities. The method to abandon mental
wandering is the practice of concentration. Distractions can be brought on
by internal or external conditions. Ordinarily, our minds are like cities of
distractions—giving rise to countless superstitions and conceptual thoughts.
Calming the city of distraction that we have within our own minds and
maintaining focus on our objectives becomes the basis upon which we can
enhance our virtuous thoughts and actions, and the basis to cultivate the
realizations on the path. When we are able to free our minds from the
objects of the delusions and distractions, we will then find it much easier
to discriminate clearly between what to practice and what to abandon.

This verse concludes by saying that seeking solitude is the practice of the
bodhisattvas. *Solitude* refers to the solitude of place. Right now, we are
under the control of the mind, and the mind itself is under the control of
the delusions. Therefore, ultimately, we are under the control of our delusions. We thus lack the wisdom to be able to differentiate right from wrong
and in general our minds are more closely associated with the delusions
than with their antidotes. So in order to gain victory, in order to conquer
the delusions, we seek solitude so as to distance ourselves from our delusions in order to cultivate their antidotes within our minds.

Why do we need to seek the refuge of solitude in order to ascertain Dharma with a clear mind of wisdom and cultivate the antidotes? Isn't it possible to live in the midst of our distractions and still learn about Dharma? Of course it is possible. To merely gain an intellectual understanding of the Dharma we needn't seek solitude. However, in order for the Dharma to become a path that will benefit our future lifetimes, and in order to be able to effectively subdue our minds, we need solitude in order to be able to develop the antidotes to our delusions.

Shantideva says:

In this way becoming weary of objects of desire,
Develop joy in solitude
Within the peaceful forest,
Empty of argument and conflict.

In sutra it is said that solitude prevents contamination, which means the contamination of our deluded states of mind. This is the greatest advantage of solitude. A contaminated, or deluded, state of mind brings only misery and physical and mental suffering. However, in solitude, we are able to keep distant from the conditions that give rise to the delusions, and thus are less likely to experience their gross manifestations. In solitude, we are also able to pacify the mind of its addiction to conceptuality and superstition.

However, seeking solitude merely for the purpose of enjoying these benefits alone is not sufficient. We must also have the foundation of a sense of aversion for the desires of the mind. Physically isolating ourselves from the world alone will not ensure mental retreat from the afflictions. If we do not have a sense of aversion for the objects of the mind's desire, we will be unable to utilize the circumstances of our solitude to bring forth any beneficial result.

The reason that we do all of these practices and all of these trainings is to become a good person, a better person. That is the objective. Even in solitude the result that we are seeking is to become a good human being. Therefore, the most essential thing that we have to learn is how to become less selfish and how to cherish and benefit others more. This is the way that we become a good human being. Benefiting others does not mean that we have to try to help each and every individual sentient being right now. It means that we should try to enhance the mental qualities that wish to do this, and on that basis expand the capacity of our minds in order to actually bring this about. If benefiting others meant that you had to actually meet every sentient being and do something to benefit them right then, we would have to say that even Buddha has failed in that respect.

If we have only the thought of cherishing ourselves, no matter what we do, everything that we seek to accomplish will only move further and further out of reach. But if we cultivate the thought of cherishing others, everything that we seek—happiness, good reputation, praise, material gain—will come to us. This is the natural reality of how things work.

From the moment our lives begin, every minute that passes brings us closer and closer to our inevitable death. If we cannot effect any kind of positive changes within ourselves while we are alive, when we die, we will depart totally empty-handed, in complete poverty. That would be a tremendous loss of opportunity.

A Brief Explanation of the Higher Training in Wisdom

In the *Commentary on the "Compendium on Valid Cognition,"* Dharmakirti states that although love and compassion are very highly regarded mental states, they cannot directly combat ignorance by themselves alone. Therefore, it is necessary to pursue the realization of emptiness. In the medium scope, this mode of practice makes up the third of the three higher trainings on the path of individual realization. In the great scope, the practice of the wisdom that realizes emptiness makes up the sixth perfection on the path of the bodhisattva.

At present, our limited understanding of the way that conventional and ultimate reality exist can be compared to a child's first attempts at drawing a house. Our ideas are very rough, and our renderings are very crude. However, let us suppose that this child perseveres in perfecting the house that he has drawn—that he draws it again and again, throughout his life, until eventually he grows up, becomes an architect, and is able to render this house on paper precisely as it should be built. In the same way, as we study the philosophical texts, contemplate their meanings, and meditate to actualize our understanding, we will, over time, be able to perfect our view.

Examining the examples, logic, and quotations in relation to the subject matter of emptiness is the first step. Even if we unable to understand clearly or in great depth at first, we should still make great effort in our listening and studying. In the future these efforts will benefit us.

An Explanation of Conventional and Ultimate Reality
According to the Diamond Cutter Sutra

> Like a star, a cataract, a butter lamp
> An illusion, a drop of dew, a water bubble
> Like a dream, a bolt of lightning, a cloud—
> View all compounded phenomena in this way.

These nine examples from the *Diamond Cutter Sutra* were taught by Buddha for the purpose of eliminating ignorance from our minds and helping us to realize the way things actually exist. Right now, due to ignorance, we are continually making incorrect assumptions about reality. We see something that appears pleasant, then we grasp at it, impute additional qualities onto it, and grasp at it even more. In this way, we generate all the poisonous states of mind and accumulate negative karma.

If you close your fist and pretend that there is something wonderful in the palm of your hand, make lots of noise and get very excited, and tell a child to come and see, merely by your behavior, the child will grow certain that you are holding something really great. On the basis of this, that child will generate great hope, expectation, and excitement, and will wait with eager impatience for you open your hand and share. As long as we habitually grasp at the true existence of all of the people, things, and events in our lives, we are just like that child, and we are susceptible to exactly the same mistake.

From Chandrakirti's *Supplement to the "Middle Way"*:

> One will find and hold two natures for all things, seeing [in them] ultimate reality and conventional reality.

In daylight, when the sky is clear, although the stars have not gone anywhere, they cannot be seen. This is analogous to what appears to the mind of an arya being in meditative equipoise on emptiness, who sees the ultimate nature of phenomena. To this kind of consciousness, there is no appearance of true existence, no appearance of duality, no appearance of conventional reality at all.

When night falls, however, and there is no sunlight, the stars shine brightly into the same sky. This is analogous to way that phenomena appear to the mind of an ordinary being, who perceives existence with the stains of the imprints of ignorance. Such an ordinary consciousness perceives what is pure as impure, what is impure as pure, what is suffering as happiness, and so forth. Due to the force of the pollutions of the mind of ignorance, conventional existence appears to an ordinary consciousness.

Thus, we can say that the analogy of the stars represents the dual nature of all phenomena: the manner in which things appear to a nonconceptual wisdom consciousness, such as that in the mind of an arya being, and the manner in which things appear to ordinary conceptual consciousness, such as that in the mind of an ordinary being with no realizations. The former is the ultimate mode of existence and ultimate truth, and the latter is the conventional mode of existence.

It is important to understand here that to the wisdom consciousness of the mind of meditative equipoise, the *appearance* of a phenomenon and its *actual mode of existence* are in complete accord. In contrast, however, to an ordinary mind, the appearance of a phenomenon and its actual mode of existence are completely discordant. Every conditioned phenomenon possesses conventional reality and ultimate reality. But this does not mean that the two aspects are unrelated.

To give another example of how to establish conventional and ultimate reality on the basis of one entity, suppose that a person named Peter comes from the West, meets a Tibetan lama, studies for a while, and generates renunciation. On this basis Peter becomes ordained and is given the name Tenzin. The basis is the same. The person is labeled Peter because he is a suitable base to be called Peter. He is later named Tenzin because he later becomes a suitable base to be called Tenzin.

From *Supplement to the "Middle Way"*:

> [If it existed,] even [one] without cataracts would perceive the falling hair. Because this is not the case, [the falling hair] does not exist.

Here, the example of the cataract represents the appearance of existence to a consciousness that is polluted by ignorance, which sees true, inherent existence in phenomena. Although this is what appears to and is apprehended by the mind polluted by the imprints of ignorance, in reality this mode of existence does not exist at all. In the same way, the appearance of the falling hair in space exists only to the eye that is obscured by cataracts. Outside of the perception of that consciousness, the falling hair does not exist at all.

The fact that inherent existence does not exist at all is proven by the fact that when the inherent existence of any object is sought by an unmistaken consciousness, it cannot be found. In the same way, the falling hair in space cannot be found when sought by the person with faultless eyesight.

From the *Sutra Showing the Display of Armor:*

All phenomena arise by
The collection of many conditions together.
Because of the collection of many conditions
There is no inherence.

The explanation of the third example—the flame of a butter lamp—is intended to eliminate the extreme of nihilism in the practitioner's mind. Although, as we have already established, phenomena do not exist from their own side or by their own characteristics or nature, neither are phenomena nonexistent. The result of the flame of a butter lamp arises from the collection of many causes and conditions: the lamp itself, the wick, the butter, the match. Although we cannot say that the flame of the butter lamp itself resides in any of these parts, it has undeniably arisen from them. In the same way, although we cannot say that any phenomenon resides inherently in any of its parts, neither can we can say that phenomena are nonexistent. Existence itself is established based on the dependent arising of causes and conditions.

From the *Commentary to "Four Hundred Stanzas":*

That which occurs like an illusion is not nondeceiving, because things that abide as [one] aspect appear as another aspect.

This means that what is noninherently existent by nature appears to be inherently existent, and is therefore deceptive. This is illustrated by the example of the illusion.

The traditional explanation of the illusion is the example of the magician who creates beautiful and terrible mirages that manipulate our emotions and cause us to experience attachment, aversion, and so forth. However, something that may seem a little closer to our lives in the twenty-first century is the example of a television program. If we see something very beautiful or pleasant on a television show, attachment and desire rise within us. If we see something unpleasant or horrible on a television show, aversion and anger rise within us. This is in spite of the fact that we are generally aware that what we are seeing on television is not actually real—it is a scripted story, or a doctored image.

This is the way that illusions function in our lives to affect us, and similarly, the way that we perceive our existence away from the television set is affected by the pollutions of the imprints of ignorance. We are propelled by the force of our karma and delusions from lifetime to lifetime, and in each of these lifetimes we experience various forms of happiness and suffering arising from our attachment, aversion, and so on. Because we do not understand the nature of conventional and ultimate existence—as illustrated by the previous examples of the star, the mirage, and the flame of the lamp—we experience every illusion as a reality, and our happiness and suffering arise on this basis.

From Maitreya's *Discrimination between the Middle Way and Extremes:*

The meaning of impermanence is the meaning of nonexistence.

A drop of drew on a blade of grass is so delicate that even the rays of the rising sun will dry it up, or a strong wind may blow it away. The happiness that we experience in our lives is similarly fragile.

In his commentary on this verse from the *Diamond Cutter Sutra,* Konchog Tenpai Dronme states:

The tiny dewdrop on the end of the blade of grass has an extremely unstable nature, such that it will instantly dry up due to even a small condition such as being touched by light. In the same way, all compounded phenomena, once they are established, without depending on a later cause, possess a transient nature. They are not even a little bit trustworthy.

The example of a water bubble also represents the nature of our happiness in cyclic existence. When a bubble arises from the water, it is very pleasant, shining, and nice. However, when it bursts, as it inevitably will, it returns to the nature of water. In the same way, as long we are in samsara, in the space between the peak of one gross suffering and the peak of the next, we experience the pleasant, shining bubble that we call happiness. However, soon enough, the bubble will burst and return to its original state of suffering. This is called the suffering of change, and it is very deceptive, because it appears in our lives disguised as happiness.

Ordinary sentient beings such as ourselves instinctively categorize our experiences as good or bad, happiness or suffering. According to these categories, we then experience feelings of pleasure or unhappiness. Beings who have realized emptiness directly, however, understand that all contaminated phenomena are in the nature of suffering, and thus, from the beginning, they do not make these kinds of distinctions. As a result, they do not experience contaminated feelings of pleasure or unhappiness. From their perspective, living in cyclic existence is like living on the point of a needle—there is never a single moment of happiness. From the very depths of cyclic existence up to the highest peak of the form and the formless realms, all of our existence is brought on by karma and delusions, and therefore can only bring suffering.

The last three examples from the verse in the *Diamond Cutter Sutra* use the three times—the past, the present, and the future—to illustrate emptiness.

The first is the example of a dream, which shows the emptiness of our experiences of the past.

From chapter 7 of Nagarjuna's *Root Wisdom of the Middle Way*:

Like a dream, like an illusion,
Like a city of ghosts—
Like that [things] will arise and like that [things] will abide.
Like that, [things] will disintegrate.

When we remember things that we dream about, we generate attachment, anger, and so forth, even though the objects of the dream are not actually real. In the same way, although all the things that we have experienced in the past exist, they do not exist in the manner in which we grasp them, which is as truly, inherently existing experiences of happiness or suffering.

The emptiness of the present is shown by the example of a bolt of lightning. According to Konchog Tenpai Dronme:

> It is impossible to identify the source of lightning in the beginning, where it abides and remains in the middle, and where it goes in the end. In an instant the whiteness appears, and after that, it immediately becomes nonexistent.

As we cannot say that a bolt of lightning arose from here, abides here, and will end here, so we are unable to pinpoint the things of the present when we search for them. The things of the present are merely what lie between the things of the past and the future, thus their existence is entirely relative and imputed. From the commentary by Konchok Denpay Dronme:

> Although a mere empty sky cannot rain, from the accumulation of clouds in that sky, rain falls. Due to that, the ripened crops are able to produce fruit continuously.

The example of a cloud shows how emptiness is like the future. In the same way that the sky alone is unable to bring forth rain, the clear nature of mind alone is unable to wander in samsara or attain nirvana. However, when the appropriate causes and conditions of delusions, karmic seeds, and imprints of lower rebirths are brought together, the ripening result of future rebirth in cyclic existence can occur.

This concludes the discussion of the training of higher wisdom in accordance with the verse from the *Diamond Cutter Sutra*.

Becoming a Mahayanist

The bodhisattva Togme Zangpo says that when we train in compassion and bodhichitta, even if those we care for should suddenly become our worst enemies, we should behold them with the extraordinary love of a mother for her child who has fallen ill. How is it possible to cultivate this extraordinary sense of love? Our love and compassion for others must be unconditional. If we have unconditional love and compassion for others, even if they rise up as our most vicious enemies, our feelings and behavior will remain the same. In contrast, when our love and compassion are based on the fact that a certain person has been kind to us, is our friend or relative and so on, then should that individual suddenly become our enemy, we will no longer be able to think of them with such warm feelings.

The love and compassion of a mother for her only child are not quite at the level of a bodhisattva's, but they are perhaps the closest thing to it that we can find in this world. The mother has no expectation from her child, no hopes of any return, so in that sense, her love is unconditional. When a child becomes crazed, screaming and attacking the mother, she feels no animosity at all—rather she feels an even greater, more extraordinary sense of love and concern. In the same way, the beings that we encounter in our lives are suffering from the chronic disease of the delusions, so rather than holding on to these manifestations of the delusions as being truly existent and taking them personally, we should practice training in unconditional, extraordinary love and compassion.

In order to establish the foundation of the practice of unconditional love and compassion, you must first become aware of the faults in your own actions of body, speech, and mind. You should understand that your own actions are rooted in the ignorance that grasps at true existence, and that this is the core motivation for most of what you do. If you understand your own three poisonous states of mind, if you understand the three types of suffering, and particularly if you understand the way in which karma and delusions control you, should you happen to see the manifestations of negativity in the actions of others, you will find it easy to be more tolerant.

In *Ornament for the Mahayana Sutras*, Maitreya explains four distinct signs of a Mahayana practitioner. These are compassion, aspiration, patience, and joyful enthusiasm. Mahayana practitioners are endowed with a very pure, unbiased sense of compassion and a strong aspiration to study and understand the profound path of wisdom. In addition, Mahayana practitioners are endowed with patience for everything that they do and have the ability to endure any kind of physical, verbal, or mental difficulty in order to fulfill the objective of benefiting others. Mahayana practitioners are also endowed with joyful enthusiasm for engaging in virtuous activities from the very beginning to the very end. These four signs establish a person in the family of the Mahayanist. Within the seven-point instructions on cause and effect,[29] at the point where the practitioner has generated the altruistic mind that takes complete responsibility to fulfill the benefit of others, which is the sixth step, all of the signs of a Mahayanist are complete.

Within the same text, Maitreya presents the four hindrances that become obstacles to entering the family of the Mahayanist. These four hindrances arise without exception from the basis of our self-cherishing mind and ego-grasping ignorance. The first hindrance is being addicted or overly habituated to the delusional minds because of self-cherishing and the ignorance that grasps at true existence. The second hindrance is being unduly influenced by negative friends. The third obstacle is lacking favorable internal and external conditions, meaning that one lacks the merit of virtue strong enough to assemble conducive conditions for practicing the path. If, for your part, you have great interest in Dharma and great interest in practicing the path, but the inner and outer conditions simply won't come together to allow you to do so, this is due to lack of the merit of virtue. The fourth obstacle is being totally under the control of somebody else. In this text the example is given of a person who is under the control of a king, such as a slave and so forth. However, in general this can be taken to mean being in any situation where you are essentially an animal hooked up to the reins that someone else is directing left or right.

In order to avoid experiencing these difficult situations, first and foremost, we must try not to become too habituated to our negative and delusional ways of thinking. We must also try to avoid negative influence from friends. In order to have all the conducive internal and external conditions, we should try to accumulate the merit of virtue. And we should avoid falling under the control of others. As a note, this doesn't mean that you have to be so independent that you eliminate your spiritual teachers!

The mind of an individual is empty of true existence. Because of this it can be molded and shaped, and positive transformation can come about. When spontaneous compassion arises in an individual's mind, he or she is established in the family of the Mahayana. Alternatively, when the intuitive, spontaneous aspiration for one's own liberation from delusions and karma arises, the individual is established in the family of the individual vehicle.

The individual vehicle is composed of the hearer's path and the solitary realizer's path. The basis of the mind that aspires for liberation is the same in both—an intense aversion for the source of the shortcomings of cyclic existence, which are karma and delusions. This aversion leads to the wish to be free of these things. A person in the last phase of attaining this liberation who wishes to accomplish that liberation completely on his or her own is established in the family of the solitary realizers. Those in the hearer family prefer to assemble all of the positive, supportive conditions of the advice of the spiritual teachers in order to attain liberation. Because these three ways of thinking are quite distinct, one person cannot generate all three aspirations at the same time.

Also, although we do present a path encompassing three distinctive vehicles that lead to various forms of liberation, we should remember that according to our system, there is ultimately only one vehicle. Although we speak in terms of the hearer's vehicle, the solitary realizer's vehicle, and the bodhisattva's vehicle, the ultimate vehicle is the one vehicle that enables us to attain enlightenment that is faultless, and fully complete in all the qualities of knowledge.

This point is debated among some of the lower schools. The Chittamatra school, for example, asserts that ultimately there are three vehicles. They say that before sentient beings enter the path, they have three distinct modes of aspiration. There are those who aspire toward the hearer's vehicle, those who aspire toward the solitary realizer's vehicle, and those who aspire toward the bodhisattva's vehicle. Once a practitioner enters any one of these paths, there are three distinct modes of practice, three distinct modes of accomplishment of those practices, and therefore, three distinct ultimate results. Therefore, they say, that there are three ultimate vehicles.

Both of the Madhyamaka schools, however, accept that ultimately there is only one vehicle. According to the Madhyamaka, even if individuals train in the hearer's or solitary realizer's path, they will eventually encounter Mahayana teachers and teachings and attain enlightenment on the bodhisattva's path.

According to the path and practice of the medium scope, the delusions within our minds and the prison of cyclic existence are objects that are to be unequivocally abandoned. However, in some texts we may see advice urging us *not* to cultivate aversion to samsaric existence. This can be the cause of some confusion. We should understand this point in the following way. Being averse to taking rebirth in cyclic existence means being averse to taking rebirth under the control of karma and delusions. When we, as ordinary beings, take rebirth in cyclic existence under the control of karma and delusions, we become ensnared in the cycle of the twelve links and experience suffering and many other undesirable things. However, bodhisattvas on the path of seeing and above do not take rebirth under the influence of karma and delusions. Their reincarnation into cyclic existence comes as a result of the power of prayer and compassion for sentient beings. Thus, those training on the bodhisattva path are advised not to cultivate aversion for samsara, as they take rebirth into the worlds for the purpose of benefiting others.

If we are born under the control of karma and delusions, as a result we experience continual suffering and cannot even help ourselves, much less benefit others. Therefore, those who aspire to the path of the bodhisattva have an even greater responsibility to abandon karma and delusions. Those training on the bodhisattva path also see the shortcomings of cyclic existence by contemplating true suffering and true cause according to the four noble truths, and by reflecting on the twelve links of dependent origination. By this means, these practitioners are able to develop a sense of renunciation in accordance with the three principal paths, which becomes the basis for their realization of bodhichitta.

The ultimate objective of a being training on the bodhisattva path is to benefit others with every single activity of one's body, speech, and mind. There are no bodhisattvas who are like us—capable of becoming overpowered, overwhelmed, and totally controlled by delusional thoughts that seek only our own interest. A bodhisattva's mind is the exact opposite of this—there is not even one iota of any kind of thought of seeking any kind of individual liberation, individual cessation of suffering, or individual attainment of peace or happiness. There is only the thought to bring about the benefit and happiness of others.

Within the Mahayana family, there are persons of definite family and persons of indefinite family. A person of definite family is one who from

the very beginning trains in the aspiration and path of the Mahayana vehicle. A person of indefinite family is one who initially trains in the aspiration and path of the individual vehicle, and then later on the path becomes
a Mahayana practitioner. Also, there are individuals of the family disturbed
by the conditions, and individuals of the family not disturbed by the conditions. An individual of the family disturbed by the conditions is one
who begins on the Mahayana path, but along the way meets some exceptional Hinayana teacher. This person then feels very inspired by the teachings of the Hinayana vehicle, and simultaneously feels hopelessly unable to
accomplish the objectives of the Mahayana. A person of the family not
disturbed by the conditions is a person to whom this does not happen.

This completes the topics of the medium scope according to the *Lamrim Chenmo.*

PART 5

The Great Scope

How Bodhichitta is the Doorway to Practicing the Great Vehicle

U P TO THIS POINT, we have discussed the path and practices of the small and medium scope extensively. Specifically, we have gone through the topics on guru devotion, the preliminary practices, precious human rebirth, and death and impermanence. On the basis of these topics, we have trained in the aspiration of the practitioner of the small scope. In addition to that, we have also discussed the practice of the medium scope in the context of the four noble truths—recognizing the shortcomings of true suffering and the necessity of abandoning true cause, attaining true cessation, and meditating upon the true path. We have also gained an understanding of the way that cyclic existence is caused, sustained, and perpetuated through the cycle of the twelve links of dependent origination, and an understanding of how to reverse them to attain nirvana. On the basis of this understanding, we have developed the aspiration of the practitioner of the medium scope—the aspiration to liberate ourselves from cyclic existence.

However, even if we fulfill this objective and are able to liberate ourselves from karma and delusions by the practices taught in the medium scope, according to the Prasangika-Madhyamika, although we may be released from karma and delusions, we have yet to abandon the imprints of ignorance completely. We have yet to embrace the state in which we are totally free of every failing and mistake, and have completely developed every positive quality.

Both the *Compendium of Perfections* by the Indian master Lopon Pawo and the *Sutra Taught for the Arhats* tell us that upon attaining the liberated state of an arhat, one has yet to accomplish the ultimate benefit for the world. Therefore, we are advised to abandon making the attainment of an

arhat our main objective. Instead, we should cultivate the wisdom that realizes emptiness conjoined with the thought of compassion, and engage in the
practices of the Mahayana path from the very beginning to the very end.

In *Ornament for the Mahayana Sutras*, Maitreya sets forth four characteristics that distinguish the universal vehicle, the Mahayana, from the
individual vehicle, the Hinayana.

The first is the extraordinary accumulation of virtue, which refers to
the fact that the extensive and far-reaching mind of compassion of a bodhisattva on the Mahayana path causes the accumulation of virtue to become
extraordinary. This is followed by the second characteristic, the fact that the
qualities of a practitioner in the Mahayana lineage become the basis of all
the qualities of the enlightened mind. In the same way, if you develop the
characteristics of a hearer or a solitary realizer, you will be able achieve the
result of a hearer or solitary realizer through meditation on that path.

The third is that the Mahayana path has a great purpose, in the sense
that the characteristics that we develop on this path allow us to fully manifest the qualities of the lineage and thereby bring about great benefit.
Great benefit refers to being able complete the accumulation of the merits
of virtue and wisdom, and thereby achieve the two bodies of a buddha—
the extensive accumulation of the merit of wisdom results in the body that
fulfills the ultimate benefit for self, and the extensive accumulation of the
merit of virtue results in the body that fulfills the ultimate benefit for others. By completing these accumulations, a Mahayana practitioner is able to
bring about a continual rain of activities benefiting sentient beings.

The fourth is the quality of inexhaustibility, meaning that in the state
of enlightenment one is able to effect a continual, uninterrupted flow of
virtue. In contrast, according to this text, in the attainments of the path of
the individual vehicle, such as the attainment of liberation without remainder, the continuum of the flow of virtue can be stopped.[30]

For some of us, it may actually seem very tempting to make the attainment of the individual cessation of suffering our goal, as opposed to spending three countless eons trying to accumulate merit on the Mahayana path.
After all, once we attain liberation, we are no longer subject to the control
of the delusions, and we experience absolute peace. However, if we examine the situation from the perspective of long-term benefit, it really is more
profitable to seek out the objectives of the mind that wishes to benefit

others from the very beginning. In so doing, we will also find that our own happiness is fulfilled. This is one of the extraordinary characteristics of the Mahayana path—by working solely for the welfare of others, there is no question that our own ultimate benefit will also be realized.

The *Compendium of Perfections* states that in the pure view of practitioners who have generated the wisdom that realizes emptiness, all existence is merely imputed. When we reach this stage, everything—suffering, happiness, liberation—is perceived as merely labeled, imputed by mind, empty of existing from its own side. Having attained such a level in our own spiritual attainment, to then work for the benefit of sentient beings is the most supreme and pure of all activities. Not doing so can be only be considered selfish.

Also, once we have generated renunciation and the understanding of wisdom realizing emptiness, we will be able to see clearly that we have had countless, beginningless lifetimes. Knowing this, we will know for a fact that every sentient being has been our mother many times over. Knowing them to be our mothers, knowing them to have nurtured us in the past with infinite kindness, and *still* not considering their suffering and wishing only to fulfill our own individual peace and happiness is really pitiful.

The thought seeking the welfare of others is rooted in the mind of compassion, and the mind of compassion is the greatest quality that we could ever develop. The reason it is said that Buddha's teachings are the one medicine for all sentient beings is because they include instructions on the methods to generate and cultivate compassion. The extent to which we will be able to benefit others and help to eliminate their suffering is entirely dependent upon the strength of our compassion.

Shantideva says:

What need for great explanation?
The childish ones work for their own benefit,
The buddhas work for the benefit of others.
Just look at the difference between them!

Among the practitioners who cultivate renunciation and the pure view, cultivating the supreme thought of bodhichitta is the difference between an ordinary path and a path to enlightenment.

Within the Mahayana there are two distinctive paths: the path of the causal vehicle of the bodhisattva and the path of the resultant vehicle of the Vajrayana. When we talk of "entering the Mahayana vehicle," we are referring to entering either the causal or the resultant vehicle. The gateway to both of these paths is bodhichitta. Whether we enter the Mahayana or not is completely dependent on whether we have bodhichitta. Once we have bodhichitta, even if we are lacking the wisdom realizing emptiness, we can still enter the Mahayana path. A practitioner who has generated the mind of bodhichitta but has not directly realized emptiness is a practitioner on the Mahayana path of accumulation. For example, practitioners who follow the Chittamatra view accept the true existence of phenomena. Despite the fact that they do not hold the highest view of ultimate truth, they can generate renunciation and bodhichitta, and enter the Mahayana path of accumulation.

In contrast, a practitioner who does not have bodhichitta in his or her mind, but does have the direct realization of emptiness still lacks the greatness of the Mahayana path. In fact, even those who attain liberation and then progress to generate bodhichitta and train in the Mahayana path are still in danger of falling back to the Hinayana path, because they are so long habituated to abiding in the peace and happiness of their own liberation.

In short, there is no way to enter the Mahayana path without bodhichitta in your mind. A bodhisattva far outshines an arhat by lineage by the measure of belonging to the Mahayana family, despite the fact that the arhat has totally eliminated every delusion from his or her continuum. A bodhisattva cannot, however, outshine an arhat by the measure of the quality of the mind until that bodhisattva has attained the level of the seventh ground and onward.[31] In sutra it is stated that even a tiny bit of diamond far outshines any other precious stone, even if it is in pieces, because diamond slivers are diamonds, nonetheless. Those beings who have bodhichitta in their minds are the same.

I wish to comment here that I hope you understand that this discussion is not meant to disparage the paths of the individual vehicle, but only to encourage you to widen your scope, and have the courage to travel the path of the Mahayana. Working toward your own individual cessation of suffering, your own individual peace and happiness alone, is not the best choice. This is the view of the practitioners of the great vehicle.

In order to develop compassion, we must first train in the awareness of suffering, and generate spontaneous renunciation.[32] When we have done this, we can then begin to think of these very same types of suffering in terms of others, and thereby begin to develop the mind of compassion.

As I have mentioned, Lama Atisha, the crown jewel of all the adepts of his time, studied the vast teachings on emptiness extensively, with many lamas, but received teachings on bodhichitta from a particular teacher named Lama Serlingpa. Although Lama Atisha had a great many masters, the one he had the highest regard for and the one he felt was most kind was Lama Serlingpa, because he was the source of the instructions on bodhichitta.

Shantideva says of the mind of bodhichitta:

The one that clears away one's ignorance—
Where is there a greater virtue?
Where is there a greater teacher?
Where is there greater merit?

So we see that there is absolutely nothing that equals the mind of bodhichitta. As we discussed earlier, those who take vows of individual liberation continuously accumulate the merits of living in those precepts. Likewise, once we generate spontaneous bodhichitta in our minds, it is always present—even when we are sleeping, even when we do virtuous activities with carelessness—under all circumstances we continuously accumulate the vast merit of bodhichitta. The virtue of the mind of bodhichitta is so great that it is even able to purify the most powerful negative actions, such as the five heinous crimes, so that they do not bring their ripening result.

When you churn the milk of the holy Dharma,
The essence is the butter of bodhichitta.

The benefits of the mind of bodhichitta are listed extensively in the first chapter of the *Guide to the Bodhisattva's Way of Life*. You should read this chapter, and in fact the entire text, and take from it great inspiration to practice the method aspects of the path.

Indeed, it is not sufficient that we merely study Mahayana philosophy, theory, and practice. It is important that we ourselves become people who embody the thought and activities of the universal vehicle. We should be cautious that our engagement in the Mahayana path doesn't become merely empty words, without meaning, without reality. What brings forth the reality of the Mahayana path within us, what makes us *Mahayanists,* is the attitude of bodhichitta—the thought renouncing self, cherishing others, and wishing to attain enlightenment solely for their benefit. The wisdom realizing emptiness held by the thought of compassion is the mind that will lead us to complete enlightenment. Therefore, it would not be false to say that the seed of attaining enlightenment is the thought of bodhichitta. Wisdom realizing emptiness is like the water, the soil, the sun—the conditions that cause the seed to grow. But the seed that ripens in enlightenment is the thought of bodhichitta itself.

Buddha Maitreya says in chapter 3 of *Ornament of Clear Realization:*

Because of wisdom, one will not remain in cyclic existence, and
Because of compassion, one will not remain in nirvana's peace.

Through the unified practice of method and wisdom, we can eradicate the affliction obscurations and the obscurations to omniscience that veil our minds, and thus attain full enlightenment. Method and wisdom are like the two wings of a bird that enable it to fly. Between the two, although bodhichitta is easier to understand than wisdom, actually cultivating bodhichitta within our minds is more difficult. Wisdom realizing emptiness is easier to develop because we can apply many different kinds of logic and reasoning in order to support our understanding and eventually gain realizations. The generation of the thought of bodhichitta, on the other hand, requires that we rely to a much greater extent on personal experience and training.

A Mahayana prayer says:

Just as I myself have fallen into the sea of samsara,
So have all sentient beings, who have been my mothers.

At the present time, our attitudes toward other sentient beings are very biased. Some sentient beings are our enemies, thus we feel aversion for them. Some sentient beings are strangers, thus we feel indifference toward them. Some sentient beings are close to us, thus we feel obsessively attached to them. All of these perspectives are mistaken. We should seek to eliminate all of these extreme, unrealistic attitudes, and cultivate loving-kindness and compassion in our minds. We should strive to hold every single sentient being as the object of our compassion and loving-kindness no matter what their relationship to us.

Every sentient being is, in reality, like a wish-granting jewel. Each one is the means to fulfilling the ultimate benefit for self and for others. Therefore, we should consider sentient beings to be more important than ourselves, and always maintain a pure attitude of respect toward them. Once we have begun to cultivate this kind of mentality, we should make prayers and requests to be able to continue to develop this attitude in this and future lifetimes.

Generally speaking, we all love and cherish ourselves. But the way we love and cherish ourselves arises from a mistaken view. Because of that mistake, we are still bound to the suffering of cyclic existence. Just as it is for ourselves, so it is in the case of other sentient beings. Other sentient beings also cherish themselves, but due to their mistaken views they too are continually caught up in the suffering of existence. We should make strong prayers to be able to bring forth the graduated path to enlightenment, which is the antidote to all of this, in our own minds and in the minds of others.

THE SIX GREAT QUALITIES

In *Ornament for the Mahayana Sutras,* Buddha Maitreya establishes six characteristics that make the Mahayana vehicle supreme. These are the greatness of the basis, the greatness of perseverance, the greatness of the result, the greatness of taking continual responsibility, the greatness of patience, and the greatness of the activities bringing about the pure result of enlightenment.

The greatness of the basis of the path refers to the fact that the Mahayana path is rooted in the practices of compassion and the development of the mind that seeks the benefit of others. All of the five Mahayana paths possess this attribute. It is this characteristic that establishes the practitioner in the Mahayana family.

The greatness of perseverance refers to the fact that a practitioner on the Mahayana path possesses great perseverance, enabling him or her to engage in whatever activity is necessary to bring about the goal of benefiting others. For example, a Mahayana practitioner first generates aspiring bodhichitta, the strong wish to attain enlightenment for the benefit of others. On this basis, the practitioner then generates engaging bodhichitta, and thereby engages in the conduct of a bodhisattva in order to complete that goal. No matter how difficult the tasks may be, the Mahayana practitioner maintains a sense of joyful perseverance. This is the greatness of perseverance.

The greatness of the result refers to the attainment of complete enlightenment through this path. This state of enlightenment is free of all failings and mistakes, and complete in all knowledge and qualities.

The greatness of taking continual responsibility refers in particular to taking the bodhisattva vow for the benefit of others. In the presence of all the buddhas and bodhisattvas, the practitioner of the Mahayana takes this vow to dedicate every activity of body, speech, and mind to activities seeking the welfare of others.

The fifth is the greatness of patience. A practitioner on the Mahayana path is able to voluntarily take on any problem, any amount of suffering, and deal with any difficult situation if doing so fulfills the benefit of others. The practice of the medium scope is to reflect on suffering and generate the strong determination to be free from it, which is renunciation. The extraordinary practice of the great scope practitioner, however, is to *voluntarily* take on suffering and problems instead of trying to avoid them. Rather than feeling burdened, the Mahayana practitioner takes suffering and problems as the method to facilitate progression on the path and, ultimately, to eliminate the source of suffering itself.

The sixth greatness is the greatness of engaging in all the activities that bring forth the pure result of the attainment of enlightenment solely for the benefit of others, and in that way being able to accomplish the ultimate benefit for sentient beings. This refers to the fact that practitioners on the Mahayana path, once they attain a certain level, are able to cause the minds of the sentient beings that they are karmically connected with to ripen. Upon ripening their minds, the Mahayanist can ultimately cause them to be liberated completely, and can subsequently cause that liberation to become the complete form of liberation.

According to Maitreya, these six points of greatness make the Mahayana path supreme. But of course, in order to engage in these practices, we first need to have trained our minds in the path and practices common to the small and medium scope, in the cultivation of renunciation and in the three higher trainings.

There are two ways to enter the Mahayana path. The first is to enter from the very beginning, meaning the practitioner begins training on the Mahayana path and follows the entire course of the Mahayana path to the end. The second is to begin training in the path of the individual vehicle, attain the state of an arhat, and then continue on the Mahayana path until the end. An individual who, on the basis of great compassion, engages in the path that unifies method and wisdom from the very beginning will attain the state of enlightenment in a shorter amount of time than the practitioner who begins from the base of the Hinayana path and enters the Mahayana path later on.[33]

Although the greatness of the result is, in reality, far out of our reach right now, it is definitely a result that we can attain in the future. As ordinary sentient beings, right now we are only able to perform activities that benefit sentient beings in a very minimal way, but upon attaining the fruit of enlightenment, we will finally be able to be of ultimate benefit. When we attain enlightenment, we can cause sentient beings' minds to ripen, and through that ripening we can cause their liberation.

Right now, as we are only training in the path, we cannot actualize these six great qualities. Even assuming that we can achieve these results within the period of one brief lifetime is perhaps expecting too much. Rather than rushing ahead, we should be very thorough, and begin with training in the path and practices that are common to the small and medium scope. Once we generate the mind of renunciation, we should reflect upon the suffering of others, and generate compassion. Having cultivated this thought, we should then train in the wisdom realizing the pure view. In this way, as we progress from lifetime to lifetime, we will complete the path and eventually attain our goal.

WHY WE NEED RENUNCIATION
TO DEVELOP COMPASSION

Renunciation is the essential foundation of pure compassion. Without an understanding of cyclic existence, and without the strong wish in our minds to be liberated from it, it will be impossible for us to develop very deep levels of compassion for sentient beings who are in the same situation, although we may be able to develop more superficial levels of tenderness for them. Cultivating renunciation is dependent upon understanding and recognizing suffering. We do not understand and recognize suffering on the basis of someone telling us that it works a certain way, or on the basis of reading about it. Recognizing suffering in order to effect renunciation has to be based on experience. We really need to have a feel for suffering, an experience of it, in order to develop renunciation. Therefore, we should not be averse to suffering, as it gives us the taste of this feeling. When everything is running very smoothly, there is no ground for renunciation. It is the experience of suffering that brings forth the transformation within our mind.

As I mentioned, it is also important to remember that in order to bring forth renunciation, it is not necessary that we experience every type of suffering. If we really get the feeling for what it means to experience even *one* type of suffering, based on the strength of that experience we can cultivate the mind of renunciation, the determination to definitely free ourselves from cyclic existence.

It is not so difficult for us to understand that suffering arises because of our delusions and because of our negative states of mind. However, understanding that our suffering arises because of karma—because of the causes of our own actions—is a little more challenging. In order to do so, we need to be very familiar with the workings of cause and effect and understand the way that karmic imprints ripen in the form of habits or tendencies similar to the cause in our minds. Then, once we have clearly established this, we should strive to understand it on an even more subtle level—that is, by understanding ignorance to be its root cause.

The reason we say that the root cause of all suffering is our ignorance of the ultimate mode of existence of things is because suffering is rooted in the way the "I" appears to us, and how we apprehend it. Although we may have a general intellectual understanding of how this works, it is really important for us to develop a more complete awareness, and to actually experience the ignorance grasping at the "I." The object that arises when we think "I" appears to exist totally independent of causes and conditions—inherently and truly existent. Not only does it *appear* to exist in this way, but also we intuitively *apprehend* it as existing in exactly that way. Because we are unable to see the way that the "I" appears and the way that we apprehend it clearly, it is hard for us to understand that the ignorance of ultimate reality is the cause of all our karma and delusions.

The way that we grasp at true existence is most apparent when we are experiencing strong emotions, such as extreme anger or extreme jealousy, in our everyday lives. These kinds of experiences are an opportunity to think about how this "I" arises, how our mind apprehends it, how it exists in relationship to the aggregates, and so forth. When we are under the sway of the negative emotions, we have the opportunity to get a very good picture of the way we grasp at the "I." At the moment, however, because we are not habituated to analyzing in this way, when opportunities arise, we are unable to make use of them. Nonetheless, with practice we can become familiar with this process. As we become habituated to the analytical process, we can begin to understand what is going on.

There is nothing false about this information. It is only logical that all of our delusions must have a cause. It is not logical to assume that the cause is the actions of the body alone. Of course, the body does act as a cooperative condition—the strength of the delusions can fluctuate depending on the body's vitality. For example, the attachment to sexual pleasure decreases as the body declines with age. However, although there are some external conditions that contribute, it is primarily our own deluded and afflicted minds that perpetuate and sustain our suffering and unhappiness. The delusions and afflictions are not in the innate nature of our minds— the mind is naturally luminous, clear, and knowing, and whatever defilements we experience are adventitious, and therefore can be totally removed or extinguished. As we begin to understand the innate nature of our mind and the fact that our defilements can be removed, we will develop a sense of confidence. This is not just a scriptural explanation, or merely theory. Even if we cannot counteract the delusions right away because we have yet to cultivate their antidotes, having a guideline of how all these things work will help us, so that should delusions manifest, at least we will understand what is happening.

Of the two types of obscurations, the principal object of abandonment in the great scope is the obscuration to omniscience. This refers to the imprints of our delusions. The main form of meditation in the great scope is the meditation on the wisdom realizing emptiness supported by the thought of bodhichitta. The principal form of attainment is the attainment of the state that is totally free of the two types of obscurations, the state of complete enlightenment.

Although on the Mahayana path we generate a sense of renunciation for cyclic existence at an even more extraordinary level than on the small and medium scope, we do not seek individual liberation from cyclic existence alone. For this reason, cyclic existence is not the main object of abandonment of the Mahayana path, nor are the delusions. When training in the path and practice common to the small and medium scopes, we think of suffering in terms of our own suffering, and thereby generate the thought of renunciation. In the great scope, by thinking of suffering in terms of the suffering of other beings, we develop the mind of compassion. This prevents us from falling into the extreme of seeking our own individual liberation.

In the medium scope section in the *Lamrim Chenmo* there is quite a lot of discussion about liberation, but nothing is ever mentioned about the resultant nirvana. We discuss the twelve links and the four noble truths in terms of the need to abandon the delusions, or solely from the perspective of the shortcomings of our afflicted states of mind. This shows that this section is intended to guide the disciple on the path and practice that is *common* to the medium scope, although the goal of our practice at this point, according to Lama Tsongkhapa, is not liberation or nirvana itself.

Shantideva says that in the course of trying to destroy our external enemies, we incur wounds upon our bodies, and yet we regard our scars and wounds as emblems of heroic deeds, as ornaments. Therefore, in the course of trying to destroy the internal enemy of our own delusions, why should we regard the suffering of mind and body that we experience as a burden? We should regard whatever difficulties we incur in the course of combating the internal enemy of the three poisons as a heroic achievement.

Although the delusions are not the main objectives to be abandoned on the Mahayana path, we should nonetheless regard the delusions as having great disadvantages and try not to come under their control. On the one hand, we should understand the shortcomings of the delusions and apply their antidotes, and on the other hand we should persevere in the activities benefiting others with the support of compassion for the suffering that they are experiencing.

ATTAINING THE FRUIT OF THE MAHAYANA PATH

In order to enter the Mahayana path, we must transform our ordinary gross minds into minds that can encompass the supreme thought of bodhichitta. Due to our strong familiarity with deluded ways of thinking over countless eons, this transformation can take time to unfold. Before we are able to complete this process, therefore, we may find it helpful to become familiar with the obstacles that hinder us from developing this supreme mental state as they are presented in the *Sublime Continuum* so that we will more easily be able to overcome them.

The first is attachment, which obscures our buddha-nature. Like the form of a buddha enclosed within a lotus, our ultimate potential is obscured by the direct and dormant forms of attachment in our minds.

The second obstacle is anger and hatred. Like a bumblebee guarding honey and hive, our anger bars the sweetness of our buddha-nature from the world.

The third obstacle is ignorance. Like layers of husk around a grain, our ignorance conceals the true nature of our minds.

The fourth obstacle is the strong force of the three poisons in our minds. Like gold covered in excrement, our most precious buddha-nature is concealed by the strong force of the three poisons.

The fifth obstacle is the imprints of ignorance. Like a treasure within the mind, our ultimate potential can only be found beneath the ground of the imprints of past delusions.

The sixth obstacle is the subtle object to be abandoned on the Hinayana path. As a seed in a shell must cast aside its external covering in order to germinate, so the mind must cast aside this object of abandonment in order for the nature of the mind to bear fruit.

The seventh obstacle is what is to be abandoned on the Hinayana path of meditation. Like rotten cloth that swathes a golden buddha, the objects of abandonment on the Hinayana path must be forsaken in order for the true nature of our minds to shine through.

The eighth obstacle is the afflictions that are to be abandoned on the first seven grounds of the Mahayana path. As a universal monarch must come forth from his mother's womb, the pollutions of the intellectually acquired grasping at true existence must be abandoned in order for the full potential of our minds to emerge.

The ninth obstacle is what is to be abandoned on the three pure grounds—the eighth, ninth, and tenth grounds of the Mahayana path. Like a golden buddha found inside an artist's mold, upon eliminating the imprints of the delusions on the three pure grounds, we actualize the complete potential of our own buddha-nature.

Reflecting on these nine points should remind us that all of our defilements are extinguishable. Attachment, anger, ignorance, and the force of these three poisonous minds are the obscurations of ordinary sentient beings who have yet to enter the path. The imprints of ignorance act as the obscuration of arhats on the Hinayana path. The abandonments on the path of seeing and the abandonments on the path of meditation are forms of obscuration that exist for arya beings on the Hinayana path. The remaining obscurations exist in the minds of Mahayana practitioners training on the ten grounds.

Please remember that there is absolutely no difference between our own buddha-nature and that of the enlightened beings, except for the fact that our own buddha-nature is totally shrouded by the obscurations of our delusions. It is so shrouded that we cannot even see the suffering nature of our own existence. What we see of our existence is totally opposite to what its reality is. Because of this, we cling and grasp at temporary pleasures and happiness.

THE NINE-POINT MEDITATION
IN ACCORDANCE WITH THE THREE SCOPES

As the combination of the method and wisdom aspects of the path is such an important feature of the training of the great scope, in order to give you a better idea how to practice this way, I want to present a short meditation from the second chapter of the *Compendium on Valid Cognition* by Dharmakirti. This practice explains the training of the small, medium, and great scopes through the application of the four aspects of the first noble truth, which, as you may remember, are impermanence, suffering, emptiness, and selflessness.

Beginning with applying the four aspects in terms of the small scope, we reflect on the gross mode of impermanence. According to the small scope, our lives are not everlasting or permanent. Because of that we reflect on impermanence in terms of our own existence. In contemplating suffering, we contemplate the suffering of the three lower realms in particular. Upon experiencing death without choice, we are reborn, and we then reflect upon the possibility of rebirth in the three lower realms. The last two aspects, emptiness and selflessness, are conjoined as the third point of the practice in the small scope—in this context they refer to being under the control of karma and delusions. Although we may not wish to be reborn in the lower realms, we have no control over the situation due to the force of karma and delusions, which have their root in ignorance grasping at true existence. The antidote to this ignorance is realizing emptiness and selflessness. The more we are able to understand these two concepts, the more we are able to understand how we lack freedom from the control of karma and delusions.

In the medium scope, we reflect on subtle impermanence. Because of impermanence we have suffering. In the contemplation on suffering in the medium scope, we contemplate the subtle suffering of pervasive conditioning. Then we reflect on the fact that phenomena in general are selfless and empty, without inherent existence.

In the great scope, our contemplation on impermanence takes the form of compassion that sees the impermanence of sentient beings. Our contemplation on suffering is the compassion involved in seeing the suffering of sentient beings, and our contemplation on emptiness and selflessness is nonobjectifying compassion, which is the compassion that sees the emptiness and selflessness of phenomena and sentient beings.

This is the nine-point meditation on impermanence, suffering, emptiness, and selflessness in accordance with the three scopes.

THE MANNER OF GENERATING
BODHICHITTA MIND

THE NEXT TOPIC IN THE TEXT is an explanation of the methods by which to generate the mind of bodhichitta. There are two aspects to the mind of bodhichitta: the wish to benefit others and the wish to attain enlightenment for the purpose of accomplishing the benefit of others. *Generating the mind of bodhichitta* means developing the mind to its greatest possible potential for the benefit of numberless sentient beings.

Bodhichitta is the thought of renouncing self and cherishing others. It is rooted in compassion and characterized by the aspiration to attain enlightenment in order to be of benefit to sentient beings. A perfect human rebirth with the leisures and opportunities is the most conducive basis from which to generate this supreme thought. It is very rare for those who are born in the celestial realms to generate bodhichitta, although it is possible for them to do so if they have very strong imprints of extensive listening and understanding and have collected very strong imprints of bodhichitta in a previous human rebirth.

THE PROPER BASES

Of the four continents in our world system, beings such as ourselves who are born in the southern continent where birth occurs from the womb and the physical bodies are composed of six basic constituents[34] have the most conducive basis on which to cultivate bodhichitta. In comparison, rebirths in the northern continent of unpleasant sounds and the other continents where it is not possible to generate renunciation for cyclic existence are not conducive bases on which to generate the mind of bodhichitta.

There are two kinds of mental bases upon which it is most appropriate to generate bodhichitta: the common and the uncommon. The common mental basis is a mind wishing to engage in virtue, having much faith in virtue, and willing to persevere in doing virtuous actions. Although we may have taken a perfect human rebirth with the eight leisures and ten opportunities, if we are able to engage in virtue only for very short periods of time, or if we are strongly habituated toward nonvirtue from past lifetimes, we do not have a sound mental basis to develop bodhichitta. The uncommon mental basis is a mind that possesses the thought of renouncing self and cherishing others, a mind that is rooted in compassion, and a mind that has cultivated the nine levels of meditative concentration and attained the bliss of the suppleness of body and mind. Although this mind has not entirely abandoned the afflictions of the desire realm, it is victorious over the delusions.

Generally speaking, according to our system, a desire-realm being has five sense perceptions and one mental perception. The sensory perceptions are far too gross to become the basis for generating bodhichitta. Even the mental perception, although more subtle, is usually not considered an appropriate basis from which to generate bodhichitta because the mental perception in a desire-realm being is so easily controlled by delusions, and because it is predominantly a conceptual state of mind. However, a *direct* mental perception in the mind of an ordinary desire-realm being, which is a much more subtle state of mind, can become an appropriate basis from which to cultivate bodhichitta. Unfortunately, it is very rare that an ordinary being is able to cultivate a direct mental perception. This being the case, it is usually taught that in order to cultivate the mind of bodhichitta, we must first cultivate renunciation. The mind of renunciation conjoined with the bliss of concentration that arises out of the suppleness of mind and body is an appropriate basis from which we can generate bodhichitta.

FOUR CONDITIONS, FOUR CAUSES, AND FOUR POWERS

There are four conditions that act as the supporting causes for generating the mind of bodhichitta.

The first condition is the condition of seeing or hearing about the inconceivable qualities of the holy body, holy speech, and holy mind of the buddhas and bodhisattvas. Once we ascertain these qualities, we will be inspired to attain them ourselves.

The second condition is having the opportunity to listen extensively to the vast collection of the Mahayana teachings. When we hear these teachings over and over again, in great depth and detail, we will be inspired to practice as the teachings instruct. By persevering in the cultivation of the mind of bodhichitta as we are taught, we will be able to actually attain the state of omniscience and perfect, loving compassion.

The third condition is having a sense of appreciation for the Mahayana teachings. We develop this sense of appreciation by recognizing that the teachings enable us not only to subdue our disturbed, negative minds, but also help us to enhance our potential to cherish others, and teach us the methods to do so. Seeing this, we understand that the Dharma is the one medicine to pacify the suffering of all transmigratory beings, and we feel that, because of their immense value, it would be unbearable if there were a break in the oral transmission of the teachings, and thereby we strive to ensure that they continue.

The fourth condition is seeing the difficulties of the time of the five great degenerations, and as a result making a determined effort to practice bodhichitta and act as an inspiration to others. Today, the three poisonous states of the mind are extremely strong in sentient beings—we have no humility, no consideration for others, and jealousy and miserliness are rampant. Even the attainment of liberation on the paths of the hearer or the solitary realizer is difficult to achieve under these circumstances. However, in the context of the fourth condition, the awareness of the difficulty of the times that we live in encourages us to become even more resolved to cultivate bodhichitta. In this context, we understand that the cultivation of bodhichitta in even one person's mind can serve as a model for others to be inspired to practice in this way.

When complete, these four conditions can act as an incentive for us to train in bodhichitta, and thus cause the mind of bodhichitta to arise. These conditions are not, however, the *direct* causes of the realization of bodhichitta since by themselves alone, they will not bring about the result of bodhichitta: they will not inspire the thought of loving-kindness and compassion in our minds, and are not powerful enough to counteract the mind that seeks the sole benefit of self. To actually generate the mind of bodhichitta, we need a much more powerful method, such as the practice of the seven-point instructions on cause and effect, which we will discuss later on in this section.

The cultivation of the wish to benefit others is one aspect of bodhichitta. The other aspect is the wish to attain enlightenment to complete this goal. Although we generate the wish to attain enlightenment in the context of desiring to benefit others, by actually attaining this goal, we also attain the ultimate benefit for ourselves. I bring up this point because there are some systems that assert incorrectly that the wish to benefit others is the only objective of bodhichitta.

In relation to this, among the three great monasteries of Tibet,[35] there is an ongoing debate about whether Maitreya, who will be the fifth buddha of our time,[36] has already attained enlightenment or not. The scholars of Sera Je Monastery accept that Maitreya is already a buddha. Their opponents, who do not accept this, argue that in one of his treatises Maitreya states that his reason for composing his great works is to purify the obscurations of negative karma. Therefore, they say that Maitreya had the thought of seeking only his own benefit and cannot be a buddha. Those who accept Maitreya as a buddha argue that, on the contrary, having the wish to benefit oneself is not contradictory to the mind of bodhichitta, is not contradictory to the Mahayana vehicle, and is not contradictory to being a buddha. What *is* contradictory to all of these is the thought of seeking *solely our own nirvana,* the thought of seeking personal peace, which is the practice of those who follow the individual vehicle. According to the Sera Je philosophers, the attainment of enlightenment does in fact fulfill the ultimate benefit for self, although the goal is attained with the sole motivation of cherishing others.

When we spoke about the cultivation of the mind of renunciation, we mentioned two basic components: the reflection on suffering in terms of our personal suffering and the determination to be free from suffering and to attain liberation. It is on the basis of understanding suffering that we generate the mind that seeks liberation. In the same way bodhichitta has two aspects: the wish to benefit others and the aspiration to attain enlightenment in order to bring this about. The aspiration to attain enlightenment arises on the basis of the wish to benefit others. This kind of cultivation of bodhichitta is known as king-like bodhichitta. In the same way that a king has the responsibility to protect his kingdom and all its people, the bodhisattva takes responsibility to benefit others by seeking to attain the state that is free of all failings and mistakes and complete in all positive qualities and knowledge. Thus, the thought of benefiting others is like a cause, and wanting to attain enlightenment is like the support actualizing that wish.

Just as there are four conditions, there are also four causes for generating the mind of bodhichitta. These are not the *actual* causes, but, again, indirectly lead us to develop the mind of bodhichitta.

Of the four causes, the first is being born into an auspicious lineage. This means being born with a mind that is naturally inclined toward caring for and cherishing others.

The second cause is being under the guidance of a Mahayana virtuous friend who embodies the ten qualities we discussed earlier.

The third cause is having great compassion for sentient beings.

And the fourth cause is not having aversion to the problems, suffering, and hardships of existence in samsara. Of course, this does not mean that we should be excited about cyclic existence either! However, when we are absolutely unable to tolerate the problems or difficulties of cyclic existence, and thereby want to abandon cyclic existence at all costs, we are in danger of falling into the extreme of seeking nirvana.

In addition to the four conditions and four causes, there are four powers that contribute to the development of this mind: the power of self, the power of others, the power of the cause, and the power of potential.

The power of self refers to the fact that although we may rely upon the guidance of a virtuous Mahayana friend, the actual attainment of enlightenment and the generation of bodhichitta are dependent upon ourselves.

The power of others refers to generating the mind of bodhichitta by the power of receiving extensive, inspiring explanations from our spiritual teachers and spiritual friends.

The power of the cause refers to having had great exposure to the Mahayana teachings in the earlier part of our lives or in previous lifetimes—having listened extensively, understood in great depth, and meditated upon them. Because of this, we have great familiarity with, and we are by nature inclined toward, the Mahayana attitude, so much so that in the later part of our life should someone talk about bodhichitta, right away by the power of imprints we are able to turn our minds this way.

The power of potential refers to generating the mind of bodhichitta not in dependence upon previous causes as such, but in this very lifetime by hearing Mahayana teachings and meeting with virtuous friends, being inspired by them, and thus engaging in the practice and development of the mind of bodhichitta.

These are the four conditions, the four causes, and the four powers that are necessary in order to generate the mind of bodhichitta. However, in order to facilitate the actual cultivation of bodhichitta in our own practice, we should also focus upon the actual methods to generate bodhichitta mind as presented by the great Lama Atisha and the bodhisattva Shantideva, which are the seven-point instructions on cause and effect and the technique of equalizing and exchanging self for others.

Establishing Buddha as a Valid Person

In order to train our minds in bodhichitta, it is helpful for us to try to get a sense of what it actually means to be enlightened. It is also important that we gain confidence in our ability to attain this state. To help us to do this, we can look briefly at the following points establishing Buddha as a valid person from Dharmakirti's *Commentary on the "Compendium on Valid Cognition."* These points essentially retrace Buddha's path to enlightenment, and allow us to see how it is possible for our own minds to realize emptiness and achieve enlightenment ourselves.

We begin with a being with the same continuum as Buddha Shakyamuni who, through diligent meditation, cultivated bodhichitta and entered the Mahayana path of accumulation. With the foundation of bodhichitta, this bodhisattva (who later became Buddha, don't forget) gradually cultivated the conceptual realization of the wisdom realizing emptiness. Familiarizing himself with this concept repeatedly through meditation, he realized emptiness directly, entered the path of seeing, and became an arya being. This is the first reasoning establishing Buddha as a valid person.

The second reasoning establishing Buddha as a valid person arises on the basis of the first. The wisdom realizing emptiness in the mind of the bodhisattva from the path of seeing to enlightenment is supported by a supreme form of method, and thus makes up the supreme accumulation of causes. Therefore, it is completely possible for that bodhisattva to attain the result of the nature body of a buddha, the total abandonment of the two obscurations with their imprints. Thus, from the path of seeing, the bodhisattva did exactly that, and with wisdom supported by the method of bodhichitta attained enlightenment. This reasoning is the bridge from the path of seeing to the result of enlightenment.

The third reasoning establishing Buddha as a valid person is that Buddha, upon attaining enlightenment, was able to bring forth a continuous flow of divine activities benefiting sentient beings. This is because he abandoned the two types of obscurations together with their imprints and attained the state of a tathagata with the three characteristics—having abandoned, having abandoned all without exception, and having excellently abandoned. *Having abandoned* refers to having abandoned all gross forms of the delusions. *Having abandoned all without exception* refers to having abandoned their seeds. *Having excellently abandoned* refers to having abandoned even the very imprints of the delusions.

The fourth reasoning is that Buddha, having attained the highest liberation, completed the accumulation of causes through attaining the extraordinary qualities of the path and thereby is able to engage in the pure activities continuously benefiting sentient beings. By this fourth reasoning we establish Buddha as a valid person because he is totally free of all mistakes, and possesses all knowledge. This is so because Buddha has abandoned everything there is to be abandoned and attained everything there is to be attained on the path, and thereby actualized liberation.

These four reasonings give us an idea of the steps to enlightenment by looking at the stages in which Buddha attained this state. This is like the example of a man who becomes fabulously wealthy having started out with nothing. If we hear of such a person, we will naturally wonder how he got there. We want to hear the details of what he studied, how he developed his special talent, and then how he built his extensive business, and so forth. When we have a picture of how one person achieved this goal, we see how it is possible that we could achieve it ourselves.

This process of attaining enlightenment exemplifies the way that mind can transform from a deluded state, which has only the vaguest idea of emptiness, to a direct perception, which is the ultimate antidote to all of our obscurations. Once we understand that this is possible, we are more easily able to have faith that someone—Buddha, for example—has completed the process, and at the same time we are also able to take inspiration from the fact that our own minds have the potential to accomplish the same thing. So we see that first Buddha generated bodhichitta. On the basis of having generated bodhichitta, he applied himself to the wisdom realizing emptiness. Ultimate bodhichitta arose on the basis of conventional bodhichitta. The union of method and wisdom brought forth the enlightened body, and with this, Buddha was able to engage in the extraordinary activities that continuously benefit others, and by that very fact, we say that Buddha is a valid person.

In Buddhism we talk extensively about enlightened beings who are free of all mistakes and failings, and have accomplished all knowledge and qualities. Yet we do not have the karmic fortune to be able to actually see the individuals who embody these qualities. However, due to the power of our own inferential valid cognition, we can see that this result is possible. Through inferential valid cognition we can think: "If I get rid of this delusion, I get this attainment, and because of this attainment I can develop this even greater attainment, and then yes, on the basis of that I can see that the result of enlightenment could happen."

This concept is very much like the way we plan a business. We say: "If I do this, I will make x amount of profit, and with this profit, I'll then make that much profit." The way we set ourselves up for practicing the lamrim from refuge on is similar.

In fact, reflecting on these four points establishing Buddha as a valid person can become like a practice of refuge for us. When we reflect on the qualities of Buddha through the four reasonings, a very pure mind of faith arises. This is like causal refuge. When we realize that we ourselves could generate bodhichitta and the wisdom that realizes emptiness, we gain faith that we ourselves could attain the ultimate result of buddhahood. This is like resultant refuge.

The Obstacles to Developing the Mind of Bodhichitta

In general, the mind of anger and the mind of vengeance that arises from the mind of anger are the greatest hindrances to generating bodhichitta. Of course, indirectly all of the other delusional states of the mind—the mind of attachment, the mind of ignorance, and so forth—are also problematic. However, usually we do not generate anger in relation to inanimate objects, but in relation to animate objects, and animate objects are always sentient beings. Love and compassion are also states of mind that we generate in relation to sentient beings. Upon analysis, we can see that the mind of anger and the mind of compassion are completely contradictory. Therefore, we should reflect on the shortcomings of the mind of anger over and over again, realizing that it destroys not only our own happiness, but also the happiness and well-being of others.

Specifically, there are three main obstacles to generating the mind of compassion: clinging to the appearances of this life, clinging to the temporary pleasures of the higher realms of cyclic existence, and our aspirations for individual liberation.

As ordinary sentient beings, we are totally under the control of the eight worldly concerns, and cling to the appearances of this life. The best antidote to the mind of the eight worldly dharmas at our level is mindfulness and awareness of impermanence and death. Since death is inevitable, there is nothing to be gained from having too many expectations or from cultivating too much suspicion and doubt. We are subject to impermanence and death and to the control of the positive and negative forms of karma. The mind of the eight worldly dharmas induces a strong grasping at the "I" within us, and under the power of this mind we erroneously feel as if everything is under our own control. Under the power of the eight worldly dharmas, we believe wholeheartedly in a substantially existent self that is not dependent on any other factors. But in reality none of this is true.

As it is often said, as long as we cling to the appearances of this life, we are not a Dharma person; as long as we cling to cyclic existence, we have no renunciation; and as long as we cling to individual liberation, we have no enlightenment. When training in the path and practice of the small scope, we subdue the mind that clings to appearances of this life. Having done so, we enter the medium scope, in which we develop the capacity to cultivate the mind that wishes to be free from cyclic existence. Then, when training in the path and practice of the great scope, we expand our capacity to include the development of compassion and bodhichitta.

The second obstacle, clinging to the temporary pleasures of the higher realms of cyclic existence, can be overcome by considering the contaminated nature of these states. Although they are relatively peaceful and enjoyable, existence in the higher realms is still under the power of the delusions. We discussed this extensively in the section on the medium scope.

The third obstacle, the aspiration for individual liberation, can be overcome by considering the sad situation of all other sentient beings who would be left to suffer in cyclic existence even if you yourself were to attain individual liberation. Although compassion is a part of the paths of the hearers and the solitary realizers, the compassion on these paths does not have the potential to bring forth the extraordinary supreme thought of enlightenment, or bodhichitta mind. The compassion on the Mahayana path does have this potential. The result of individual liberation, or the state of an arhat, is a valid result, but it is limited in the sense that the practitioner has yet to free him- or herself from every failing and mistake, and has yet to develop every positive quality. Therefore the state of an arhat does not fulfill the ultimate benefit for self and others. The result of complete enlightenment is superior because it *does* fulfill these benefits.

The technique that we use to generate bodhichitta in our own minds is completely dependent upon our mental capacities. One method is to train in the path and practice of the small and medium scope, and then train in the great scope on that basis, beginning with equanimity and progressing through the practices of recognizing sentient beings as one's mother, remembering their kindness, repaying their kindness, generating the infinite sense of loving-kindness, great compassion, the extraordinary supreme thought, and the result of bodhichitta whereby we wish to attain enlightenment solely and completely for the welfare of others. Having generated that kind of bodhichitta, we engage in the conduct of the six perfections. Then we seek out the perfection of wisdom, the wisdom realizing emptiness. This is one method.

Those of higher mental capacity proceed from the same common ground of the small and medium scopes, on the basis of which they train in the first five points of the seven-point instructions. They subsequently generate compassion and the extraordinary supreme thought of taking complete responsibility for sentient beings. Before they generate the actual mind of bodhichitta, however, these practitioners examine whether it is possible to attain the state in which they can fulfill their responsibility to sentient beings or not. They analyze the cause of the suffering of sentient beings, which is the ignorance that grasps at true existence and its imprints. They analyze whether it is possible to eliminate the two types of obscurations. They understand that it is absolutely necessary to attain enlightenment, but they check to see whether or not they have the potential to do this. Once they establish that they *can* generate the wisdom realizing emptiness, and that they can attain cessation, they apply themselves to the examination of all the logic and reasoning that supports the cultivation of the yogic direct perception of emptiness. In this way, they establish that it is indeed possible to eliminate the two types of obscurations, and then proceed to the training in conventional bodhichitta.

For those who train in this manner it is very important to have a strong conviction that the result of enlightenment is feasible from the beginning. When that becomes very clear, the practitioner can generate compassion and the extraordinary supreme thought, and thereby bodhichitta. The development of bodhichitta becomes a reasonable ambition when they realize that such an enlightenment is within their reach. This is another method to practice on the path.

STAGES OF TRAINING IN BODHICHITTA MIND

Understanding the Seven-Point Instructions on Cause and Effect

The seven-point instructions on cause and effect have their source in Buddha, from whom the lineage continues to Maitreya, Asanga, Lama Atisha, Chandrakirti, Chandragomin, and so forth. The seven-point instructions are a cause and effect relationship bringing the result of enlightenment. The cause of enlightenment, in this case, is the bodhichitta possessing two aspects: the wish to benefit others and the wish to attain enlightenment in order to bring this about. This bodhichitta arises from the extraordinary supreme thought of taking responsibility for sentient beings. The extraordinary supreme thought arises from the mind of great compassion. The mind of great compassion in turn arises from the infinite sense of loving-kindness toward others. Loving-kindness arises from the wish to repay the kindness of sentient beings. The wish to repay their kindness arises from remembering the kindness of others. And the basis for being able to remember their kindness is the ability to recognize all sentient beings as our mothers.

Before we begin training our minds in the seven-point instructions on cause and effect, we should try to understand these stages clearly, and become familiar with their order. Once we have done this, we can begin the actual practice.

The Mind of Compassion

The substantial cause of bodhichitta is compassion, which itself arises from an infinite sense of loving-kindness that sees the poverty of true happiness in sentient beings. As compassion is the substantial cause of bodhichitta, it is therefore regarded as the root of the Mahayana path. Developing the mind of compassion begins in the path and practice of the medium scope: thinking about our own suffering in great depth and expanse, and then applying this to others who are also in cyclic existence. Just as we do not wish suffering for ourselves, we wish others to be free of suffering as well. Yet in order sincerely to wish this for others, we must first develop a feeling of closeness toward them, and an awareness of their infinite kindness. We must wish to repay that kindness. On that basis we will then be able to wish that they be separated from suffering from the very depths of our hearts. Loving-kindness has two aspects: the wish that others have happiness and the feeling of cherishing and caring for them, which arises in recognition of the fact that they lack it.

In the composition of texts, the authors traditionally begin with prayers of homage to the gurus, the buddhas, and the bodhisattvas. However, in *Supplement to the "Middle Way,"* Chandrakirti pays homage to the mind of compassion, because it is the root that bears the fruit of the conquerors and the fruit of enlightenment, and is essential at the beginning, middle, and end of the path.

Compassion is important at the very beginning of the path because cultivating the wish to benefit others depends upon the extraordinary supreme thought of taking complete responsibility for their welfare. The amount of responsibility we are willing to take on is completely dependent upon the strength of our compassion. Without infinite loving-kindness and without the strength of compassion, we will be unable to develop a complete sense of responsibility, and as a result we will be unable to generate bodhichitta, and unable to accumulate the three countless eons of merit.

Compassion is important in the middle of the path because the speed at which we are able to progress along the path is completely dependent upon how much compassion we have cultivated in our minds. In order to generate the Mahayana path of seeing for the first time, we need to generate an extraordinary sense of great compassion, which cannot bear the suffering of sentient beings. Bodhisattvas in the form and the formless realms even take rebirth in the desire realms in order to enhance their compassion, because a human rebirth is the most conducive basis for enhancing this mind.

Of the five Mahayana paths, the first, the path of accumulation, has three parts: small, middling, and great. When we attain the middling path of accumulation, our bodhichitta becomes what is called *gold-like bodhichitta.* Just as the nature of gold is such that it cannot be altered in any way, once we attain the middling level of the path of accumulation, the nature of our conventional bodhichitta also cannot be changed.

In addition to preventing us from giving up the thought of bodhichitta and seeking our own individual liberation, compassion enables us to quickly accomplish the realizations of the paths and grounds and to complete the accumulation of the merit of virtue and the merit of transcendental wisdom. This is another reason that compassion is important in the middle of the path.

Compassion is important at the end of the path because it is the motivation that inspires enlightened beings to engage continuously and single-pointedly in the activities benefiting sentient beings. Were it not for their compassion for sentient beings, they would simply remain undisturbed in a peaceful state of meditative equipoise.

Generally speaking, we all like compassion, we all understand how great compassion is, and we all appreciate it no matter what philosophical school we belong to. However, what I am trying to emphasize here is exactly how much compassion can actually change our minds. Not only is compassion a cause for bodhichitta, but it also enhances all the other good qualities we already possess.

We can speak of three types of compassion: the compassion that sees sentient beings, the compassion that sees the impermanence of phenomena, and nonconceptual compassion that sees the nature of reality—meaning emptiness. These types of compassion are categorized in dependence upon the type of wisdom from which they arise. To clarify, we can take the example of someone who has a chronic illness. As an outer manifestation of this ailment, this person develops frightening sores on the body. When the physician looks at the patient, the physician does not fixate on the appearance of the sores, which are fairly minor in the doctor's eyes, but focuses on the internal conditions that are creating them, which are the doctor's greatest concern. However, to someone who is not a doctor, but just a passer-by, the manifestation of the frightening sores may be a very big deal indeed, and may upset that person very much. That person's mind will be entirely occupied with the appearance of the sores on the patient's body, rather than with the underlying illness.

When compassion is accompanied by a deep and profound understanding of wisdom, the compassion itself will also be profound. This compassion is like the perspective of the doctor. When compassion is accompanied by limited wisdom, the compassion itself will be much more superficial. This compassion is like the reaction of the person passing by.

Nonconceptual compassion refers to the compassion that arises as a result of one's understanding of the emptiness of inherent existence. Of the three levels of compassion, nonconceptual compassion is the most profound, discerning, and pervasive. Having understood emptiness in terms of our own suffering, we behold the suffering of sentient beings, and see how they suffer due to ignorance grasping at true existence, and how they are bound by this ignorance to cyclic existence. The compassion arising from this kind of understanding is very subtle, powerful, and dynamic.

The compassion that sees the impermanence of phenomena, which is the second, is a bit grosser. This is the compassion that arises as we develop the awareness of the transient nature of sentient beings, an awareness of their impermanence, and the awareness that they lack independent or substantial existence. This level of compassion is still a very deep sense of compassion, but it is less subtle than nonconceptual compassion.

The types of compassion that I have just explained are necessarily developed on the basis of meditative equipoise. To practice the first type, you would begin by meditating with great strength on the emptiness of inherent existence, and then, upon arising from meditative equipoise, you would then examine sentient beings and phenomena with the mind affected by that point of view. In the same way, to practice the second type, you could meditate on the impermanent nature of phenomena or on the lack of independent or substantial existence of phenomena, and then once you have finished that meditation, you could arise and look at sentient beings from that new perspective.

The most basic of these three types of compassion is the compassion that merely beholds sentient beings. This kind of compassion observes sentient beings, but does not take into account the specific factors of their existence such as impermanence or lack of independent or inherent existence.

The mind of compassion that cherishes others is pervasive in the sense that every sentient being already possesses it to some degree. However, in most of us, this mind is limited by the pollution of the multitude of conditions that we place upon it. Just as we say that within the twelve links, the eighth and the ninth links of craving and grasping ripen the tenth link of existence, in the same way, within the seven-point instructions on cause and effect, the causes of remembering sentient beings as one's mother, remembering their kindness, wishing to repay their kindness, and the infinite sense of loving-kindness ripen our thoughts of compassion from their limited potential into something that is limitless and great. Thus, when we generate compassion, it is not a *new* compassion that we are creating out of nothing, but rather our ordinary, limited compassion ripened to its full potential.

It is stated in some scriptures that when we are afraid, we should meditate on compassion, as compassion is the antidote to every possible fear. In the same way, when we are anxious, we should meditate on compassion. When we feel a sense of weakness or uncertainty in ourselves, we should meditate on compassion. Compassion counteracts all of these negative states of mind and many more. If we are able to generate compassion in the face of the many difficulties and problems that we experience in our lives, our troubles will become much less overwhelming.

I heard a story about a group of refugees from Tibet who escaped with two leaders—one who was extremely compassionate, and one who was very intelligent but less compassionate. They took turns at each end of the group—one leader took charge of the group from the front, while the other leader stayed at the back to make sure that everyone made it to the border. The leader who had more compassion was extremely concerned for everyone, taking care of the weaker people who couldn't travel so quickly, including an old woman who joined the group along the way. At a certain pass near the border the group was forced to travel very quickly, and there was an argument between the two leaders. The one who was more compassionate insisted on taking the old woman, and the other one said that if they took her, the whole group would have to travel slowly, and as a result they all might get caught. They continued on in two groups, and somehow the one who was more compassionate ended up in front with the faster group, while the less compassionate one ended up behind with the slower group, making sure that everyone made it across. The next day there was a huge snowstorm, and the old lady couldn't keep up at all. It took the entire night for her group to get across. The first group reached a safe area and waited for the other group to join them. When the second group finally arrived, the first leader asked after the old lady, and was told that she had been left behind. Hearing this, that leader became very upset and said he was going back to look for her. He had such an extraordinary mind that he took complete responsibility for this one person. He asked for volunteers to join him for the full night's journey back, and maybe five or six people volunteered. Unfortunately, they never made it across the border.

The main point of this story is to demonstrate the way that a mind filled with compassion is able to act under the most difficult of circumstances with great strength of mind, nobility, and confidence. Therefore, should you find yourself experiencing fear, anxiety, and depression, you should strengthen your sense of compassion for others in order to combat these thoughts. Depression and fear arise because the mind is weak. But compassion endows the mind with courage and strength. For all of these reasons compassion is important on the Mahayana path at the beginning, the middle, and the end. No matter how many difficulties and problems arise, the strength of the mind of compassion is able to take them on. Whether we are able to actually succeed in accomplishing our goals or not is secondary.

When we are just beginning the meditations on bodhichitta, we should remember to continuously reflect upon the shortcomings of the obstacles of the negative minds, which are the exact opposite of what we are trying to cultivate. We should have a unified practice, on the one hand becoming familiar with the seven-point instructions on cause and effect, and on the other hand also being very cautious about obstacles. These two things must be done together. If we only engage in the seven-point instructions on cause and effect without being cautious of the obstacles that our negative minds can create, we are building a castle made of sand. It will not take much for it all to come tumbling down.

Also, as we are training our mind in this method of generating bodhichitta, we should not become so single-pointed that we neglect the other aspects of the path. We should continue to study and reflect on other parts of the path simultaneously, especially as taught in the *Guide to the Bodhisattva's Way of Life*. We should read the chapters on patience and mindfulness and reflect on them. We should contemplate the chapter on conscientiousness so that we do not begin to feel lazy about the practice of the seven-point instructions on cause and effect, and we should reflect on the first chapter on the benefits of the mind of bodhichitta to inspire us. In this way, the other aspects of the path will become a great support to our practice of bodhichitta.

What is the difference between the compassion generated on the basis of the seven-point instructions on cause and effect and everyday compassion? Everyday compassion, in general, arises from our awareness of the result of the gross manifestation of suffering, and is a very limited level of compassion. The compassion that we develop in reliance upon the seven-point instructions on cause and effect, however, arises on the basis of our awareness of the *causes* of suffering: delusions and nonvirtuous karmic actions. To develop this kind of compassion we must have strong faith in cause and effect, which is regarded as the root of all of our happiness and well-being. Therefore, training in the ascertainment of cause and effect as it is taught in the small scope is essential to provide a strong foundation for the mind of compassion. Again, without creating the foundation of the experience of the realizations of the small and the medium scopes, it will not be possible to generate the path and practice of the great scope. It is said that when Lama Atisha used to meet individuals and gain insight into the incredible, immeasurable nonvirtuous karma that they had accumulated, his concern for them would overwhelm him, and tears would come to his eyes.

One session of meditation on compassion should be preceded by reflection on perfect human rebirth, impermanence and death, and the cause and effect of our actions, and, based on that, cultivation of the mind of refuge. Upon reflecting on cause and effect, we reflect on the causes of suffering—nonvirtuous karma and delusions—and in this way reflect on true suffering and the true cause of suffering by thinking in terms of the suffering that we ourselves have experienced. We thereby cultivate renunciation. We can also reflect on the twelve links of dependent origination. When we have shaped our mind to a certain degree through these contemplations, we can then begin to think about suffering and the true cause of suffering or the twelve links in terms of other sentient beings' experiences. Only then will our minds have the appropriate basis on which to contemplate the recognition of sentient beings as our mothers, remembering their kindness, and cultivating the wish to repay their kindness, and only then will we have the foundation for meditating on love and compassion.

The seven points of the seven-point instruction are as follows: the first is recognizing sentient beings as one's mother; the second is remembering their kindness; the third is wishing to repay their kindness; the fourth is generating the thought of infinite loving-kindness; the fifth is generating compassion; the sixth is generating the extraordinary supreme thought of taking responsibility for sentient beings; and the seventh is generating the mind of bodhichitta. The first few points—recognizing sentient beings as our mother, remembering their kindness, wishing to repay their kindness, and cultivating an infinite sense of loving-kindness—are not the main causes of generating compassion; rather, they are the bridge that connects our contemplations.

We can count the instructions as seven by regarding the last point—generating the mind of bodhichitta—as the result, and the previous six points as the cause giving rise to that result. Alternatively, we can consider the first four points—recognizing sentient beings as one's mother, remembering their kindness, wishing to repay their kindness, and the thought of infinite loving-kindness—as the cause of compassion, which is the fifth, and the last two—the extraordinary supreme thought and the generation of the mind of bodhichitta—its results. The instructions from the *Lamrim Chenmo* follow this second system.

Actually Training in the Seven-Point Instructions on Cause and Effect

DEVELOPING EQUANIMITY

There is only one gateway to the Mahayana path of sutra or tantra, and that is the gateway of bodhichitta. The objective of bodhichitta is the attainment of enlightenment for the benefit of sentient beings. In order to develop the wish to benefit others, we need to create the basis. This does not mean an external basis of other sentient beings, but a basis within our own minds. Right now we do not have the basis for cultivating the mind that totally seeks the welfare of others because our perspectives are extremely biased. We constantly place the people that we come into contact with into mental categories of enemy, friend, or stranger. As if that weren't enough, within these categories themselves we further discriminate—creating divisions of "best" friend, "close" friend, "worst" enemy, and so forth. With these kinds of thoughts in our minds, it will be impossible for us to develop the true wish to benefit all other sentient beings. If we wish to develop bodhichitta, instead of favoring some and distancing others, we must necessarily cultivate the attitude of equanimity for all beings.

There are four objects in relation to which we should cultivate equanimity. We can cultivate equanimity in dependence upon self, in dependence upon others, in dependence upon the conventional mode of existence, and in dependence upon the ultimate mode of existence.

Cultivating equanimity in dependence upon self means thinking that in the same way that we ourselves want happiness, others want happiness also. In the same way that we wish for good things, others wish for those things also. In the same way that there are some things that we do not want, others are the same in not wanting these things. By thinking this way, we try to eliminate our bias toward "enemy," "friend," and "stranger," as all beings are the same in terms of wanting happiness and not wanting unhappiness.

Cultivating equanimity in dependence upon others means thinking as follows:

Because of some small reason, today I have divided all these sentient beings into enemies, friends, and strangers. In reality, there is not a single being who has not been most close and dear to me in my past lifetimes, and who will not be close and dear to me in future lifetimes. In this lifetime, too, there is great potential for closeness. Therefore, there is absolutely no reason to discriminate between them.

Cultivating equanimity in dependence on the conventional mode of existence means recognizing the fact that we discriminate between sentient beings, and recognizing that we all, ourselves included, want happiness and don't want suffering. Also, we should contemplate the fact that every sentient being is the same in possessing the luminous, clear nature of mind, and that all of our obscurations are temporary.

Cultivating equanimity in dependence upon the ultimate mode of existence means understanding that our own minds and the minds of others—friends, enemies, or strangers—are empty of inherent existence and possess buddha-nature. The mind that we cherish so much—thinking that it is *my* mind—is not different from the minds of others in terms of its intrinsic purity, nor is it any different in the sense that it is empty of inherent existence, dependent upon causes and conditions, and does not exist independently.

Equanimity means eliminating the biased mind that discriminates, that encourages us to feel close to some and distant from others. A mind of equanimity considers oneself and others to be the same, and it is completely free of the extreme attitudes of being overly attached to some and very distant from others. We can bring forth equanimity in our attitude by reflecting on the basis of these four points.

Generally speaking, there are three types of equanimity: the equanimity of compounded phenomena, the equanimity of feeling, and immeasurable, limitless equanimity. The equanimity that we need as the basis of bodhichitta is limitless equanimity. This is the same as the equanimity that is spoken of in the four immeasurable thoughts, although the method of training the mind is somewhat different here.

In the prayer of the four immeasurable thoughts, we wish sentient beings to develop equanimity, to be free of the extremely disturbing minds of feeling close to some and distant from others. But here, as a basis for training our minds in bodhichitta, we focus on equanimity in our own attitudes. In the four immeasurables the basis is the external object, while in the practice of bodhichitta the basis is ourselves. In the presentation of this text there are no specific instructions given in terms of the four immeasurable thoughts, but it seems clear that once we cultivate our own minds in the attitude of equanimity toward others, we will naturally wish the same for other sentient beings because we appreciate the virtue of this practice. In the same way, we can cultivate immeasurable rejoicing, immeasurable love, and immeasurable compassion in our minds.

Just as we said that compassion has three aspects—seeing sentient beings, seeing phenomena, and seeing the nature of reality—it is said in the teachings of Lama Kelsang Jamyang Monlam that we can also apply the same three aspects to the rest of the four immeasurable thoughts. He says that this is so stated within scripture, although the text name is not specified. However, this is logically applicable. Although the practice of the four immeasurable thoughts is not the actual body of practice for generating the mind of bodhichitta, it makes a very good addition.

To actually cultivate the mind of equanimity, we can begin by imagining a stranger in front of us. Right now, at our ordinary level, our states of mind are very extreme—we feel extreme attachment, clinging, anger, or total indifference. When we think of an enemy, we fall into the extreme of aversion, and when we think of a friend, we fall to the other extreme of attachment and so forth. Thus, in order to help cultivate a balance in our attitude, we bring to mind a stranger. If we think of a stranger, we can assume the attitude of equanimity free of these two extremes. While having that picture of equanimity, we can then apply that same feeling toward friend, enemy, and so forth.

After we have done this, we should then bring to mind the friend to whom we feel particularly close and attached. We should think that the feelings of closeness and inseparability that we are experiencing right now have arisen because of conditions and that there is nothing solid or concrete about the fact that this friend is very close and dear to us. There is nothing permanent or stable about it. In terms of past lifetimes there have been many occasions on which this particular being has done us much harm. In terms of future lifetimes also, this being will be the cause of much suffering for us. We should think that there is absolutely no justification for holding this person so close and dear and clinging to him or her. In reality there is nothing solid, concrete, or permanent about our closeness with this person. It has only arisen due to conditions. Realizing this, we can rein in our sense of feeling overly close, overly attached, and obsessed with this person, and try to cultivate a sense of equanimity similar to that which we would have toward a stranger.

In relation to the stranger our mind has a better balance—not feeling particularly close and not feeling particularly distant. It is in relation to friends and enemies that our mind falls into extremes. In the path and practice of the medium scope we discussed the six types of shortcomings. If we wish, we can think about the first of these, the uncertain nature of our existence, and apply it to the strong, permanent feelings that we have toward the friend or enemy. Doing this may help to remove some of that sense of solidity.

Most of all, we should think that this external object that we think of as "friend," who is very close and dear, who has such an impact on our feelings of happiness and suffering, and from whom we cannot bear to be separated, does not exist from his or her own side. Our friend exists due to karma, due to delusions, and most of all due to the projection of our own mind. This very close dear friend, who seems so solid, is in reality like a dream, like an illusion. By thinking of the uncertainty of this relationship, and by thinking of the way in which it is imputed, we can counteract the extreme feeling of attachment to what we know as friend.

However, we should take care that our practice of cultivating equanimity does not invalidate friends and enemies entirely, making them nonexistent. That is not the objective. By cultivating equanimity, we are merely trying to target the obsessive mind of attachment that we have in relation to the friend, or the aggressive mind of anger that we have in relation to the enemy, and neutralize it.

The Three Causes
Recognizing Sentient Beings as Our Mothers

If we consider our own experience, we will find that when the people who are very close and dear to us have problems or experience suffering, it is very difficult to bear. Generally speaking, this is particularly so when we consider the experience of our own mothers—who have raised us, fed us, and cared for us since our birth. This being so, we begin the seven-point meditation with the recognition of every sentient being as having been our mother. The objective is to be able to see every sentient being the way we see the beings in our lives who are most dear to us.

Of course, even if we do not consider sentient beings as most precious and dear to us, we may still have a sense of concern for their suffering and wish them to be free from it. This very thought can be made very, very powerful and great if we are able to take it one step further and develop the ability to hold sentient beings as close as we would our own relatives and friends. This is very important for strengthening the mind of compassion. Moreover, this particular meditation technique has the blessings of the oral lineage. In case we may feel that we can cultivate sentient beings in this image by some other method, we should consider these instructions to carry such blessings.

To be able to develop the recognition of all sentient beings as our mothers, of course, we must first accept the existence of past and future lives. At the moment, our minds are so concentrated on what is going on in the lifetime that we happen to be experiencing at the moment that we are simply unable to comprehend that we have had other lives. Although we might not completely reject their existence, we have doubts. Yet we talk quite freely about attaining enlightenment, omniscience—free of all mistakes, fully endowed with all positive qualities. We *wish* to attain this state. Although we may not be fully convinced that this kind of enlightenment exists, we have far less doubt with regard to such an attainment. We hold it as something very close to our hearts because it is something we wish for ourselves. In order not to get stuck on the first point of this seven-point series, unable to accomplish any of the latter points of practice, we must try to think in the same way with regard to bodhichitta, and develop the strong aspiration to develop bodhichitta in our minds.

In order to make the subject appealing, we can examine the resources of other instructions, such as the *Guide to the Bodhisattva's Way of Life,* especially the first chapter on the benefits of generating the mind of bodhichitta and the chapters on mindfulness, conscientiousness, and patience. As we gain enthusiasm for these practices, slowly, slowly we eliminate our doubt or wrong views with regard to past and future lives. As the strength of our compassion increases, as our wish to attain bodhichitta becomes greater and more committed, our belief in past and future lives will become more solid.

For example, when we study the lamrim, the graduated path to enlightenment, the first point is devotion to our spiritual teacher, and seeing the guru as buddha. Although that is the first point, in order to fully develop this kind of devotion to the spiritual teacher, it is usually necessary that we study further points along the path. As we do so, we are able to better appreciate the practices of guru devotion. However, if, from the beginning, we were to focus only on guru devotion, trying to see the spiritual teacher as buddha, and not take into consideration any of the latter subjects of the lamrim, we would have an extremely difficult time of it and would probably get stuck.

Also, at the very beginning of the *Lamrim Chenmo* it is said that even if we do not have the kind of guru devotion that is able to see the spiritual teacher as a buddha right now, at the very least we should eliminate the mind that sees faults. In the same way, in the seven-point instructions on cause and effect, even if we are still unable to recognize sentient beings as our mothers, at least we should try not to develop the firm view that the opposite is true—that in fact sentient beings are definitely *not* our mothers. We should not think that because *we* are certain that this view is incorrect, it really is not true. We cannot follow this type of reasoning to validate what exists and what does not exist. There are many phenomena in the universe that we do not know about that do indeed exist.

In not seeing sentient beings as our mothers, we have everything to lose. In seeing sentient beings as our mothers on the basis of the reasoning of past and future lifetimes, the mind is opened to infinite virtues, the obstacles that our own ignorance has created are removed, and we have the opportunity to develop greater goodness. It is to our own advantage to take this on. Furthermore, if we are looking for proof, there are people in this world who remember their past lives very clearly.

Generally speaking, it is very important for us to cultivate the skills to enable us to move through our Dharma practice. Like the weeds that obstruct a plant that is trying to flower, in the same way we may experience many obstacles that impede our development of love and compassion. By the force of the inspiration that we receive from seeing the benefit of the mind of compassion in the beginning, in the middle, and in the very end of our spiritual path, we should take care not allow any of the weeds of our mistaken thoughts to hold us back from progressing on the path.

Please keep in mind that when we talk about past lives, we are not talking about knowing the physical aggregates of a past life. And when we talk about future lives, we do not mean knowing the physical aggregates of a future life. This is a very gross level of recognition of a past or future life. When we talk about past and future lifetimes, we are speaking in the context of the *aggregate of consciousness* and its continuum. This life's consciousness did not begin at our birth, and death is not the end of it. To understand the continuum of the aggregate of consciousness, we need to understand the continuum of our minds as being without beginning and without end. In order to ascertain this clearly, it is best if we have attained some level of single-pointed concentration. Through the subtle levels of mind that we develop in concentration, we can experience for ourselves the fact that our mental continuum is merely luminous, mere experience, and that it continues from lifetime to lifetime without interruption. However, even if we do not have single-pointed concentration, we can try to ascertain the reality of the continuum of consciousness by simply reflecting on the continuum of our mind from the time of our waking up this morning. Retrace that continuum to the day before, to the weeks, to the months, and to the years before that. When you have done that, you can then try to retrace it to the time before birth, and your previous life.

Chandrakirti says that our existence is beginningless. The continuum of consciousness that depends on the five aggregates is without beginning and without end. What obscures us from recognizing sentient beings as our mothers are the experiences of death and birth. Yet the fact that we simply cannot recognize sentient beings as our mothers in no way proves that they are not our mothers.

Through recognizing sentient beings as our mothers, remembering their kindness, generating the wish to repay that kindness, and generating the mind of infinite loving-kindness, we develop great compassion, and wish sentient beings to be completely free of all suffering. As a result of the mind of compassion we develop the extraordinary supreme thought, and due to that we are able to generate the mind of bodhichitta.

To cultivate the first of the seven-point instructions on cause and effect, you should use the person in your life who is the dearest and closest as your model. As I mentioned, it is traditional to take the image of the mother as the one who fulfills that role, but if this is not your personal experience, you can use someone else—your father, your sister or brother, your friend, whomever. Your success in this practice will be dependent on how much equanimity you have already generated within your mind, and the extent to which you have freed your mind from the extremes of aversion and clinging. It is not necessary to have the feeling of recognizing every single sentient being as your mother: a general feeling is sufficient, as long as you feel quite certain that every sentient being at one time or another has been this very close and dear person in your life.

Developing equanimity in your attitude and recognizing and accepting sentient beings as your mother are the most important points of this practice. They are also the hardest. If you can practice and achieve a stable experience of these two points, you will be able to realize the remaining points very easily.

Remembering Their Kindness

We remember the kindness of sentient beings in the context of the way in which they have nurtured us in countless lifetimes up until today. Using the mother as the example, we think about how she would much rather experience sickness herself than have her child suffer with illness. If there were any choice in the matter, then without any doubt, without any hesitation, the mother would most happily take the place of the child. In general the attachment between mother and child is of a better quality than other, ordinary forms of attachment, because the mother is able to sacrifice herself totally for her child. Ordinary attachment has many conditions, but between a mother and a child, there are far fewer.

When we look at how parents care for their children, we can see that they give up many things—sleep, privacy, holidays, and so forth. Taking these examples, we can reflect on the kindness of our own mothers. Of course when we don't consider things from a spiritual point of view, we might think that our parents asked for this job. But in reality our parents didn't particularly ask for us. As bardo beings we searched for a place to be born and they were what we found. There was a whole network of delusions and karma involved in bringing together this kind of relationship. It is never only the parents' business.

Wishing to Repay Their Kindness

After reflecting on the kindness of mother sentient beings as extensively as we can, the third point is to develop the incentive to repay that kindness.

We should not wish to repay the kindness in some temporary way, but rather in a way that benefits sentient beings in the long term. Anything that benefits sentient beings in the long term can only be in the category of liberation and enlightenment.

When we think about the situation of sentient beings, we should think of a blind person, lacking the eye of wisdom that sees what to abandon and what to practice. Mother sentient beings are blind in that respect, and they stand at the edge of a steep precipice, ready to fall into the depths of cyclic existence. As we consider their pitiful existence, we should also consider that as a result of having some basic knowledge of the path and practice of the small and medium scopes, which has endowed us with some amount of wisdom and skill, we are far better off than they are. That being the case, how could we not cultivate the wish to repay their kindness?

Of course, in order to think about this point properly, we first need to understand true cessation in terms of its potential to eliminate the two kinds of obscurations and so forth. As long as the goals of true cessation and liberation are very clear in our minds, we can sincerely wish these things for mother sentient beings.

ACTUALLY GENERATING THE MIND
THAT WISHES TO BENEFIT OTHERS
Loving-Kindness
In cultivating the actual mind of bodhichitta, the first three points of recognizing sentient beings as our mothers, remembering their kindness, and wishing to repay their kindness create the foundation of the mind that wishes to benefit others. The actual cultivation of the mind that wishes to benefit others occurs by way of the next three points: developing infinite loving-kindness for sentient beings, developing great compassion, and developing the extraordinary supreme thought of wishing to free them from suffering.

The objects of our infinite sense of loving-kindness are the sentient beings who lack true happiness. The aspect of the mind of loving-kindness is wishing sentient beings to have happiness and the causes of happiness.

When we cultivate infinite loving-kindness, wishing the very best of every happiness to sentient beings, we begin by wishing it for those who are very close and dear to us. Gradually we expand our wish to include our friends in general, to strangers, and then even to include our enemies. However, it isn't necessary to practice this sequence all the time. Later on, as our capacity grows, we can vary it.

We should begin our training in the infinite sense of loving-kindness by familiarizing our mind with two basic concepts: the clear ascertainment of how sentient beings do not have happiness, and the wish that they achieve the happiness they lack. When we think about how sentient beings lack happiness, we should think about all sentient beings—from ordinary sentient beings who have not entered any path up to and including arhats and even bodhisattvas. When we think only about sentient beings who lack ordinary, temporary, contaminated happiness, we are considering a limited number of sentient beings. When we only think about sentient beings who lack the happiness of liberation, we are also considering a limited number of sentient beings.

After thinking about what sentient beings lack, we wish that they may attain it. We wish them the cessation of suffering. We wish them the complete means of ultimate happiness.

Some practitioners generate compassion first and loving-kindness later. But generally speaking, it will probably be more effective to generate loving-kindness first and then cultivate compassion. In either case, there must be a basis of care, concern, and cherishing. Without this foundation we cannot generate either love or compassion.

The merits arising from cultivating equanimity, cultivating the recognition of all sentient beings as having been our mothers, remembering that kindness, wishing to repay them, and meditating on loving-kindness are far greater than the merits generated from an accumulation of merit in relation to a merit field of a hundred billion million worlds. Furthermore, Nagarjuna states in his *Precious Garland* that even the merit arising from feeding every single sentient being three meals a day would not compare to the merit of meditating on infinite loving-kindness for even a short time.

Please remember that the loving-kindness that we are referring to here is that which arises as a result of recognizing sentient beings as one's mother, remembering their kindness, and wishing to repay their kindness. All of these points are established on the basis of equanimity. We are talking specifically about a meditation with these foundations.

Great Compassion

The next point is cultivating the mind of great compassion that wishes sentient beings to be free of suffering.

It should be clear to us by now that the reason that sentient beings lack true happiness is because they experience so much suffering. The suffering that sentient beings experience is an obstacle to their experience of true happiness. Therefore, the mind of great compassion wishes sentient beings to be completely free from suffering and its causes.

When we generate compassion only in relation to gross suffering—the suffering of suffering—our compassion is very limited. When we extend it to include the suffering of change, our compassion covers more ground. If, however, we can generate compassion in relation to the third form of suffering—the suffering of pervasive conditioning—our compassion will become even more extensive. When we wish sentient beings to be free of even the *causes* of the suffering of pervasive conditioning, the compassion that we generate is truly capable of extending to every single sentient being, from ordinary beings who have yet to enter the path to those on the verge of enlightenment.

The depth and expanse of our great compassion is completely dependent upon our contemplations on the medium scope—how much we have thought about suffering in terms of our own experience. When we, ourselves, have gone through a particular sickness or disease, and we then see somebody else having the same problem, we are easily able to relate to his or her experience. In the same way, depending on how much we have familiarized ourselves with the experience of the path and practice of the small and medium scopes, we are able to effect the practice of the great scope that much more. The degree to which we have thought about the specific and general types of suffering in the medium scope and what it means to abandon their causes makes all the difference in what we are able to cultivate in the form of love and compassion in the great scope. It is often said that the profundity of the tantric path relies upon the basis of the path of sutra. In the same way, all of the magnificence and glory of the great scope is entirely rooted in the path and practice of the small and medium scopes. Without the foundation of these two, the path of the great scope is mere empty words.

The Supreme Thought That Takes Responsibility for Others

The supreme thought of taking responsibility for all sentient beings comes as a result of enhancing great compassion from the point of thinking how wonderful it would be if sentient beings were free of suffering to the point when that sense of cherishing and care has reached its highest potential. Having the spontaneous thought: "May I, myself, *cause* sentient beings to be free of suffering," is the mark of having generated the supreme thought of taking responsibility for others.

In order to cultivate the extraordinary supreme thought in our minds, we have to begin with renunciation. Based on that, we cultivate the first part of the seven-point instructions on cause and effect—equanimity, recognizing sentient beings as our mother, remembering their kindness, wishing to repay their kindness, and cultivating the infinite sense of loving-kindness and compassion. Only on that basis can we generate the experience of the extraordinary supreme thought.

When we cultivate great compassion, we generate the strong wish that sentient beings be free of suffering, thinking how wonderful it would be if this were so. It is only in the cultivation of the extraordinary supreme thought that we take the complete responsibility to make the objectives of the mind of compassion a personal reality. To use an analogy, compassion is like seeing the things that you want to buy and thinking that you would like to buy them to decorate your house, but the extraordinary supreme thought is actually making the decision to buy these things. Of course, in order to take complete responsibility for freeing all sentient beings from suffering, we ourselves have to be standing on our own two feet. Thus, we must attain enlightenment in order to bring about the cessation of suffering and the ultimate happiness of other sentient beings.

The extraordinary supreme thought of taking responsibility for others is related to the wish to repay the kindness of mother sentient beings, but it is an even greater, more exceptional state of mind. We are familiar with the first of the four immeasurables: "How wonderful it would be if sentient beings had happiness and were free of suffering." However, thinking that it is essential that sentient beings have happiness and are free from suffering and that oneself alone will take complete responsibility to bring this about is the compassion of the extraordinary supreme thought. The extraordinary supreme thought is the wish to free sentient beings from suffering developed to its greatest potential.

Some of you may think that this kind of thought appears very easy to generate. Others may think that it seems totally impossible. If you think that it's going to be quite easy, and then you find when you actually apply yourself on the path that it is in fact very difficult, it can cause you to totally lose hope, give up, and have negative thoughts. So, from the beginning, you should remember that the basis on which you are working is your own mind, which is completely under the control of self-cherishing thoughts. It is this mind that you have to turn inside out and upside down to be able to generate the extraordinary supreme thought of taking total responsibility for the ultimate welfare of others.

So what is the advice from Lama Tsongkhapa in this section? The advice is to engage ourselves in a continuous, uninterrupted form of practice, making effort to develop the thought to benefit others in our minds. We are advised to engage in this practice with continuity, and to practice not only in meditation, but also to carry on with basic goodness and kindness in our attitudes in the post-meditation periods. Living by this practice, the weeks become months, the months become years, and the years become a whole lifetime of practice in the thought to benefit others.

Training in the Mind That Strives for Enlightenment

After cultivating the aspiration to benefit others on the basis of the supreme thought, the next phase is developing the aspiration to attain enlightenment for sentient beings.

In order to fulfill the ultimate benefit of others, we must attain enlightenment. Developing the aspiration to do this is similar to cultivating a form of refuge. This being the case, I will mention again how important it is that we have a clear idea of what it means to be enlightened. In order to cultivate the aspiration to attain enlightenment, we must first be certain that the result can actually be attained. Previously we discussed the four reasons establishing Buddha as a valid person, and what it means to attain the enlightened state. By understanding the four reasons we can ascertain all the stages on the path to enlightenment, and that it is possible for us to progress on the path and reach the final goal.

When trying to develop the aspiration to attain enlightenment, we may also find it helpful to cultivate the understanding of the ultimate Buddha object of refuge, the ultimate Dharma object of refuge, and the ultimate Sangha object of refuge as we discussed earlier, and to cultivate the faith that aspires to attain the qualities of these objects. All of this, of course, has to be undertaken on the basis of the wish to benefit others—on the basis of love, compassion, and the extraordinary supreme thought, and also on the basis of understanding that the innate nature of our own mind is clear and knowing. We should know that all of our mental delusions and faults are temporary and adventitious, and that we have the complete potential to attain enlightenment.

In the training in the path and practice of the great scope, the infinite sense of loving-kindness, compassion, and the extraordinary supreme thought are the three mental states that make up the *actual* generation of the mind benefiting others. As I mentioned, the basis for cultivating the mind benefiting others is the recognition of sentient beings as one's own mother, remembering the kindness of those beings, and repaying their kindness.

In order to bring our determination to benefit sentient beings to fruition, we aspire to attain the enlightened state, the result of the four bodies of a buddha. When the altruistic aspiration to attain enlightenment only for the benefit of sentient beings arises spontaneously, effortlessly, and intuitively in our minds, we have generated conventional bodhichitta. We thus enter the Mahayana path of accumulation and become a bodhisattva, an object worthy of veneration and homage by celestial beings and humans, and from this point forward all of our activities become totally virtuous, whether we are eating, sleeping, or walking around. Not only do we become the basis of the label *bodhisattva* at this point, but we truly embody what this label implies.

In the same way, when we generate spontaneous faith in the objects of refuge in our minds, regardless of whether we take part in a refuge ceremony or not, we naturally become Buddhists. But if we have no thought of refuge and no faith in refuge, even if we take part in the ceremony, we cannot become Buddhists. Likewise, once we have generated bodhichitta, regardless of whether we go through the ritual or not, we become a bodhisattva. On the other hand, going to the ceremony without having generated bodhichitta will not turn us into bodhisattvas in and of itself.

Of course, please don't forget that in order to create the foundation for this practice in the great scope, it will be necessary for you to train your minds well in the path and practice common to the medium scope. And in order to create the basis for *that* practice, you will need to train in the path and practice which is common to the small scope.

We should begin our training in bodhichitta by listening extensively to teachings on this subject, and cultivating understanding of the topics. We should then reflect upon whatever we have listened to again and again through analytical meditation. Finally, we should familiarize our minds with whatever understanding we gain from this through meditation over and over again for a long time.

Overcoming Obstacles to Our Practice of Bodhichitta

The bodhisattva Togmay Sangpo states that all of the myriad forms of suffering that we experience arise as a result of wishing for our own happiness. Our personal problems also arise from our own self-centered minds, the ignorance grasping at a truly existent self. It is these two—the self-cherishing mind and the ignorance grasping at true existence—that cause of all of our troubles, and lead us to cause suffering in the lives of others.

As ordinary sentient beings training in the path to enlightenment, sometimes, while applying ourselves in the path of Dharma practice, we experience a lot of difficulties and problems, directly and indirectly. If we are not careful, we might end up thinking that all of the problems that we are experiencing come as a result of having met the Dharma or because we are trying to obtain enlightenment. In reality, however, it is our own ignorance grasping at true existence induced by the self-centered mind of self-cherishing that causes the suffering that we experience in ordinary worldly life as well as in our spiritual practice.

As it stands now, even while trying to engage in Dharma practice, we are still under the control of our own self-cherishing minds. We naturally seek better food, better clothing, a better reputation, and better shelter. Our minds are full of expectations, doubts, or suspicions, creating obstacles at the very beginning of the spiritual path. In the middle, the self-cherishing mind makes it impossible to unify our thoughts and actions with the Dharma. At the end, our self-cherishing mind makes it difficult to complete our Dharma practice. Seeing how it causes harm in the beginning, middle, and end, we should apply ourselves in order to gradually eliminate this mentality, which is like the loophole through which all our practices fall.

Although it is true that our minds are clouded by the ignorance that is the root of all our delusions, we should remember that we also have within us the potential to develop its antidote—the wisdom realizing selflessness. However, thinking that merely by listening to and contemplating the teachings on emptiness we will be able to extinguish the root of ignorance, overcome self-cherishing, and free ourselves from the eight worldly dharmas immediately is completely mistaken. In accordance with the *Ornament of Clear Realization,* in order to abandon our delusions we must begin with the grosser levels. We cannot expect to generate the most subtle form of wisdom right away, and thus eliminate the roots of ignorance immediately. Instead, we should begin with eliminating the manifest forms of the delusions and of ignorance, and gradually develop more subtle realizations over time. In this way, we will eventually be able to eliminate all of our suffering from its very root.

When we meditate on bodhichitta and find there is absolutely no effect of the meditation on our minds, we should backtrack. We should think, "Why is it that my mind has not been affected by my meditation on bodhichitta?" We should then check to see how much renunciation we have cultivated, how much we have attempted to get rid of the clinging and grasping to the pleasures of cyclic existence. If the results of the latter meditations are not forthcoming, we should go back and examine the foundation.

If we examine the reasons we are lacking compassion, we will see that a big part of the problem is that we are lacking renunciation. Renunciation comes on the basis of having contemplated suffering in terms of our own suffering, and the reason we have not yet developed it is that we have yet to abandon the thought clinging to the appearances of this life, the interests of the eight worldly dharmas, and the self-cherishing mind. Thus we can see the root of all of our problems—whether in terms of our Dharma experiences or our worldly experiences—lies within the self-cherishing mind.

The text goes on to say that all of our greatest attainments, such as the accomplishment of enlightenment, come as a result of wishing for the happiness of others. Generating the wisdom realizing emptiness is one of the causes of enlightenment, but wisdom realizing emptiness exists in the mind of those who attain liberation on the paths of the hearers and the solitary realizers as well. The difference between these practitioners and the practitioners of the Mahayana path is the mind of bodhichitta that seeks the benefit of other beings. This bodhichitta arises as a result of compassion, and compassion in turn arises as a result of renunciation. Renunciation arises as a result of giving up the thought clinging to the appearances of this life. Giving up the thought clinging to the appearances of this life, in turn, arises as a result of giving up our self-centered ways of thinking. In this way, more cherishing of others and less cherishing of oneself is the primary factor for setting forth on the spiritual path. We should think about these graduated stages of practice backward and forward until we can recall them clearly and easily in our minds.

Recognizing the Mind That Results from this Training

The development of infinite loving-kindness, great compassion, and the extraordinary supreme thought compose the complete wish to benefit others. This altruistic mental state is supported by the mind wishing to attain enlightenment for the purpose of others, which is the mind of conventional bodhichitta. Conventional bodhichitta is a primary mind. The mind seeking the benefit of others is a secondary mental factor. Love, compassion, and the extraordinary supreme thought are all secondary mental factors. Even the wish to attain enlightenment for the benefit of others is a secondary mental factor, accompanying the primary mind of conventional bodhichitta.

Perhaps you are wondering at this point how exactly it is that the infinite sense of loving-kindness, compassion, and the supreme thought taking responsibility for beings are mental states that benefit others. The mind of loving-kindness wishes the very best result of happiness, liberation, and enlightenment—the ultimate form of happiness—for other beings. Thus it qualifies as a mind benefiting others. In the same way, the mind of compassion also qualifies as a mind benefiting others because it wishes for others to attain a state of total freedom from the very roots of suffering, which are the imprints of the delusions. The extraordinary supreme thought taking responsibility for others also wishes both of these things, and takes complete responsibility to bring all sentient beings to that state of ultimate happiness and complete cessation of suffering. Therefore this mind, too, is a mind benefiting others.

When we shape our minds into this beautiful thought wishing to benefit others based on the cultivation of equanimity, the recognition of sentient beings as one's mother, remembering their kindness, wishing to repay their kindness, the infinite sense of loving-kindness, great compassion, and the extraordinary supreme thought, our minds take on a very pure aspect. Whatever virtuous activities that we do by way of accumulation of merit or purification become very powerful if they are done on this basis. As well, every beneficial action that we engage in physically or verbally becomes much more powerfully positive because the receptacle of our mind has become priceless, like a treasure vase.

Within this lifetime, with this body, with this mind, we have the potential to generate bodhichitta. Once we accomplish this, wherever we go, whatever we do, we constantly generate virtue. As we become more familiar with the extraordinary supreme thought based in love and compassion, it becomes spontaneous. When this happens, we are able to complete the accumulations of the two types of merit very quickly.

In the beginning, we have to put a lot of effort into getting our minds to think like this. It takes months and years to train our minds to see things in this way. But by reflecting over and over and over again, eventually these thoughts become habitual, and we find ourselves able to engage in walking meditation on love and compassion or traveling meditation on love and compassion. In fact, everything we do becomes a meditation on love and compassion.

To inspire us, let us look at a section from *Ornament for the Mahayan Sutras,* in which Maitreya lists four attributes of the mind of conventional bodhichitta.

The first of the four is a great sense of joy. The mind that has generated conventional bodhichitta experiences great joy engaging in every activity to benefit sentient beings, no matter how difficult it may be. Right now, in contrast, the activities benefiting sentient beings are difficult because we are unable to separate ourselves from the motivations of the eight worldly dharmas and our own self-cherishing.

The second attribute of the mind of conventional bodhichitta is perseverance and enthusiasm for engaging in the beneficial activities of the meditation and post-meditation periods. Bodhichitta is divided into two types: aspiring bodhichitta and engaging bodhichitta. The mind of aspiring bodhichitta wishes to attain enlightenment to be of ultimate benefit to others. With the mind of engaging bodhichitta, however, we actually engage in the actions that will lead to that accomplishment. With perseverance and enthusiasm, we are able to quickly accomplish the accumulation of the two types of merits and attain enlightenment.

The third attribute of the mind of conventional bodhichitta is that it is extremely meaningful to benefit and bring about the happiness of ourselves and others. Our own benefit is fulfilled because when we generate bodhichitta, we naturally abandon self-cherishing thoughts. And the less self-cherishing we experience, the less often our minds give rise to delusions, and the greater our happiness will be.

The fourth attribute of the mind of conventional bodhichitta is that it is the cause of accomplishing the state of full enlightenment. Enlightenment is the result of having completed the two vast accumulations of merit, the merit of virtue and the merit of wisdom. An enlightened being has completely abandoned the two types of obscurations and embodies omniscience, great compassion, and perfect power to be of ultimate benefit for self and others. This result cannot be attained on the basis of wisdom realizing emptiness alone, but only on the basis of wisdom supported by bodhichitta.

In order to practice the Mahayana path, we first eliminate the thought clinging to the appearances of this life, the thought clinging to future lifetimes, and we then cultivate the mind of renunciation and the mind of wisdom realizing emptiness. In addition to these contemplations, we should also cultivate our aspiration to develop bodhichitta by constantly reminding ourselves of the extensive benefits of this mind by way of these four attributes.

As I mentioned, the mind of conventional bodhichitta is a primary mind. It cannot be a secondary mind. Its objective is the attainment of the full and complete state of enlightenment, the state of total freedom from all failings and mistakes, the full completion of all knowledge and positive qualities. This means the attainment of the nature body, the transcendental wisdom body, the body of enjoyment, and the emanation body of a buddha.

Because conventional bodhichitta is a primary mind, it is considered a cognitive aspect of the main mental consciousness. This being the case, it is always accompanied by the five omnipresent mental factors, which are feeling, discrimination, intention, attention, and contact. Within the categories of feeling, however, it is impossible that the mind of conventional bodhichitta be accompanied by the feeling of suffering. When initially cultivating the mind of conventional bodhichitta, we experience the feeling of equanimity. Then, later on, when we generate the spontaneous, uncontrived, effortless mind of conventional bodhichitta, we experience the feeling of happiness.

Why is it impossible for the secondary mental factor accompanying the primary mind of conventional bodhichitta to be the feeling of suffering? Of course, when we are first generating the mind of bodhichitta, we actually generate this mind by thinking about suffering. Despite this, the mind of conventional bodhichitta that solely and completely seeks the welfare of others takes on such a complete sense of responsibility to extinguish suffering that it does not undergo the experience of suffering itself. It does not experience suffering precisely *because* it has willingly taken on the responsibility to eliminate the suffering of others.

The secondary mental factor of discrimination that accompanies the primary mind of bodhichitta discerns the goal of attaining perfect enlightenment. In fact, all of the five omnipresent mental factors accompanying this mind have the goal of enlightenment as their objective.

Of the two aspirations of the mind of bodhichitta—the aspiration to benefit sentient beings and the aspiration to attain enlightenment in order to actually benefit them—the aspiration to attain enlightenment is the secondary mental factor accompanying the primary mind of conventional bodhichitta. In accordance with the texts on mind and mental factors or *lorig (blo rigs)*, a main or primary mind cannot be accompanied by more than one aspiration at a time. However, all of the major scriptures that address this topic, such as the *Ornament of Clear Realization* and so forth, discuss conventional bodhichitta as being a mind that has two aspirations—the aspiration to benefit sentient beings and the aspiration to attain enlightenment. They explain this by stating that the aspiration wishing to benefit others is a *cause* for the aspiration wishing to attain enlightenment, while the aspiration wishing to attain enlightenment is the aspiration that actually accompanies the mind of conventional bodhichitta.

Loving-kindness, compassion, and the extraordinary supreme thought serve as the three causes of the main aspiration to enlightenment, and are all secondary mental factors. Because they are all secondary mental factors the aspiration to benefit sentient beings is also a secondary mental factor. Because they are all secondary mental factors, they accompany a primary mind of bodhichitta. Any primary mind has five determining factors: aspiration, belief, remembrance, concentration, and wisdom. All of these five secondary mental factors exist in relation to the object that is realized.

It is important to understand why bodhichitta is so essential to our practice, particularly since we are constantly exposed to the opportunity to take tantric initiations in which we are asked to generate conventional bodhichitta, visualized as a moon disk, and ultimate bodhichitta, visualized as a white vajra standing in its center. We need to know what kind of mental states these are, where they begin, and where they end. In order to have the basis for cultivating such a visualization, we should have a complete understanding of what bodhichitta mind is about. As Lama Tsongkhapa says, it is not sufficient for us to be students of the Mahayana teachings, but rather we ourselves as individuals should become Mahayanists in our attitude. Making this a reality depends entirely on the strength of our understanding of bodhichitta.

Distinguishing between Types of Bodhichitta
As a bodhisattva who has entered the Mahayana travels that path, the bodhichitta in that being's mind progresses through four stages of development. The bodhichitta on the first two Mahayana paths, the paths of accumulation and preparation, is called the *bodhichitta immersed in faith.* On the fourth to the seventh grounds, the path of seeing up until the path of meditation, the bodhichitta is called *bodhichitta of the extraordinary supreme thought.* On the last three grounds, the eighth, ninth, and tenth, which is the path of meditation, the bodhichitta is called the *mind that has ripened in every aspect.* The bodhichitta on the path of no more learning is called the *bodhichitta that has abandoned all obscurations.*

Generating aspiring bodhichitta, generating the extraordinary supreme thought of bodhichitta, generating bodhichitta that is fully ripened in every aspect, and generating the mind that is free of all obscurations are *not* practices that are exclusive of wisdom. The method aspects of the mind on the path must be developed in conjunction with the wisdom realizing emptiness. During the cultivation of aspiring bodhichitta on the paths of accumulation and preparation, the accompanying wisdom still perceives subject-object duality. The wisdom that accompanies the extraordinary supreme thought that is generated on the path of seeing, however, is the wisdom directly realizing emptiness. This kind of wisdom does not perceive subject-object duality. Although the wisdom that accompanies the bodhichitta that is ripe in every aspect on the first seven impure grounds is also direct and no longer polluted by the gross form of grasping at true existence, the innate form of grasping at true existence, which is more subtle, still remains.

Aspiring bodhichitta and engaging bodhichitta are distinguished from one another on the basis of the bodhisattva vow. Up until the point of taking the actual bodhisattva vow, the bodhichitta that we generate in our minds is aspiring bodhichitta. Once we have taken the bodhisattva commitments, the bodhichitta that we have in our minds can be labeled engaging bodhichitta, although, depending on the level of mind of the practitioner, it may not actually be engaging bodhichitta at this point. Engaging bodhichitta is distinguished by the practitioner's actual engagement in the practices to attain enlightenment for the benefit of all beings. When our conduct does not embody these activities, but we still have the wish in our minds to attain this state for the sake of others, our bodhichitta is aspiring or wishing bodhichitta.

Actually, there is some history of disagreement between scholars as to the distinctions between aspiring and engaging bodhichitta. In the writings of the great Indian masters, there are many different presentations regarding Mahayana mind generation. When Lama Tsongkhapa clarified them, he did not make it definitive. Among the great monasteries, the Sera Je School and the Drepung School follow different scriptures in reference to the subject of Mahayana mind generation. According to Panchen Sonam Drakpa, whose interpretation is followed by the scholars of Drepung Loseling, the mind in meditative equipoise on the Mahayana path of seeing does not possess conventional bodhichitta. According to this point of view, there is no such thing as the mind of bodhichitta that holds the mind of meditative equipoise on emptiness: in the mind of meditative equipoise there is no presence of conventional bodhichitta at all, or any other mind— the mind of equipoise is alone. According to the Drepung tradition, for a mental state to exist it should be directly manifest. That being the case, the debate follows, a being on the first ground in meditative equipoise must not have conventional bodhichitta, or refuge, or any other mental state, because none of these is manifest at this time.

According to the writings of Sera Je Jetsunpa, whose interpretation is followed by the scholars of Sera Je, conventional bodhichitta actually does exist in the mind of a being in meditative equipoise on the path of seeing. In order to exist, according to Jetsunpa, a mind does not necessarily have to be directly manifest. Therefore, all sentient beings who are in meditative equipoise on emptiness on the path of seeing also possess aspiring bodhichitta at that time.

With regard to the question of whether these two types of bodhichitta take the form of one or two continuums when developed in one being's mind, all the presentations say that the two types of bodhichitta are one substantial continuum. According to Jetsunpa, the continuum of bodhichitta in a being's mind is the continuation of the continuum that the practitioner developed while practicing the seven-point instructions on cause and effect. When a practitioner engages in the practices of ethics and generosity in the post-meditation periods, the bodhichitta that accompanies these activities becomes engaging bodhichitta. During meditative equipoise on emptiness, that bodhichitta becomes aspiring bodhichitta. In other words, it is engaging bodhichitta when the practitioner is directly engaging in physical or verbal activities, and it is aspiring if the individual is practicing meditative equipoise. The substantial continuum of bodhichitta is always there, in the practitioner's mind, and it becomes engaging or aspiring bodhichitta depending on what the individual is practicing.

The two aspects of bodhichitta were taught by Buddha in the *Array of Stalks Sutra,* and were further clarified by Shantideva in the following verse:

As one understands the difference
Between one who goes and one who wants to go,
So the wise should understand
The difference between these two.

Training in the Method of Exchanging Self with Others

BENEFITS AND DISADVANTAGES

The practice of equalizing and exchanging self for others originated with

Buddha, and the lineage was passed down through Nagarjuna, Shantideva, Atisha, and Dromtonpa. Early on, this technique was regarded as a secret instruction, meaning that it was taught exclusively to those disciples whose minds were fully ripened or who had the potential to undertake these practices, as opposed to being taught in public. After Dromtonpa the tradition was maintained as secret advice in the Kadampa lineage. From Chekawa onward, however, for fear of the lineage being lost completely, it slowly began to be taught publicly.

The section on equalizing and exchanging self for others in the *Lamrim Chenmo* begins with explanations of the benefits of doing this practice and the disadvantages of not doing it.

From Shantideva's *Guide to the Bodhisattva's Way of Life*:

Those who wish to protect
Themselves and others quickly
Should rely upon the secret practice
Of exchanging self for others.

And also:

Whatever happiness is found in this world
All arises from wishing for the happiness of others.
Whatever suffering is found in this world
All arises from wishing for one's own happiness.

When we consider the shortcomings of self-cherishing, we should begin by thinking about the fact that we have been cherishing our own selves since beginningless time. And yet with this thought only concerned for our own welfare, with this selfish interest that has accompanied us for countless lifetimes, nothing fruitful has arisen. No good has come of it at all. The reason that we are still lacking true freedom is because of this self-cherishing mind. Not only has no positive result been forthcoming from this attitude, but we have experienced great loss because of it. Since cherishing the self has borne no fruit and caused us so many losses, and since we have to cherish someone, why not cherish others? Examining the benefits of the mind that cherishes others through the use of logic and reasoning, through scriptural authority, and through our own inferential cognition, we will surely see that this is the most reasonable conclusion.

In terms of this lifetime, no matter how much happiness and worldly comfort we seek—whether in the form of better food, better clothing, better shelter, a better reputation—and no matter how much we accumulate, it is never enough. This is because of the self-cherishing mind. No matter what we come to possess, as long as self-cherishing is still prominent in our attitudes, we continually suffer from a basic lack of satisfaction. Even having just about everything, we still feel something is missing. If, however, we are able to succeed in the practice of exchanging self for others, putting the needs and wants of other beings before our own desires, the lack of contentment that we feel in our minds today will disappear, and we will experience only joy. The dissatisfaction that we feel now will become the experience of happiness.

Renouncing self and cherishing others does not mean that you should allow others to do whatever they like to you. Rather, when you cherish yourself, you work for the fulfillment of the positive causes and conditions that bring positive results for yourself in the long run, and the elimination of the negative causes and conditions that bring negative results for yourself in the future. By renouncing self-cherishing, and trying to cherish others, you do the same thing in terms of other sentient beings. Your focus becomes working for the fulfillment of the positive causes and conditions that will bring the result of future happiness for other beings, and eliminating the negative causes and conditions that will bring the result of future suffering into their lives.

Shakyamuni Buddha himself is an example of someone who has fully developed the mind cherishing others. In comparison to the way that Buddha cherished others, what we conceive of when we think of this concept is very childlike.

Cherishing others doesn't mean being tolerant of all their activities and giving them whatever they want. When you cherish others, you encourage them to abandon the ten nonvirtuous activities of body, speech, and mind. You inspire them to practice the path of three higher trainings of ethics, concentration, and wisdom, and the bodhisattva's path. You should encourage and inspire other beings to abandon what is to be abandoned in their thoughts and actions and to take up what is to be cultivated on the path of positive mental development.

In order to cherish others from the depths of your heart, you must have the wish to benefit them. It doesn't mean that whatever you do has to bear fruit. At this point, whether the intended result arises or not is secondary, as long you have the sincere wish to help others. In this world, all of the great beings—from Buddha to Manjushri to Maitreya to Nagarjuna, from all of the great Indian masters to the great Tsongkhapa himself—have achieved their greatness on the basis of renouncing self and cherishing others. All of their accomplishments have been based on this mentality.

Becoming Familiar

The habit of cherishing ourselves is not an inherently existent state of mind. It is not a mind that exists from its own side. The only reason we have self-cherishing at all is because we are so used to it, so accustomed to thinking about the world from this point of view. We have become habituated to functioning under the power of self-cherishing because we have invested countless lifetimes into this pattern of thought, and we have strengthened our self-cherishing mind with the support of many causes and conditions. That being the case, once we do in fact create the causes and conditions and begin to habituate our thoughts and actions toward the mentality of cherishing others, it will not be impossible to change our minds. If we create the causes, the result is not impossible. It is the natural course of dependent arising that by familiarizing ourselves over and over and over again with the thoughts and actions of cherishing others, eventually this state of mind will naturally arise. So please don't think that this is beyond your reach. Just as through habit you have come to cherish yourself, through habit you can actualize cherishing others.

The fact that sentient beings wish to experience happiness and do not wish to experience suffering is a natural reality. It cannot be changed through causes and conditions. Our self-cherishing minds, however, are not a natural reality at all but have been brought about by habitual karmic patterns. When we change the object of self to the object of others, and we cultivate the habit of thinking of their welfare before our own, we can definitely conceive of the thought that cherishes them.

Although we are habituated to our self-cherishing perspective, we will see, upon examination, it is a mental state that is actually quite unsatisfactory. The thought cherishing others, however, is the basis upon which many extraordinary qualities can be developed. To be able to exchange self for others, to be able to renounce self-cherishing, is only a matter of becoming habituated to that thought of cherishing others and distancing ourselves from that habit of cherishing the self. It doesn't require three countless eons of merit or the direct realization of wisdom realizing emptiness—it's just a matter of cultivating the habit. It is definitely within our capacity to develop the ability to exchange self for others and renounce self-cherishing, with this body in this lifetime.

For example, imagine that there was some person in the earlier part of your life who used to frighten you tremendously—such that merely hearing the name of that person would bring great fear to your heart. Then in the later part of your life this very same person became someone from whom you were inseparable. If your mind can change to such a degree within one lifetime in terms of its perspective on one person, then why not also in the case of renouncing self and cherishing others?

Generally speaking, when we say, "my body," we have a very strong sense of cherishing our physical form. In relation to identifying ourselves with these aggregates, we make a great differentiation between "me" and "my" aggregates, and what "others" are in relation to "me" and "my" aggregates. Yet even the aggregate of form, strictly speaking, has nothing to do with our bodies. In reality, "my body" arises from the sperm and egg of our parents, and thus is the continuum of what is in fact "other's body." Through our habitual pattern of thinking, we have come to identify what in fact belongs to others as our own, and have come to cherish it. If we can regard what is in fact another's body as "mine" and come to cherish it, then we should see how it is not at all impossible to cherish other beings.

Furthermore, from the perspective of ultimate truth, what is "I" and what is "others" are not inherently existent "I" and "others." What is "I" is dependent upon the other, what is "others" is dependent upon the "I"— they exist in dependence on each other and have no inherent existence from their own side. When we say "this side" or "the other side," the existence of this side depends on the other side, and the existence of the other side depends on this side. You could not designate "this side" if there were no "other side." This side has no inherent existence; the other side has no inherent existence. In the same way, the color blue exists in dependence upon being distinguished from the color yellow, and the color yellow exists in dependence upon being distinguished from the color blue. The interdependence of "I" and "others" is even closer than this!

When we think like this—about how "I" and "others" do not inherently exist, how there is such close interdependence between labels, how we have through habit come to regard what in fact is another's body as our own—we can see how "I" and "others" are not at all mutually exclusive. We can see that in fact there is no great difference between "I" and "others" at all. There is not a solid, concrete distinction between these two. Since there is no independently existent "other" and no independently existent "I," there is no valid basis for holding ourselves of great importance, for cherishing ourselves and renouncing others.

Perhaps our very gross minds begin to think that since the suffering of others does not benefit me or harm me or affect me in any way, there's no reason for me to be bothered by it, and that there is simply no reason for me to cherish them. If we find ourselves thinking like this, we can recall the fact that even while we are young, although the suffering of old age is not affecting us right then, we pay into the pension that will provide for us when we are old. We can apply the same reasoning to the logic of cherishing others.

Our gross minds may then counter by insisting that these are two different things: my old age is the continuum of my present existence, and therefore it *does* affect me. But when we talk about the aggregates, there is no inherently existent self. The aggregates and so forth all exist due to dependence, due to imputation, whether we are talking about the present situation or our own future continuum. There is no inherently existent "me" in my youth, there is no inherently existent "me" in my old age. All of this exists merely by dependence. In the same way, although what is "me" and others is not one continuum, still there is no inherently existent "me" and "others." "Me" and "others" exist in dependence. Myself in my youth and myself in the future, in old age, are interdependent. We should apply this same logic to ourselves and other sentient beings.

To clarify, we are not saying here that there is no existence of self or others. What we are saying here is that there is no *inherently existing* self and others. The only way that self and others exist is through interdependence.

Dedicating all our merits to the benefit of others is another way to counteract the self-cherishing mind. Sometimes I am asked whether dedicating merits to others will really benefit them or not. The entire Buddhadharma is founded on cause and effect, and inclusive of this law is the fact that one can never experience a result for which one has not created a cause. And so, even though we dedicate our merits to others, we are the ones who actually accumulate the merit. However, we can say in general that since we have had countless, beginningless lifetimes, we have always had some connection to sentient beings. The connections of the immediate lifetime, whether Dharma connections or worldly connections, also affect the situation. By virtue of these connections, dedicated merit *can* benefit the person to whom you dedicate it. It may not have an extremely strong, direct effect, but indirectly it has some benefit. However, it is even more important to understand that the dedication of merits *will* directly affect our own mind of self-cherishing, and enhance the mind wishing to give to others.

From *Guide to the Bodhisattva's Way of Life*:

As the state of buddhahood depends equally
On sentient beings and on the buddhas,
How is it then that I do not respect
Sentient beings as I do the buddhas?

Since both the buddhas and sentient beings equally enable us to attain the result of enlightenment, why should we revere the buddhas so much, taking them as our objects of refuge, making offerings, and being very humble, while at the same time being immensely disrespectful to the sentient beings around us, who are the other half of the cause for our enlightenment? Why should we make such a distinction between them?

Furthermore, if we merely cultivate our minds in renunciation and the wisdom realizing emptiness, and if the mind that cherishes others is not strongly established, the highest result we can possibly attain will be the result of an arhat on the path of the individual vehicle. The omniscient state of full enlightenment is not possible without the firm foundation of the mind of cherishing others.

We should become as familiar as possible with the many disadvantages of cherishing the self and the many great benefits that arise from the practice of cherishing others, and understand them.

STAGES OF THE ACTUAL PRACTICE OF EQUALIZING
AND EXCHANGING SELF WITH OTHERS

Although the seven-point instructions on cause and effect were taught by Chandrakirti, and the technique of equalizing and exchanging self with others was taught by Shantideva, in the *Lamrim Chenmo* the two methods are often presented in a combined practice having eleven parts. Training the mind in this method is an extremely effective way to develop and sustain the mind of bodhichitta.

The first point is creating the basis of the mind of equanimity as presented in Kamalashila's *Stages of Meditation*. We should be familiar with the method for doing this, as we have discussed equanimity extensively already.

The second point is the recognition of all sentient beings as our mothers, which we have also discussed, followed by the third point, remembering their kindness. In the usual form of remembering kindness from the seven-point instructions of cause and effect, we focus on remembering the kindness of sentient beings as our mothers in particular. We concentrate on the fact that sentient beings have been our mothers countless times, and have so selflessly nurtured us. In the combined practice, however, we remember the kindness of sentient beings in an extraordinary way: we think about the kindness of sentient beings even while they were *not* our mother. In respect to this, we should reflect on the fact that all of our comfort and happiness, great or small, comes in dependence on an infinite chain of direct and indirect kindness from other sentient beings. When practicing the combined technique, it is most effective if we think about kindness in these two ways: by focusing on the kindness of mother sentient beings in terms of that particular relationship, and then recalling how, even outside of that role, sentient beings are responsible for every single happiness that we experience.

The fourth point is the wish to repay that kindness, as we have already discussed.

The fifth is equalizing self and others in the sense of understanding that we are all the same in wanting happiness and in not wanting suffering—that there is no difference between ourselves and others in that way. Furthermore, we should contemplate the reality that we are not inherently existent, that what is "I" and what is "others" is totally interdependent.

The sixth point is thinking of the manifold disadvantages of cherishing the self, which should be clear by now.

The seventh is thinking of the manifold advantages of cherishing others, which should also be clear.

The result of thinking in these ways brings us to the eighth point. This is the actual practice of exchanging self with others in which we visualize taking on the sufferings of others from the base of the mind of compassion. Although we do not possess omniscience, great compassion, or the perfect power to know sentient beings' exact needs or their mind level and predispositions at the moment, as beginners on the path or as ordinary sentient beings we can nonetheless enhance the mind of compassion through this visualization practice.

We should begin our practice by imagining that we are taking on the suffering of people who are very close and dear to us. When we can generate a genuine and heartfelt sense of this, we can then extend our practice to include strangers, then further extend it to all of our enemies. In this way we will cultivate a very pervasive sense of compassion, even extending to beings born in the hot hells and the cold hells—taking on the suffering of all the beings of the six realms as well as all of the bodhisattvas up to the tenth ground.

This meditation on compassion should have the effect of opening our hearts. If we feel uncomfortable taking on the suffering of others even at the level of imagination, it means that we have not fully embraced the mind of compassion. The reason there is discomfort or doubt in our minds is because we lack compassion, and the reason that we lack compassion is because we lack the strength of the mind that cherishes others. We lack the capacity to cherish others because we cherish ourselves so strongly. We have a very strong sense of cherishing the self because we have not succeeded in our practice of equalizing and exchanging self for others. Therefore, we should go back to the root, reinforcing our thinking by repeating the contemplations regarding the advantages in cherishing others and the disadvantages of cherishing self.

If we have cultivated the mind of compassion, but are still experiencing obstacles in our practice of taking on the suffering of others, we are advised to begin with taking on our own future suffering—whatever suffering is to come in the later part of the day, in the week ahead, in the month ahead, or in the years ahead. It is easy to accept taking on our own suffering because it has to do with ourselves. As we become habituated to taking on our own future suffering, we can gradually begin to take on the suffering of beings that are very close and dear to us, then extend that to strangers, to enemies, and to all the beings of the six realms.

Even though we are only practicing the visual technique of taking on the suffering of others, and thus not *actually* relieving them of suffering, this practice is nonetheless a basis upon which we can accumulate extensive merit. Our practice of this technique will improve with familiarity and habit. Although in the beginning stages we will not be able to bring about a perfect result, there are cases in which the karmic connection is extraordinarily strong and in which the mind of the practitioner has been developed so completely that the visualization can actually become real. You may have heard about the bodhisattva Togmay Sangpo, who cried out in pain and took the bruises onto his own body when someone threw a stone at a stray dog. In the cases of those bodhisattvas who have fully encompassed the mind of great compassion that wishes to take on every suffering of others, these kinds of things can happen in reality.

Having familiarized ourselves with the technique of taking on the suffering of others, we should then practice giving happiness, which is the ninth point. Actually, the order in which we practice the two points—giving happiness with love and taking suffering with compassion—is not set. It is fine to begin either way. However, from the point of view of convenience, it is usually recommended that we first take on suffering with the mind of compassion, and then give happiness from the resources of the mind of infinite loving-kindness.

Giving happiness, too, at this stage, is only a visual form of giving. With the love that wishes happiness for others, we visualize that we are giving our body, our possessions, and our merits of the past, present, and future to bring forth the result of ultimate happiness in the lives of others. In real life, giving happiness can even be the *wish* to give, if it is not possible to really give something.

Having practiced in this way for a while, we should then recall that although by means of this practice we are developing our mind's capacity to take on the suffering of others and to give them happiness, that is all we are doing. In reality, at present, we cannot actually bring about these results. Therefore, the tenth point in this meditation is the cultivation of the extraordinary supreme thought, by which we make the resolution to take on the complete responsibility to liberate sentient beings from suffering.

To clarify, the practice of giving and taking with loving compassion is the actual manifestation of the mind wishing to benefit others. When we do this practice, of course, any benefit to others that we are actually able to bring about occurs only through our imaginations. To be able to take on the suffering of sentient beings in our lives for real, we need to attain the state of perfection in which we have abandoned everything that is to be abandoned and realized everything that is to be realized. Once we have attained this state, we can actualize the objectives of our love and compassion. Therefore, the eleventh point is training the mind in the wish to attain enlightenment solely for the welfare of others. This is also known as the Mahayana mind generation. When the thought aspiring to attain enlightenment for the benefit of beings is established very firmly like the king of mountains in our minds, we can quickly complete the realizations of the paths and grounds and reach the ultimate attainment.

The Benefits of Generating Bodhichitta

The main goal of the combined practice of the seven-point instructions and exchanging self with others is to generate bodhichitta. Many benefits are taught in the scriptures in order to inspire us to generate this virtuous mind. We should study these and try to understand them in order to be further inspired to generate the mind of bodhichitta. This is specifically stated by the Fifth Dalai Lama in the text from the lamrim tradition known as the *Instruction from Manjushri.*

The first benefit of the bodhichitta bearing the two aspects is that the wish to attain enlightenment solely for the welfare of others is regarded as the gateway of the Mahayana path. Thus, once you have generated bodhichitta, you become a practitioner who has entered the Mahayana path.

The second benefit is that the practitioner who has the mind of bodhichitta is endowed with the name of a bodhisattva, and becomes the heart-child of the buddhas. Generally speaking, of course, there is no sentient being who is not a heart-child of the buddhas, but by cultivating the mind of renunciation and bodhichitta, we become the heart-child in a special sense, as we are well on our way to fulfilling all of the hopes and wishes of the enlightened beings.

The third benefit is that a being who attains the state of a bodhisattva for the very first time outshines the arhats on the paths of the hearer and the solitary realizer. For example, when a prince is born, by his birthright he exceeds the greatness of his ministers, despite their many and various qualifications. In the same way, upon generating the mind of bodhichitta, the greatness of a bodhisattva exceeds that of the arhats on the other paths.

The fourth benefit is that upon generating the mind of bodhichitta, the practitioner becomes a supreme field of merit for others. The sentient beings of our time do not have the karmic fortune to encounter the supreme emanation of the historical Buddha, nor have most of them cultivated the level of concentration known as the concentration of the continuum of Dharma, which enables them to see enlightened forms. However, the bodhisattvas who have attained the path of accumulation and the path of preparation *are* a supreme field of merit that sentient beings can access, and in relation to whom they can accumulate merit. When we generate bodhichitta, we ourselves become part of this merit field.

The fifth benefit is that by generating the mind of bodhichitta we are able to quickly accomplish the accumulation of the two types of merit—the merit of virtue and the merit of wisdom. It is on the basis of bodhichitta that we are able to train in the practices of the six perfections and thereby accomplish the accumulation of the merit of virtue, and it is also on the basis of bodhichitta that we are able to undertake these practices in conjunction with the wisdom realizing emptiness, and accomplish the accumulation of the merit of wisdom.

The sixth benefit is that we are able to purify the obscurations of our negative karma very quickly. Even very powerful negative karma can be completely purified by the mind of bodhichitta. Even if for some reason we cannot purify every result of our negative actions completely, with the mind of bodhichitta we can purify them at least to the extent that their effects become very, very light. Just as a prisoner who has received an extremely heavy punishment seeks parole for good behavior, in the same way, by applying the four opponent powers and generating the mind of bodhichitta, we are able to effect a very strong purification and lessen the effects of our negative karma.

The seventh benefit is that all of our wishes will be fulfilled very easily, without hindrance. This refers to our wishes that are in accordance with the Dharma.

The eighth benefit is that we will be protected from all harm and obstacles. Ordinarily, due to our delusions and self-cherishing, we experience interferences, harm from enemies, harm from human and nonhuman sources. But generally speaking, since harm and obstacles arise because of negative, self-cherishing minds, if we work only to benefit others, it is far less likely that others will harm us or try to create obstacles in our lives.

Once in Tibet there was a town whose inhabitants were experiencing a great deal of harm from nonhuman beings. In the West such a place would be said to be haunted, I think. In the houses of the people in this town, the taps would turn on until the water flooded everywhere, and things would move all over the place by themselves. Even during the daytime the people in this town were very frightened, keeping all the doors locked and so forth, which of course did no good whatsoever. Finally, the inhabitants of the town invited a lama to come and help pacify the disturbances of the place. Generally, in accordance with tantric practice, there are many complicated rituals that one can do to counteract all these disturbances, but the main practices of this particular lama were the meditations on bodhichitta and emptiness. Therefore, when he arrived in the town, he simply sat down and began to meditate. When he was finished, because he hadn't done a lot of rituals or rung bells or banged drums and so forth, the people of the town doubted whether anything had happened, whether he had succeeded in subduing whatever forces were disturbing them. But after he left, the entire town was completely changed, and became a very peaceful place.

Obstacles such as frightening dreams and so forth also come due to the mind's overactive, superstitious way of thinking. As Milarepa stated, conceptual thoughts are the gateway for every kind of harm. Just as we say that in order to receive the blessings of the buddhas, our own mind needs to be opened by faith, in the same way our superstitions, hopes, and expectations open our mind to all harm. We can counteract this harm by meditating on emptiness, or meditating on bodhichitta. This is the very best kind of puja. When prayers are requested to remove sickness or obstacles, the very best kinds of prayers are these meditations on emptiness and bodhichitta.

The ninth benefit is that, with bodhichitta, we will be able to complete all of the paths and grounds very quickly.

The tenth benefit is that bodhichitta is the source of all the forms of happiness of transmigrating beings. It is like the very rich field from which one can harvest the well-being of sentient beings.

The Mahayana mind generation is the gateway to both the causal vehicle and the resultant vehicle of the Mahayana. If we are fortunate enough to enter the resultant vehicle of the Guhyasamaja Tantra, on the basis of which we can accomplish enlightenment within this one brief lifetime, even if we have the negative karma of the five heinous crimes, due to the profundity of the practice we can still purify and attain enlightenment. Yet we cannot practice this way if our mind is separated from the thought of bodhichitta. In fact, the tantric path is so profound and quick *because* of the mind of bodhichitta. Therefore, our progression on the Mahayana and the Vajrayana paths becomes entirely a question of whether we have the mind of bodhichitta or not.

The wisdom realizing emptiness is common to both the Mahayana and the Hinayana vehicle. It is also the ultimate result of both vehicles. Bodhichitta, however, is exclusive to the universal vehicle of the Mahayana. We cannot attain enlightenment without holding bodhichitta as the very core of our practice. Whatever realization of the paths and grounds we are able to accomplish and whatever roots of virtue we are able to accumulate are completely dependent upon the mind of bodhichitta. In the Madhyamaka root text it is said that the hearers, the solitary realizers, and the buddhas all arise from the source of the mind of bodhichitta. Therefore, we should realize the importance of bodhichitta and the need to hold it as the very core of our practice.

There are two types of people who practice the path. There are those who practice in a very intense way, seeking to attain enlightenment within this very lifetime, and then there are others who do not engage in an intense daily practice and progress more slowly, attaining enlightenment over lifetimes. Those who have the intensity for practice, in order to realize the fruits and results of such practice, cannot do so without the mind of bodhichitta. Without the mind of bodhichitta, even the most profound deity yoga practice will not bring results.

THE MEASURE OF GENERATING
BODHICHITTA MIND

The measure of generating bodhichitta is when, having trained in the practices of the seven-point instructions on cause and effect and the practice of exchanging self for others, you experience the spontaneous wish to attain enlightenment in order to benefit all beings. Once you have the spontaneous wish to accomplish this for the benefit of others, your bodhichitta is labeled *earth-like bodhichitta,* and you enter the first of the five Mahayana paths, the path of accumulation.

THE MANNER OF HOLDING BODHICHITTA
THROUGH RITUAL

Through Ritual, Obtaining What One Has Not Obtained

Among the six different realms of existence, rebirth in the human realm is said to be the most conducive for cultivating the mind of bodhichitta. This is particularly so in the case of a human being who has met the Dharma, and who has met the graduated path to enlightenment as presented by Lama Tsongkhapa. When we have attained a life in which we have all of the conducive external and internal conditions, the very least that we should do is to try to cultivate the three principal paths of renunciation, bodhichitta, and the pure view in our minds. And even if we cannot cultivate the perfect realization of these three paths in our minds, at the very least we should try to accomplish the cultivation of the mind of bodhichitta.

In order to stabilize aspiring bodhichitta within our minds, we engage in a ritual ceremony whereby we commit ourselves to this mind. This aspiring bodhichitta will become the basis of our bodhisattva vows in the future. The discussion of the ceremony whereby we commit ourselves to aspiring bodhichitta has three parts. The first part is the discussion of taking on the bodhichitta mind, which has not been obtained before. The second part is the discussion of how to protect the mind of bodhichitta from declining. And the third part is the discussion of how to purify it should it decline.

In order to maintain the aspiring bodhichitta that we have cultivated, which will be the base upon which we cultivate engaging bodhichitta, we must take the commitment to this mind from someone who already holds the vows of engaging bodhichitta and who lives in the practices of the bodhisattva conduct.

Before we commit ourselves to bodhichitta mind we should also possess certain qualities. We should have developed renunciation for the realms of cyclic existence—the desire, the form, and the formless realms—in our minds. We should have reflected on suffering in terms of our own suffering, and have developed compassion due to having reflected extensively on the suffering of others. We should also have some experience of the wisdom understanding emptiness, or at the very least have the mindfulness of impermanence and death and the recognition of the fact that we are not going to live forever.

There are three parts to the ritual ceremony in which we make the bodhisattva commitment: the preliminaries, actually committing oneself to this mind, and the concluding rites.

The place in which we take the bodhisattva vows should be well decorated with extensive offerings. The offerings should be free of the pollutions of motivation and free of the pollutions of substance. Of course, if we have material offerings we should give them, but the very best offering is the offering of our mind of faith. In the place where we take the bodhisattva vows we should have a holy object in the aspect of Buddha, who is the founder of the teachings and who symbolizes the roots of compassion. The holy object symbolizing Buddha should be well made, filled with blessed mantras, and offered to the holy beings. Also, as on the Mahayana path where there is strong emphasis on the combined practice of method and wisdom, in order to represent the holy Dharma we should also have a text expounding the perfection of wisdom.

From your side, as the person who is making this commitment, you should regard this occasion as a very special, joyous day. In your worldly life when the occasion of a celebration arises, you feel great excitement. You prepare for it by having a shower, putting on your best clothing, and so forth. You should be exactly like that and even more so when you make this commitment to the mind of bodhichitta.

In the preliminary part of the ceremony, the main focus is the generation of the extraordinary uncommon mind of refuge, which is different from other forms of refuge. You should begin by visualizing an extensive refuge merit field with the guru in the very center in front of you. Then, with your hands joined in the mudra of prostration, and with strong faith in your mind, you should verbally recite the seven-limb practice of accumulation and purification. It is important at this point that you visualize the lama from whom you take the bodhisattva commitment as Buddha. You then invite the deities, make prostrations and mandala offerings, and recite the request for the bodhisattva vows three times.

After making the request, cultivate the extraordinary form of refuge in your mind. As always, refuge is the basis for taking all of the vows and precepts. As you visualize the field of refuge in front of you, bring to mind their qualities as stated in the *Sublime Continuum* by considering the eight uncompounded qualities of the Buddha object of refuge, the eight inconceivable qualities of the Dharma object of refuge, and the eight qualities of the Sangha object of refuge. Reflecting on the qualities of the objects of refuge, recall that your objective is to attain the fully enlightened state of a buddha in order to liberate all beings from cyclic existence. In order to accomplish such a purpose, cultivate the recognition of Shakyamuni Buddha as the founder of the refuge, the Dharma as the actual refuge, and the Sangha as the support.

Then, with the mind of faith and aspiration, you should kneel and call the attention of the preceptor with your hands in the mudra of prostration. You should keep in mind that through this ritual, you are not merely generating the determination to attain enlightenment for the benefit of other sentient beings, but you are also making the commitment never to abandon this mind until you attain that state.

In the ritual itself, you begin by calling upon all of the buddhas and bodhisattvas, as well as your preceptor, to please pay attention to you. You state your name, and then vow that in the same way that all the buddhas and bodhisattvas have generated the mind of awakening, you will do the same for the benefit of sentient beings, and that you will attain enlightenment in order to liberate them. Usually the commitment goes something like this:

Just as the buddhas and bodhisattvas of the past, present, and future generated the pure mind of bodhichitta, likewise I, myself, wishing to engage in these pure activities, also generate the mind of bodhichitta in order to be able to practice like them.

You should repeat the actual vow of bodhichitta three times after the preceptor. The purpose of such repetition is to stabilize and make your commitment more clear in your mind.

The ritual concludes with the preceptor presenting the advice for cultivating the mind of bodhichitta.

How to Protect What One Has Obtained

The ceremony of the commitment to bodhichitta should inspire within us the decision to never ever forsake the mind of bodhichitta, no matter what may befall us. If a beggar who is blind and living in utter poverty by some fortune finds a wish-fulfilling jewel in the garbage, it would be unbelievably precious and valuable to him. We, ourselves, are like this beggar who lives in poverty—we lack the wisdom realizing emptiness, we lack realizations, and we are totally controlled by karma and delusions. By some karmic fortune, we have met with the teachings of Buddha, and in particular we have met with the teachings of the glorious Lama Tsongkhapa. We have had the opportunity to generate the mind of bodhichitta. In having found such a rare opportunity, considering the pitiful situation that we are in, throwing it all away would be a tremendous loss.

Once on the Mahayana path, bodhichitta can only be destroyed when, from the depth of our hearts, we totally give up on the thought benefiting sentient beings. Giving up on the thought benefiting sentient beings *does not mean* having negative thoughts toward them. Ordinary bodhisattvas who generate anger toward sentient beings are still considered bodhisattvas. Having negative minds toward sentient beings doesn't extinguish bodhichitta. Bodhichitta can only be extinguished when we completely give up on the thought to benefit others. Forsaking the mind of bodhichitta and forsaking sentient beings are the worst of all the transgressions causing decline in one's bodhichitta, because these two have the power to make the bodhisattva vows completely useless. We need to be particularly careful since our mind is always under the control of karma and delusions, and it is very easy for the deluded mind to think, "There is absolutely no way I want to benefit this person," in relation to individuals that we do not care for.

From the beginning of the *Six-Session Guru Yoga:*

In order to be able to liberate all transmigrators from the fears of
   samsara and nirvana's peace,
From now until attaining buddhahood,
I will generate the mind wishing to attain enlightenment,
Never forsaking it, even at the cost of my life.

Of course, merely not giving up on the thought of bodhichitta is not a
sufficient practice. As well, we need to work toward empowering and
enhancing whatever level of bodhichitta we have managed to develop in
our minds. In order to do this, once we have made the commitment to
bodhichitta mind, we should do the practice of generating bodhichitta
mind three times each day and three times each night. If possible, we
should practice the extensive version in which we generate the visualization
of the field of merit, cultivate the infinite thought of loving-kindness and
compassion, and take the bodhisattva vows again each time. If, however,
we cannot find the time to do this in its most complete form, at minimum we should recite the refuge and bodhichitta prayer, *Sang gye cho dang
tsog kyi chog nam la* et cetera,[37] three times each day and three times each
night to fulfill our commitment. Also, if we remember to generate refuge
and bodhichitta at the start of whatever activity we do throughout the
day—practicing generosity, listening to teachings, making prostrations—
we thus ensure that that activity becomes a Mahayana practice.

Since most of us sleep straight through the night we might have difficulty keeping our commitment to generate bodhichitta mind three times
at night, but we can surely do this three times a day. The words of this
prayer are very profound and powerful. The prayer is phrased in this way
to emphasize the importance of never forsaking sentient beings and never
forsaking our bodhisattva vows.

Generating bodhichitta in this way and promising never to forsake the
mind of bodhichitta even at the cost of your life are not a *direct* antidote
to the delusions. However, practicing in this way will help you to refrain
from generating negative states of mind that have not yet been generated.
And, should a negative mind already have been generated, these practices
can help you control it so it doesn't get any worse. Your constant recollection of your commitment to such a mind and to never ever forsake it even
at the cost of your life is also a general antidote to all the delusions.

For example, let's say that one day your mind is predominantly under the control of strong craving and grasping. Then, out of habit, you begin your regular recitation and generation of your commitment to bodhichitta. As you generate bodhichitta in your mind, it dawns upon you to wonder that if your mind remains sunk in craving and grasping, how can you ever bring sentient beings to enlightenment? Although this practice may not be a direct antidote, it will definitely help to remove your mind from the control of the delusion.

If we practice like this on a day-to-day basis, we will begin to see what types of thoughts and behavior are an advantage to us, and what types of thoughts and behavior are a disadvantage. In this way, we will be able to enhance our bodhichitta, strengthen our bodhichitta, and free our bodhichitta from all obstacles. We will accumulate vast stores of merit, ensuring that our bodhichitta will never degenerate.

This completes the points of advice on protecting bodhichitta from decline.

The second series of advice from the *Lamrim Chenmo* is given for us to follow in order to ensure that we will never be separated from the mind of bodhichitta in any of our future lifetimes. In order to ensure that, we must abandon the four black dharmas that create obstacles to encountering bodhichitta in future lifetimes, and practice the four white dharmas that ensure that we will meet with bodhichitta in future lifetimes.

The first of the four black dharmas is telling lies to your abbots, your preceptors, or your spiritual teachers—the beings who have taken the role of caring for you in your spiritual practice. An example of lying to them would be if you are not actually doing your practice, but tell them how wonderfully well it is going—deceiving them with information you know very clearly not to be fact. It doesn't matter whether the lama or the preceptor has actually been deceived or not; as long as you fulfill the act from your side, you incur the transgression.

The second black dharma is causing other people who have done virtuous things in their lives to regret those actions. Again, it doesn't matter whether you are able to succeed in that activity or not; as long as you intentionally try to generate the mind regretting a virtuous act in someone else's mind, you incur this transgression.

The third black dharma is saying harmful, unpleasant, and untrue things about a person who has generated the mind of bodhichitta. In order to complete the third black dharma, three criteria must be fulfilled. The first is that you must express these things with the motivation of one of the three poisons. The second is that you must say these negative things about a person who has generated the mind of bodhichitta. The third is that you say these things to someone else who has generated aspiring bodhichitta.

The fourth black dharma is employing guile and pretentiousness, meaning that you do something negative and blame it on someone else, or that you pretend to have a quality you do not have. These two activities are completely contradictory to the pure altruistic aspiration of bodhichitta and thereby are regarded as the fourth of the four black dharmas.

After having taken the bodhisattva commitment, if you engage in the four black dharmas, not only will the bodhisattva precepts that you have taken in this lifetime degenerate, but you can be assured that in future lifetimes you will also be separated from bodhichitta. Even if people who have *not* made the commitment to the mind of bodhichitta engage in any of these four black dharmas, the result will be that they remain apart from the altruistic mind of bodhichitta.

The four white dharmas stand in direct opposition to the four black dharmas, and are the advice on what one should practice.

The first is not deceiving by lying either directly or in the form of a joke to your abbots, preceptors, or virtuous friends even at the cost of your life.

The second is abandoning all pretense and guile even in the form of a joke, and living with complete and total honesty in relation to all sentient beings even at the cost of your life.

The third white dharma is praising the qualities of the holy body, speech, and mind of the buddhas and bodhisattvas of the ten directions, and making sure that everyone in the four directions knows these qualities. It is also explained that if a good opportunity should arise in which it would be appropriate to talk about the good qualities of the buddhas and bodhisattvas and you do *not* do so, you incur a transgression. However, if you are in a situation in which it is not totally appropriate to talk about the qualities of these buddhas and bodhisattvas, then by not speaking you incur no transgression.

The fourth white dharma is ripening sentient beings' minds. This particular practice includes taking caution not to be the cause of generating negativity in the minds of others. To cause others to experience positive mental states is the best, but taking care through the course of your actions not to directly or indirectly cause them to think negatively is also part of the fourth white dharma.

When we incur transgressions in the category of the aspiring bodhi-sattva vows, or when we do not live in accordance with the advice of the vows, we accumulate a lot of negative karma. After having taken the aspiring bodhisattva vows in the form of a ceremony, we can purify them with the four opponent powers. Although this section of the *Lamrim Chenmo* primarily addresses the ritual for taking the aspiring bodhichitta vows, we may also have the opportunity one day to take the engaging, or actual, bodhisattva vows. When we do so, we should remember that if we take these vows and break them, we incur a downfall that cannot be purified by the method of the four opponent powers alone.

Combining an Entire Life's Practice into the Five Powers

The practice called combining an entire life's practice into the five powers is a condensed explanation of how to practice Dharma. Any kind of practice that is accompanied by the five powers becomes very profound, simply by the power of these actions. You can do this practice wherever you are, and however you live. All that is needed is your own buddha-nature, your own potential to attain enlightenment. The five powers are the power of the motivation, the power of the white seed, the power of habit, the power of the antidote, and the power of prayer.

As a Dharma practitioner, your motivation should be the very first step of whatever action you undertake. What should your motivation be? Thinking, "I will do good until tomorrow," is a very limited motivation. At the very least, you should have the intent to strive for virtue until death. If you can, you should cultivate the motivation thinking:

> For the rest of my life, and particularly today, I will strengthen and develop the awareness of the enemy of my own delusions. I will try to recognize my own negative states of mind, and realize the problems and suffering that they create, and how they are rooted in the ignorance grasping at true existence and the self-cherishing mind.

Also, for the rest of my life, and especially today, I will cultivate thoughts of compassion, kindness, and love for others.

Setting this kind of motivation is in itself a virtuous activity, and will thus enable your physical and verbal activities to become virtuous as well.

The power of the white seed is dedicating all of your virtue as a means to counteract your delusions and your self-cherishing mind, as well as to further enhance your capacity for love, kindness, and compassion. You should dedicate not only in order to ensure your own happiness and well-being, but also to ensure the temporary and ultimate benefit of others.

The third power is the power of habit or familiarity, which means acquainting your body, speech, and mind with white virtuous actions and motivation. This refers to taking care to ensure that whatever knowledge you gain does not become a means to enhance the eight worldly dharmas in your mind. Instead, whatever you learn should be directed toward eliminating your ignorance. It is the natural course of things that your mind will become familiar with whatever you are studying over time. Highly realized lamas are able to reflect on the entire lamrim in the time it takes to mount a horse, simply due to their mind's power of familiarity.

When I was a student at Tantric College, it was the custom that the daily tea be served in huge bowls to each person. Each monk had to finish his tea and put the bowl away by the time the chanting master was done with his, which was not very long. These bowls were quite big and the tea was quite hot, and in the beginning all of us new students were very worried because we couldn't finish it. But month by month, as time went on, by the power of familiarity it became easy.

Right now you may think that it is very difficult even to focus single-pointedly on a single object for a short while. But as your mind becomes more and more habituated to the process, you will be able to engage in single-pointed meditation for longer and longer periods of time. In fact, all of the extraordinary qualities and levels of mind develop due to the power of habituation.

The fourth power is the power of the antidote. This means cultivating mindfulness, awareness, remembrance, and introspection. In order to ensure that delusions do not arise, or to stop them once they have arisen, we apply the antidotes of these four mental factors. When a watchdog sees an intruder, it begins to bark immediately. In the same way, these states of mind are our internal watchdogs, guarding against the manifestations of our self-cherishing minds. In order to carry forth the power of the motivation, to carry forth the power of the white seed, and to carry forth the power of habit, we must employ the power of the antidote.

The fifth is the power of prayer, by which we dedicate all of our virtues so that we will be able to eliminate our self-cherishing mind and be able to fully develop the mind that cherishes others.

If we practice the five powers in combination with bodhichitta, we can be certain that nothing that we do during the course of the day will be wasted, and that we will accumulate very powerful merit. If we can bring these five powers into our daily practice, our whole month is made meaningful, our whole year is made meaningful, and in due course our entire lifetime will be made meaningful as well.

AFTER GENERATING BODHICHITTA, THE MANNER OF TRAINING IN THE CONDUCT OF A BODHISATTVA

In Dharmakirti's *Commentary on the "Compendium on Valid Cognition,"* it is stated that bodhisattvas who are endowed with the mind of compassion that cherishes sentient beings cultivate this state of mind and engage in activities to pacify their suffering using the practice of the six perfections.

According to the Tibetan tradition, there are two parts to the training in the Mahayana path: training in the general path and training in the Vajrayana path. Training in the general path refers to the training in the path and practices of the bodhisattvas: generating the mind of bodhichitta, taking the bodhisattva vows, and practicing the conduct of a bodhisattva. Although there are many forms of conduct of a bodhisattva, they can all be included within the six perfections. Through the practice of the six perfections, the bodhisattva is able to complete the two types of accumulations, the accumulation of merit and the accumulation of wisdom. It can be said that all of the activities of a bodhisattva are included within the activities of these two accumulations. Although it could also be said that a bodhisattva's conduct can be subsumed within the practices of the three higher trainings, Maitreya states in *Ornament for the Mahayana Sutras* that the presentation of the bodhisattva's conduct through the explanation of the six perfections is the most effective method to bring forth the understanding of this topic.

SIX REASONS THAT THE NUMBER IS DEFINITE

In accordance with the *Ornament for the Mahayana Sutras,* there are six reasons the conduct of a bodhisattva is presented in the comprehensive form of the six perfections.

The first reason is that the six perfections are a means to attain higher rebirth. Higher rebirth in this context means a rebirth endowed with four states of auspiciousness: the auspiciousness of material affluence, the auspiciousness of body, the auspiciousness of one's entourage or surroundings, and the auspiciousness of being able to complete every activity that one begins. A bodhisattva who is born with a perfect human rebirth combined with these four auspicious conditions has a great advantage in practicing the path. However, if we ordinary sentient beings are born with these conditions, in some cases they can serve merely to subject us further to the control of our own delusions, instead of helping us. In order for these auspicious conditions to benefit us, we must be endowed with the eye of wisdom and have the understanding of what is to be practiced and what is to be abandoned. Without the eye of wisdom, although we may enjoy the four auspicious results in this lifetime, the only thing that we will accomplish is wasting the results of our past positive karma.

The second reason the conduct of a bodhisattva is presented in the comprehensive form of the six perfections is that the practice of the six perfections fulfills the benefit of both self and others. Specifically, the first three of the six perfections—generosity, ethics, and patience—directly benefit others. The fourth, perseverance, works both ways, for self and others. And concentration and wisdom directly fulfill the benefits of the self. Please keep in mind that the fact that perseverance, concentration, and wisdom fulfill the benefit of the self does not mean that they are not of benefit to others as well. Rather, this explanation is meant to show that the latter three perfections are *more* connected to the self, while the first three perfections are *more* connected to others.

The third reason is that the practice of the six perfections also fulfills the specific benefit of others. As bodhisattvas, we benefit others through the practice of generosity by providing them with whatever they need. Through the practice of ethics, we protect others from harm through the three doors of our body, speech, and mind. Through the practice of tolerance, we eliminate anger and violence toward other beings. Through the practice of perseverance we are able to develop the strength of mind continually pursuing the activities that benefit others. Through the training in concentration, we are able to develop subtle levels of mind that endow us with clairvoyance and psychic powers enabling us to know the needs and wishes of sentient beings. Through the training in wisdom, we are able to develop superior insight into reality, which in turn leads us to the realizations that will enable us to ripen the minds of sentient beings. The perfection of wisdom will also enable us to endow sentient beings with whatever realizations they have not achieved and eliminate their wrong views.

The fourth reason in accordance with the *Ornament for the Mahayana Sutras* is that the six perfections are inclusive of the entire body of Mahayana practice. For example, when we practice generosity without seeking reward or seeking the benefits of the eight worldly dharmas, we are also practicing the higher training in ethics. As a result of engaging in the practice of ethics with such purity, we naturally develop a sense of tolerance toward other sentient beings that will not falter even should they show us disrespect or disregard. This is the practice of patience. On the basis of such a mind, we also develop perseverance, the ability to take great joy in whatever virtuous activity we engage in. As a result of taking joy in virtue, we will naturally be drawn to develop our minds in the perfection of meditative concentration in order to complete the perfection of wisdom.

The fifth reason is that the six perfections are inclusive of all of the method aspects of the practice.

The sixth reason is that the six perfections are inclusive of the practices of the three higher trainings. The higher training in ethics is made up of the training in generosity, ethics, and patience. The result of this practice will be that the roots of whatever virtue we have created will not be destroyed by anger. The perfection of perseverance, because it enhances the virtue of that practice, is applied to all of the three higher trainings of ethics, concentration, and wisdom. The perfection of concentration is equivalent to the practice in the higher training in concentration. Though there are different types of concentration, the very best concentration is the perfection of concentration as practiced on the bodhisattva's path. Finally, the perfection of wisdom is equivalent to the higher training in wisdom. Again, although there are all kinds of wisdom, the very best wisdom is the perfection of wisdom included within the perfections.

The reason for asserting thus that the practices of the six perfections include, in essence, the three higher trainings, is to appeal to people of different mental attitudes. For some, the three higher trainings sound like an appealing form of practice, whereas the six perfections may not inspire them.

THE ORDER OF THE SIX PERFECTIONS

Next, I will give an introductory presentation of the order of the six perfections in accordance with the explanations of the Indian scholar Haribhadra—Lopon Sengye Sangpo in Tibetan—and Maitreya's *Ornament of Clear Realization*. There were twenty-one commentaries written to *Ornament of Clear Realization*. Of these, the one written by Haribhadra is regarded the most highly by Lama Tsongkhapa. In the Gelug tradition, the two sources used to explain the practices of the perfection vehicle are *Heart Explanation of "Ornament"* and *Golden Rosary of Eloquence* by Lama Tsongkhapa. These have as their source the *Commentary on the Clear Meaning* by Haribhadra, which in turn is a clarification of the *Ornament of Clear Realization*.

According to Haribhadra's text, sentient beings are bound to cyclic existence by attachment and desire to material objects. Even should we be fortunate enough to generate some form of the wish to be free from cyclic existence and train in the path to benefit sentient beings and attain enlightenment, we encounter difficulties with others who have negative minds and behave badly toward us. As a result, we then are unable to maintain our practices because we lack the perfection of perseverance.

To counteract these obstacles on the path, we practice the six perfections in the following way. The practice of the perfections of generosity and ethics enable us to accumulate sufficient merit to enter the Mahayana path. Upon entering the path, we practice the perfection of patience and the perfection of perseverance in order to continue to develop our minds. Finally, we are forced to confront the basis of our delusions, the ignorance grasping at true existence, which brings forth suffering in our own lives and in the lives of others. The antidote to the ignorance grasping at the truly existent self is the wisdom realizing emptiness. Cultivating this wisdom on the basis of single-pointed concentration enables us to generate the direct antidote to grasping at true existence.

From the perspective of the *Ornament for the Mahayana Sutras*, this series can also be examined as a demonstration of the gradual stages of practices in the perfection vehicle as follows. When we are not attached to material objects, we are free of the mind of miserliness, and are able to practice generosity. This in itself creates greater satisfaction, less desire, and more contentment in our minds. Contentment is the basis of living in pure ethics, in which we focus on abstaining from the negative actions that arise out of the mind of desire and attachment. The practice of ethics naturally creates the basis for the practice of patience. The diligence that we develop through our practice of patience, in turn, naturally creates the basis for the practice of perseverance. Our practice of perseverance creates the basis on which to generate single-pointed concentration, which enables us to undertake analysis in a very effective way. This brings forth the perfection of unmistaken and complete wisdom itself in our minds. In this way, all the previous perfections act as the basis of the latter ones.

Yet another reason the six perfections are set up in this particular order is to demarcate a lower and a higher practice, a more gross and a more subtle practice. "Higher" and "lower" refers to what is easier to practice and what is more difficult to practice. The practices that are easier are regarded as lower or grosser forms of practice, and the practices that are more difficult are regarded as supreme or more subtle forms of practice. However, these kinds of differentiations are made in a very general context. Specifically, there is not such a great difference when, for example, you practice the perfection of generosity and apply the emptiness of the three spheres to that practice. That practice of generosity could not be said to be easier or lower than the practice of wisdom.

The method of training in the conduct of the perfections is presented by way of two topics: how to train in the general conduct, and how to train in the last two perfections in particular. In order to ripen our own minds, we train in the six perfections, and in order to ripen the minds of others, we train in the four activities to subdue sentient beings.

THE GENERAL CONDUCT:
THE PERFECTION OF GENEROSITY

Our training in generosity begins with trying to understand the nature of the practice of generosity and the method by which we should engage in this practice.

The Nature of Generosity and the Way to Practice It

Generosity is the wish to give, unhindered by attachment and miserliness. Completing the perfection of generosity does not require the practitioner to give away everything he or she owns, nor does it require the elimination of poverty in the world. Rather, the perfection of generosity is complete when you have enhanced the wish to give to its fullest potential in your own mind. When you are training in the practice of generosity, whether or not you actually have a physical object to give makes absolutely no difference.

The basis for the practice of the perfection of generosity is established by abandoning the mind of attachment to the body and the possessions, and by contemplating their impermanent nature and the fact that this body and our possessions are the results of karma and delusions and are under their control. The main obstacles to generosity are thoughts of miserliness or stinginess. However, abandoning miserliness alone is also not sufficient to fulfill the perfection of generosity. As miserliness is a secondary mental factor to the mind of attachment, when the affliction of attachment is overcome, miserliness is also overcome. Thus, there are many arhats who have abandoned miserliness in their minds so that such thoughts will never arise again, but by this alone these practitioners have yet to fulfill the perfection of generosity. In fact, it is not necessary to completely abandon miserliness in your mind before you begin to develop the wish to give. The sheer force of the wish to give, when developed to its full potential in your mind, can itself act as an antidote to the gross manifestation of miserliness.

In the beginning of our training in the perfection of generosity, it is most important to encourage ourselves to develop the mind that wishes to give by understanding the advantages or virtues of such a mind, and, in conjunction with this, reflecting upon the shortcomings of miserliness.

In *Precious Garland*, Nagarjuna states that if we practice generosity and dedicate the merits to the benefit of each mother sentient being, we will accumulate extensive merit in dependence upon each of these beings. Should this merit be able to take a physical form, the entire universe would be too small to hold it. In other words, the perfection of generosity is a very quick way to accumulate a great deal of merit. Thinking in this way should give us the strength of mind to begin to try to abandon our thoughts of attachment and miserliness to our body, possessions, and roots of virtue.

If that doesn't work, we can try to take inspiration from the life story of Shakyamuni Buddha. At the age of twenty-nine, Shakyamuni Buddha, who was then Prince Siddhartha, gave up his entire kingdom, considerable wealth, and his parents, wife, and child to practice the path and attain realizations. If Buddha was able to surrender the most precious things in his life to work for the benefit of other beings, then we who aspire to practice this path should certainly be able to part with a few meager possessions.

Furthermore, in thinking about the benefits of practicing generosity, we should consider the effort that we expend taking care of our material belongings in this world. We spend a great deal of time and energy attempting to protect, secure, and maintain everything that we own and value. And yet in so doing, we only really succeed in generating a lot of negative thoughts, engaging in countless negative actions, and accumulating great stores of negative imprints, which will serve to keep us involved in similar activities in our future lives. If, instead, we were to focus on protecting, securing, and maintaining the perfection of generosity in our minds, we would find that the gains from doing so would far exceed anything that we could imagine. In India they say: "All that is not given is lost."

The Six Pure Qualities
and How One Perfection Is Inclusive of Six

In order for the practice of generosity to become the *perfection* of generosity, it should be endowed with six pure qualities. These are the purity of the basis, the purity of the substance, the purity of the purpose, the purity of the method, the purity of the dedication, and the purity of every aspect.

The purity of the basis refers to the purity of our motivation, which means that our motivation to practice generosity should be the wish to attain enlightenment solely for the welfare of others, completely cherishing other sentient beings and renouncing our own self-interest. Of course, this bodhichitta must be rooted in the mind of compassion.

The purity of the substance applies to the object that is actually given. What we give should be appropriate to the immediate situation and to the time—we should give whatever is most needed or whatever is most lacking.

The purity of the purpose means that whatever you give should bring immediate and long-term benefit to all mother sentient beings.

The purity of the method refers to the practitioner's awareness of the emptiness of the three spheres. This means that as we are engaging in our practice of generosity, we should remember that the person performing the act of generosity is empty and therefore does not exist from his or her own side, that the recipient of that action of generosity is empty and does not exist from his or her own side, and that whatever is being given is also empty and therefore does not exist from its own side.

The purity of the dedication means that you should conclude your practice of generosity by dedicating whatever virtues you have created to enlightenment for the benefit of all sentient beings.

The sixth pure quality, which is the purity of every aspect, refers to the fact that through the roots of this virtue, one creates the potential to eliminate the two types of obscurations and thus attain the unsurpassable state of enlightenment.

Again, an action should be endowed with these six pure qualities to become a perfection. If a generous action is performed and is not endowed with these six qualities, it is merely an ordinary generous action.

Additionally, it is important to understand that according to the training of the perfection vehicle, the supreme practice of any one of the six perfections should be inclusive of the practice of the other five.

For example, a bodhisattva training in the perfection of generosity will cultivate the aspiration of the Mahayana, and abstain from the aspiration of the individual vehicle in which one wishes to attain personal cessation of suffering alone. In so doing, this bodhisattva is also practicing the perfection of ethics. Along the path, when others criticize or become upset with this bodhisattva, his or her mind remains undisturbed. This is the practice of patience. As the bodhisattva continues training in the perfection of generosity, his or her aspiration to improve that practice and the great joy with which that bodhisattva engages in the conduct of that practice are the perfection of enthusiastic perseverance. The single-pointed focus with which the bodhisattva engages in the practice of generosity and the dedication of the merits of this practice to enlightenment are the perfection of concentration. And finally, the bodhisattva's awareness of the emptiness of the three spheres of agent, object, and action fulfills the perfection of wisdom.

The Individual's Practice of Generosity

There are many different ways to practice the perfection of generosity, according to our circumstances in life, our natural disposition, and so forth. We can practice generosity with material things, or we can practice generosity with Dharma. Generally speaking, bodhisattvas living as householders are advised to practice generosity with material things. Bodhisattvas living as ordained people, however, should practice the generosity of Dharma. Ordained bodhisattvas are not advised to pursue the practice of the generosity of material things because trying to accumulate a lot of material things, even only in order to give them away, could create obstacles to the activities of listening, understanding, and meditating upon the teachings.

The Kadampa master Sharawa said that he would not discuss the benefits of giving with ordained people who seek out material accumulation and justify their actions by insisting that this is a method to benefit others. Instead, this great master stated that it would be more suitable to expound the shortcomings of accumulating and grasping at material things to these disciples.

For ordained people, taking an active interest in seeking material gains is detrimental to living in pure ethics. However, bodhisattvas who, due to their particular karma, are blessed with a lot of material things without having to make any effort to seek them out should practice the generosity of material things.

I have heard it said in the teachings that there were three conditions that caused the decline of the Buddhadharma in India after the time of Shakyamuni Buddha. The first was that practitioners lost the ability to distinguish the practices of sutra and tantra clearly, which resulted in widespread practice of the Vajrayana without the foundation of sutra. Secondly, the ruling families of the many states of India began to take interest in other philosophical and spiritual traditions, and move away from the Buddha's teachings. And thirdly, people who were ordained monastics in the Buddhist tradition began to accumulate material possessions.

Giving Dharma

There are three main types of generosity, which are distinguished from one another by what is given. The three types of generosity are giving the Dharma, giving protection from fear, and giving material things.

Giving Dharma means giving the teachings of the Buddhadharma in particular, but it can also mean giving any other kind of teachings—explanations on the medical sciences, astrology, art, basic life skills, and so forth. Anything that you teach another person with the pure motivation seeking solely to benefit that person is a part of giving Dharma. Encouraging others to live in ethics, to practice generosity, to be patient, and to persevere in virtuous activities are also all part of the generosity of Dharma.

Giving Protection from Fear

The generosity of giving protection from fear means giving others a feeling of security, or easing their apprehension or anxiety. If you visit someone in a hospital, talk to them, calm their mind, and try to dispel their concerns over whatever is happening to them, you are practicing the generosity of giving protection from fear. Or, if you offer support to others who are experiencing problems in their lives or suffering, by talking and listening to them you are also practicing giving protection from fear. Giving physical shelter from frightening situations is also giving protection from fear, as is giving directions to people who are lost and wandering around. Generally speaking, anything you do with a pure motivation to help another person handle or overcome a problem is part of the practice of giving protection from fear.

Giving Material Things

To Whom to Give
Appropriate recipients of material generosity are of ten kinds:

1. Friends and relatives who have benefited you
2. Enemies who have harmed you
3. Strangers
4. People living in pure ethics
5. People not living in pure ethics
6. People who have fewer realizations than you

7. People who have realizations that equal yours
8. People who have more realizations than you
9. People who are richer than you are
10. People who are living in poverty

The Kind of Thoughts with Which to Give and the Kind of Thoughts to Abandon

There are three types of thoughts that should accompany your practice of generosity. These are the thought observing the necessity, the thought observing the substance, and the thought observing the field.

The thought observing the necessity refers to your awareness of the necessity of your attaining enlightenment for the benefit of others. This is the first kind of thought that should accompany your practice of generosity.

The thought observing the substance refers to what you actually give. Since you have dedicated your body, speech, mind, and all of your possessions to the benefit of others in order to develop your full potential to give, you should consider all of these things to be things that no longer belong to you. You should think that they actually belong to others, and that you are merely holding them for the time being. When you practice generosity in combination with this kind of thought, you will not find it very difficult to give things away.

The thought observing the field refers to the objects of your generosity—namely, other sentient beings. Since you have already dedicated all of your possessions to the benefit of other beings, you should consider those beings to be a field in which you harvest virtue. With this thought in mind, you should give with love to your enemy, with compassion to those who are suffering, with happiness to those who have great qualities in their minds, and with equanimity to those who have helped you in this life.

As it is taught that there are specific types of thoughts that will help to support and develop your practice of generosity, and that therefore you should cultivate, it is also taught that there are specific thoughts that will hinder your practice, and that therefore you should abandon. The first of the thoughts to abandon is the wrong view that does not believe in the positive results of your actions. This kind of thought manifests in the following form: "I don't believe in generosity, creating merit, or that this practice will bring material wealth in the future, but I'll give something anyway." Giving with this kind of a mentality is not useful.

You should also abandon undertaking an act of generosity with the intention to harm, instead of to benefit. You should abandon thinking that practicing extensive acts of generosity alone is the means to liberation from cyclic existence. You should abandon practicing generosity with a mind of pride or with a mind that disparages the recipient of your generosity. You should abandon practicing generosity with a competitive mind and giving things away in order to show off.

Also, you should abandon undertaking acts of generosity—whether giving material things or giving the Dharma—with the hope of developing a good reputation. You should abandon practicing generosity with a mind lacking enthusiasm. And you should abandon regretting the act of having given.

You should also abandon giving with the hope of reward, or the hope that something will come in return. In fact, you should not even hope for the ripening result of your karmic actions. You should also abandon doubts with regard to the virtue of generosity, such as thinking that if you give too much, you might become very poor.

It is also important to avoid deciding to give and then taking a long time to actually do it, as in the meantime many things can happen and you may lose your opportunity. You should avoid giving after you've made the recipient engage in actions that contradict the Dharma, or negative or deluded activities. You should also avoid giving something and then talking about all the many times you gave before, again and again and again, so that the recipient of your generosity gets very tired of hearing about it.

It is most important that you give with a strong motivation to benefit the recipient of your generosity. Furthermore, when the opportunity to give presents itself, you should rejoice and feel very happy that you have come across such an extraordinary opportunity. It is also very important that any act of giving that you engage in with your body, speech, or mind should be done with great respect, and with a pure heart. Also, if you yourself are able to actually make the offering it is better to do so rather than sending the gift with someone else.

What to Give and What Not to Give

It is appropriate to give anything that will not cause the recipient to create the karma to be born in the lower realms, and that, when given, will bring about immediate happiness and long-term benefit. If you are faced with a situation in which what is given creates a problem or suffering in the short term, but enables the individual to accumulate merit and abandon nonvirtue in the long term, it is worthwhile to give. It is not appropriate to give things that will become an immediate cause of suffering and a cause of suffering in the long run. If giving something will bring immediate happiness, but long-term harm, it is also not appropriate to give that object.

You must also consider the appropriateness of the time and the occasion when giving. For example, the bodhisattvas on the paths of accumulation and preparation have taken the wishing bodhichitta vows, the engaging bodhisattva vows, and have practiced to strengthen the mind wishing to give. However, until the time when they have generated the pure mind of the extraordinary supreme thought taking responsibility for sentient beings,[38] should they be asked to give their life or their flesh and blood, they should not undertake the actual activity of giving of the body. Furthermore, even if they have developed very pure compassion to its full degree, have no miserliness, and have developed the complete mind of giving, if giving the body means benefiting a very limited few and not giving the body means being able to benefit limitless other sentient beings, they should not give the body.

The following are situations in which it is not appropriate to give. If someone asks for all of our possessions, and we know that as a result this individual is going to engage in negative activities harming other sentient beings, we should not give. We should not give the evening meal to monks and nuns, or to those who have taken the eight Mahayana precepts, as doing so can encourage those practitioners to break their vow of not taking food at inappropriate times. We should also not give food or drink to practitioners who are restricted from consuming them by other vows or precepts.

In terms of giving Dharma, it is inappropriate to give Dharma teachings to someone who requests them but has no intention at all to practice, and merely seeks to gain knowledge of the intellectual controversy and the points of argument.

It is also not appropriate to give things that do not fulfill any benefit. For example, when people ask for poison, or weapons, we should not give them. We should also not give to funds that are used to destroy the environment, the water, animals, and so forth.

Antidotes to the Obstacles to Generosity

The first chapter of *Ornament of Clear Realization* says:

Never abandon a beggar, although you yourself might have nothing.

The main practice of generosity is strengthening and increasing the wish to give in our minds. Because generosity is a mental state, even if you are a penniless beggar, you can still accumulate the merit of generosity, because all it entails is enhancing the mind.

There are four obstacles to strengthening our wish to give.

The first obstacle is not being familiar with giving, and thus finding it difficult to practice. When we have something to give and we make the choice not to, this is primarily because we are not habituated to giving. If we have not given extensively in past lifetimes, or in the earlier part of this lifetime, we will be unhappy at the prospect of doing so and be unable to practice generosity. The antidote to this obstacle is to understand what is going on here, and reflect on the fact that if our mind and behavior do not change, it will only be possible that we experience similar results in the future.

The second obstacle is the fear that we don't have enough to give, and that if we give what we have, we will become poor. The antidote to this kind of mental state is to meditate on the fact that as long as we are in cyclic existence, we are certain to experience suffering, and that the reason that we remain in samsara is because of our inability to engage in virtue. We should consider how practicing generosity is an opportunity to engage in virtue, and that even though we might not have much ourselves, if we don't make an attempt to create virtue now, our future lifetimes will not bring about any better result. The reason that we are in this to begin with is because we have not engaged in virtue in the past. Even if we die because of having given away the little that we have, at the time of death and after death that very action will benefit us.

The third obstacle is the mind of attachment to whatever is to be given. To counteract attachment we should think about its shortcomings—how the results of attachment can only be suffering and negativity. To reduce attachment to the body, we can contemplate the four types of mindfulness in terms of the body: its impermanence, its impurity, its selflessness, and the fact that it is not independent. In terms of our possessions, we should contemplate the fact that regardless of what happens, we will inevitably have to part with everything that we own. We can think over and over again about the ways that we can be separated from our possessions. Moreover, we should consider how we will experience great mental anxiety at the time of death when we will be forced to separate from all of the things that the mind of attachment has bound us to. We can also think how great familiarity with attachment will only bring us more suffering and problems in our future lives.

The fourth obstacle is not being able to comprehend the positive karmic results of the action of giving. The antidote to this is to contemplate impermanence—specifically, to consider the fact that all phenomena are disintegrating moment by moment, and that all of your wealth and belongings, in particular, will definitely be separated from you at some point in the future.

Generally speaking, if we don't have material things, it's a problem. And if we do have them, it's also a problem. If we compare the two, however, which problem is greater—having or not having? Having is a greater problem, primarily because we are never satisfied with what we have. We are always trying to improve our possessions, to increase them, and to hang onto them. We might actually find that if we have fewer material belongings, our minds will be more at peace. Of course, maybe I am just saying that because I don't have much!

Generosity in the Form of Thought

The generosity that we practice merely in the form of thought refers to practicing generosity through the power of visualization. Specifically, this can mean visualizing the people and places in the world that are afflicted with great poverty and visualizing giving them everything that is needed. In this way, we can practice the visualized form of giving to all the beings of this universe.

Furthermore, in *Compendium of Trainings,* Shantideva recommends that we train in the practice of generosity of the body, since the body is something that we really cherish, protect, and care for. We should visualize someone in front of us begging for our eyes, begging for our hands, and begging for our hearts. Then we should visualize ourselves giving what they are asking for. Please keep in mind that although we are not actually giving away our body parts, this is a mental exercise intended to strengthen our capacities to one day be able to do so.

On occasions when we are in retreat and we wish to strengthen our mind's ability and wish to give, we should practice this visualized form of giving. This is a way of enhancing the wish to give with very little exertion, while simultaneously accumulating great merit. Bodhisattvas who are well endowed with wisdom practice this type of giving. It says in the text that although giving through visualization is most appropriate for those who do not have material things to give, those who *do* have things to give can practice it as well.

As ordinary sentient beings, at the moment we do not have the strength of mind to practice the extensive forms of the perfection of generosity, such as generosity of the body, possessions, and the roots of virtue. Regardless, at our level we must continue to train our minds even though we lack that strength of mind. If we don't train our minds, there will not be any way to develop these qualities within ourselves. As we train our minds, and as the strength of the wish to give grows, eventually we will begin to embody these qualities. In due time, we will be able to give without reservation from the depths of our hearts—we will effortlessly be able to give our body, our possessions, and our roots of virtue. We will have absolutely no hesitation. Having cultivated such a complete perfection of the mind of generosity, from the depth of our hearts we will dedicate everything that we have totally for the benefit of others. And whatever we use in terms of basic necessities, we will use only with the thought to benefit others.

In fact, once you have attained the perfection of generosity, it is no longer possible to experience the thought of "mine." Even now, while training in the path of the bodhisattvas, we should think of all of our possessions as belonging to others, since we have already dedicated them for others' benefit. According to some traditions of Vinaya, if a fully ordained monk uses his possessions thinking they are his instead of thinking they are others', that monk can incur a transgression in the category of a defeat.[39]

If our belongings have indeed been dedicated for the benefit of others in the completion of the perfection of generosity, to use them for selfish purposes would be inappropriate. However, using these things with the wish to benefit others is permissible. This is the advice from Shantideva's *Compendium of Trainings*. For example, when there are workers in a household, a particular worker doesn't ask permission from the homeowner for every little item that he or she uses. It's not necessary. Because this worker is working for the benefit of the owner, using those items is appropriate.

It is further stated that since we, as ordinary sentient beings, do not have the capacity to actually give our body, possessions, and roots of virtue, through visualization we should train our minds so as to develop the kind of strength to be able to give in this way. It says in the text that we shouldn't think that this practice is without essence, because merely attempting to strengthen our minds to be able to give in this way is very admirable.

Again, when we undertake the practices of virtue such as generosity and so forth, we should always adorn our dedication with reflection on the emptiness of the three spheres, the agent, action, and object—ourselves, the virtuous act, and the enlightenment to which we dedicate. Reflecting on the emptiness of the three spheres is a way to protect the merit of virtue. When the merits of virtue are accumulated and reinforced by the mind of wisdom through reflection on the emptiness of the three spheres, they cannot be destroyed by our delusions so easily.

This has been a very elaborate explanation of the perfection of generosity.

THE GENERAL CONDUCT:
THE PERFECTION OF ETHICS

The discussion of ethics is divided into the following topics: the nature of ethics, the method by which to engage in the practice of ethics, the classification of the types of ethics, and how to accomplish the perfection of ethics.

The nature of ethics, as with generosity, is also described as being a quality that must be cultivated within our minds. Ethics is the wish to abandon harming other sentient beings. Again, in order to complete the perfection of ethics, it is not necessary that you become capable of releasing every sentient being from harm. Rather, to complete the perfection of ethics, you must develop the *wish* to abandon harming sentient beings to the greatest possible extent.

In general, there are three types of ethics: the ethics of abstaining from activities that are the basis of harm, the ethics of undertaking virtue, and the ethics of benefiting others. The general explanation of the practice of ethics relates primarily to the first of the three types of ethics—the ethics of abandoning harm toward other sentient beings. This wish is essentially the mind's aspiration to abstain from every activity that will cause suffering to others—especially the ten nonvirtuous actions of body, speech, and mind, and within those, the seven vices of body and speech in particular.

Once we have generated the mind of bodhichitta that seeks the ultimate welfare of sentient beings, there is absolutely no way that our practice of ethics can degenerate. And yet if our practice of ethics should decline, even the basis of benefiting ourselves would be destroyed, so how would it ever be possible for us to fulfill the benefit of others? Furthermore, we place great emphasis on observing pure ethics because it is the core of all of our spiritual practices as well as the foundation of the six perfections and all of our mental development.

When undertaking the practice of ethics, we must continually work to strengthen our wish to keep pure morality, to observe and protect pure ethics. We do this by constantly bringing the shortcomings and manifold disadvantages of the lack of ethics to our minds, and by contemplating the advantages or the blessings of living in pure ethics. When our minds become very familiar with the gain and the loss with regard to practicing or not practicing pure ethics, our wish to observe pure morality will be strengthened.

The first of the three categories of ethics, the ethics of abstaining from the activities harming sentient beings, refers to all the vows and precepts that we take, such as the pratimoksha vows, lay precepts, and bodhisattva vows. Abstaining refers to refraining from engaging in all of the thoughts and actions that are by nature bad, or those that are prohibited because of the rules of discipline. Whatever commitments and pledges we take in front of a preceptor or an abbot fall into the category of the ethics of abandoning harm or the ethics of abstaining.

The second category, the ethics of undertaking virtue, is also connected to the practice of enthusiastic perseverance, or taking joy in virtue. This means making the effort to cultivate the practice of those paths that have not yet been generated in our minds, such as the practices of the six perfections. Working to enhance and develop whichever of the six perfections we have already generated is also part of the ethics of accumulating virtue.

The ethics of benefiting sentient beings means removing all the obstacles that set beings far apart from the attainments of this lifetime and future lifetimes—of higher rebirth, liberation, and enlightenment. Benefiting sentient beings refers to fulfilling all of the positive conditions in order to make it easy for them to attain these states.

Of the three types of ethics, the ethics of abstaining from activities that harm sentient beings is the most important. This practice of ethics acts as the foundation for the other two types. Within the training in the ethics abstaining from harming sentient beings, there are two further divisions: abstaining from the thoughts and actions that are by nature negative and nonvirtuous, and abstaining from those that are negative because they contradict vows or commitments that we have taken. Of the two, it is more important to abstain from the thoughts and actions that are by nature bad.

In the context of thoughts and activities that are to be abandoned because they contradict vows we have taken, some of the actions that are prohibited in the lower vehicles are allowed in the higher vehicles. But in the case of those thoughts and actions that are by nature bad, there are no such allowances made under any circumstances at all. Whether in the context of the individual vehicle or the universal vehicle, these actions are to be abandoned because they are by nature nonvirtuous. You should not even have the motivation or intention to engage in such activities, much less actually do them.

The six pure qualities discussed above should be applied to the practice of ethics as well. Of the six, the first is the purity of the basis. As a practitioner of pure ethics, you should not take pride in living in pure ethics, and you should not expect respect and regard from other people just because you are living in pure ethics. Rather, you should live in pure ethics with the thought of bodhichitta, of renouncing self, of cherishing others, with the thought to benefit others, and the wish to attain enlightenment. This is the motivation with which you should practice living in ethics.

The rest of the six you can apply on your own.

Then also, just as with the practice of generosity, even if we cannot practice the perfection of ethics in its most complete form, we should see how the bodhisattvas on the ten grounds practice ethics and aspire to become like them. In reality, however, we should focus on what we are capable of. In our case, we should focus on abandoning the ten types of nonvirtuous activities of body, speech, and mind. We should practice at this level, applying remembrance, mindfulness, and awareness.

On the one hand, as a result of abandoning the ten nonvirtuous actions, we eliminate suffering and problems in this lifetime and in future lifetimes, and we ensure happiness in this and future lifetimes. Moreover, we eliminate the result of experiencing the habit similar to the cause. On the other hand, if we engage in negative actions over and over again, we create strong propensities in our minds to develop the same bad habits in all of our future lifetimes. Focusing on the abandonment of the ten nonvirtuous actions eliminates those habits, and brings greater and greater happiness.

I am not going to discuss the practice of ethics very extensively in this section, because I have already covered this topic in the commentary on the medium scope. If we were to go into detail, we would have to discuss details of the bodhisattva vows and so forth. Generally speaking, however, if you would like further explanation of this practice, you should turn to Lama Tsongkhapa's *Medium Treatise on the Stages of the Path to Enlightenment* and his *Small Treatise on the Stages of the Path to Enlightenment.*

THE GENERAL CONDUCT:
THE PERFECTION OF PATIENCE

The next topic is the training in the perfection of patience. The divisions are explaining the nature of patience, the disadvantages of not practicing patience, the categories of patience, and how to practice it.

The Nature of Patience and the Benefits of Practicing It

Patience is also a quality that must be cultivated within the mind. There are three types of patience. The first is the patience of not retaliating in the face of receiving harm. The second is the patience of voluntarily taking on problems or suffering. And the third type of patience is the patience that is willing to undergo whatever difficulty may arise in the course of one's Dharma practice.

The main obstacle to practicing the patience that does not wish to retaliate is anger. The main obstacles to practicing the patience voluntarily taking on hardships or suffering are anger, lack of confidence, and feeling that we are incapable of doing so. The obstacles to practicing the patience of enduring difficulties in our Dharma practice are lack of faith and lack of interest in the Dharma.

The perfection of patience is complete when we are able to cease the mind of anger. As in the previous perfections, completing the perfection of patience does not mean that every sentient being will stop harming you or disturbing you. Rather, the perfection of patience is complete when we stop experiencing anger in reaction to the activities of other sentient beings, and when our capacity for tolerance has been developed to its fullest potential.

In the beginning, the best method to encourage us to develop our practice of patience is to familiarize our minds with the manifold advantages of the benefits of patience, and the numerous disadvantages of not practicing it. Thinking repeatedly about the benefits of practicing it will inspire us to try to practice patience when the opportunity arises, instead of getting angry.

In *Bodhisattva Grounds*, Arya Asanga lists some of the benefits of the practice of patience as follows. First, Asanga asserts that when practicing patience, our minds of anger cease, and thus there is less outer disturbance. Second, when we practice patience extensively, we will have fewer enemies and less discrimination toward others. Third, having practiced patience extensively in this lifetime, when the time of death arrives, we will be free to pass away without any sense of regret. And finally, as our practice of patience increases and flourishes, the happiness that we experience will also increase and flourish.

On a practical level, the practice of patience is very important to ensure harmonious existence within the community or society in which we live. In fact, our happiness within a community or within a society is largely *dependent* upon our ability to practice patience. Where the mind of patience thrives, a happy community or happy society will also thrive. Anger arises from our inability to tolerate differences between ourselves and others in terms of beliefs, attitudes, and conduct. But if we think about it carefully, we can see that these differences exist even within one individual. The way we think in the morning, for example, has undergone many transformations by the end of our day. If there can be so much fluctuation in the thoughts and ideas and activities of one person, then it is only reasonable to expect that this will also occur when there are two people involved, and even much more so when we consider an entire country or world. If we understand and accept this reality, we will begin to see how important it is to give the people around us space for their own unique ways of doing things.

However, practicing patience doesn't mean that we should let people walk all over us. If we find that this is happening, we should definitely put a stop to it. However, our response should be free of the mind of anger. If we are lacking patience, we will not be able to correct anyone else. When we are free of anger, however, all of our physical and verbal actions can be done with the sole thought of benefiting other beings. In the place of the violent mind of anger, we should cultivate the wish to help others.

In order for even two people to live a happy life together, it is necessary for them to let go of a great deal of self-cherishing. One person's peace of mind and happiness is very much dependent upon the other person, and the second person's mental peace and happiness is very much dependent upon the first person. If we focus solely on our own happiness, the problems will begin. This is how the story goes. The practice of patience is very important, not only in spiritual life, but also to ensure the success of our worldly life. It is also a very important practice in this lifetime and in future lifetimes.

The ripening result of practicing patience is having a physical appearance that is very pleasing to the eyes of others that draws people to you, or causes others to admire you. Because of this you will never be lacking in friends. This experience is the result that is similar to the cause.

Patience protects our mind from its own delusional states. While we are practicing patience, we are protected from coming under the control of the afflicted states of mind. Also, particularly when we practice the patience of voluntarily taking on suffering and problems, even negative experiences will not become obstacles for us or cause us to become unhappy. Because we are able to keep our minds in an undisturbed, subdued state, we will be able to engage in many positive thoughts and actions in our lives. And because of this, at the end of our lives we can die without any regret.

By understanding the virtue, necessity, and benefits of the practice of patience, and the logic and reason as to why we should practice patience, we will develop the wish to apply ourselves very diligently to this practice. This is stated in Shantideva's *Guide to the Bodhisattva's Way of Life*. As a result of practicing patience, you will experience happiness in this and future lifetimes, and you will bring happiness into the lives of the other sentient beings that you encounter.

The Disadvantages of Not Practicing Patience

In Togmay Sangpo's *Thirty-Seven Practices of Bodhisattvas,* it is stated that in order to harvest the merit of virtue, bodhisattvas consider every harm, every difficulty, and every problem that they encounter to be a wish-fulfilling treasure. The reason for this is that through these experiences, they have the occasion to complete the perfection of patience. In general, it is the practice of bodhisattvas to utilize every opportunity in which they meet with other beings to enhance upon the mind aspiring to attain enlightenment. At the beginning stages of the practice, while they are still influenced by karma and delusions, these bodhisattvas reflect continually upon the benefits of the practice of patience and the shortcomings of not practicing it.

In *Guide to the Bodhisattva's Way of Life,* Shantideva says:

If it can be fixed
What is the need for unhappiness?
And if it cannot be fixed
What is the help of unhappiness?

If a situation can be remedied, we should remedy it, and if this is the case, there is no basis for unhappiness or worry. However, if a situation cannot be remedied—if there are great obstacles and the conducive conditions cannot be brought together to ensure success—what need is there to be unhappy or to worry, since nothing can be done? That is the advice given when undertaking works for self or for others.

Unhappiness is the basis of the mind of anger. Just as food nourishes our body and empowers it, in the same way our unhappy mind nurtures the mind of anger and hatred. There are infinite disadvantages to the mind of anger, not only in terms of our Dharma practice but also in terms of our worldly existence. By remembering the shortcomings of this mind, and by applying mindfulness and awareness, we should work to remove the conditions that give rise to it.

The internal enemy of anger and hatred has no function other than to harm us physically and mentally, and to destroy all of the virtue that we have accumulated over many lifetimes. In terms of our experience with external enemies, there are occasions when they harm us and other occasions when they are busy with other things. The internal enemy of our anger and hatred, however, has no other function but to harm us continuously. The mind of anger induces the mind of vengeance, the mind of revenge, and the mind that holds a grudge. The actions that stem from these kinds of thoughts cause us to create even more nonvirtue.

How should we deal with anger when it arises? We should experience the conditions disturbing our happy state of mind as an echo or as a dream. From the Prasangika point of view, all the forms and situations that we experience are merely labeled, merely imputed by the mind. Therefore, rather than allowing the degeneration of our reputation, criticism that we may receive from others, personal loss, or personal suffering to become the cause for generating an unhappy mind, we can cultivate the view that sees these experiences as existing like an echo or like a dream.

Particularly if we are seeking to cultivate the virtues of love and compassion in our mind, it is essential that we extinguish every aspect of anger and hatred and infuse our mind with patience. Of course, attachment is also an obstacle to the cultivation of love and compassion because it creates a differentiation between self and others, and thereby we feel close to that which we identify with "self" and averse or distant toward that which is "others." However, anger is a much more direct obstacle. Generally speaking, anger is usually accompanied by ill will—the wish to harm— while attachment is not accompanied by such a mind. Therefore, anger is the direct opposite of the mind of love and compassion. Anger is the expression of the wish to harm, while love and compassion are the expression of the wish to benefit others.

It is said that there is no evil like anger, and that there is no virtue like patience. Patience is held in particularly high regard as a practice of virtue for ordinary sentient beings lacking bodhichitta, such as ourselves, who are almost entirely under the control of our delusions.

It is possible, though unlikely, for bodhisattvas on the Mahayana paths of accumulation and preparation to generate anger, because they have yet to abandon the seeds of the mind of anger. The effect of doing so would be the destruction of the accumulation of the merit of virtue that has been collected over many lifetimes.

Shantideva says:

All good conduct
That has been accumulated over a thousand eons
Through generosity and offering to the tathagatas
Is destroyed by anger in a moment.[40]

Of the two types of accumulation of merit—the merit of virtue and the merit of transcendental wisdom—the merit of virtue is the type that can be destroyed by anger. The merit of transcendental wisdom cannot be destroyed by anger. The reason that this is so is because the merit of virtue is not the direct antidote to the three poisonous minds. Therefore, powerful negative states of mind become a cause to destroy it. In contrast, because the wisdom realizing emptiness is extremely powerful, and the direct antidote to all of the delusions, even powerful negative states of mind such as anger cannot destroy it.

How can merit be destroyed by anger? This is explained differently according to different textual traditions. In one explanation it is said that anger delays the ripening results of merit. For example, a virtuous activity that we do in the early part of our life, which would ordinarily ripen in the later part of our life, can be affected by anger so that it does not ripen until the following lifetime. In this context, *destroyed* doesn't mean that the merit will not ripen into a result when it meets with the conducive conditions, but rather that it will be delayed for a long time. Of course, it is not possible for positive karma *not* to ripen into a result at all if it meets with the right conditions, because it is a karma that has been accumulated. Therefore, merit is destroyed only in the sense that its positive fruit is experienced a long time later. The proponents of this position argue that if the mind of single-pointed concentration—which is a conventional mind—cannot eliminate the seeds of our delusions, how could anger—which is also a conventional mind—eliminate the seeds of our virtue? According to this interpretation, anger cannot harm the seed of a virtuous action, and therefore this is the correct way to understand the effect that it has on a karmic result.

In our own tradition, however, the view that anger does not harm the seed of virtue is not accepted. If conventional minds cannot harm the seeds of karma, it is argued, how do we explain karmic purification? In applying the four opponent powers to purify our negative karmic accumulations, we say that although purification does not totally *remove* the seeds of negative karma, it does *harm* them. And because it harms the seeds of negative karma, even if we meet with the conditions that could ripen the result, the seed has been made ineffective through purification, and we will not experience its result. Therefore, according to our own system, the negative mind of anger *must* harm the seed of virtuous karma in the same way.

Again, when we complete a negative karmic action, we create a seed as well as a negative karmic imprint. Experiencing the ripening result of that karma does not remove its seed or its imprint. However, should that seed and the imprint meet again with the ripening conditions, it will not ripen again because the fruit has already been experienced. Regardless, the seed remains.

Our tradition asserts that the anger that destroys the merit of virtue must harm the karmic seed. Because it affects the karmic seed, some positive result that otherwise would have been experienced very soon is instead made distant. According to this interpretation, because the positive result that we were to experience is lessened, the karmic seed must have been affected. In the same way, through applying the four opponent powers we can render our karmic seeds unable to produce a result, although we cannot eliminate them entirely.

The concept of anger destroying merit is also sometimes explained in terms of the fact that the experience of anger propels the result of a habit that is similar to the cause into the future, which means that we will experience more anger in the future and thus less happiness. Because each experience of anger strengthens our familiarity with it, we are more likely to experience it again at a later point, and as a result our merit is lessened.

In general, Lama Tsongkhapa advises us to rely heavily on the words of Buddha himself in conjunction with logical analysis in order to understand the way that this process works. According to Lama Tsongkhapa, if we first understand Buddha's presentation of the way that negative karmic seeds are affected by the power of purification, we can then apply the same sort of logic and reasoning with regard to the way our negative minds affect our positive virtuous karma.

If you are interested in the way karmic seeds function, you can find more details in the commentaries on Madhyamaka by Sera Jetsunpa and Drepung Gomang Jamyang Shepa.

When Shantideva talks about one moment of anger destroying a thousand eons of merit, or Chandrakirti mentions one moment of anger destroying a hundred eons of merit, the merit that they are discussing is the merit accumulated in the mind of a bodhisattva. If this is the result in the case of an extraordinary being's experience of anger, then, as you can imagine, the result in the case of ordinary sentient beings is all the greater.

All of these points are mentioned in order to inspire you to practice patience, because there is so much to be gained from this practice, and also so much at stake.

Even if after all of this discussion we still find it difficult to comprehend or accept how the negative mind of anger affects our merits of a thousand eons, we can certainly focus on the immediate ways in which it interferes with our lives. For example, angry thoughts create a disturbing, unsubdued state of mind—when we are angry we have no happiness, no peace, no sleep, and we become totally unstable. Seeing how anger affects us in this way should inspire us to work to extinguish it. In the case of a practitioner who has totally given up the thought clinging to the appearances of this life, to whom the infinite future lifetimes become so important, these explanations about the merits of a thousand eons being destroyed in one moment of anger are very effective. For others, the immediate disadvantages of anger, such as the unsubdued mind, lack of peace, lack of happiness, lack of sleep, and unstable mind, provide incentive to practice patience.

The Patience of Not Retaliating

Again, there are three kinds of patience: the patience of not retaliating when we are harmed, the patience of voluntarily taking on difficulties, problems, sickness, and so forth, and the patience that is able to bear hardship in the course of developing ourselves in Dharma practice.

The first type of patience is not retaliating when we are harmed. When we lack this kind of patience, if we are harmed physically, mentally, or verbally, we will not be able to tolerate it. Also, should we encounter a person toward whom we have aversion, and should they be experiencing good things, we will feel that this is totally unbearable. Should this person be undergoing very difficult times, however, we will feel happy.

We should be encouraged to develop the patience of not retaliating by considering the fact that without it, we will never be happy. In the long run, it is much more to our advantage in life to cultivate patience, and not retaliate. When others harm us, at the very least we should keep our minds calm and undisturbed. At the very best, we should be able to care and cherish the source of that harm.

How do you train your mind to remain undisturbed in the face of great harm? You must take the time to analyze the situation. When you do so, you will see that the individual who harms you is completely out of control. Because the one who harms you is controlled by other conditions, that person is harming you without any choice in the matter at all. The conditions that bring this about are the delusions in the person's own mind, that person's previous karmic seeds, and your own contributing karma. All of these come together to cause this person to harm you involuntarily. When you examine the situation in this way, it should be very clear to you that the person who is harming you has absolutely no choice in the matter at all. When you understand how this person is merely subject to the conditions around him or her, you will realize that it is totally invalid for you to react to this harm with anger. It is totally invalid for you not to care for and cherish this person.

For example, if a person who is mentally ill attacks me, it would be absolutely stupid and foolish for me to get angry with this person, because this person is not in control of his or her mind. There is no valid basis in the actions of this person to justify my becoming angry. Moreover, as this situation is so pitiful, and the person is completely powerless in the face of that insanity, it is most appropriate that I should have the mind of care and cherishing, and wish to help this person in some way.

In order for the understanding that the person harming us is completely without control to sink into my mind, of course, it is important for me to have reflected upon the disadvantages of my own anger. I should reflect how, when I am angry, I feel completely unified with that anger—the anger and the person—me—seem to be the same thing. I should also reflect how it feels to be free of the mind of anger. It is on the basis of examining my own experience that it will be possible to generate an understanding of others when they get angry.

When we aspire to practice the Mahayana path, particularly when we aspire to practice bodhichitta, renouncing self, cherishing others, and wishing to attain enlightenment for the benefit of others, it is essential that we do not retaliate for the harms that we have received from our external enemies. This is a very important part of practicing the path of the great scope.

The Patience of Willingly Taking on Suffering

In our ordinary samsaric lives, most of us have very few experiences of leisure and happiness and many, many experiences of suffering. If we can learn to transform that suffering into some kind of beneficial or positive experience, we will be much better off. Some suffering that we experience arises as a result of very powerful karma, and as long as we are under the influence of our delusions, it may not be reversible. If we can practice the patience of willingly taking on suffering, although we still may be forced by our karma to experience a suffering result, the *degree* to which we experience that suffering will be much less.

With the practice of willingly taking on suffering, we will never be overwhelmed by the suffering that we are bound to experience as long as we are bound in samsara. Instead, we will be able to use our negative experiences as the path to accumulate virtue, and quickly free ourselves from this unfortunate state in order to help other beings.

The Patience of Enduring Hardships in One's Dharma Practice

If we are unable to practice the patience that endures hardships in the course of our Dharma practice, we will be unable to practice Dharma at all. In these degenerate times, we are certain to experience great obstacles to our practice of abandoning nonvirtue and cultivating virtue. However, when we make an effort in such times of difficulty, the merits that we create are even more powerful. In these degenerate times, by the incredible blessings of the buddhas and the merit of our own past karma, we have had the opportunity to meet and practice the Dharma. We have also been able to begin to apply ourselves in the practices of examining the nature of our own mind, recognizing our delusions, seeing their shortcomings, and applying the antidotes. This being the case, we really must consider ourselves to be extremely fortunate.

However, sometimes when we engage in Dharma practice, we experience a lot of interferences and obstacles, both internal and external. Even if we are able to free ourselves from one obstacle, another one is usually right behind it. Obstacles can manifest in a negative or positive form. When things are going too well in our lives, our practice can be harmed because we do not have the incentive to practice Dharma; at other times, things become so difficult that we lose the recognition of our great fortune in finding this existence. Whether obstacles manifest under good or bad circumstances, the essential thing is never to give up applying ourselves to the practice of subduing our minds. Practicing Dharma is like walking a tightrope. We must be careful not to fall into either of the two extremes: finding ourselves in circumstances that are so good that we are totally distracted from our Dharma practice, or encountering so many problems that we give up on it completely.

Generally, most people lose the inspiration of their Dharma practice due to experiencing difficult circumstances. When we first meet the Dharma, we have a great sense of perseverance in our practice, a great sense of determination to subdue our minds. However, we may encounter health problems, financial problems, or problems from friends or relatives—a lot of entanglements. Generally speaking, these experiences become obstacles. Whatever obstacles we may experience, we must realize that they are not truly, inherently existent obstacles. In terms of their ultimate mode of existence, all of these obstacles are merely imputed by our minds. However, they do exist conventionally, which means that they can function to harm us. The attitude we take in relation to those problems is very important. Rather than working only from the point of view of trying to fix the problems, we must also try to change the way our minds perceive them. If we have skill, we can transform any negative circumstances into the path of spiritual development.

Usually, when problems appear in our lives, we blame them on others.

We are totally habituated to blaming everything on external conditions. But as it is said many times over in the teachings, all of our problems and suffering arise only from our own negative karma. The ripening results of the lower realms arise only from our own negative karma. Likewise, higher rebirth and happiness arise only from our own positive karma. Therefore, when we experience obstacles in the course of our lives, and particularly in our Dharma practice, we should reflect upon the fact that whatever we are experiencing is only the manifestation of our own past negative actions. We should apply an understanding of the reality of the law of cause and effect to all of our misfortunes and suffering. We understand that karma is definite, that we never experience any kind of result for which we have not created the cause, and that whatever cause we have created, its result is never lost to us. So when we run into unfortunate experiences in life, we should apply all this understanding, and we should look upon our misfortune as a way of exhausting that karma.

Happiness and suffering do not come without causes and conditions, and they do not arise out of nowhere. In the same way, virtuous and nonvirtuous karmic accumulations are not without causes and conditions, nor do they arise independently. nonvirtuous actions have their causes in the negative states of mind. These in turn are rooted in self-cherishing and the ignorance grasping at true existence. The karmic imprints of ignorance are the direct and indirect causes bringing forth nonvirtue and suffering. When we understand the result of suffering in this context, knowing how it has come about, it can help us to reconfirm the understanding of cause and effect, and to have faith in karma. Likewise, it can also help us to identify the real enemy—our own ignorance—and its antidote. When we expand upon whatever fortune or misfortune we experience in such a way, we stabilize our own Dharma practice and ensure that under no circumstances will we ever give up the thought to practice Dharma.

As beginners on the spiritual path, the thing most likely to set us back on the path is encountering problems or difficulties. Therefore, as if we were climbing down a hill, in order not to trip we take care with every step. We should apply this awareness to our Dharma practice, and take care to engage all the activities of our body, speech, and mind only in virtue. For those who are wise, even adverse circumstances become a cause to generate virtue.

When we practice Dharma and make certain advances or improvements in our knowledge, a sense of self-importance in what we have accomplished may arise. If this occurs, it is important to maintain an awareness of suffering, particularly since we are supposed to be practicing love and compassion. Just as we do not wish suffering for ourselves, neither do other sentient beings. In this way, encountering obstacles can help us cut through our sense of pride and self-importance. In the tantric path we transform the three poisonous minds into the path to enlightenment. At our level, we transform adverse circumstances into the path of our spiritual development.

A sign of a really pure practitioner is that when things are going really smoothly, when there is only happiness and comfort, that practitioner is very unhappy with the situation. And then, when there are a lot of problems and difficulties, that practitioner is very happy. A pure practitioner understands that when there is only comfort and happiness, we are exhausting positive karma. But when there are a lot of problems and difficulties, we are exhausting negative karma. Moreover, under difficult circumstances, we ensure that our delusional minds of pride and so forth are subdued. We experience a heightened sense of awareness of the suffering of others, more compassion, and further incentive to engage in virtue and abandon nonvirtue.

As worldly beings, when someone praises us, we feel very happy, and when someone criticizes us, we feel unhappy. But a pure practitioner will take joy in criticism and be unhappy at receiving praise. When we are criticized, we become aware of the failings and mistakes that we are ordinarily unable to recognize or face up to. When we are criticized, we are introduced to that reality.

Whatever circumstances arise in our life, good or bad, we must try to take them as the path to enlightenment. From the philosophical point of view, when fortunate or unfortunate circumstances occur, we can examine their nature as being empty of inherent existence, empty of independent existence, and merely imputed. Although they are merely imputed, we can also understand that they are totally functional, bringing about the result of happiness or suffering. We can also realize them to be like a dream, like an illusion, or like a mirage—although they appear, they lack true existence. In this way, when we reflect upon our experiences from the point of view of their nature, whether they are extremely good or extremely bad, we will not be totally overtaken by the experience of that happiness or suffering.

Also, during our experience of the extremes of fortunate and unfortunate circumstances, we can take the opportunity to witness the ignorance grasping at the inherent existence of the "I," which is most apparent at these times of strong emotional engagement. Normally, when our mind is not influenced by these kinds of strong emotional conditions, our intuitive mode of grasping at true existence is not apparent at all.

If we have skill, we will be able to use every opportunity in our life, good or bad, to progress further on the path to enlightenment. In this way, we can think of ourselves as artists making statues of buddha—when we are able to take everything that we experience as our path to enlightenment, it is like molding our future enlightenment with our own hands.

THE GENERAL CONDUCT: THE PERFECTION OF ENTHUSIASTIC PERSEVERANCE

The Nature of Perseverance and the Benefits of Practicing It

Enthusiastic perseverance is characterized by a quality of joy that arises in our minds upon engaging in virtuous activities for the benefit of others. Perseverance is the secondary mental factor that moves our body, speech, and mind to happily engage in virtue.

In the *Ornament for the Mahayana Sutras* Maitreya states:

Among the collection of all the virtues, perseverance is supreme...
Through perseverance, you will come to possess supreme purity.
Through perseverance, you will overcome the view of the transitory
   collection.
Through perseverance, you will obtain supreme enlightenment.

If we engage in virtuous activities without a sense of joy, they become activities that are virtuous only by nature. But if these activities are accompanied by enthusiastic perseverance, they become virtuous by motivation as well. Once our minds are familiar with perseverance, we will never be defeated by the delusions, and will always be victorious over them. We will never feel incapable of accomplishing good works, but on the contrary, will have the confidence and intent to complete them. When we have perseverance, we can attain anything we set our minds to. Without perseverance, however, we will attain nothing at all. Perseverance enables us to free ourselves from the bondage of cyclic existence and to practice the unified path of method and wisdom in order to attain enlightenment. The benefits of practicing enthusiastic perseverance are limitless.

However, the shortcomings of not practicing perseverance are just as many. The opposite of perseverance is laziness, and a mind of laziness cannot help anyone. With laziness, we will be unable to accomplish the practices of any of the six perfections, and it will take a very long time to become enlightened. With the mind of laziness, we will be unable to be of immediate or ultimate benefit to others, and whatever we have managed to accomplish will only decline and degenerate.

The Three Types of Perseverance

There are three types of perseverance: armor-like perseverance, the perseverance of accumulating virtue, and the perseverance of benefiting sentient beings.

Armor-like perseverance is the strong motivation to engage tirelessly in the profound path of wisdom and the extensive path of method until enlightenment in order to be of benefit to sentient beings. If we can generate even a facsimile of the mind of armor-like perseverance, we will be able to accumulate limitless merit and purify our obscurations very quickly, and generate realizations that will never degenerate. This will be especially true if we have generated bodhichitta and made the commitment to engage in the activities benefiting sentient beings through the conduct of the six perfections. Armor-like perseverance is what makes it possible to engage in the conduct of the six perfections no matter how difficult the path may become. Without perseverance, however, we will be unable to fulfill the aspirations of the mind of bodhichitta, or complete any practice of the conduct of a bodhisattva.

According to the *Sutra of the Inconceivable Mind*, we can cultivate armor-like perseverance through contemplating the following thought:

If I regard all of beginningless time until today as one day, and thirty of those days become a month, and twelve of those months become a year—even if it takes one hundred of those years, if I can generate bodhichitta and attain the concentration of the Dharma continuum enabling me to see the face of a buddha, and hear the speech of the holy Dharma, then it will all be worthwhile. By attaining this state, if I can then understand sentient beings' predispositions, aspirations, and levels of mind, and if through all of this knowledge I can ripen the mind of one sentient being and lead that being to enlightenment, then it will all have been worthwhile.

Once we understand a little about the path and practices that will lead us to enlightenment, most of us develop the wish to attain our goal as quickly as possible. But then, when we hear that it is necessary to accumulate three countless eons of merit in order to attain enlightenment, we become completely exhausted and want to forget about the whole thing. This is primarily due to lack of perseverance, particularly armor-like perseverance. The cultivation of armor-like perseverance is intended to build up our strength of mind to undertake virtue and travel the path for the benefit of sentient beings over a very long duration of time. When we have developed this kind of perseverance, we will feel absolutely no discomfort when we hear about accumulating merit over three countless eons. It will make no difference to us one way or the other. Generally, it is impossible to set a deadline for the time when we will have completely subdued our mind of its delusions and developed all of our positive qualities. Since this is so, how will we be able to accomplish all of these things without armor-like perseverance?

For example, when we do purification practices applying the four opponent powers, the instructions say to engage in such practices until we see definite signs of purification. It doesn't say to do them only *x* number of times. If we truly intend to practice in this way, we cannot do so without the mind of armor-like perseverance.

Interestingly, a certain quality of the mental state of armor-like perseverance can be compared to the worldly mind of dissatisfaction that keeps us constantly seeking new things, people, and experiences in our lives. The mind of dissatisfaction motivates us day and night to pursue the interests of the eight worldly dharmas throughout our lives until our deaths. The mind of armor-like perseverance is similar in strength and impetus, although the activities that it inspires us to engage in are, of course, virtuous and positive. However, someone who has completed the perfection of armor-like perseverance will, in a certain way, never be content, and will be driven to accumulate more and more virtue until the final goal is reached.

Those on the paths of the hearers and solitary realizers also practice armor-like perseverance, although their practice could not be called the *perfection* of perseverance, because they are lacking the support of the unified practice of method and wisdom.

Once we have developed armor-like perseverance, we can accomplish the second of the three types of perseverance, the perseverance in accumulating virtue.

The third type of perseverance is the perseverance of benefiting sentient beings. There are eleven ways to practice it. The first way is by doing activities that contribute to the happiness of sentient beings and that eliminate their suffering. Secondly we can benefit sentient beings who are ignorant or confused about the correct method to free themselves from suffering. We can also practice the perseverance of benefiting sentient beings by working to bring them immediate and long-term benefit, by helping them when they are afraid, when they are miserable and depressed, or when they are living in poverty. The seventh way in which we can practice the perseverance of benefiting sentient beings is by providing shelter overnight. We can also practice perseverance by giving mental support, which means going along with the views of people who are very lonely or sad even if their ideas aren't quite the same as your own in order to benefit them in the long run. The ninth way to practice is by inspiring and encouraging sentient beings to do positive actions so that they may enter the path of pure virtue. We can also help sentient beings who have entered a mistaken path or are doing negative activities by disengaging them from those things. And finally, we can benefit sentient beings through our clairvoyance and psychic powers.

Obstacles to the Practice of Perseverance

The method for managing the obstacles to perseverance is to recognize them and then abandon them. Ordinary beings who have yet to enter the path commonly experience two main obstacles when training in this kind of mind. The first is being able to accomplish the practices of the path but choosing not to do so, and the second is thinking that we are incapable of accomplishing the practices of the path at all. The first obstacle is a type of laziness. It is the laziness of being attracted to ordinary activities instead of virtuous activities. The second obstacle is the laziness of procrastination.

The first obstacle occurs as a result of our attachment to temporary forms of happiness or comfort. When the mind is distracted and concerned only with seeking a temporary or limited kind of happiness, this obstacle will arise. The antidote to this obstacle is to strengthen our meditation on perfect human rebirth. Think well about the eight leisures, the ten endowments, and how our perfect human rebirth can be very easily lost—that it is impermanent and subject to death, and that when death does happen, our black and white karma takes control. Contemplating the rarity of the opportunity of our perfect human rebirth in conjunction with impermanence and death will counteract the mind's clinging to useless and base activities. Another method to counteract this kind of attachment is to contemplate the benefits of the Dharma, and the fact that Buddha's teachings are like a treasury that fulfills the temporary and ultimate benefits of beings. Thinking in this way can help us to loosen our attachment to the transient, temporary pleasures of this life.

Feeling that we don't have the intelligence or strength of mind to complete the path is also an obstacle. Sometimes we may think about the resultant state of an enlightened being who is completely free of faults and has developed every quality, and then we may despair, thinking how we have removed no faults and generated no qualities in ourselves. The comparison between our goal and ourselves in the present may make us feel that there is absolutely no way that we can attain enlightenment. We should be very careful in this situation. If this thought should manifest directly, it will cause our bodhichitta to become invalid.

The method to counteract this obstacle is to think about Buddha, who, in having eliminated all faults from his mind and attained all the positive qualities, would not state anything but the truth. And Buddha has stated that even flies and bees and ants have the potential to attain enlightenment. If Buddha has said that about these sentient beings, what need is there to mention our own case, our own capacity to attain enlightenment?

Another way to counteract this obstacle is to contemplate the conventional nature of our own minds, which are luminous, clear, and knowing. We can also contemplate the fact that the mind's ultimate nature is empty of inherent existence. For inspiration, it is also useful to think about the examples of the buddhas and the bodhisattvas who accumulated merit over countless eons in order to reach enlightenment, such as the bodhisattva who offered his body as food to a starving tigress and her cubs. Reflecting on the perseverance that these great beings displayed can inspire us to do the same, and thus counteract the laziness of disparaging ourselves.

Knowing that we are under the control of our own karma and delusions, and therefore bound to samsara's suffering, at the very least we should understand what sort of problems or difficulties we will have to tolerate on the path. We should understand that as long as we are in cyclic existence, we are definitely going to suffer. And we should resolve that no matter how long it takes to be free from this situation, we will practice patience as we encounter such difficulties. Encouraging this kind of mind can also avert the laziness of disparaging ourselves.

Sometimes we justify our laziness by blaming the causes and conditions that exist in our environment, when in reality there is no excuse: we are only lazy. Every unfortunate situation that we encounter is a result of our own karma and delusions that propel us endlessly through cyclic existence. There is no one to blame but ourselves. If, however, we are able to develop our perseverance on the path and cultivate the realizations of renunciation, bodhichitta, and the pure view, the suffering that we experience will become less and less, and we will begin to realize the illusory nature of samsara.

Cultivating Confidence in Our Practice

If we seriously intend to train our minds in the practices of the six perfections, it is important that we develop confidence in what we are doing. Ordinarily we consider pride to be an afflictive emotion that we should abandon, but in fact there are certain types of pride that can actually support our practice.

The first type of pride that we should cultivate in our practice is the pride of action. Again, although we use the label "pride," please do not confuse this state of mind with the affliction that is to be abandoned. The pride of action holds the thought, "I, myself alone, will attain enlightenment to benefit beings." Thinking this, we are endowed with the complete certainty that we will be able to bring this about.

If we are going to do a retreat or some practice, we depend on a lot of external factors in order to accomplish such things. But in some cases the mind can become overwhelmed by all of the things that are needed. When we have the pride of action, then, yes, we still need all these external conditions to come together, but whether we do that retreat or not is not completely dependent upon them. We focus on accomplishing the practice of that particular retreat, and whether the other conditions come together or not does not disturb our mind so much.

The second type of pride that we can cultivate in order to support our practice is the pride in our own potential to benefit others. Endowed with this thought, we are confident in our capabilities to help other beings. If we do not have this kind of confidence, it will be very easy for us to be overwhelmed by small obstacles on the path.

The third type of pride is the pride in our ability to be victorious over our delusions. For example, if ten people are in a race, before the race begins each one of those ten people cultivates the confidence that they are going to win. Although they think this way, in reality these people do not have a clear conviction of that fact. In the same way, we can build up our confidence in our ability to be victorious over our delusions without actually having a clear conviction that we will actually be able to accomplish this. This kind of pride or confidence will enable us to make positive progress on the path to enlightenment, and, in conjunction with the other two types of pride, will help us to strengthen our practice of enthusiastic perseverance.

In the *Guide to the Bodhisattva's Way of Life*, it says:

Just as the tathagatas before
Cultivated the mind of enlightenment and
Practiced in proper order
The conduct of the bodhisattvas,

In the same way, for the benefit of others,
I will generate the mind of enlightenment

And train in proper order
In that practice.

Our ability to practice enthusiastic perseverance is strongly related to the strength of our aspiration to attain the goal that we seek, which in this case is the state of enlightenment for the sake of all sentient beings. This aspiration, in turn, is largely dependent on our faith in the way that our actions will ripen into the experience of particular results. When we have faith and understanding in karmic cause and effect, we will see how cultivating the altruistic mind that seeks the welfare of others is the cause that will ripen in the result of the five paths and ten grounds in our minds, thereby enabling our enlightenment. In the same way, with this awareness, we will understand that the ripening results of our nonvirtuous actions will be negative results that are similar to the cause, negative habits, and so forth. This will encourage us to aspire to engage in actions that are virtuous and positive, and abandon actions that are nonvirtuous and negative.

If we have faith and belief in our goals, we will naturally develop the wish to attain them. This wish, when strengthened, will become an aspiration, and this aspiration will inspire us to develop perseverance in attaining those results. If we then support our perseverance with the three types of pride, we can maintain a steady stream of practice, and joyfully practice virtue all the way up until enlightenment.

Our enthusiasm for practice and our perseverance on the path should not be like a hailstorm—falling from the sky all at once with absolutely no constancy. When we apply ourselves to virtuous activities, it is essential that we maintain a continual stream of perseverance rather than making effort in the form of one huge push toward a particular goal, leaving no energy remaining to act as a basis for the future.

The perfection of perseverance is essentially the practice of combating the enemy of our own delusions. When we fight with external enemies, our goal is to destroy them so that they will be unable to harm us again. When we do battle with the internal enemy of the delusions, our goal is to gain victory over them so that we will never come under their control again. When we are trying to destroy our internal enemies, such as the obsessive mind of attachment, perseverance can help us to ensure that once we have conquered one delusion, a second one will not arise in its place. Persever-ance will help us to be certain that we will not fall under the control of the three poisons as we practice the path to enlightenment, and, at the other extreme, that we do not focus on eliminating one particular delusion to the exclusion of all the rest. The practice of enthusiastic perseverance in con-junction with mindfulness will also enable us to understand the conven-tional and ultimate modes of existence, have faith in cause and effect, and remember the vows and precepts that we have taken. Although our own thoughts and actions at present may not encompass the perfection of per-severance, we can definitely aspire to develop the perfection of this prac-tice as the buddhas and bodhisattvas have done.

CALMING THE MIND

THE PERFECTION OF CONCENTRATION

THE CONCENTRATION CHAPTER of Shantideva's *Guide to the Bodhi-sattva's Way of Life* begins:

Having cultivated perseverance in that way
Place the mind in meditative concentration.
The mind that is distracted
Remains within the fangs of the afflictions.

Without single-pointed concentration as a foundation, we will be unable to bring forth the complete realizations of renunciation, bodhichitta, and emptiness in our minds.

A mind that has not trained in concentration is a mind that is constantly distracted, a mind caught in the delusions—clinging to the appearances of this lifetime, the benefits of the future lifetimes, the wish for individual liberation, and so forth. When our minds are distracted, it is like being in the mouth of an alligator—from such a position, we will easily be eaten. If we are distracted, it is very easy for negative thoughts to arise even while we are engaging in virtuous activities. If, however, we are able to isolate ourselves physically and mentally from the source of our delusions, we may have a chance at keeping our actions from coming under their control.

The practice of calm abiding can be categorized as either an "inner" or an "outer" practice. It is designated an inner practice if it is a Buddhist practice, and an outer practice if it is practiced by someone who is not a Buddhist. In general, the cultivation of single-pointed concentration is common to many spiritual paths. The nature of concentration is that it is a virtuous state of mind that cannot be moved away from its object. The perfection of concentration can refer to a state of calm abiding, a state of superior insight, or a unified state of calm abiding and superior insight.

Single-pointed concentration has two main functions in the mind of the practitioner. The first is that it endows the practitioner with mental and physical bliss, and the second is that it enables the practitioner to attain qualities, in the sense that it acts as the basis of the attainments of clairvoyance and psychic powers. In *Treasury of Knowledge,* Vasubhandu presents a clear explanation of the method to cultivate clairvoyance on the basis of concentration. Even ordinary sentient beings who wish to cultivate clairvoyance can do these meditations, and through the power of these practices develop the clairvoyance that knows ten moments of someone else's mind.

As in the case of previous five perfections, the perfection of concentration should be endowed with the six pure qualities.

Training the mind in calm abiding should precede the cultivation of superior insight, because the subtle bliss of mind and body—the basis upon which superior insight is generated—is only attained through the training in the nine methods of mental placement. The way this occurs is as follows. By cultivating our minds in calm abiding, we are able to establish single-pointed focus on our object of meditation. This single-pointedness acts as the basis for our development of superior insight. While maintaining single-pointed focus, the wisdom of individual discrimination is able to analyze its object with great clarity, totally free of distraction and mental sinking. This is the meditation of superior insight. The Tibetan word for superior insight is *lhagtong (lhag mthong),* which means seeing more, seeing further, or seeing in a superior way.

The way our minds are in our present situation, our analytical capabilities are hindered by the coarseness of our mental consciousness. Right now, the mind that analyzes the object is a very gross mind, whereas the object that we wish to analyze—the meaning of emptiness—is very, very subtle. A very gross level of mind does not have the clarity or focus to be able to analyze a very subtle subject. We can imagine how this is so by thinking of the analogy of using a flashlight with low batteries to see a path in the dark.

Sometimes we may feel that we have listened to a great many teachings, that we have gained great understanding, and that we have done many meditations, and yet we wonder why we have had no experience of realizations.

When we feel that way, we should recall the subtlety of the subjects we are dealing with, and then look at the mind that we are using to examine them. We should then resolve not to be so easily disappointed or discouraged by our lack of results. If we analyze the graduated path, we can see that the steps are very sound, that the practices are based on valid logic, and that if we actually apply ourselves to practicing the steps as they are set forth in the texts, results will be forthcoming. Generating armor-like perseverance, we should develop continuity in our practice. When we have continuity in our practice, we will definitely have results.

To generate the created forms of renunciation, bodhichitta, and the wisdom realizing emptiness, we do not necessarily need calm abiding or superior insight in our minds. However, we cannot generate the *spontaneous* or uncreated realizations of these topics on the basis of our ordinary gross mind. In order to bring forth spontaneous realizations, it is absolutely imperative to cultivate calm abiding and superior insight. Right now our minds are like monkeys. We do a little bit of something here, then we leave it incomplete, and go elsewhere. We begin many things and leave them all unfinished. Training our minds in calm abiding will help us to overcome this bad habit, and create a firm foundation for our practice of wisdom as well.

If you look at the texts from the Sutrayana tradition of Tibetan Buddhism, you will see that there are volumes upon volumes of scriptures and commentaries that take the wisdom realizing emptiness as their main subject. The reason that Nagarjuna and his disciples placed so much emphasis on the analytical process of the mind of wisdom is because the objective of the Buddhist path is to eliminate the most subtle form of the delusions from the mind, and not merely their grossest manifestations. The gross manifestations of the delusions can be eliminated with the concentration that arises from the fully developed mind of calm abiding. But since we are seeking to uproot our negative states of mind completely, it is imperative that we cultivate the investigative mind of wisdom as well.

In the beginning, we should strive to cultivate an understanding of whatever teachings we have listened to. Then we should practice concentration, taking whatever we have understood as our object, and cultivate strong familiarity with it through single-pointed focus. Finally, through the process of meditation, the realization of that subject matter will arise.

The obstacles to the practices of both concentration meditation and analytical meditation are distraction, excitement, and mental sinking. Although both mental distraction and mental excitement are secondary mental factors, there are distinctions between them. Mental distraction can be associated with either a virtuous or a nonvirtuous object. Mental excitement, however, is usually associated with the mind of attachment.

Accumulating the Appropriate Conditions

The next topic is the way to create conducive conditions for generating the mind of calm abiding.

In order to cultivate concentration properly, a conducive external environment is imperative. A conducive internal mental attitude is also imperative. The external condition that is most essential for the cultivation of concentration is a pleasant environment—meaning a place that is harmonious with your mental disposition, and where you can easily attain food and other means of survival. While training in concentration meditation, on the one hand, you shouldn't live so meagerly that you physically harm yourself, or that you become physically incapable of doing the practice. On the other hand, you shouldn't feed yourself to the point of indulgence. Overeating can become an obstacle to your meditation as well—creating the desire for more sleep, inducing more general laziness, and so forth. It is important to find a balance between the two extremes. Your food should be very simple, not a continental breakfast, for example, with many things to deal with. Also, you should ensure that whatever you eat or drink while on retreat is not acquired through wrong livelihood, and that whoever is sponsoring you is not acquiring their means through wrong livelihood.

The place where you meditate should not be a place where there has been war, a lot of crime, or a lot of activities that are considered negative by nature. If you try to meditate in a place like this, your mind will not be able to overcome the negative conditions of the area. Some of the first Tibetans to escape from Tibet and take refuge in India ended up in a refugee camp that had previously been a prison. During the British rule, thousands of people had been held there. Many of the Tibetan monks who stayed in this refugee camp at that time felt greatly disturbed by this environment.

The best places to meditate are places where past meditators have undertaken long periods of retreat. However, you shouldn't seek out a place that is extremely isolated, so that you are constantly worried about wild animals, scorpions, spiders, and thieves. If there are people living around you, of course, they should be people who aspire to practice as you do. You should not put yourself in a retreat place with people with whom you do not have good rapport. Especially in the beginning, it can be very helpful to have people nearby whose ethics and perspective on the world are similar to your own. Early on it may be difficult to stay totally alone, so it might be useful to have someone there with whom you can discuss ideas and practices as you go along. This kind of interaction can be very beneficial for your practice.

You should choose a colder climate rather than a warm, sticky place. The cold eliminates a lot of insects and so forth, and it also ensures fewer health problems. High elevation is also an advantage, as is a place where there is less noise.

When setting out for your retreat, you should bring all the instructions for your meditation with you along with all of your resources, such as lam-rim texts and *lojong (blo sbyong)*—mind-training—texts, and so forth. Of course, it goes without saying that you should have received all the instructions on the practice before you undertake retreat.

Internally, in order to train in concentration, you must have a sense of contentment in your mind and not be constantly overcome by strong thoughts of attachment and desire to the pleasures of the five senses. When you have less desire, you naturally have fewer obstacles, and you will be able to engage in a more focused meditation. You should not have too many things to do outside of your practice. Also, while cultivating concentration, it is very important to be living in pure ethics.

In the beginning, your practice of concentration should focus on attaining a state of mind that is a combination of focus and clarity—in which the object appears clearly to the mind *and* the mind is able to remain firmly on the object. The combination of these two is essential. As you progress in your practice and develop further levels of concentration, the attainment of concentration and clarity alone is no longer sufficient. To be free of the subtle forms of mental distraction and mental sinking, you must then develop strength in your concentration and strength in your clarity. When there is no strength in your clarity, your visualization will appear but it will not be sharp.

The Way to Meditate

THE IMPORTANCE OF MINDFULNESS

In order to have a faultless practice of calm abiding, we need to develop very strong concentration supported by very strong mindfulness and wisdom. Wisdom in this case refers to the function of mind called introspection, which acts as a kind of security guard for the mind—watching for faults or weaknesses that may arise in our concentration. We should train in the mindfulness possessing three qualities. Our mindfulness must be able to remember the aspect of our object of concentration. It must have the ability to hold that aspect, and it must not be distracted by other objects.

You should seek to develop a concentration that is stable and lasting. In order to be able to bring this about, mindfulness is very important. Of course, even in terms of our ordinary perception, every primary mind is accompanied by five determining factors, one of which is mindfulness. Although this kind of mindfulness does fulfill the function of helping you to hold the object that you are perceiving, it is not stable or continuous, and cannot hold the mind on its object for an indefinite amount of time. Ordinarily, when the primary mind changes its object from one thing to another, that mindfulness changes its object as well. In the practice of concentration meditation, we must strive to develop a more developed type of mindfulness that can fulfill the function of remaining focused on the object of concentration for a long period of time.

In the beginning, when we engage in the practice of single-pointed placement of the mind for the first time and begin the battle with our conceptual thoughts, we must apply concentration, mindfulness, and introspection in equal amounts. As we gain stability, we should check repeatedly to make sure that we have not lost our object. Simultaneously, we must be careful not to overexert ourselves, because if we tighten the mind too much, we run the danger of falling into the extreme of mental sinking.

This process is similar to what you go through when setting up your television set. The picture on your TV is controlled by many different buttons: one button fixes the image so it doesn't shake, another adjusts the color, another adjusts the brightness, another button makes the image appear very sharp. Cultivating concentration is similar. We need to fine-tune our minds until they do not move at all. It is very important to support our concentration with just the right amount of mindfulness—not too little, not too much. Accomplishing the right balance depends on how well we have trained in the mindfulness of the experienced practitioner, which in turn depends upon how well we have trained in the mindfulness of the new practitioner and the general form of mindfulness.

On the first and second levels of the nine levels of mental placement, which we will discuss shortly, we practice the general form of mindfulness. On the third through the seventh levels we practice the mindfulness of the new practitioner. On the eighth level we practice the mindfulness of the experienced practitioner. At the ninth level of mental placement, we are able to apply mindfulness in just the right amount. We are able to place the mind in concentration effortlessly, for however long we wish. On the seventh and eighth levels of mental placement, the practitioner also has the right balance of mindfulness, but effort is required to maintain it. In the first and second levels of mental placement, applying the right balance of mindfulness is totally impossible.

Although we call these stages of mindfulness *general, new,* and *experienced* forms, and although each stage is superior to the one that precedes it, it is important to remember that, in reality, it is the same mindfulness all the way through. The difference is that in the later states of mental placement mindfulness has been developed to its fullest extent, while in the earlier stages it has not.

In some other Buddhist traditions an even more extraordinary form of mindfulness is taught, in which the mind is developed to the point where the practitioner is able to observe conceptual thoughts arising from the mind and subsequently receding back into the mind itself. This is observed as occurring in the same way that a bird takes off from an island and flies away into the sky, only to return to land on the same island. Another illustration is the way that the waves rise and recede back into the same sea. In sutra, the practitioner's skill is compared to a man with a single shield who is able to ward off thousands of arrows that are shot at him merely by the force of his mindfulness. The end of the story about this man, just as a note, mentions that despite his great dexterity he meets with a bad end— he becomes distracted when a woman that he is attached to passes by, at which point he loses his mindfulness and is killed.

The Object of Meditation

In order to develop the kind of mindfulness that will bring about the extraordinary concentration of calm abiding, you should choose a meditation object that you already have some familiarity with. It is easier to strengthen mindfulness on the basis of a familiar object than on the basis of an unfamiliar object. The object can be an external object or a mental object. Of course, the object that your mind is most familiar with is the mind itself. If you choose to take the mind as your object, the aspect of the mind that you should focus upon is its clarity and experience. Whatever object you choose, you should try to cultivate an awareness of the fact that what you are visualizing is actually not a gross form, but rather the appearance of your own mental consciousness. Your object of concentration is your *mind's image* of a stick or a stone or a buddha.

If you are a more experienced practitioner, you will find it easier to eliminate distractions and hence cultivate concentration by taking an internal mental object, rather than an external object, as the focus of your concentration. Using an internal object as your object of concentration will lead you to develop the ability to take the mind itself as your object of concentration. Once you are able to do this, you will eventually gain some experience of the nature of your mind. Once you have a clear experience of the nature of your mind, you will then be able to begin to reduce conceptuality, and in so doing reduce the negative karmic imprints that ripen in your continuum.

However, when you are beginning, it may in fact be easier to use an external object as your object of concentration. If you do choose to use an external object, you should pick an object with positive qualities, such as a statue or a picture of a buddha, so that as you familiarize your mind with this object, you also accumulate positive imprints. As you gain great familiarity with that external object, it will eventually begin to appear as a mental image. Once you begin to concentrate on a mental image, you will probably notice that you are experiencing a lot of conceptual thoughts related to the past, present, and future. As you persevere, however, these distractions will begin to arise less and less frequently, and you will begin to realize that what is actually appearing is your mind's experience of that mental object. Eventually, when this is fine-tuned, you will understand that this appearance is the mind's knowing, clarity, and experience alone.

This can be understood better by looking at the analogy of a flowing river. If you want to look at the bottom of the river, you must somehow stop the water from coming and going. When you have stopped the water from flowing in and flowing out, the bottom of the river clearly appears. In the same way, when you are able to focus on your mental image, and your mind is free from all the conceptual thoughts related to the past, present, or future, you have the opportunity to see the conventional reality of the object clearly.

The sutras describe four kinds of objects of concentration. The first kind is pervasive objects. These are directly manifest objects not requiring any kind of analysis, such as gross phenomena or forms. The second kind is the objects for overcoming objects of attachment. This means, for example, taking the subtle impermanence of your object of attachment as your object of concentration in order to counteract your delusions. The third type is called the object of the wise practitioner, which refers to the conventional or ultimate reality of an object. And the fourth type of object is the object for the purification of delusions. This kind of object is exclusive to those practitioners who have generated calm abiding.

Additionally, there are five objects of concentration that are chosen in accordance with whatever delusions are strongest in our minds. The first of these is related to attachment. Since attachment is characterized by the mind superimposing qualities upon an object that it does not actually have, to counteract this, we reflect on the impermanence and impurity of the object. Once we have established its transitory or contaminated nature by intellectual analysis, we take that conclusion as our object of concentration. This is the method to overcome attachment by the practice of single-pointed concentration.

The second object of concentration is related to anger and hatred. If we have been habituated to the delusions of anger and hatred over many lifetimes, we will constantly see others as possessing faults and mistakes to a much greater degree than is realistic. This is the basis of anger and hatred. To counteract these delusions, we reflect on love and compassion, and once we have successfully generated love for that person, we take that love as our object of single-pointed concentration.

As an antidote to the confused mind of ignorance, we should meditate upon the twelve links of dependent arising, forward and in reverse. The method for doing this was already discussed. After meditating on dependent arising, we should come to the conclusion that ignorance is the root cause of cyclic existence. We should then engage in single-pointed concentration either on the fact that ignorance is the root of cyclic existence or on the fact that if we extinguish ignorance, we also eliminate the root of cyclic existence.

The fourth object of concentration is the antidote to the delusion of pride. In order to counteract the mind of pride in our own knowledge, we can think about any phenomena in general of which we have no knowledge.

The fifth object of concentration is the breath, which we take as our meditation object in order to overcome the distraction of too many conceptual thoughts.

Of course, the very best object of concentration is the mode of existence of the two truths. When we counteract a mind of attachment merely with analytical meditation on the impurity of our object of attachment and then concentrate single-pointedly on that, we cannot affect the mind of pride, or the mind of anger, or any other mind with the same meditation. Meditation on conventional or ultimate truth, however, is an antidote to all of the delusions.

The Obstacles to Concentration

In the actual meditation of developing our mind in the stages of mental concentration, there are five obstacles to abandon and eight antidotes to apply.

Of the five obstacles, the first is laziness. This refers to the laziness of being attracted to useless, base activities and the laziness of procrastination. The second obstacle is constantly forgetting the instructions. The third is mental excitement and mental sinking, which are explained further below. The fourth is not applying the antidotes when you experience mental excitement or sinking, and the fifth is continuing to apply the antidotes even when your mind is not experiencing any kind of sinking or excitement. This might occur, for example, if you put too much effort into your practice of mindfulness on the ninth level of mental placement, when no effort is required, and thereby create an obstacle.

The characteristics of the minds of mental excitement and mental sinking are as follows.

The object of mental excitement is usually an object of the mind of attachment. The aspect of this mind is that it craves that object. Its function is to create an unsubdued or disturbed state of mind. Gross mental excitement is usually a nonvirtuous state of mind. Subtle mental excitement is not virtuous or nonvirtuous, but neutral.

Gross mental sinking means that we have single-pointed placement of the mind on its object, but no clarity. The experience of this is like looking at something without our glasses: we can't see clearly. Subtle mental sinking means that we have the single-pointed focus of mind and clarity, but the mind holding the object lacks strength. Subtle mental sinking is usually virtuous. Gross mental sinking is not nonvirtuous, but it is an afflicted mind.

Ordinarily, when cultivating calm abiding, the practitioner is able to make clear progress up to the point of being able to abandon the gross forms of mental excitement and mental sinking. At this point, however, many people make the mistake of thinking that they have established a faultless form of concentration, when in reality they are experiencing a subtle form of mental sinking. This is a great mistake, because even if we remain in such a state for a very long time, we will not even accumulate the causes to be reborn in the meditative states of concentration of the form and formless realms.

In the beginning, we might find ourselves making great effort merely to get our minds to stay focused on the object of concentration. As a result our minds get wound up too tight, and we experience subtle forms of mental sinking. In order to experience total clarity of the object of concentration, which is a completely clean, clear state of mind, we must counteract this. Focusing on developing the clarity of mind with regard to its object of concentration also helps to strengthen the wisdom aspect of the mind. As a result of that, however, it is also possible that we might trigger the obstacle of mental excitement and totally lose the object of concentration.

Again, introspection is the function of the mind that watches and notices what is going on and brings forth the intention to apply the antidote, while mindfulness is the function of mind that corrects whatever faults we have found. When we experience the subtle form of mental excitement, we will experience a clear state of mind with a firm hold on the object, with distractions arising in the background. At that time, we need to strengthen our introspection, which is the function of mind that checks to make sure that things are going along as they should be—a kind of mental spy.

As beginners, when we experience the subtle form of mental excitement and are unable to recognize it, it becomes a gross form of mental excitement, at which point we totally lose our placement, clarity, and focus. To avoid this, we should be on guard for the experience of subtle mental excitement, and if we notice that we are experiencing it, we should take a break from the session to get rid of it.

To counteract the experience of subtle mental sinking in which we have mental focus and clarity, but lack strength, we can think about perfect human rebirth and the benefits of the practices of calm abiding and superior insight.

As we practice placing the mind, we should develop the ability to identify these obstacles as they arise in our meditation. In order to ensure a faultless meditative concentration, mindfulness and introspection are imperative.

Sometimes calm abiding meditation is misunderstood as only having to do with single-pointed meditation on an object. In fact, this is incorrect. In order to remove many of the obstacles of single-pointed concentration, we need to apply other forms of meditation as well. Although the objective of this practice is to develop the mind's capacity in single-pointed concentration, this practice is not composed of that meditation alone. Also, before we engage in the practice of developing the mind in calm abiding, we should train the mind in the path and practice of the small, medium, and great scopes. When we experience very strong forms of mental excitement, it often becomes necessary to rely upon the instructions of the medium scope's path and practice as an antidote. When we experience the gross and subtle levels of mental sinking, we can counteract this by thinking about the benefits of the practice of bodhichitta, perfect human rebirth, the benefits of enlightenment, and the benefits of liberation. This proves that the belief that analytical meditation is an obstacle to single-pointed concentration is a misunderstanding.

Another method by which we can counteract mental excitement and mental sinking is through closing the doors of the six perceptions. A great deal of mental excitement can arise on the basis of information we receive through our eyes, ears, and tactile sensations alone. Mental sinking and mental excitement can even arise in dependence on what we eat or drink. Of course, the way that things affect us is very much dependent on the individual. People whose minds are very bright and energetic usually have more problems with mental excitement. People who are naturally lazy and sluggish have more problems with mental sinking.

Whether we are experiencing gross or subtle mental sinking, or gross or subtle mental excitement, the antidote to all of these obstacles is mindfulness and/or introspection. If our powers of introspection are superior, we will recognize gross and subtle mental sinking and excitement as soon as they arise. By the power of mindfulness, we will then be able to apply the appropriate antidote and continue with our meditation. Concentration meditation is like driving a car—most of the work is in getting it started. Once it's running, things are a little bit easier.

There are eight antidotes to the five obstacles, the first five of which are the antidotes to laziness. *Antidote* is used to describe a mind that is the opposite of what is being eliminated. For example, emptiness is the antidote to the ignorance grasping at true existence. Therefore, the mode of apprehension of the wisdom realizing emptiness stands in direct opposition to the mode of apprehension of the ignorant mind. A mental state that is developed as an antidote can be developed limitlessly. Although these eight particular antidotes don't fulfill the criteria of an *ultimate* antidote because they do not eliminate the obstacle so that it never arises again,[41] they do eliminate the obstacle in the immediate situation.

The five antidotes to laziness are faith, perseverance, aspiration, suppleness, and mindfulness.

Faith refers to the faith that wishes to attain concentration. When we have faith in the qualities of concentration, we will naturally aspire to attain it. In order to inspire faith in the benefits of concentration, we can reflect that although it is possible to learn a great deal about the way phenomena exist and so forth on the basis of our gross mind at present, everything that we learn will become so much more profound on the basis of concentration. On the basis of concentration, we will be able to manifest the extraordinary, limitless potential of our minds. Contemplating thus, and examining the way that every limitless quality of our mind can be forthcoming solely on the foundation of calm abiding, we will definitely aspire to develop it.

Perseverance is the quality of mind that enables us to engage in that attainment of calm abiding most joyfully.

Aspiration is the wish to engage in the practice of single-pointed concentration. As a result, we will naturally develop the suppleness of the mind and body. *Suppleness* means being able to engage in physical or mental activities without difficulty. The fifth antidote to laziness is *mindfulness,* which guards against forgetfulness.

The sixth antidote is *introspection,* which guards against mental excitement and sinking, and the seventh and eighth antidotes are *applying the antidote immediately* and *knowing when not to apply the antidote.*

When we cultivate our minds in meditative concentration, we may develop clairvoyance and psychic powers as byproducts of our efforts, but they should become not the main goals of our practice. The purpose of cultivating calm abiding is to develop the concentration necessary for realizing renunciation, bodhichitta, and the pure view of emptiness. However, knowing that the development of calm abiding can lead to the extraordinary development of our minds can also help us to eliminate laziness.

When we begin training in the nine levels of mental placement, the first and second levels are primarily concerned with trying to get the mind to stay on its object of focus. At this time, it is hardly ever necessary to apply the antidotes to our mental obstacles. The entire struggle at this point is composed of trying to get the mind to stay put. On the second, third, and fourth levels of mental placement, however, once we have gained some stability of mind, we apply the antidotes and combat all the obstacles of mental excitement and sinking. This is the focus of these levels. Up until the seventh level, we have to depend upon applying the antidotes to the obstacles in order to maintain our concentration. On the eighth level, in which we practice the mindfulness of an experienced practitioner, when obstacles arise within the mind, it is no longer necessary to apply individual antidotes to the individual types of obstacles: a general antidote should suffice. For example, from the very beginning of the session, we set the very strong motivation to undertake a faultless kind of concentration. This in itself acts as a general antidote to all of the obstacles of the mind and is quite sufficient to eliminate them once we are at this stage. The practitioner on this level is like the man with the shield who is attacked with arrows from all sides—there is no need to ward off each of the arrows individually; he is so skilled in the use of the shield that he is able to stop them all more or less at once. Because it possesses this characteristic, meditation on the eighth level is much smoother and has far fewer interruptions than meditation on the preceding levels.

The Nine Levels

The first of the nine levels of mental placement is *placing the mind.* In the early stages of developing concentration, as you begin to try to settle your mind down, you will probably feel that you have suddenly become more distracted than ever, and you may be discouraged. Actually, what is happening at this point is that as a result of beginning to focus single-pointedly, you have simply become aware of the activity that has been going on in your mind all along. On the first level of mental placement, it is very important to limit the duration of the time of your meditation. At the beginning, it is better to have many short sessions, rather than just a few long sessions.

On the second level of mental placement, the level of *continual placement,* the length of time that your mind is able to remain on the object increases. The object of your meditation remains the same, but your mind has greater staying power on the second level.

The third level is *re-placement.* On this level you work primarily to strengthen your mindfulness. Applying the force of mindfulness, you repeatedly place your mind on the object of concentration and hold it there for as long as possible. The term *re-placement* refers to taking the mind from its distracted state and placing it back on its object.

The fourth level is *close placement,* which is characterized by making an effort to improve the clarity of the object of concentration as it appears to your mind.

The fifth level is *subduing the mind.* On this level, your focus is strengthening the clear appearance of the object of concentration, and subduing all of the obstacles that arise is relation to it. On this stage you are so well practiced that when obstacles arise, you are able to apply their antidotes right away and continue with your meditation. Gross forms of mental sinking are eliminated on this level.

The sixth level of mental placement is *pacified mind.* On this level, obstacles that arise are overcome merely by reflecting on their shortcomings, and the meditation session is not interrupted. On the sixth level, gross forms of mental excitement are completely eliminated.

The seventh level of mental placement is *thoroughly pacified mind,* in which you are able to eliminate the obstacles of the mind with ease, remaining in meditation.

The eighth level is *single-pointed placement of the mind.* On this level, you work to eliminate the subtle forms of mental excitement and mental sinking. With a little effort, you are able to engage in single-pointed concentration whenever and for however long you wish.

On the ninth level of mental placement, *placement with equanimity,* merely by generating the wish to engage in a six-hour meditation, for example, you are able to do so. After the initial motivation, your meditation continues without effort. The mind on the ninth level is regarded as the most subtle mind of the desire realm. As you become habituated to this level of meditative concentration, you attain suppleness of mind, on the basis of which you develop suppleness of body and the bliss of the suppleness of body. Due to generating the bliss of the suppleness of the body, you generate the bliss of the suppleness of mind. As a sign of having attained the bliss of the suppleness of mind, the crown wind becomes pacified, which acts as a condition for the inner bliss of the suppleness of mind to arise.

The suppleness of mind and body are not physical experiences. Of the categories of phenomena—consciousness, physical matter, and noncompositional factors, which are not matter or consciousness—the suppleness of mind and body are noncompositional factors. The bliss of the suppleness of mind and the bliss of the suppleness of body are consciousnesses.

The mind of calm abiding is not a direct perception, but a conceptual state. However, in comparison to our own ordinary conceptual states of mind, the conceptual states of the mind on the seventh, eighth, and ninth levels of calm abiding are very subtle.

Upon initially attaining calm abiding, the yogic practitioner needs to reacquaint his or her mind with it repeatedly, until strength through familiarity is cultivated.

The Six Powers and the Four Forms of Attention
In addition to attaining calm abiding on the basis of the nine levels of mental placement, it is also necessary to cultivate the six powers and the four forms of attention in order to complete one's practice of concentration.

These methods support the generation of the single-pointed concentration of calm abiding.

The six powers are the power of listening, the power of contemplation, the power of mindfulness, the power of introspection, the power of perseverance, and the power of habit.

The power of listening helps us to accomplish the first of the nine levels of mental placement. *Listening* refers to receiving the instructions on the shortcomings of the desire-realm mind and body, which will lead us to cultivate the wish to be liberated from the desire realm, and seek the means to be free from it. Please do not misunderstand, thinking that in order to attain the first level of mental placement, we need *only* rely on the power of listening. Besides this, we still need to apply the power of perseverance and so forth. However, of the six powers, listening is the most important on the first level.

The second level is attained with the support of the power of contemplation. The object of contemplation is the object of concentration.

We attain the third level with the particular support of the power of mindfulness, which helps us to recognize obstacles to our meditation that appear in the form of mental excitement or sinking, and free ourselves from them.

The power of introspection is applied especially on the fourth and the fifth levels. We generate the power of introspection in order to counteract the gross minds of mental sinking or excitement.

The sixth and seventh levels are attained with the support of the power of perseverance.

The eighth and ninth levels of mental placement are attained with the support of the power of habit or familiarity. On the eighth level of mental placement, due to our familiarity with the object, our concentration is basically faultless. By the ninth level, by the power of familiarity, we are able to ensure faultless concentration without any effort.

Next are the four forms of attention.

On the first and the second levels of mental placement, because the mind does not stay put on the object of concentration, we need to apply a lot of effort. Therefore we apply the first form of attention, concentrated attention, which is a mental alertness that holds its object very tightly.

From the third to the seventh levels of mental placement, the duration that we are able to stay in concentration is longer than the duration that we are unable to stay in concentration. However, our concentration is constantly interrupted by gross and subtle levels of mental sinking and excitement. To counteract this, we apply the second kind of attention, repeated attention.

On the eighth level we are able to remain in meditative concentration, but with effort. This type of attention is called uninterrupted attention.

The fourth form of attention is effortless attention. We apply this form of attention on the ninth level of mental concentration.

The Measure of Having Attained Calm Abiding

The measure of having attained calm abiding is when, with the support of the bliss of body and mind, you are able to hold your mind on the object of meditation for as long a period of time as you wish.

Calm Abiding on the Worldly Path and on the Dharma Path

There are two methods by which a practitioner can utilize calm abiding meditation to destroy the delusions. The first is utilizing calm abiding on a worldly path, and the second is utilizing calm abiding on a path that leads beyond the world. Utilizing calm abiding on a worldly path means using concentration to eliminate the gross manifestations of the delusions. In contrast, when we use calm abiding on the path beyond samsara, we use it as the basis from which to generate renunciation and the wisdom realizing emptiness, and thereby to eliminate our delusions from their very roots.

On the worldly path, the main motivation for cultivating the mind of calm abiding is to attain a peaceful mental state. The practitioner on this path determines the mind of the desire realm to be an absolutely gross, unsubdued, and unpeaceful state of the mind. In contrast, he or she considers the subtle levels of the mind of the form and the formless realms to be peaceful and subdued, and thus aspires to attain these states. This practitioner trains his or her mind and attains a certain level of calm abiding, on the basis of which he or she is able to engage in an analytical meditation on the shortcomings of the desire realm and the advantages of the form and the formless realms. Through the power of that analysis, the practitioner obtains the suppleness of mind, due to which he or she attains the suppleness of body, followed by the bliss of the suppleness of the body, and the bliss of the suppleness of mind.

In general, our familiarity with calm abiding will draw our minds closer to generating superior insight. When we attain the stage of calm abiding upon which gross dualistic perception ceases, we attain ten signs. At this point, all of the objects of the five sense perceptions and all of the signs of past, present, and future become a mere appearance. This is not quite like the realization of the Chittamatra view,[42] but rather as the mind gains extraordinary clarity, everything that it perceives becomes a mere appearance. Regardless of what we are feeling physically, our mental state is not affected. Because the mind is so familiar with the meditative states, even our sleep can become a state of concentration.

The mind of calm abiding is not considered to be a mental state of the desire realm; rather it is considered to be a mind of the form and formless realms. How is it possible that our own gross desire-realm minds can transform into a mind of the form and formless realms by the power of the nine levels of calm abiding?

In answer to that, some say that since we've had countless, beginningless lifetimes in cyclic existence, we have had many occasions upon which to attain the mental states of the form and the formless realms. Therefore, as we already have attained them, we have the imprints of these mental states in our continuums. According to this argument, the conditions of the ninth level of single-pointed concentration ripen previous imprints of non-desire-realm minds.

Another answer is the thesis that is accepted by our own philosophical system. According to our system, when we generate the single-pointed concentration of the ninth level, which is the most subtle level of the desire-realm mind, the bliss of body and mind is attained. At this point, the continuum that is similar to the previous state of the desire-realm mind does not transform into the mind of calm abiding, but the substantial continuum does.

According to this view, the continuum that is similar to the previous state is a desire-realm mind, and a desire-realm mind cannot transform into a mind of the form and the formless realms, because the mental states of the form and the formless realms are so much more subtle. Therefore, the mind of calm abiding is the result of the transformation of the substantial continuum. According to our system it is possible for the substantial continuum of a desire-realm mind to transform into the mind of the form and formless realms just as, for example, an ordinary mind can become the mind of an arya if it is trained in the path, through familiarity and meditation. Since the mind of a sentient being with so many delusions and imprints can transform into the nature of an enlightened mind, why shouldn't a gross desire-realm mind be able to transform into the subtle mind of calm abiding?

An individual who has attained the mind of calm abiding no longer possesses the most subtle level of the mind of the desire realm. In the same way, someone who has attained the ninth level of mental placement is free of the previous eight levels of mental placement. Someone who has attained the eighth level is free of the gross mind of the seventh level, and so forth. All of the latter states of mental placement are totally free of the earlier states. However, the earlier states have not degenerated; rather, they no longer exist because the substantial continuum of that mind has been transformed into the next.

In the same way, someone on the five paths who has attained the second of the five paths, the path of preparation, does not have the mind of the first path, the path of accumulation. However, although we say that this individual does not have the mind of the path of accumulation, within the mind of the path of preparation the substantial continuum of the path of accumulation does exist.

There are two kinds of valid cognitive consciousnesses: direct valid cognizers and subsequent valid cognizers. A direct valid cognizer cognizes an object for the first time, newly and infallibly. A subsequent cognizer cognizes that which has already been apprehended. On the path of seeing, we see emptiness directly for the first time by the power of a direct valid cognizer. However, on the path of meditation, we apprehend emptiness (which has already been realized) with a subsequent valid cognizer. Likewise, on the paths of accumulation and preparation, emptiness is realized only through a generic image by a valid *conceptual* cognizer. Because it is only a generic form of understanding emptiness, the cognition is conceptual, but because that conceptual mind is realizing something infallibly and newly, it is also direct. On the path of preparation, since we are still seeing that generic form, we have a subsequent conceptual cognizer. In case you are wondering, in a buddha's mind, there is no such thing as subsequent cognizer—everything is a direct cognition.

A conceptual valid cognizer becomes a subsequent conceptual valid cognizer, which then becomes a direct valid cognizer, which in turn becomes a subsequent valid cognizer. How does this happen? It happens in the same way that the subtle mind of the desire realm becomes the mind of the form and the formless realms through the transformation of the substantial continuum, rather than the transformation of continuum that is similar to the previous state. The continuum that is similar to the previous state does not become the latter one, but the subsequent continuum transforms to become the latter states of mind.

Take the example of the gross and subtle levels of mental sinking. As beginners training to strengthen our minds in concentration, initially we work so hard trying to concentrate that our minds become too tight and we experience sinking. It is the substantial continuum of the concentration itself, the mind holding the object too tightly, that transforms into the gross mental sinking.

Some practitioners seek to generate calm abiding with the limited objective of seeking peace from the delusions. For others, the motivation is seeing the qualities of the result of the individual vehicle of the Hinayana, the causal vehicle of the Mahayana, or the resultant vehicle of the Vajrayana. However, since we are practicing the great scope of the Mahayana as taught by Lama Tsongkhapa, our motivation to develop calm abiding should be the altruistic wish to attain enlightenment solely for the welfare of others.

Understanding this, in order to achieve the results of the Mahayana path, we may apply ourselves with great perseverance in the accumulation of causes, and in the removal of the obstacles to attaining the results of the great vehicle. But when results do not happen fast enough, our effort lessens, and our practice begins to lack diligence and continuity. Then, when we hear that we must accumulate three countless eons of merit to attain enlightenment, we may feel that there is no way we can ever finish in this lifetime, get discouraged, and feel like giving up. This kind of attitude is not helpful. When we become too focused on the result of the path alone, we develop the feeling that we have to attain it very quickly. And when we don't attain it soon enough, our perseverance begins to lag. We create obstacles for ourselves when our minds become too obsessed with the result of the path.

The reason that we are unable to realize the results of the path in our own minds is because we are lacking the foundation. Therefore, it is essential that we begin our training with the path and practice of the small scope in which we eliminate any thought of clinging or grasping toward the appearance of this life. Then, in accordance with the path and practice of the medium scope, it is essential that we generate within our minds a definite sense of determination to be free of cyclic existence. Only then, on the basis of cutting off the thought that emphasizes the appearances of this life, do we have the capacity to seek out the nine levels of mental placement in order to attain calm abiding. If the goal is only to attain calm abiding, at the very least we must have the determination to be free from the afflicted minds of the desire realm.

The main obstacles to cultivating higher levels of concentration are mental excitement and mental sinking. But to focus only on eliminating mental excitement and sinking and not to take into account the causes of the delusional minds that bring about mental excitement and sinking is a mistake. Therefore we should cultivate a sense of renunciation to be free of these deluded states of mind. When an individual attains calm abiding, there is no longer any gross manifestation of the delusions of the desire realm. Therefore, determining to be free of these negative states of mind is essential to achieving that state.

The cultivation of calm abiding and superior insight is prevalent in the Theravadin traditions—in Thailand and Burma, and so forth. Many of the Hindu traditions also have skillful methods for cultivating calm abiding. It may be helpful for you to take ideas from these sources as well.

When practitioners use calm abiding on the worldly path to extinguish the gross manifestation of the delusions, they normally perceive the suffering desire realm as the object to be abandoned, and look upon the peace of the form and the formless realms as a state to be attained. This kind of practitioner will begin with developing calm abiding through the cultivation of the nine levels and so forth as we have already discussed. On the basis of calm abiding, the practitioner engages in an investigative analytical process, which enables him or her to attain the first of the six types of attention of the mind of near-attainment. Once the practitioner reaches the second of the six types of attention of the mind of near-attainment, he or she has attained superior insight, and from this point on practices a unified form of calm abiding and superior insight.

The delusions of the desire realm are divided into three: the great, the medium, and the small. Within the great delusions, there are the great-great, great-medium, and great-small. Within the medium delusions, there are the medium-great, medium-medium, and medium-small. Within the small delusions, there are the small-great, small-medium, and small-small. When the mind of the unified practice of calm abiding and superior insight is fully developed, it becomes the complete antidote to the first group of the great delusions. When this occurs, the practitioner attains the third of the six types of attention of the mind of near-attainment. This is followed by the development of the antidote to the three medium delusions, and the attainments of the fourth and fifth of the six types of attention of the mind of near-attainment. This, in turn, is followed by the development of the antidote to the small delusions, the sixth of the six types of attention of the mind of near-attainment, and the attainment of the direct meditative equipoise of the first of the four levels of meditative absorption. At this stage, the individual no longer experiences any kind of gross manifestation of the delusions of the desire realm.

The practitioner then goes on to progress through the second, third, and fourth levels of meditative absorption of the form realm.

Following this, one attains the first level of the formless realm. The four levels of the formless realm are limitless space, limitless consciousness, nothingness, and the peak of samsara. The attainment of limitless space acts as an antidote to the delusions of the fourth level of meditative absorption in the form realm. The attainment of limitless consciousness acts as an antidote to the delusions that are present at the level of limitless space. The attainment of nothingness acts as an antidote to the delusions that are present at the level of limitless consciousness. The attainment of the peak of samsara acts as an antidote to the delusions that are present at the level of nothingness.

The only antidote to the delusions of the peak of samsara is the wisdom that realizes emptiness. Thus, on the worldly path, the practitioner generates a limited kind of renunciation and manages to abandon the delusions of cyclic existence only up to the point of the stage of nothingness. In order to abandon the delusions of the peak of samsara, that practitioner must rely upon a path that will lead him or her beyond cyclic existence. To do this, it is necessary to cultivate the antidote of the wisdom that realizes emptiness.

Shantideva says:

Therefore, in order to clarify all obscurations,
I will withdraw my mind from mistaken paths.
I will constantly rest in meditative equipoise
Upon the perfect object.

THE FINAL PERFECTION

THE PERFECTION OF WISDOM

From the beginning of the ninth chapter of the *Guide to the Bodhisattva's Way of Life:*

All of these practices
Were taught by the Lord for the sake of wisdom.
Therefore, with the wish to pacify suffering,
Cultivate wisdom.

Lama Tsongkhapa says that even if we train our minds in renunciation and bodhichitta over a long period of time, if we do not realize the ultimate mode of existence of phenomena, it will not be possible for our thoughts of renunciation and bodhichitta to become a cause for liberation or enlightenment. Therefore, we must persevere in the realization of dependent arising and emptiness. Even in the individual vehicle, with the thought of renunciation alone, we will only be able to advance to the first of the five paths, the Hinayana path of accumulation. In order to proceed to the second of the five paths, the Hinayana path of preparation, it is necessary to generate superior insight into emptiness. Likewise, with the cultivation of the mind of bodhichitta alone, we can reach only the first of the five Mahayana paths, the path of accumulation. We cannot enter the Mahayana path of preparation without the wisdom realizing emptiness.

In the context of the *Lamrim Chenmo,* when we speak of the wisdom realizing emptiness, we are also speaking of the mind of superior insight, or *lhagtong.* In this context, *superior insight* refers to a single-pointed and supple subject mind whose object is emptiness. Superior insight is always attained on the basis of calm abiding. For our purposes, superior insight can also be called "wisdom" when we speak of it in a very general way. In other contexts, however, it is not necessary that superior insight or the mind of wisdom always take emptiness as its object.

The study of superior insight should be approached through the analysis of definitive subjects, meaning emptiness. Definitive subjects deal with ultimate truths, and the best way to engage in the investigation of ultimate truths is through studying the explanations of Nagarjuna, Chandrakirti, and Asanga. In the great monasteries of Tibet, before entering the Madhyamaka class, the student must have completed the entire study of the six perfections in the *Ornament of Clear Realization*. When this is done, before study on Madhyamaka begins, many prayers are made, including extensive praises to the twenty-one Taras and recitation of the *Heart Sutra*, to ensure that whatever study is undertaken becomes effective for eliminating ignorance.

Even if we have some kind of general understanding that ignorance grasping at true existence is the root of cyclic existence, and even if we recognize that the wisdom that realizes emptiness is the means to eliminating this ignorance, we will not be able to actually cut the root of cyclic existence through study alone. Following the tradition of the monasteries, we must be sure to make prayers and requests for success to our gurus and deities in combination with extensive practices of accumulation of merit and purification in order to be able to listen, contemplate, and meditate to bring about realizations of this topic.

Definitive and Interpretive Meanings of Scriptures

The instructions for realizing the ultimate mode of existence can be found in the sutras, the direct teachings of Buddha. According to the Prasangika-Madhyamaka system, the system the *Lamrim Chenmo* follows, the sutras on the ultimate nature of reality are classified as definitive sutras, while those whose main subject matter is the conventional mode of existence are classified as interpretive. Thus, for the Prasangika-Madhyamaka school, the sutras of the first turning of the wheel of Dharma are interpretive, the teachings of the middle turning of the wheel of Dharma are considered definitive, and the teachings of the third or the last turning are considered interpretive.

According to the other Madhyamaka school, the Svatantrika-Madhyamaka, this distinction is based on different factors. According to the Svatantrikas, a definitive sutra is one that teaches ultimate truth directly or one that can be taken literally. Conversely, an interpretive sutra is a sutra that cannot be taken literally. For example, although the subject matter of the *Heart Sutra* is the ultimate nature of existence, because the words of the sutra cannot be taken literally it is considered an interpretive sutra according to the Svatantrikas. The Prasangikas, by contrast, view the *Heart Sutra* as definitive on the basis of its subject matter.

One of the disadvantages of being born a sentient being in our era is that we are generally considered to have a lower mental capacity than the sentient beings who lived at the time of Buddha. This being the case, it is difficult for us to determine the definitive meaning of the *Sutra on the Perfection of Wisdom* directly. Therefore, it is extremely helpful for us to rely upon commentaries on Buddha's words to clearly understand their meaning. In the Indian and Tibetan traditions, there were many great masters who wrote commentaries on Buddha's definitive sutras. The best of these are by those teachers foretold by Buddha, such as Nagarjuna, Aryadeva, Buddhapalita, and Chandrakirti. Lama Tsongkhapa wrote extensively on this subject as well in texts such as the *Lamrim Chenmo*. Studying such sources is the easiest means for us to quickly realize Buddha's ultimate intention.

Chandrakirti says that any teaching on emptiness that does not accord with the view as taught by Nagarjuna is a degeneration of the ultimate view, and cannot ever become a cause for liberation or enlightenment. Chandrakirti's statement is authoritative because he was an incomparable scholar, praised as a master who gave faultless explanations of Nagarjuna's view.

In order to establish emptiness on the basis of scriptural authority, Nagarjuna wrote the *Compendium of All Sutras*. In order to establish emptiness on the basis of logic and reasoning, Nagarjuna wrote the six treatises. Of these, the first four treatises—*Root Wisdom of the Middle Way, Thorough Investigation, Seventy Verses on Emptiness,* and *Eliminating All Arguments*—take up the subject matter of establishing ultimate truth itself. *Root Wisdom* specifically deals with negating true existence by refuting the assertion propounded by the Vaibashika and the Sautrantika schools that functioning entities are truly existent. The second treatise, *Thorough Investigation,* presents the negation of the proofs that the Vaibashikas and the Sautran-tikas present to substantiate the true existence of functioning entities. The third treatise, *Seventy Verses on Emptiness,* has its source in the seventh chapter of *Root Wisdom,* and analyzes the way that phenomena function—the way that they are produced, abide, and cease—even though they do not truly exist. The fourth treatise, *Eliminating All Arguments,* is derived from the first chapter of *Root Wisdom,* and establishes how the concepts of nega-tion and existence are valid in terms of phenomena that do not truly exist. The last two of the six treatises are *Precious Garland* and *Sixty Verses on Logic.* These texts demonstrate how the realization of emptiness is the root of the attainment of liberation. In addition, there are the two very impor-tant commentaries on these texts written by Chandrakirti: *Supplement to the "Middle Way"* and *Clear Words,* which elucidate the meaning and the words of Nagarjuna's *Root Wisdom,* respectively.

According to the sutras, phenomena can be classified as belonging to one of three categories: manifest, slightly hidden, and extremely hidden. Manifest phenomena should not be disproveable by direct valid cognition. Slightly hidden phenomena should not be disproveable by inferential valid cognition. And extremely hidden phenomena should not be disproveable by an inferential valid cognition based on belief. In order to establish any subject as valid, depending on its category, it should not be disproved by any of these three types of cognition. Every subject in every sutra is an object of one of these three cognitions. If it cannot be harmed by one of the three cognitions, according to our own system, the subject matter of that sutra can be taken literally.

Establishing the View of Emptiness

STAGES OF REALIZING EMPTINESS

Chandrakirti says that from the root of ignorance, the three poisonous states of mind and the six root delusions arise and become the conditions for suffering in our own lives and in the lives of others. Our delusions arise from holding the transitory aggregates of the mind and body as "I" or "mine." Therefore, a yogi must learn to identify the nominal "I," which *does* exist on the basis of cause and effect, as opposed to the inherently existing "I," which does not. As we gradually come to distinguish the "I" that is to be negated and the nominal "I," which actually exists on the basis of cause and effect, we evolve to the stage at which we can cut the root of cyclic existence forever.

The definition of beginningless ignorance is holding the notion of an inherently existing "I" based on the transitory aggregates of the mind and body. This ignorance is the first of the twelve links of dependent origination. It is the root of our wrong view, the root of our self-cherishing. Its result is the three poisonous states of mind, and *their* result is suffering and unhappiness. To eliminate the mistaken consciousness of ignorance and its imprints, we need to cultivate wisdom on the basis of compassion and bodhichitta.

In order to eliminate the ignorance that grasps at a truly existent "I," we first need to clearly recognize the mode of existence of the nominal "I." On the basis of the nominal "I"—the "I" that exists based on cause and effect—ignorance superimposes a totally fabricated mode of existence. This mental projection creates the strong instinctive sense of an inherently existent "I," which in turn triggers all the other delusions. Thereby, with the *causal* motivation of ignorance grasping at true existence and the *immediate* motivation of ignorance of cause and effect, anger, hatred, and so forth arise, and we thus accumulate karma, and are propelled through cyclic existence.

It is the same with phenomena other than the "I." Ignorance superimposes a totally fabricated mode of existence onto the basis of something that exists only nominally. We then perceive this phenomenon to be inherently existent, at which point we experience the delusional minds of attachment, hatred, pride, and so forth, and as a result we accumulate karma.

It is said in the scriptures that all the extraordinary, beautiful things in our environment, such as flowers and fruit, do not exist inherently, from their own side, at all, but exist only as a mere designation of a valid label upon a valid basis by a valid mind. Whether we find a particular object pleasant or unpleasant is completely imputed by our minds. From the side of the object itself, there is not an atom that is inherently pleasant or unpleasant. However, even though objects that we hold to be pleasant or unpleasant do not have an atom of existence from their own side, having merely been imputed, they are still able to effect the results of benefit or harm. All phenomena are the result of dependent arising, although their nature is empty. Whether an individual experiences happiness or suffering, pleasure or displeasure, depends completely on the karma of that individual.

One of my philosophy teachers told me this story. Once he was taking a walk with his teacher. As they came upon an opening where they could see the valley below, his teacher said, "Isn't this beautiful and pleasant?" My teacher answered, "Yes, very much so," at which point his teacher replied, "This beauty and pleasantness do not exist from the side of the object, but arise only from within your own mind."

If we search within the elements of earth, water, fire, wind, space, and consciousness—among all of these, the person who enjoys the view cannot be found. If we ask whether such a person exists at all, we must say yes, of course such a person exists—of course there is a person who is enjoying the view. But if we ask whether this person exists from the side of the basis of imputation—the aggregates, the elements, and so forth—we must come to the conclusion that there is no person who exists in this way.

It is like a rainbow. We can see a rainbow, but we can't catch it with our hands. We can see the "I," yet when we look for it, there is nothing solid or concrete to hold onto. When the mind has a strong sense of grasping at true existence, or a strong egotistic grasping at a truly existing self, or when a strong selfishness arises, under the power of these emotions we feel a very solid, concrete sense of "I." All of our negative actions arise due to this ignorance grasping at true existence.

Conventional phenomena can appear to beings in one of three ways: as truly existent with no grasping, as truly existent and with grasping, or as not truly existent with no grasping. Ordinary sentient beings both perceive things as truly existent and grasp at that true existence. This is like someone encountering television for the first time. That person will experience strong grasping at the appearance of whatever is happening on the screen. A joke will bring forth great joy, or, depending on the plot, great feelings of anger or attachment will arise. Whatever is going on appears to truly exist, and the mind will grasp at it so strongly that we will experience all of these emotions.

To a being who has realized emptiness directly but has not stabilized that realization, such as an arya bodhisattva on the path of seeing, conventional phenomena will *appear* as truly existent, but the bodhisattva will not grasp at that appearance or believe in it. To a being in meditative equipoise realizing emptiness directly, phenomena will not appear as truly existent, and he or she will not grasp.

So how, then, do we realize emptiness? We begin by cultivating the wisdom that arises from listening and studying. The kind of mind that we use to do this is an inferential cognition. The emptiness that appears to us at this point still remains within the duality of the subject-object relationship. On that basis, however, we cultivate a second kind of wisdom, that which arises from contemplation. The emptiness that appears at this point is still dualistic, but it is more subtle than the previous one. Finally, we cultivate the wisdom that arises from meditation, which is an even more refined state of mind. This usually occurs on the second of the five Mahayana paths, the path of preparation. Generating the wisdom that arises from meditation is equivalent to attaining the *heat* level of this path. From the heat level on the path of preparation we proceed to the level of *forbearance* and *supreme dharma*. Although there is still duality in our perception at this time, it is so subtle that it is not detected. When this consciousness becomes completely free of even the most subtle duality, it becomes the mind directly realizing emptiness. This consciousness is extraordinarily powerful.

Right now, we experience two modes of grasping at true existence—conceptual and innate. The direct realization of emptiness is the antidote to the mind's mode of grasping at true existence at the conceptual level.

In order to attain enlightenment or even liberation from cyclic existence, realizing emptiness is essential. And in order to engage in the graduated steps that lead to realizing ultimate truth, you first need renunciation. Even if you do not have the complete form of renunciation as a base, at the very least you should have some sort of artificial mental experience of renunciation. When you have some experience of renunciation at any level, you generate the strong wish to be free from the three poisonous states of mind, and you thereby are motivated to practice in order to recognize the cause of these minds, which is ignorance. This will eventually lead you to generate the recognition of what in your subjective experience is to be negated, as well as the proper way to apprehend the object. This is the way to realize emptiness.

Chandrakirti says:

All of the faults of the delusions arise
From the view of the transitory collection.

To summarize, in Madhyamaka philosophy it is said that due to our view of the transitory aggregates, we project an "I" that exists independently of any causes and conditions. This "I" then seems to exist in such a way that we feel certain we can actually find it under investigation. Grasping at the "I" we experience a strong feeling of "mine"—"my" body, "my" ideas, "my" friends. This grasping at "I" and "mine" engenders attachment and aversion and all the other delusions, binding us to cyclic existence.

Some sutras say that even generating a suspicion that emptiness *might* be true, we make a crack in our cyclic existence. For example, imagine that someone is terrified of a snake that he has seen enter his room. Then someone else comes along and says, "I don't think there is a snake here; I can't see it." Although the first person is still not certain whether there is a snake or not, just hearing the second person's conviction that there is no snake can help him to generate doubt in his own point of view, and begin to release his mind from fear.

THE TWO TRUTHS
Aryadeva says in *Four Hundred Stanzas* that understanding the two truths is the basis for understanding the four noble truths, which are the foundation of all Buddhist practice. The two truths illuminate the conventional struggle of cyclic existence and the method by which we can surmount this struggle.

Understanding Conventional and Ultimate Truth
If something can be categorized as an ultimate truth, it brings liberation from cyclic existence. If it is a conventional truth, it can have either of two aspects: binding one in samsara or liberating one from it. Let us look at the etymology of the Tibetan phrase for conventional truth, *kundzob denpa (kun dzob bden pa). Kun* means all, *dzob* means obscuring, and *denpa* means truth. Therefore, although we say *conventional truth,* the Tibetan equivalent literally translates as totally obscured truth, or something that is true for a totally obscured mind. From the perspective of such a mind,

a conventional truth is in fact true. However, from an ultimate perspective, it is false, because it does not exist as it appears.

The Prasangika system considers all direct valid perceptions except the direct perception of emptiness to be mistaken states of consciousness, because their object appears to be truly existent. Therefore, although we call the visual perception of a vase, for example, a direct valid perception, due to the fact that the vase appears as truly existent, it is a mistaken perception according to the Prasangika system. Let us look at this more closely. To the sense consciousness ascertaining a vase—which is a direct valid perception—the vase appears to be one-hundred-percent unmistaken. Yet when we begin to recognize the conventional reality of the vase, even a little bit, we realize that the vase, which is the object of this direct valid cognition, has a mistaken appearance. In realizing this, whatever sense of trust or belief we might have in our perception of the vase is shaken.

When we understand conventional truths, we understand that there are mistakes in our perception. When we realize ultimate truths, all the mistakes in our perception are totally eradicated. In order to generate the realization of ultimate truth, free of all mistakes, we must first learn what those mistakes are. We need to recognize, first of all, that we *have* mistaken perceptions. In our lives, our experience of happiness or suffering is due to the relationship between our subjective mind and external objects. Our delusions arise as a direct result of the way that objects appear to our minds, and the way that we apprehend those objects to exist. As a result of the delusions, we accumulate the karma that causes and sustains cyclic existence.

Ultimate truth can be understood only on the basis of conventional reality. Let's look at the vase again. A vase is considered a conventional truth because it does not exist as it appears. This means that to a direct sense perception, such as that in the mind of an ordinary being perceiving the vase, the vase appears to be inherently existent. Upon analysis, however, not even an atom of inherent existence can be found in this object. On a grosser level, we can say that something that is inherently existent should by definition also be independently existent, but if we analyze the vase, we will see that it clearly has a dependent nature.

Thus, we begin by trying to realize the conventional nature of the vase, recognizing that there are mistakes in our perception of it. We then try to eliminate those mistakes through applying logic and reasoning, the most supreme type of which is the reasoning of dependent arising. By applying logic and reasoning, we eventually realize that the vase does not exist the way it appears to us. Having realized the conventional truth of the vase, we understand that there is something to negate. However, before we can generate the complete recognition of what is to be negated, we must realize the mistake that is being made by the mind perceiving that vase. Once we ascertain this with certainty, we will be able to realize the vase's ultimate nature.

When we are sick, the first stage is recognizing that we are not well. This is followed by a second stage of determining exactly what our sickness is, whether something is wrong with our lungs or our heart or whatever. Realizing conventional truth is like knowing that we are sick, that something isn't right. Recognizing the object to be negated is like determining exactly what illness we have. Realizing ultimate truth is equivalent to curing that illness.

In reality, conventional truth and ultimate truth are mutually exclusive. This means that there is not one single phenomenon that is both an ultimate truth and a conventional truth. Not only are conventional and ultimate truth mutually exclusive, but they are *directly* mutually exclusive. Please be careful not to get confused here—earlier we discussed how we can establish the two truths on the basis of every conventional phenomenon, and now we are saying that they are directly mutually exclusive. Let me explain why.

The way in which a vase and a pillar, for example, are mutually exclusive and the way in which conventional truth and ultimate truth are mutually exclusive are not the same. It is true that you cannot find one entity that is both a vase and a pillar, and in the same way one thing cannot be both a conventional truth and an ultimate truth. However, as long as any phenomenon exists, it must be either one of the two—a conventional or an ultimate truth. This cannot be said of vases and pillars.

In terms of true existence and non-true existence, by the act of negating true existence we establish that an object is not truly existent. By establishing that it is not truly existent, we negate its true existence. That is how it should be. When the mind eliminates one type of existence, it automatically implies some other type of existence. And when it establishes one type of existence, it automatically negates that kind of nonexistence. For example, when we realize that a phenomenon is permanent, we negate the idea that this phenomenon is impermanent. And when we apprehend that a phenomenon is impermanent, we negate the idea that it exists permanently. In the same way, when we establish emptiness, we must understand what type of existence we are refuting. To realize emptiness and the two truths, it is very helpful to understand this.

It is also helpful to understand how affirming and nonaffirming negations function. A nonaffirming negation is a mere negation—for example, "there is no vase" is a nonaffirming negation, because it negates something without implying anything else. An affirming negation, however, negates one thing but simultaneously implies the existence of something else. The example that is commonly used to illustrate this is the statement, "The heavy man doesn't eat lunch." What is negated here is the fact that the man eats lunch, and what is affirmed through implication is the fact that he must eat at other times.

Emptiness, noninherent existence, and non-true existence are nonaffirming negations.

How Perception Experiences an Object

All of the many problems that arise in our minds are rooted in the fact that the way our minds perceive and believe in things is completely different from the way those things actually exist. Therefore, it is important when seeking to understand the two truths that we have a clear idea of the way that a direct perception experiences its object and the way that a conceptual perception experiences its object. In order to define in detail the way that direct and conceptual perceptions engage in their objects, we can look at the third chapter of *Commentary on the "Compendium on Valid Cognition,"* in which Dharmakirti describes the way the mind establishes existence. According to this text, when a consciousness perceives an object in harmony with the way that object exists in reality, it is a direct perception. And when a consciousness perceives an object in a way that is not harmonious with the way that object exists in reality, it is a conceptual perception.

For example, because the consciousness that realizes the conventional truth of a vase by direct valid cognition perceives the vase dualistically, it is tainted by the pollutions of ignorance, and is regarded as a mistaken mind. However, a direct valid cognition that realizes emptiness would *not* be considered mistaken. That is, a valid cognition directly perceiving a vase or any conventional truth is mistaken, but a direct valid cognition realizing emptiness is not. There are no mistakes in the mind that directly realizes an ultimate truth by direct valid cognition because it is totally free of duality. That is how the two are different.

Please don't feel too overwhelmed by all of this information and all of these difficult words. Maybe some of you find this very unpleasant. I am not as skillful as His Holiness the Dalai Lama at explaining such things. But you shouldn't think, "How can I ever learn this?" Don't be too tight with all this information, and don't be too loose. Remain somewhere in between.

When I finished my studies, I went to help my teacher Geshe Sopa Rinpoche. At the Center at that time we didn't have a translator, so Geshe-la told me to go ahead and teach without one. I could only manage "How are you?" and "Where are you from?" in English, and I thought there was no way I could possibly teach the Dharma in English. I listened to many, many cassettes of teachings by His Holiness with a translator. I listened and listened and thought to myself, "How can this translator handle all these Indian masters' names?" To myself I thought, "I can't do this," but I didn't give up.

These days, I can say Vasubandhu and Chandrakirti with no problems. I think all of you will have the same experience. Just by hearing a couple of lectures or reading a few books on a topic, you shouldn't assume that you will understand all of these things right away. When you are grappling with a subject from a different tradition, from a different language background, to think that you must learn and understand it all immediately can cause you to become very frustrated. You will be putting yourself through unnecessary trouble. At the beginning the teachings on emptiness may sound like nothing but a whole lot of technical terms that don't make much sense, but later on, when you begin to get a feeling for it, you will start to understand that these terms relate directly to your mind, and are applicable to many situations in your life.

Also, all of this information shouldn't remain up there somewhere in a cloud creating more confusion. As you study, it should settle down into a clear understanding. Because the study of emptiness can be a very intellectual undertaking, in order to ensure that it does not become merely dry intellectual knowledge, offering you no benefit, your study and practice of emptiness should be done within the framework of the lamrim, the graduated path to enlightenment.

Understanding the two truths is completely relevant to the psychology of our mind and the way that we relate to external objects. This topic should never become mere intellectual information because it describes the reality of our life—it describes our minds, and the way our minds perceive objects. The point of the two truths is to realize our mistakes—that things do not exist the way they appear, or the way that we believe them to exist.

As long as something exists and appears, it has to be either one of the two truths. If it is a conventional, or obscured, truth, the appearance and the mode of existence of that phenomenon are in discord, and if it is an ultimate truth, its appearance and the mode of existence are the same. Even enlightenment and all the qualities of enlightenment are categorized as being either conventional truth or ultimate truth.

How Cognition Designates Conventional and Ultimate Truth

Conventional and ultimate truths are designated as such by cognition. The object itself, from its own side, is not a conventional truth, nor can it from its own side be an ultimate truth. It becomes a conventional or ultimate truth only in dependence on being posited by a subject mind. In the mind of an ordinary sentient being, the cognition that designates a conventional truth cannot also designate an ultimate truth. This is so because in order for a cognition to know an object as an ultimate truth directly, it must be completely free of the pollutions of ignorance. A conceptual mind, in contrast, is always polluted by ignorance.

For a bodhisattva on the path of preparation, the cognition that realizes emptiness is a conceptual cognition. Although we could say that this conceptual cognition does at this point know an ultimate truth, in the end, this conceptual cognition will not realize ultimate truth directly. The mind that actually realizes ultimate truth directly will be the mind of meditative equipoise on the path of seeing, which is a direct perception directly realizing emptiness. Therefore, although the mind in meditative equipoise on the path of preparation does cognize emptiness, the emptiness that it cognizes does not exist the way it appears, and therefore it is not cognizing an ultimate truth. To clarify, a mind that knows an ultimate truth directly cannot ever be a conceptual mind.

Generally, a mind that knows an ultimate truth directly is far more refined than an ordinary conceptual mind. However, it doesn't have to be refined to the degree of being totally enlightened. For example, an arya being's transcendental wisdom of meditative equipoise realizing emptiness directly is a completely nonconceptual, valid state of mind that knows emptiness. It can designate an object as an ultimate truth. The mind that realizes an ultimate truth directly is totally free of the appearance of what is to be negated, totally free of duality, and totally free of the appearance of conventional truth.

All of the states of consciousness of a buddha are considered conventional truths. The form bodies of a buddha are also conventional truths. However, the nature body of a buddha is considered an ultimate truth, because the nature body of a buddha is itself the emptiness of true existence of that enlightened mind. The nature body has two aspects. The first is the naturally pure aspect, which is the enlightened mind's emptiness of true existence. The second aspect is the temporarily pure aspect, which refers to the cessation of all of the defilements and obscurations, the enlightened mind that has attained the cessation of all the temporary adventitious delusions. According to the Prasangika system, both of these aspects of the nature body are ultimate truths. Because they are ultimate truths, the way they appear and the way they exist have to accord. As conventional truths, the appearance and mode of existence of the other three bodies of a buddha are not in accord.

Of course, although phenomena may be categorized as conventional truths, to the transcendental wisdom of an enlightened mind there is no such thing as the appearance and the mode of existence being in discord. To an enlightened mind, the way things appear and the way things exist are in complete accord. In terms of categorizing conventional and ultimate truth in dependence upon the subject mind that apprehends it, from the perspective of an enlightened mind, every phenomenon is an ultimate truth, because to an enlightened mind there is no discord at all. If we are incorrect in our analysis, we might be led to assume that the reason that the nature body of a buddha is considered an ultimate truth is because it is essentially emptiness, and the reason that the other three remaining bodies are considered conventional truth is because they are not emptiness. However, this is not necessarily the case. When we direct our minds to the four bodies of a buddha, there are four possible direct valid perceptions that we can experience: the direct valid perception seeing the nature body, the truth body, the enjoyment body, and the emanation body. To the direct valid perception seeing the nature body, there is *never* any appearance of true existence, any appearance of conventional reality, or any appearance of duality. But it is *possible* that the other three bodies can appear as truly existent or as conventionalities. Therefore, the nature body of a buddha is always categorized as an ultimate truth, while the other three are generally categorized as conventional truth.

On the one hand, we say that everything exists by mere imputation, including ultimate truth. But when we designate objects as conventional or ultimate, we do so on the basis of whether their appearance and their mode of existence accord or not. For example, there are two types of direct valid perceptions of a vase: the direct valid perception of the eye consciousness that sees a vase, and the direct valid perception of a mental consciousness that realizes the emptiness of the vase. Both of them are the same in that they are direct valid perceptions, but the direct valid perception *seeing* the vase through the eye consciousness is polluted by ignorance, the appearance of true existence. The direct valid perception that realizes the emptiness of the vase, however, is free from the pollution of ignorance. So in this case there is also a difference in the object. In order for the subject mind to be an ultimate truth, the object must be the emptiness of the vase, not just the vase itself. And in order for the emptiness of the vase to be established, the subject mind must be an ultimate truth.

Understanding the two truths in this way enables us to discriminate between what is good or bad, what is happiness or suffering, who is my friend or my enemy. Our experience of happiness and suffering is different depending on the way we impute it. As our wisdom increases, our discrimination improves, and we are able to eliminate many more causes for suffering and create the basis for much more happiness. When we experience harm from an enemy, for example, it can be very helpful to know a little about the conventional reality of our existence, to understand that whatever appears to our mind is an obscured truth. The ability to see reality so that what appears and what exists accord completely will only occur when we generate the mind that is able to directly experience emptiness. Up until that point, everything we experience will be strongly influenced by ignorance.

The Two Truths According to the Philosophical Schools
In order to cultivate the wisdom that pacifies all the causes of suffering, we need to understand the mode of existence of the two truths. As Chandrakirti states, if we do not understand the mode of existence of the two truths, then whatever view we generate will be mistaken, and thereby, whatever wisdom arises will be ineffective in eliminating the two types of obscurations.

Shantideva says:

Conventional reality and ultimate reality
Are accepted as being the two truths.
Ultimate reality is not an object of mental experience.
Mind itself is said to be conventional.

In Tibetan Buddhism there are four main philosophical schools or tenet systems. In the first turning of the wheel of Dharma, the disciples were primarily aspirants of the individual vehicle, so Buddha taught the four noble truths, stating that phenomena exist by way of their own characteristics, that they truly exist, and that they ultimately exist. In accordance with these teachings, the Vaibashika and Sautrantika schools emerged.

In the middle turning of the wheel of Dharma, Buddha taught that phenomena do not inherently or truly exist. The philosophical schools of the Prasangika-Madhyamaka and Svatantrika-Madhyamaka emerged in accordance with this view.

According to the last turning of the wheel of Dharma as taught in the *Sutra Unraveling the Thought of the Buddha,* among other texts, all phenomena can be divided into three categories: dependent phenomena, thoroughly established phenomena, and imputed phenomena. According to these teachings, dependent phenomena are truly and inherently existent. Thoroughly established phenomena are also truly and inherently existent. Imputed phenomena, according to this view, are the only phenomena that do not inherently or truly exist. In accordance with these teachings, the Chittamatra school emerged.

In your studies, you will probably come across this classification frequently. Whether one is a Vaibashika or a Sautrantika or a Chittamatra or a Madhyamika is dependent upon the theory or view that one holds. The differentiation among these four schools of thought is based on view, not on conduct.

At one time, the teachings went into decline in India and were subsequently revived primarily by Nagarjuna, who was born approximately four hundred years after Buddha's passing, and Asanga, born approximately nine hundred years after Buddha's passing. Nagarjuna and Asanga are often referred to as the two great charioteers. Nagarjuna, in particular, was responsible for a great resurgence in the Madhyamaka view in India. He was followed by the great Indian masters Buddhapalita (ca. 470 C.E.), Bhavaviveka (ca. 500 C.E.), and Chandrakirti (ca. 600 C.E.), who all commented on Nagarjuna's explanations. According to the slightly different ways in which the Indian masters interpreted these teachings, the Madhyamaka school is divided into two: the Svatantrika-Madhyamaka school follows the explanations of Bhavaviveka, while the Prasangika-Madhyamaka school follows the explanations of Buddhapalita and Chandrakirti. Shantarakshita (740–810 C.E.) and Kamalashila (760–815 C.E.) were also great Svatantrika philosophers. However, although they followed the Svatantrika philosophical view in general, they did not accept external existence, meaning the existence of phenomena without depending on the ripening of karmic imprints, and as a result, even within the Svatantrika system there are subschools.

The *Lamrim Chenmo* is categorized as belonging to the philosophical system of the Prasangika-Madhyamaka. Generally speaking, the purpose of the different presentations of the philosophical viewpoints is simply to eliminate ignorance. The four Buddhist schools of thought are like four major hospitals, each of which has a different way of diagnosing the sickness of ignorance. It is very valuable to study the philosophical mechanics of ignorance in detail on the basis of the graduated path to enlightenment. Please be careful, though. Some individuals take a great deal of interest in the philosophical view of emptiness but not much interest in mind training or in lamrim, and as a result the information that they learn becomes a lot of dry intellectual philosophy that does not nurture their minds in any way. The most skillful way to approach the teachings of the lamrim is to use them as the key to unlock the doors of all the philosophical viewpoints. In this way we can enter the path and over successive lifetimes attain enlightenment.

As we have discussed, the practice of ethics is the foundation for every positive quality and all knowledge that we could wish to attain. But our practice of ethics can be hindered if we have faults in our view. In order to complete the perfection of ethics, we need to have a pure view.

Usually, when we differentiate between the Mahayana vehicle and the Hinayana vehicle, we do so on the basis of conduct. But it is also possible to differentiate the Mahayana from the Hinayana on the basis of their philosophy. From this point of view, the Sautrantika and Vaibashika schools are categorized as Hinayana schools of thought, while the Chittamatra and Madhyamaka schools are categorized as Mahayana schools.

To continue, both the Mahayana and Hinayana schools accept the self-lessness of persons, although the *way* in which they assert the selflessness of persons varies. The main point of philosophical divergence between these two schools is their understanding of the selflessness of phenomena. The selflessness of phenomena is accepted in the Mahayana schools, whereas in the Hinayana schools it is not. Because the Vaibashika and the Sautrantika schools accept that all things have inherent existence, true existence, and existence by way of their own characteristics, they cannot accept that phenomena are selfless. However, they do not accept that a "self" or an essence of a phenomenon exists on the basis of each and every single phenomenon, but only on the basis of dependent phenomena—that is, phenomena that arise due to causes and conditions, phenomena that are regarded as matter or form. As long as a phenomenon fulfills these three requirements of possessing external existence, true existence, and existence by way of its own characteristics, in their view that particular phenomenon cannot be selfless.

In order for us, as beginners on the path, to gain some understanding of conventional and ultimate truth, I would like to give a short introduction to the way that these concepts are approached in each of the four Buddhist philosophical schools.

The Two Truths in the Vaibashika School
According to the Vaibashika school, conventional and ultimate truths are differentiated as follows. When a conceptual mind sees an object such as a vase through an image, upon analysis it is able to distinguish the minute constituent particles, or atoms, that make up that vase. In the process of

differentiating the particles, the mind that apprehends the vase itself is lost. This is an example of conventional truth for the Vaibashika school.

Ultimate truths are phenomena such that if they are apprehended by consciousness, the mind apprehending them is not lost. Directionally partless particles of atoms or a consciousness without duration of time are examples of ultimate truths.

When the Vaibashikas establish selflessness, they do so on the basis of the emptiness of an "I" that is permanent, independent, and substantially existent. A secondary Vaibashika school regards selflessness as the emptiness of a substantially existent, self-sufficient "I." Because in both of these cases, the mind apprehending the selflessness is not lost, these modes of existence are regarded as ultimate truths.

The Two Truths in the Sautrantika School

In comparison to the Vaibashikas, the Sautrantika school is said to hold a higher view. Sautrantikas do not accept the possibility of a consciousness that has no duration, because they assert that consciousness is a continuum. According to them, if consciousness was not a continuum, then instead of a *beginningless* consciousness, one would have to posit a beginning of consciousness, and many contradictions would follow from that.

The Sautrantikas regard entities that are not ultimately able to perform a function as conventional truths. Although they designate the emptiness of a self-sufficient, substantially existent "I" as the subtle mode of selflessness, the mere negation of that self-sufficient, substantially existent "I" is considered to be a conventional truth. Other examples of conventional truth in this system are permanent phenomena and uncompounded space, for these too cannot ultimately perform a function.

According to the Sautrantikas, ultimate truths are all phenomena that are ultimately able to perform a function. According to this system, all compounded phenomena—those that arise from causes and conditions—all products, and all external phenomena are ultimate truths.

The Two Truths in the Chittamatra School

The followers of the Chittamatra school, as mentioned above, divide all phenomena by way of three characteristics. These are dependent phenomena (which arise from causes and conditions), thoroughly established phenomena, and imputed phenomena. According to the Chittamatras, all dependent phenomena and all imputed phenomena are conventional truths, and thoroughly established phenomena are ultimate truths. The Chittamatras also assert that objects of the minds of beings who have realized the truth directly are ultimate truths, while objects of conceptual mind are conventional truths.

The Chittamatras do not accept any kind of ultimate truth that does not depend on the imprints of the mind. For the Chittamatra school, the Sautrantika view of externally existent ultimate truths is the main object to be negated. According to the Chittamatras, the vase and the visual perception perceiving the vase are of one substance. The visual perception perceiving a vase and the existence of the vase are therefore simultaneous. According to them, the vase and the visual perception perceiving that vase are caused by one substantial cause, which is the imprint in the fundamental consciousness. The fundamental consciousness is a mental consciousness that is neutral by nature and whose continuum is uninterrupted until the point when the practitioner attains nirvana. This fundamental consciousness is also what the Chittamatra school labels "self."

One of the unique tenets of the Chittamatra school is its assertion that things exist by the power of the manifestation of imprints from the fundamental consciousness. They categorize imprints into three groups: imprints that are of a similar type, imprints grasping at self-existence, and imprints of habit or familiarity.

According to the Chittamatras, all of our valid perceptions—mental states that are direct and unmistaken—arise from the fundamental consciousness as a result of the imprints of a similar type. The imprints grasping at self-existence, however, give rise to all the poisonous states of mind—such as attachment. The Chittamatras assert that it is by the power of imprints grasping at self-existence that we generate delusions, create karma, and cause and perpetuate cyclic existence. The third imprint, the imprint of habit or familiarity, can be virtuous or nonvirtuous. This kind of imprint enables us to experience the intuitive grasping at a truly existent self and all the delusions. It allows us to feel intuitively angry, or intuitively kind.

These imprints are interconnected: the imprints of habit are connected to the imprints of a similar type, which in turn are understood to be connected to the imprints grasping at self-existence. Personally, however, I don't see a strong connection between the imprints of a similar type and the imprints grasping at self-existence.

As I mentioned, according to the Chittamatras, the vase and the visual perception perceiving the vase exist simultaneously. They are of one substance, and they are established by the ripening of a single imprint. The imprint that ripens in this case is the imprint of a similar type. According to the Chittamatras, the reason we experience suffering and not happiness in our lives is that we do not know the ultimate nature of existence, and, not knowing it, we hold onto things as existing separate from the nature of the mind. For example, we hold the object of our anger and ourself, the person who is getting angry, as existing outside of the mind rather than realizing that the object of our anger and the person getting angry both arise due to the manifestation of the same imprint from the fundamental consciousness. Due to this ignorance, and due to the imprints of the view of self-existence, we experience unhappiness.

Chittamatras consider thoroughly established phenomena to be ultimate truths. For them, emptiness is truly existent. Because they posit the basis of emptiness—dependent phenomena—to be truly existent, they maintain that its emptiness must be truly existent as well, because the mode of existence of the basis of emptiness has to accord with the mode of existence of the emptiness itself. According to the Chittamatra School, emptiness is not merely labeled by the mind; rather it is something that exists from the side of the object.

From the Chittamatra point of view, space and other uncompounded phenomena—phenomena that don't arise from causes and conditions—are examples of phenomena that are not truly existent, because these things are mere imputations. Space is a mere imputation because it is a mere negation of contact or obstruction. According to the Chittamatras, all imputed phenomena are not truly existent.

The Madhyamikas in Brief

According to the Madhyamaka system, when the way that a particular phenomenon appears and the way in which it actually exists are in accord, it is an ultimate truth. When the way that a phenomenon appears to exist and the way in which it actually exists are different, it is a conventional truth. To a gross conceptual consciousness, phenomena appear in one way and exist in a totally different way. To nonconceptual mental states, such as the direct perception of an arya being in meditative equipoise, the way phenomena appear to exist and the reality of their existence accord.

In fact, for all four philosophical schools the manner of asserting conventional and ultimate existence is strongly connected to the relationship between the subject and the object. When there is a mistaken mode of apprehension between the subject and object, it is usually considered conventional truth. When there is no mistake, it is an ultimate truth.

The Madhyamaka philosophers fall into two main divisions: the Svatantrika-Madhyamaka school and the Prasangika-Madhyamaka school. Generally, the Svatantrika school follows the commentaries on Nagarjuna's *Root Wisdom* written by Bhavaviveka, Shantarakshita, and Kamalashila, while the Prasangika School follows the commentaries on Nagarjuna written by Buddhapalita and Chandrakirti. This will be discussed in more detail shortly.

Why do we call the Svatantrika-Madhyamaka school a school of the Madhyamaka or the Middle Way, when, in accordance with the view of our own system, the Svatantrikas have not identified what is to be negated perfectly, and are still inclined toward the extreme of eternalism? And if we were to do so, why wouldn't we call the Chittamatra system a school of the Middle Way as well? In fact, a Madhyamaka school is distinguished as such by the fact that it is a Mahayana philosophical system that does not accept the true existence of phenomena even on a conventional level. The Svatantrikas fulfill this qualification, as they do not accept truly existing conventional phenomena, although they do accept the existence of phenomena by way of their own characteristics. The Chittamatra school, in contrast, posits the true existence of functioning phenomena on a conventional level, and therefore cannot be considered a school of the Middle Way.

The Svatantrika philosopher Bhavaviveka takes the Chittamatra tenet that posits the existence of phenomena as merely manifestations of the imprints from the fundamental consciousness (and therefore not externally existent) as his main object to be negated. According to Bhavaviveka, it is possible to have external existence that is not empowered by the manifestation of the imprints in consciousness. Bhavaviveka argued that if the Chittamatra view were correct, we would have to accept two ways of apprehending an object. When a phenomenon was imputed and then investigated, it would appear one way, and when a phenomenon was imputed but not investigated, it would appear another way. Every phenomenon would have this discrepancy under these two circumstances. For example, my seeing a pillar would arise under the power of a karmic imprint that allows me to see that pillar. Therefore, upon analysis, we would have to say that this pillar would be exclusive to me, and me alone. It would not be seen by others. So at first, if we were to say, I saw this pillar, you saw this pillar, or everyone saw this pillar, the pillar we would be referring to would be a pillar that has not been analyzed. But upon analysis, we would have to say that each of us would be seeing our own pillar.

According to Bhavaviveka, in order for a phenomenon to exist, it is not necessary that it exist due to the power of the manifestation of the imprints within consciousness. By this assertion, Bhavaviveka is implicitly accepting external existence. Usually when we talk about the Svatantrika system, however, we are referring to the viewpoints presented by Kamalashila and Shantarakshita. In accordance with their viewpoints, there is no doubt that external existence is completely untenable.

The Chittamatra view of emptiness being truly existent and the basis of emptiness also being truly existent is refuted by the Svatantrika-Madhyamaka school in general. The Svatantrikas do not accept any kind of true existence, even conventionally. When they refute the true existence of functioning phenomena, which means dependent phenomena, that in turn refutes the true existence of emptiness itself. This is because when you refute the true existence of the basis of emptiness, you also refute the true existence of emptiness itself. So as a method of refuting the true existence of emptiness, the Svatantrikas begin by refuting the true existence of the basis of emptiness.

Unlike the Chittamatras, the Svatantrika system accepts only six consciousnesses—five sensory consciousnesses and one mental consciousness. The Svatantrika-Madhyamaka system does accept imprints, but it does not accept a fundamental consciousness in which they are stored. According to the Svatantrikas, the imprints abide within the mental consciousness itself.

The Svatantrika system posits a subtle level of emptiness. Their view of ultimate existence is that phenomena exist by way of their own characteristics inherently, yet are empty of existing by way of their own uncommon characteristics. They accept inherent existence, and existence by way of its own characteristics, but they do not accept phenomena existing on the basis of their own *unique* modes of existence.

What does it mean to say that a phenomenon does not exist by way of its own unique mode of existence? According to the Svatantrika view, a combination of both the subject and object gives rise to existence. This is in opposition to the possibility that the object exists by way of its own unique mode of existence. Rather than saying that, the Svatantrikas assert that phenomena exist as a result of both the subject and object. According to them, an object cannot exist by way of its own unique basis, nor can a mind perceiving an object exist by way of its own unique basis. Existence occurs as a result of both subject and object.

According to the Svatantrikas, if an object were to exist on the basis of its own unique mode of existence, it would be truly existent, which is impossible because according to this system there is no such thing as true existence. When the Prasangikas say that a phenomenon exists only by the power of mind, they mean that when that particular phenomenon is investigated by ultimate analysis, it cannot be found. But according to the view of the Svatantrikas, when phenomena are investigated by ultimate analysis, they *can* be found. From the Svatantrika point of view, although phenomena do exist by the power of imputation, they do not exist *merely* by imputation. The Svatantrikas do not accept any kind of existence arising solely on the basis of the mind. They feel that it is impossible to apply cause and effect if you assert this view.

To summarize, the Svatantrikas accept inherent existence, which means that the object can be found upon analysis, but they do not accept true existence, which to them means that the object exists by its own unique mode of existence.

In the ninth chapter of the *Guide to the Bodhisattva's Way of Life,* Shantideva says that there are two ways to establish conventional and ultimate truth. These are the way an ordinary being establishes them and the way a yogi establishes them. In this case, *ordinary being* refers to a follower of the Vaibashika or Sautrantika schools, and *yogi* refers to a practitioner of the Madhyamaka system. The two truths as established in the Vaibashika and Sautrantika systems can be faulted by the Chittamatra school through logic and scriptural citation. The Chittamatra viewpoint can be faulted both by scriptural authority and by logic of the Svatantrika view. And the

Svatantrika viewpoint of the two truths is in turn contradicted both by scriptural authority and the logic and reasoning of the Prasangika system. In this way, each of the lower schools' assertion of the two truths is faulted by scriptural authority and the reasoning of the higher schools.

ACTUALLY ESTABLISHING SUCHNESS
The Reason It Is Necessary to Recognize the Proper Object to Be Negated
In order to realize emptiness correctly, we must begin by recognizing what it is that we are trying to refute, what it is that things are empty of. There are two parts to this: refuting the subject and refuting the object. It is best to begin with the recognition of that which is to be negated in our subjective experience of the object—the consciousness, or mind, that grasps at phenomena as being inherently existent. Once we recognize that, it will be easy to recognize its object: inherent existence itself. In order to recognize the subject mind that is to be negated, we first need to identify the three poisons and understand that their cause is ignorance. Also, we need to try to understand that the way that phenomena appear to our mind and the reality of the way that phenomena actually exist are two different things.

From the beginning then, we have to be clear that what we want is ultimate happiness, and what we do not want is suffering. Also, we should understand through our analysis of our lives and the world around us that although the causes of our suffering appear to be external, in reality they are all internal. These internal causes are the three poisons, within which we are particularly concerned about ignorance—the consciousness itself *and* the object that it apprehends.

One of the dangers of this kind of meditation is that it is very easy to make the mistake of over-negation, by which we can completely refute the dependent arising of causes and conditions and fall into the extreme of total nonexistence or nihilism. Another danger is that, fearing the mistake of the nihilistic view, we under-negate, falling to the other extreme of eternalism or belief in permanent existence. In order to recognize the proper object to be negated, we need to find the balance between too much and too little negation.

In general, there is one type of logic used for analyzing ultimate existence and another type of logic used for analyzing conventional existence. Let me clarify what I mean by the logic examining ultimate existence.

For example, the basis of the imputation of the "I" is the aggregates. Upon this basis, we instinctively grasp at an "I," or "me." If, after searching for it, we were actually able to find the "I" among the aggregates of mind and body, the "I" would truly exist. This is the logic for investigating ultimate existence. If the object is found by the consciousness analyzing ultimate existence, the object must be truly existent.

In reality, every phenomenon that exists or appears *cannot* in fact be found by such an analysis. For example, the wisdom of meditative equipoise single-pointedly focusing on the ultimate nature of a vase sees the ultimate nature of the vase, but it does not see the vase itself. The mistake of over-negation is usually made because we assume that since the logic analyzing ultimate existence does not see the vase, even the conventional vase does not exist.

Some of the ancient systems of Tibet held this mistaken view that phenomena do not exist at all. They supported this conclusion by saying that because a consciousness analyzing ultimate existence does not see the object, the object does not exist at all. This is like throwing out the baby with the bath water. These practitioners confused the fact that the meditative consciousness analyzing ultimate truth was unable to see the vase with the vase itself. They asserted that because a wisdom consciousness in the mind of a superior being in meditative equipoise analyzing ultimate existence does not apprehend the conventional mode of existence of things, things do not exist. Those who disagreed with them asked how they could then explain the fact that our eye sensory perception, for example, sees the production of a vase, the vase itself, the function of the vase, and so forth. And these practitioners replied by quoting the sutras, saying that all of our sensory perceptions are conventional, obscured truths, and therefore are totally unreliable.

To further establish the nonexistence of phenomena, these schools cited the four reliances:

> Don't rely on the person, rely on the Dharma.
> Don't rely on the words of the Dharma, rely on their meaning.
> Don't rely on the interpreted meaning, rely on the definitive meaning.
> Don't rely on conceptual perception, rely on ultimate perception.

It was the fourth reliance that was of particular interest to these scholars. Ultimate mental perception refers to the wisdom consciousness of meditative equipoise, and since the conventional vase does not appear to this consciousness, they asserted that the vase was nonexistent.

In regard to functioning phenomena, that is, products arising from causes and conditions, the old systems say that there are no products because there is no production from self, production from other, production from both, or production from neither. This is actually stated in the first chapter of Nagarjuna's *Root Wisdom.* Since all these modes of production have been negated by Nagarjuna, these systems assert that the logical conclusion is that there are no products, and no existence. This is one type of view asserting that phenomena do not exist at all.

According to Lama Tsongkhapa, one cannot differentiate between *existence* and *conventional existence,* because they are in fact the same. If something is conventionally existent, it is existent, and if it is existent, it is conventionally existent. However, due to the mistake of overnegation of the object of refutation, some systems assert that there are no causes and conditions, and no products. In order to eliminate this view, the section on superior insight of the *Lamrim Chenmo* says that in order to realize the results of the form body of a buddha, we must rely on a practice that is dependent upon conventional truth. And in order to attain the truth body of a buddha, we must rely on a practice that is dependent upon ultimate truth. Therefore, we need to understand the basis of the two truths. Conventional truth should not negate ultimate truth, and ultimate truth should not negate conventional truth. The two should complement one another.

According to the mistaken view of some of the earlier schools, direct valid perception realizing ultimate truth negates conventional reality. But by establishing the ultimate mode of existence of phenomena from this viewpoint, the practitioner simultaneously negates conventional existence. And, while accumulating the merit of transcendental wisdom, the practitioner destroys the merit of virtue. Instead of unifying method and wisdom, this practice makes them mutually exclusive. This kind of practitioner clearly does not understand the two truths. Instead of the two truths being complementary, they negate one another. Thinking like this, there is no way to actualize the result of the two bodies of a buddha.

The Svatantrika-Madhyamaka school and those below it assert that the Prasangika view of the emptiness of inherent existence, true existence, and existence by way of its own characteristics necessarily implies that there is no dependent arising. The Vaibashika schools that assert external existence would say that with this view, there is no way for the Prasangikas to establish compounded existence. They would argue that there is no way that there could be birth, death, or destruction, and no way to apply any sort of causality. They say that with this view, the four noble truths could not exist, the two truths could not exist, and refuge could not exist.

The Prasangikas respond that even though phenomena are empty of inherent existence, samsara and all the states beyond it do exist, true suffering and the true cause of suffering do exist, and the true path and true cessation as well as the two truths exist. According to the Prasangikas, they all exist because they all exist conventionally. Even though phenomena are not inherently existent, cause and effect is totally applicable conventionally. Just because phenomena are not inherently existent does not mean that they do not exist at all.

According to the Prasangikas, if phenomena were inherently existent, one would not be able to apply causality to things and events. *Because* phenomena are dependent upon causes and conditions, *because* phenomena are dependent arisings, for that very reason, they are empty of inherent existence. Because they lack existence from their own side, dependent arising applies. Because phenomena are empty of inherent existence, the twelve links of dependent origination can function. According to the Prasangika system, things do not exist inherently, but that which is *not* inherently existent cannot necessarily be said to be nonexistent. An example of something that is not inherently existent and does exist is a vase. An example of something that is not inherently existent and does not exist is a rabbit's horns.

According to some of the early schools of thought, since things do not exist in the face of the transcendental wisdom of an arya being in meditative equipoise, they qualify as being nonexistent. From Lama Tsongkhapa's viewpoint, establishing existence based on whether an arya being's transcendental wisdom mind of equipoise perceives an object or not amounts to establishing existence only selectively. The emptiness realized under these circumstances could only be on the basis of certain phenomena—meaning ultimate phenomena—whereas emptiness should be pervasive.

One should be able to apply emptiness uniformly on the basis of each and every phenomenon.

In our own Prasangika system, we demonstrate the emptiness of a phenomenon—a vase, for example—from two different angles. The emptiness of a vase cannot be established just by the fact of the vase being merely imputed and empty of inherent existence alone. When we say that a vase does not exist inherently or that the vase is empty of true existence, we are establishing emptiness by talking about the emptiness of the vase in particular. This kind of negation is one angle. From another point of view, when a transcendental wisdom mind in equipoise meditates on the emptiness of that vase, the fact that this mind does *not* see the vase itself is also the emptiness of the vase. To this mind, there is no appearance of a vase. Not only is there no appearance of the vase, but also this mind has no concept of the vase. It does not even comprehend the vase. Therefore, the mind that realizes the emptiness of a phenomenon does not realize the basis of that emptiness, which is the phenomenon itself. There is no appearance of the basis of that emptiness.

The fact that the vase is nonexistent to the wisdom mind of an arya being in equipoise does not mean that there is no vase. It is more subtle than that. That mind comes to single-pointed equipoise after having gone through an analytical process. When that mind seeks the vase, it is not able to find the imputed label "vase" in the basis. That mere negation in itself is the vase not existing inherently.

According to the Svatantrika school, the arya being's transcendental wisdom mind of equipoise *does* see the basis of imputation, which is the vase itself. According to them, that wisdom mind is a direct perception, and all direct perceptions take manifest phenomena as their objects. Therefore, hidden or extremely hidden phenomena like subtle selflessness cannot be the object of a direct perception of single-pointed transcendental equipoise. However, in the Prasangika system, if the basis of imputation could be established by the mind of an arya being, then the existence of the basis of imputation and its appearance would be in accord. Thus, it would have to be truly existent, and as a result, all conventional phenomena would have to be truly existent. Therefore, the Prasangika system asserts that no vase appears to an arya being's transcendental wisdom mind of equipoise. This is how Prasangikas negate the assertion that an arya being's transcendental wisdom of equipoise perceives the basis of imputation, and that there is no appearance of emptiness to that mind.

The old systems assert the nonexistence of phenomena, and due to the fault of over-negation they eliminate even conventional existence. Therefore, these systems cannot be considered Madhyamaka systems.

The Three Criteria

In *Root Wisdom,* Nagarjuna cites three criteria that a phenomenon would necessarily possess if it were inherently existent: it would have to be unaffected by causes and conditions, it could not be dependent on any other factor, and it would have to be something that does not transform into another mode, even temporarily.

According to the Prasangika system, there is no phenomenon that is inherently existent, or that exists in a particular way by its very nature. According to the Prasangika, even when we say that someone is "naturally" short-tempered, upon further investigation, there is nothing essentially or inherently short-tempered in that person. There is nothing that exists in that person that is not subject to change. Since that person's nature is dependent upon causes and conditions, it by definition cannot be inherent, since inherent natures are independent. It cannot be natural, or innate, because it *can* be changed.

Moreover, the mind itself is also empty of existing inherently and empty of existing by way of its own nature. If we think carefully about this, we will see that the very fact that our minds possess no inherent existence allows for the fact that we can change them, eliminate our delusions, and become enlightened.

Once again, according to the Prasangika system, if phenomena were actually inherently existent, they would have to fulfill the three criteria listed above. However, according to the Prasangika, this is logically impossible, for if things possessed these three criteria, cause and effect would no longer apply, and our experience of the world as we know it would be totally repudiated.

However, although these are the criteria that phenomena would need to possess in order to be inherently existent, according to the Prasangika system, these criteria need not be present in order for our minds to *grasp* at things as if they were inherently existent. There are two modes of grasping at inherent existence. The first is intellectual, or philosophically acquired, grasping at inherent existence, sometimes also called "learned." The second is innate grasping at inherent existence. Innate grasping is the ignorance that is considered to be the root of cyclic existence. All sentient beings possess the innate form of grasping at the "I" that wants happiness and does not want suffering. However, the object of this grasping—the "I" that we grasp—does not itself meet the three criteria for inherent existence.

Lama Tsongkhapa states in the *Essence of Eloquence:*

> If something existed in the way that grasping at true existence perceived it, it would have to exist as follows: it would have to withstand scrutiny by the logic analyzing the ultimate, be a partless functioning thing, and possess the three criteria.

He goes on to state that refuting these criteria does not in itself bring forth the realization of selflessness within our minds, and that therefore these criteria cannot be considered the measure of inherent existence. If these criteria were the full measure of inherent existence, he asserts, then every sentient being's mind should apprehend these things when apprehending inherent existence. But this does not occur. The old philosophical traditions of Tibet, however, made the mistake of asserting that ultimate existence could be established by negating these criteria. According to Lama Tsongkhapa, taking these criteria as the full measure of inherent existence implies a very narrow view of what is to be negated, and the philosophical traditions that did so did not understand the full intention of Nagarjuna's writings, which clarify the Buddha's intent in the Perfection of Wisdom sutras.

What was the Buddha's objective in teaching emptiness, anyway? He wasn't just on a philosophical trip. Buddha taught emptiness in order to pacify the elaborations and the projections of the deluded mind. This point is generally agreed upon by all Buddhist schools. However, among the schools, the teachings that are considered effective in fulfilling this function vary widely, and, as a result, so do the interpretations of emptiness.

According to the Svatantrika system and those below it, for example, if *empty* means *empty of inherent existence,* all phenomena that are empty would also be totally nonexistent. If something lacks inherent existence, according to these schools, karmic cause and effect cannot function, and thus they fall into the extreme of nihilism. The Svatantrikas and below thus assert that the version of emptiness taught by the Prasangikas merely serves to creates further elaboration in the mind, instead of serving to pacify it.

According to the Prasangikas, however, the Svatantrikas have not understood Buddha's objective in teaching emptiness. The Prasangikas say that the Svatantrikas and those below fail to see the relationship between dependent arising and emptiness and thus fail to understand that the very fact of the dependent arising of something substantiates its emptiness of existence from its own side. The subtle dependent arising of things implies that those things are dependent upon mere imputation. Things dependent upon mere imputation cannot be inherently existent, because by definition they exist in dependence on the subject perceiving them, and not from the side of the object.

Just in case you are wondering why we are bothering to analyze other people's mistaken views, you can think of it as if you were watching someone else play a game that you, yourself, aspire to learn. A great deal can be learned from watching others play. You watch, and you think, "He should have used a little bit more force there," or "She should have used a little less force there." When studying the lamrim, examining the arguments presented from many different points of view can help us to clarify our own understanding. Of course, it is impossible to thoroughly understand the perspective of these schools and the way that they understood the scriptures and ultimate reality in the time it takes to read a few pages.

In the evolution of Buddhism in Tibet, Tibetan scholars swung back and forth between extremes in seeking to understand the philosophical view of the Madhyamaka without error. In the same way, as Buddhism spreads to the West, similar problems will occur. However, the most essential thing to understand about the philosophy of emptiness is that its purpose is to eliminate ignorance and to subdue our minds. There is no medication that will get rid of our ignorance. There is no laser surgery. Ignorance must be eradicated by internal methods that arise from the mind itself. As long as we understand that ignorance is the cause of all our suffering and problems, that it is the cause of all our delusional states of mind, and that the antidote to ignorance is the philosophy of emptiness, our study of this subject will be effective.

In our lives, our own minds are our biggest problem. The reason is because our minds make so many mistakes in the way they relate to the external world. The solution to this is to refine and improve the mind's relationship with its objects. This is the sole method for establishing stable and enduring happiness. And even if there is only one person in the whole world working hard, persevering in generating the experience of the realization of emptiness, this one person has the potential to eliminate suffering for countless other sentient beings.

Recognizing What Is to Be Negated According to the Two Madhyamaka schools

The Philosophical Split Between the Madhyamikas

As I mentioned above, the Svatantrika system follows the commentaries on Nagarjuna by the masters Bhavaviveka and Kamalashila, while the Prasangika system follows the commentaries by the masters Buddhapalita and Chandrakirti. I will try to explain the origins of the dissent briefly. If you are interested in reading further on this topic, Tsongkhapa's commentary on Nagarjuna's *Root Wisdom,* which is called the *Ocean of Reasoning: The Great Commentary on Root Wisdom,* and Khedrup Je's *Dose of Emptiness* clearly explain Buddhapalita's interpretation of Nagarjuna, Bhavaviveka's criticism of Buddhapalita's interpretation along with Bhavaviveka's own interpretation, and Chandrakirti's criticism of Bhavaviveka along with Chandrakirti's own interpretation. The monastic textbooks of the Gelug tradition also present their own slightly different perspectives on the points made in these texts.

The basis of the disagreement begins with a verse by Nagarjuna in the first chapter of *Root Wisdom,* in which Nagarjuna refutes the Samkhya school's idea of the production of things.

Things are not produced from self,
Or from other;
They are not produced from both;
Or produced without cause.

In Buddhapalita's *Commentary on "Root Wisdom of the Middle Way"* he interprets the first line—"things are not produced from self"—as follows:

Things are not produced from themselves because their production would become meaningless and endless. There is no purpose to functioning phenomena that exist in their own nature being produced again. If it already exists and again must be produced, it will be produced continually.

Here Buddhapalita develops the logical consequence of the Samkhya position that all things are produced from themselves in order to demonstrate the fallacy of the Samkhya position. The mode of reasoning that he employs to make this point is called consequential reasoning, in which an absurd consequence of the opponent's position is presented in order to cause the understanding of the correct view to arise in the opponent's mind. This mode of reasoning is a crucial element in the approach to realizing emptiness as taught in the Prasangika system.

Some time after Buddhapalita, the great scholar Bhavaviveka came along and took issue with Buddhapalita's commentary. In so doing, Bhavaviveka presented his own elucidation of Buddhapalita's ideas, which is called Bhavaviveka's interpretative consequence. The main vehicle for Bhavaviveka's refutation is his text entitled the *Lamp of Wisdom*.

In *Lamp of Wisdom,* Bhavaviveka asserts that the reasoning behind Buddhapalita's consequence—which is "because they are produced from themselves"—is not logical, and cannot be established by valid cognition. Essentially, Bhavaviveka's understanding of Buddhapalita's explanation is based on his own form of autonomous reasoning. Bhavaviveka says that in order to make it a correct consequence—in other words, a consequence in autonomous form—we need to have a reason that we can validate by valid cognition. Therefore, Bhavaviveka suggests that we change the reason from "because they are produced from themselves" to "because they are already established as themselves." Thus, the consequence becomes: "It follows that the reproduction of things would be meaningless, since they are already established as themselves."

Buddhapalita's second point of reasoning, which is an overextension, is to be understood as an infinite regress. The second reason is: "It follows that the production of things would involve an infinite regress, for even though things exist, they would have to be produced again." That is the correct consequential syllogism that supports this point of reasoning.

When Bhavaviveka interprets Buddhapalita's commentary, he cuts out the word "again" from this consequence. Therefore, in Bhavaviveka's view, the second reason becomes: "It follows that the production of things would involve an infinite regress, for even though they exist, they would have to be produced."

In retrospect, however, we can see that in fact the inclusion of the term "again" is quite crucial to the intended meaning of this sentence. Chandrakirti, when commenting on this issue in *Clear Words,* clarifies that this statement should necessarily be interpreted from the position of the opponent (the Samkhyas) because Buddhapalita lacks his own thesis. This means that Buddhapalita, in using the word "again," is showing the absurd consequence of the re-production of things from the perspective of the opponent.

Bhavaviveka set forth further criticism of Buddhapalita in his *Lamp of Wisdom* on the basis of three points. Please remember, however, that although Bhavaviveka does present these criticisms, in so doing he does *not* present a clear distinction between the Autonomous (Svatantrika)-Madhyamaka and the Consequentialist (Prasangika)-Madhyamaka schools. Bhavaviveka's first point is that Buddhapalita, in his consequence refuting production from self, neither gives us an actual reason—he presents only a consequence, with no affirmative evidence—nor employs any examples, which is what one is supposed to do in the context of syllogistic reasoning. Therefore, according to Bhavaviveka, what Buddhapalita has done is incorrect.

Bhavaviveka's second criticism of Buddhapalita is that in refuting production from the thing itself, Buddhapalita is refuting the position of the Samkhyas, but that he has not examined the Samkhya's actual position well. According to Bhavaviveka, Buddhapalita has simply used the words "production from self" without understanding what the Samkhyas mean by this phrase.

In his third criticism, Bhavaviveka, who is very concerned with logic and reasoning, criticizes the twofold reasoning that Buddhapalita presents. According to Bhavaviveka, the reasoning of the consequence should actually be inverted in order to make a logical statement. In other words, instead of saying: "Things are not produced from self because it would be meaningless and because it would involve an infinite regress," he should be saying: "Things are not produced from self because production *is* meaningful and because production *does not* involve an infinite regress."

In his commentary on Nagarjuna's *Root Wisdom,* Lama Tsongkhapa asserts that, in addition to inverting the reasoning, Bhavaviveka means that the predicate to be proven should also be inverted. However, Je Rinpoche points out further complications in this approach by saying that the predicate to be proven need not be inverted in the same way as the reason. In other words, inverting the reason simply means that rather than saying production is meaningless and that it would involve an infinite regress, you just negate those straightforwardly, so it becomes "production is meaningful, and it does not involve an infinite regress." But according to this logic, the predicate to be proven—"things are not produced from self"— would also be inverted, becoming "production from self," which we obviously don't want to prove. What we do instead is construct a predicate to be proven that makes our statement: "It follows that the production of things is not just the mere exclusion of production from self, because production is meaningful and because production is not an infinite regress." Again, this is Bhavaviveka's interpretation of what Buddhapalita should present as his predicate.

But now we have a problem. By constructing the predicate in this way, we have constructed a statement that is an affirming negation. We discussed the distinction between affirming negations and nonaffirming negations earlier. According to Bhavaviveka, by employing the use of an affirming negation, Buddhapalita contradicts Nagarjuna and thus contradicts Buddha himself.

Some years later, in his commentary *Clear Words,* Chandrakirti responded to Bhavaviveka's interpretation of Buddhapalita with his own refutation of these three points. Through his response we develop the actual distinction between the Consequentialist and the Autonomous-Madhyamaka.

It seems that one main problem between these scholars was that Bhavaviveka did not have a clear distinction between his own view and that of Buddhapalita. Bhavaviveka assumed that Buddhapalita accepted autonomous reasoning—his own form of reasoning—when in fact this was not the case. As a result, Bhavaviveka's criticisms of Buddhapalita are all on the basis of autonomous reasoning, while Buddhapalita's reasonings were in fact consequential. Bhavaviveka essentially asserts that the refutation of the Samkhya's argument should be by way of autonomous reasoning, while Buddhapalita and Chandrakirti assert that it can be refuted through consequence. Bhavaviveka insists that Buddhapalita could not engage in this refutation by way of consequence, because Buddhapalita's reasoning was nonexistent, or his logic was faulty. But Lama Tsongkhapa and other scholars insist that Bhavaviveka did not interpret Buddhapalita's logic properly to begin with.

Chandrakirti clearly felt that there was a great difference between Bhavaviveka and Buddhapalita in terms of the question of autonomous reasoning. But Bhavaviveka, according to Je Rinpoche, did not feel that there was such a great difference at all between himself and Buddhapalita. You should also be aware that there are actually two different translations of Chandrakirti's *Clear Words* into Tibetan, and there is some discussion around this issue that rests upon the discrepancies between the translations. I will not go into detail about that here, but it might be useful for you to keep that in mind.

Of course, on the basis of what I have explained here, you will not get a very clear idea about the origins of the division between the two schools. Actually, I have not even broken the surface of this debate. However you should understand that there are two basic points of dissent. The first is the difference in the forms of reasoning—autonomous and consequentialist—that are considered valid to establish ultimate truth. The second is the deeper level of distinction, on the basis of view. In essence, Bhavaviveka and the Svatantrikas accept some level of inherent existence, while Buddhapalita, Chandrakirti, and the Prasangikas do not. This is further elucidated in Chandrakirti's refutation of a common base in *Clear Words*. For a more extensive understanding of this issue, you should study the commentaries of Buddhapalita, Bhavaviveka, and Chandrakirti directly. This is only a very general summary of the points of disagreement. Without extensive philosophical background and contextual understanding, it will be very difficult to get a grasp on this subject matter.

Refuting the Svatantrikas

In general, the basis of our practice is the two truths, and the path we should follow is the path of method and wisdom, or bodhichitta and emptiness. The two results that we seek from the path are, respectively, the *rupakaya* and the *dharmakaya*—the form body of a buddha and the truth body of a buddha. The Prasangika view of the two truths is regarded as the most refined among the four philosophical schools. However, in order to establish a firm ground for the Prasangika view, it is essential and also very helpful to understand the explanations of the two truths as presented by the other tenet systems. On this basis, we can develop a clearer view.

For example, as we have discussed, the Svatantrika system asserts inherent existence on the basis of dependent arising. The Prasangika system, in contrast, asserts the *absence* of inherent existence on the same basis—dependent arising. The difference between their views is a matter of subtlety. Of course, it's very easy to say in words that something is a gross or a subtle dependent arising, but to actually to experience dependent arising on any level is very difficult.

According to our system, when we establish subtle dependent arising, the base of the dependent arising itself should not be contradicted by ultimate analysis, meaning that it should not be truly or inherently existent. This ensures that we do not fall into the extreme of believing in permanence or inherent existence. Conversely, the base of emptiness, such as the base of the imputed label "vase," should not be faulted by conventional analysis, in order to ensure that we do not fall into the other extreme of total nonexistence. Finally, the base of emptiness should be known conventionally in the world as that thing. The reason for this is because in the Prasangika system, everything is merely imputed, everything exists by mere labeling. In order to prevent taking this to an extreme—for example calling the vase a "chair" and justifying this by the fact that it exists merely by imputation—we say that it should be commonly known in the world as that thing.

For example, according to the Prasangika system, we impute "I" on the basis of the mind and body, and so when we search for the "I" among the mental and physical aggregates, we cannot find the "I." Why is this? Since the "I" is merely imputed on the aggregates, it can be faulted neither by logical analysis establishing ultimate existence nor by logic proving its conventional existence. Also, this "I" exists merely by renown, merely by labeling, on the basis of the aggregates. Therefore, based on these criteria, Prasangikas claim that the merely imputed "I" does exist conventionally. To put it another way, the "I" exists in dependence upon the basis of imputation, the imputed label, and the imputing mind. And although it exists merely as an imputation, it is nonetheless able to perform all the functions of the "I." When we investigate it, however, we cannot point to any one thing and say we have found it.

The Svatantrikas and the Prasangikas agree that the logic refuting ultimate existence is necessary in order to eliminate the view of eternalism, and that the logic establishing conventional existence is necessary in order to eliminate the view of nihilism. But the Svatantrikas and the Prasangikas disagree as to whether phenomena exist by the power of being known by that label. Svatantrikas say that if an object exists, that existence must be established partially from the side of the object. To them, crediting existence to the mind's imputation alone is too extreme. If you do so, they say, how can you ever uphold cause and effect relationships? To them, it is more realistic to assert that, yes, phenomena are imputed by the mind, but in addition to this, phenomena also exist from their own side.

In the Prasangika system, phenomena exist solely on the basis of labeling. According to this view, we experience happiness or suffering due to our habitual grasping at things as being solid, concrete, and inherent. When something unpleasant happens—for instance, if we hear someone say something very rude about us—because of our view that solid, concrete, inherently bad things were said about us, we suffer. We think our unhappiness is due to the harshness of the words that were spoken, while in fact our unhappiness is due to our strong grasping at these words. If we were not grasping, the words would not affect us. Without grasping, they become just words. For instance, if you insult someone who doesn't understand your language, no matter what you say, it will not bother them.

It is very important to realize this point—that what actually creates the unhappiness we feel is our own grasping. Although there may be external conditions involved, it is really our own mind that determines the extent to which we are affected by the things going on around us. If it were necessary to combat every external condition that is a potential cause of harm to us, there would be no end to it. Therefore, the only solution is to protect our own minds. And the best way to do this is through the wisdom that realizes emptiness.

Although all phenomena are categorized as either conventional or ultimate truths, as ordinary sentient beings we interact most often with conventional truths. The Svatantrikas divide conventional truths into two types: correct conventional truths and wrong conventional truths. The Prasangikas' differentiation is similar in meaning, but the two divisions are labeled "objects that are correct in the view of the world" and "objects that are wrong in the view of the world." According to the Prasangikas, categorizing something as "correct" conventional truth would imply that it exists as it appears. In the Prasangika system, no conventional phenomenon has this status.

Examples of wrong conventional truths, according to the Svatantrikas, are a reflection in a mirror, a dream, or a mirage. We are not so easily fooled by wrong conventional truths, no matter how bright and beautiful they are, because they are obviously mistaken—they clearly do not exist the way they appear.

According to the Prasangika system, objects that are wrong in the view of the world can be subjects or objects. Minds that grasp at the permanence, independent status, or substantial existence of a person are mistaken subjects that are wrong in the view of the world. This is so because you don't need to have realized the meaning of emptiness to recognize that these are mistaken; meditation on impermanence and so forth is sufficient. According to the Svatantrika system, however, these examples would not be accepted. This system asserts that wrong conventional truths are only views that are grossly mistaken in the ordinary world: for example, thinking that the face in the mirror is a real face and thinking that an elephant in a dream is real. Ordinary people understand that the reflection of a face in the mirror is not a face and that the elephant in the dream is not an elephant.

By examining these points, you should understand that the Svatantrikas present a much less subtle view of wrong conventional truth than the Prasangikas.

In order to establish an understanding of ultimate truth, we can begin on the basis of less refined phenomena, such as establishing the nonexistence of the elephant in the dream. In a very gross way, we know that even though the elephant in the dream appears, it does not exist. As we investigate more deeply, we will begin to understand that even the things that are correct in the view of the world possess a mode of appearance that does not correspond with the reality of their existence. Of course, this is much harder to grasp and requires extremely painstaking investigation, for at a superficial level the appearance and the mode of existence of conventional objects seem to accord. When we analyze carefully, however, we see that, in fact, the way that conventional objects appear and the way that they actually exist do not accord in the least.

Some people also use the analogy of the "I" that is dreaming to illustrate the disparity between the way that things appear and the way they actually exist. When we dream, we experience a very strong sense of the "I" doing this and that, going through the experiences of the dream. We are certain, in the dream, that what we are experiencing is real. When we wake up from the dream, however, we realize the illusory nature of everything that has happened, and that all of the events and experiences of the dream were in fact false. Though not perfect, this is a good analogy to the experience of realizing emptiness.

Speaking of dreams, it is possible for some individuals, having gone through the process of extensive analysis, even to be able to use the occasions of their dreams to realize emptiness. The dream consciousness is a very strong, powerfully focused state of mind, and it is possible to utilize this consciousness to analyze the emptiness of the "I." However, this kind of meditation takes a great deal of training. First we have to gain control of our dreaming minds, and know that we are dreaming, and then we have to intentionally direct our dreams to do these kinds of meditations.

This is really becoming something, isn't it? Before I was telling you how difficult it is to realize emptiness, and now I am saying that you can do it in your sleep!

Other Systems
In order to cut the root of cyclic existence, we need to realize emptiness in accordance with the view of the Prasangika-Madhyamaka system. The purpose of generating a very subtle view is to eliminate a subtle mental projection, what is called the *object to be negated*. In order to even *recognize* the subtle object to be negated, we first need to recognize the gross object to be negated. To accomplish this, we will take another look at the other philosophical schools.

According to the Vaibashikas and the Sautrantikas, the objects to be negated are permanence, existence without causes and conditions, and existence without depending on parts and particles. These schools regard grasping at permanence and grasping at existence without depending on causes and conditions and without depending on parts and particles as the root of all suffering. It is this mistaken understanding of the relationship between subject and object that they hold to be the basis of all the delusions. In addition, some subsets of these schools posit a more subtle object to be negated. To them, what is to be negated is a person that is substantially and independently existent—in other words, an "I" or a person that exists without depending on its basis of imputation.

According to the Chittamatra School, the object to be negated is external existence—again, meaning the existence of phenomena without depending on the ripening of karmic imprints.

With the Madhyamaka system, there are again two schools of thought. The Svatantrikas follow the Indian master Bhavaviveka in negating any unique mode of existence from the side of the object without any involvement by mind. The Svatantrika system does not accept true existence, or existence by way of an object's own unique mode of existence. However, the Svatantrikas do accept the existence of an object from its own side, or inherent existence.

According to the Prasangika system, there is no true existence, there is no inherent existence, there is no existence from the side of the object. Apart from mere imputation, there is no existence, inherent existence, innate existence, existence from an object's own side, or existence by way of an object's own characteristics. As it says in Lama Tsongkhapa's *Prayer of the Beginning, Middle, and End:*

> Having totally abandoned the extreme of mistaken views
> That hold an intellectually constructed emptiness as supreme,
> Having become terrified by the profound meaning of the way that
> things exist,
> May I realize that phenomena are primordially empty.

During his lifetime, to the common perception, Lama Tsongkhapa seemed to be an ordinary person. In actual fact, we could never say that Lama Tsongkhapa was ordinary. But according to his biographies, Je Tsongkhapa manifested making mistakes in realizing the view of emptiness, and by recognizing and correcting those mistakes, he rose to establish the pure view of the Madhyamaka system. In our own practice too, when we train in the wisdom that realizes emptiness, it is very possible we will make mistakes. One meditator I know completed the entire course of monastic studies and then went to a hermitage to meditate. He later told me that after having meditated on emptiness in retreat, he discovered that the Prasangika view he thought he had so well established in his mind was in fact a Svatantrika view!

Each time we listen to, contemplate, and meditate on the teachings, we have the opportunity—through the power of purification and the accumulation of merit—to realize them as if we were listening to, contemplating, or meditating on them for the first time. Sadly, when we study Dharma, we often make the mistake of disregarding teachings that we have heard before in favor of new ones. But the purpose of studying Dharma is to bring about realizations in our minds. Therefore, we not should approach our studies as if they were novels or newspapers—reading something once and then forgetting about it. The point of studying Dharma is to cultivate the theory and the practice of the Buddha's teachings within our own minds, and if we want to do this, it is imperative that we work to deepen and refine our understanding by listening, contemplating, and meditating over and over again. A more extensive and profound understanding of the teachings will arise within our minds as the force of our purification and accumulation of merit increase.

When we study in the monasteries, our teachers tell us to read the same subject, the same chapter, fifteen, twenty times, then debate, debate, debate, and come back and read it again. Each time we get a different insight. We don't just highlight the key points and leave it at that. Someone told me of a Christian priest who said that when he rereads the Bible, even though he may have read a particular passage many times before, it has a different meaning for him every time. This is exactly the way to approach it. Even if there is not much difference in the subject matter from one day to the next—the words and letters may be all the same— there is a difference in our own minds. We experience fluctuation in our comprehension because our understanding is dependent on many internal and external factors that affect whether or not we see clearly. Our mental state, our physical state, the time of day—all of these make a difference. Because of this, when we sit down to study Dharma, we should do so at minimum with the thought of renunciation, even if we can only manage a contrived form of it. Doing this will have a huge effect on the clarity of our mind and on how much we are able to absorb. It is foolish to think that merely because Lama Tsongkhapa realized emptiness and has now given us a presentation of it that is faultless, and that therefore all we need to do is read or listen to this information once and we will somehow effortlessly realize.

In the beginning, it very hard to correlate the philosophical information that we receive in teachings to the practical reality of our meditation. For example, this meditator that I spoke of earlier completed the entire course of monastic studies and knew exactly what the Svatantrika viewpoint was and how to negate it, but when he engaged in serious meditation, he realized that he was actually holding their view. Studying the Dharma is, in a sense, like learning how to plow a field by having someone draw diagrams in the ashes of a wood stove. Plowing a few ashes and actually plowing a field are worlds apart. It is the same with receiving the instructions on these philosophical viewpoints and trying to practice them in meditation.

We are very fortunate to have the opportunity to rely on the resources of the scriptures, to be able to read them, and to be able to understand them. We must be careful, however. While studying emptiness, we need to investigate and analyze the teachings repeatedly and continue to build a strong support of merit and purification. By this method we will be able to arrive at the most refined level of the view. As exemplified by Lama Tsongkhapa's biography, in the beginning we should enrich ourselves by studying the teachings extensively and cultivating a clear understanding, and then we should apply ourselves to practice day and night unceasingly. After all, if we think about it, how could the great result of attaining the ultimate happiness of the enlightened state be possible on the basis of limited study, understanding, and meditation?

A very young monk once told me a quotation from Milarepa:

> While I'm walking I do a meditation, while I'm sitting I do a
> meditation.

The practice of being able to meditate continually throughout every activity arises from establishing great familiarity with the material through extensive listening and contemplation. His Holiness the Dalai Lama, for example, might be walking down an aisle with people crowded around on all sides, but it is easy to see that his mind is completely absorbed, working tirelessly for the Dharma and sentient beings.

Establishing Our Own System

In the Prasangika system, there are two types of objects to be negated: those that are negated by the path and those that are negated by logic. Those negated by the path are the two types of obscurations—the affliction obscuration and the obscuration to omniscience. Those negated by logic are (from the point of view of the subject) the grasping at inherent existence and (from the point of view of the object) the inherent existence of phenomena. *Logic,* in this context, refers to the logic that establishes ultimate existence. From the point of view of the subject, there are two kinds of grasping, learned and innate. Learned grasping is eliminated by logic, and innate grasping is eliminated by the path. Learned or intellectually acquired grasping does not necessarily refer to a view that is acquired through following a philosophical tradition. For even though a person has never even heard the term "inherently existent," as long as that person has not realized emptiness, he or she possesses the intellectually acquired form of grasping at true existence.

To accomplish the identification of the object to be negated, the first thing you need to do is establish a clear picture of the object that is posited by your innate grasping at true existence. Before you can realize that this object does not exist, you must first get a picture of what it feels like when it seems to exist. Kuntang Jampelyang wrote a beautiful text utilizing the example of water and trees to demonstrate the understanding of subtle emptiness. He says that when you go to the ocean to seek its treasures, first and foremost you must be knowledgeable about the dangers of the ocean. After learning all the dangers of the sea and taking precautions against them, you then take to the sea and begin your quest. In the same way, before you can find the treasure of subtle emptiness, you first need to recognize what is to be negated, which in this case is the object of the mind's innate grasping at true existence.

According to the lamrim tradition, we meditate on impermanence as the antidote to grasping at permanence, and we meditate on the impure nature of phenomena in order to counteract the mind that grasps at phenomena as being pure. If we perceive something as extraordinarily beautiful and thereby generate strong attachment toward it, in order to eliminate that attachment we can meditate on impermanence; we can consider how this mind is the basis for suffering, and how it is totally mistaken. Thinking like this, we can subdue the attachment in the short term, but there is no way we can abandon this delusion until we have realized emptiness completely.

In a sutra, someone once asked Buddha if one should apply the meditation on impermanence as an antidote to a mind obsessed with a magician's illusion of a beautiful woman, if one does not recognize that the woman is an illusion. Buddha replies that one cannot abandon the mind of attachment completely through this method. Although we can meditate on the impermanence of this illusory woman, as long as we hold her aggregates to be truly existent, we cannot abandon the delusion. Even if we meditate on emptiness while holding the base of the aggregates as truly existent, it won't work. Why not? If you have an abscess with a very deep infection but you only disinfect the surface, the wound might feel cleaner, but as long as the roots of the infection are still there, it will not heal. In the same way, according to the Prasangika system, only the perfect meditation on emptiness can eliminate the roots of cyclic existence.

How to Establish the View in Your Own Mind
The next topic is the method for generating the view in one's own continuum.

The Four-Point Meditation
The main method to generate the view in one's own continuum that is taught in the *Lamrim Chenmo* is the seven-point meditation. However, I thought it might be helpful for your practice to also give a brief explanation of the four-point meditation, or analysis, which was taught by Lama Tsongkhapa in his middle-length treatise on the lamrim. Therefore, we will begin with that.

As the name suggests, there are four points to this meditation. The first point is recognizing what is to be negated. The object to be negated must be negated on the basis of both the subject mind and the apprehended object. From the side of the subject mind, as we have discussed, there are two levels at which the negation should take place: grasping on an intellectual or learned level and grasping on the innate level. Of the two, the latter is the most important. The object to be negated on the innate level is the innate grasping at the "I" as being inherently existent. What should *not* be negated is the conventional "I."

The innate grasping at the "I" as inherently existent is present in the mind of every sentient being at all times, even in dreams. Again, the best way to begin to get some idea of the way that the inherently existent "I" appears is to use situations in which you experience strong emotions. For example, if you are being severely criticized for something you didn't do, in the midst of your hurt and anger you may notice the presence of a strong feeling of an "I" that is being blamed and criticized. Alternatively, when someone says pleasing things about you, you experience a sense of the "I" that everyone thinks is so wonderful. Under normal conditions when you are not experiencing strong emotions, the innate mode of grasping at an inherently existent "I" does not appear so clearly to the mind.

Can we do two things at once, experience the event and examine our "I"? When we are walking with someone we love in a beautiful park, we are listening to the person's conversation and enjoying it, on the one hand, and, on the other, we are taking pleasure in the environment of the park. We can have both experiences together. While experiencing strong emotions, we should be able to experience that extreme happiness or suffering with one part of our mind, while with another part of our mind, we can and should be able to analyze how this inherently existent "I" is appearing to us, and how it is grasped.

Sometimes when we apprehend the inherently existent "I," it is totally identified with our body, and at other times it is totally identified with our mind. For example, when someone tells us we are ugly, we think, "I'm not ugly." In this case we have associated the "I" with the body. Then if someone says, "No matter how much I teach you, you never learn, you're so stupid," we think, "I'm not stupid," thus associating the "I" with the mind. In both of these cases, whether we identify the "I" with the body or with the mind, we have still not ascertained what is to be negated. When recognized correctly, however, the "I" that is to be negated, the inherently existent "I," which exists by way of its own nature from its own side, is *not* associated with the body, nor is it associated with the mind. That "I" should appear to be totally independent of the mind and the body, as something completely apart from them. We should feel a sense of the "I" that is independent and solidly, concretely, inherently existent, an "I" that wants happiness and does not want suffering. When we recognize this kind of "I," we have recognized the object to be negated.

It is very common to make mistakes in the ascertainment of what is to be negated. Sometimes we over-negate, and other times we do not negate enough. Although the inherently existent "I" that is to be negated will not appear clearly without us making an effort, this "I" that is to be negated is, nonetheless, the main condition for generating all of our delusional states of mind, which in turn create karma, which in turn causes and sustains our cyclic existence. Therefore it is very important to identify it properly. Generally, it is said that even if it takes months and years to develop a clear recognition of the object to be negated, we shouldn't be disappointed. It is worth the time it takes, because the latter three points of the four-point meditation come much more easily once the object to be negated has been determined.

The second of the four points is ascertaining the pervasion. Ascertaining the pervasion means establishing the fact that if the object to be negated were to exist in the way that it appears to exist—as an inherently existent "I"—it would have to exist in one of four ways:

1. As inherently separate from the aggregates of body and mind
2. As inherently one with the aggregates of body and mind
3. As both separate and one
4. As neither separate nor one

We must examine the "I" and see if the way it actually exists accords with any of these four possibilities. When we need to catch a thief, we shut one door here, we shut the other door here, and somewhere in between the two we catch our criminal. In the same way, through this fourpoint meditation we exclude the possibilities of the "I" existing as one with the aggregates or apart from them.

In order to establish the logical pervasion, I will reiterate that it is very important that we have clearly recognized the object to be negated and that we hold it very firmly in our minds. If we do *not* have a clear picture of what is to be negated when we engage in the second point of analysis, it will be difficult for us to complete this point.

When we meditate on the four points, in general, our meditation should be a combination of analytical and single-pointed meditation. For example, upon determining what is to be negated, we should concentrate single-pointedly on the appearance of the inherently existent "I," and the innate mode of grasping at it, so that we have a clear idea when we do the latter points of analysis. In the same way, having ascertained the second point of the pervasion, we should engage in single-pointed concentration on the result of that analysis. It follows in the same way with the latter two points.

The third point is establishing that the inherently existent "I" does not exist as one with either the mind or the body that are its basis of imputation. We can establish this by examining our own mind and body and our own sense of "I." If we say that this inherently existent "I" exists as one with the aggregates, then we cannot differentiate the "I" and the body. We cannot say "my body" if we assert that the "me" and the "body" are one and the same. An inherently existent oneness cannot have different parts. We can see from our own life experience that there is no such mode of existence in which the "I" and the aggregates are a single entity.

The fourth point is establishing that the inherently existent "I" does not exist as something different from the aggregates of mind and body that are its basis of imputation. Upon analysis, we will see that it is quite impossible to say our "I" is wholly different from the aggregates or the activities of the aggregates. If we designate an "I" that is totally independent from the aggregates of the mind and body, it would no longer be logical to say, "I am sick," "my leg is broken," "my hand hurts," and so forth. Therefore, an "I" that exists as something inherently different from the aggregates is not reasonable either.

The conclusion that we will arrive at by the end of this meditation is that if the inherently existent "I" does not exist as one with these aggregates *and* if it doesn't exist as something separate from them—as we have determined through our analysis—the only other alternative is that such an "I" does not exist at all. When we have determined this point clearly and are certain of it, we should familiarize our minds with it single-pointedly.

Please do not think that you will take a shortcut by starting with the easier points first and leaving the difficult ones for later. It doesn't work that way. In order to ensure your success in this meditation, you must stick to the sequence of the four-point analysis. However, after the first two points—the ascertainment of what is to be negated and the ascer-

tainment of the pervasion—the order in which you apply the next two—
the logic of inherently existent oneness or inherently existent difference—
is less important.

The Sevenfold Reasoning

Chandrakirti's sevenfold reasoning on selflessness is the main meditation
technique presented by Lama Tsongkhapa in the *Lamrim Chenmo* as the
means to realizing emptiness. As in the four-point analysis, the recognition
of what is to be negated and the ascertainment of the pervasion of its mode
of existence constitute the foundation of this meditation.

Although the traditional basis for applying the logic of the seven points
in this meditation is a chariot, please keep in mind that you can also apply
this logic to the "I" and the aggregates in order to establish the selflessness
of persons. Also, since chariots are not the preferred means of transporta-
tion in the world these days, I will explain this meditation on the basis of
a car. When you imagine a car as your basis of meditation, it will be the
most effective if you imagine a car that is very precious and important to
you, one toward which you have very strong grasping and which would
cause you to become very upset should even a scratch appear on it. The
seven points of logic are as follows.

1. The car does not exist inherently because it is not one with
   the basis upon which "car" is imputed.
2. The car does not exist inherently because it is not something
   other than the basis upon which "car" is imputed.
3. The car does not exist inherently because it is not inherently
   dependent on its parts.
4. The car does not exist inherently because its parts are not
   inherently dependent on the car.
5. The car does not exist inherently because it does not inherently possess its parts.
6. The car does not exist inherently because the mere assembly
   of the parts does not constitute the car.
7. The car does not exist inherently because the shape of the car
   is not the car.

To go about this meditation, you first need to ascertain the object to be negated. This can be done by bringing the image of your precious car to mind. When you think about that car, you think about an inherently existent car. You are not concerned with the shape of the car, or with its parts and particles; you imagine the *car* itself, existing independently of causes and conditions and wholly from its own side. The concept of inherent existence is completely fused with your image of the car. When you have established this, you should try to ascertain the pervasions, which are the first two points. This means thinking that if there is such an inherently existent car, it must exist either as one with the basis of designation or as something totally separate. One you have established this, you can apply the rest as follows: the car is not inherently dependent on the parts of the car, nor are the parts of the car inherently dependent upon the car itself. The car does not inherently possess its parts. The parts of the car coming together do not constitute the car. And if there is a dent on the car, that's not the car, either, and so forth.

Ordinarily, our innate mode of grasping at this car as being inherently existent is a cause of great suffering. We can imagine our mind holding tightly onto the inherent existence of this car as a tightly closed fist. And we can imagine that applying each of the seven points of logic is like releasing one finger, releasing another finger—gradually loosening the hold of the innate grasping at inherent existence, which is the source of all the delusions, until we no longer apprehend the inherent existence of the car at all.

If you find that your meditation applying the seven aspects of logic is having little or no effect on your grasping mind, you should backtrack a little. This is probably the fault of not having established the earlier points thoroughly. Therefore, you should return to the clear ascertainment of the object to be negated and start again from there.

The Twenty Emptinesses

The founder Buddha, with infinite compassion and with great skill, presented ultimate truth on the basis of three divisions of emptiness in the *Sutra on the Perfection of Wisdom:* the twenty emptinesses, the sixteen emptinesses, and the four emptinesses. The presentation of the twenty emptinesses is the most extensive among the three, and subsumes the latter two categories. In order to realize emptiness, it is not reasonable to assume that we will be able to go through every single phenomenon that exists in the world and negate its inherent existence one by one. This being the case, the presentation of the twenty emptinesses is particularly useful, because it can help us to understand and realize emptiness in terms of categories. The twenty emptinesses are established on the basis of various objects, such as the user, the utilized, the sensory powers, consciousness, and the directions. Although there are twenty different bases of emptiness taught here by Buddha, there are not twenty different objects to be negated. The object to be negated for each of the twenty emptinesses is the same, and thus the "emptiness" itself is also the same. The base upon which that emptiness is established, however, is different. "Twenty" refers to twenty different bases of phenomena.

The first of the twenty emptinesses is the *emptiness of the internal*. The emptiness of the internal is the emptiness that is established on a base that is pervaded by consciousness. Ordinarily, a base that is pervaded by consciousness can be form or that which is not form. In this case, the emptiness of the internal is established on the basis of that which is not form—the consciousness, or mind.

The second is the *emptiness of the external*, which is established on the basis of the objects of the sense perceptions—form, sound, smell, taste, and touch. The basis of the emptiness of the external should not possess consciousness, thus it refers to inanimate phenomena.

The third is the *emptiness of the internal and the external*. This emptiness is established on the basis of the sense powers. It is known as the emptiness of the internal and the external because the sense powers are considered internal from the point of view of the external object and external from point of view of consciousness. Therefore, the sensory powers are the basis for the emptiness of the internal and the external.

The first three emptinesses subsume all possible bases upon which emptiness can be established. According to the *Sutra on the Perfection of Wisdom*, a bodhisattva establishes the emptiness of the internal on the small path of accumulation, the emptiness of the external on the medium path of accumulation, and the emptiness of the internal and external on the great path of accumulation.

The fourth is the emptiness that is established on the basis of emptiness itself. This is commonly known as the *emptiness of emptiness*. When we establish emptiness on the basis of a phenomenon, the emptiness of the basis itself is the emptiness of emptiness. Also, upon finding the emptiness of a phenomenon, the mere negation that comes as a result of investigating this emptiness and *not finding* the imputed label "emptiness" is the emptiness of emptiness. Buddha taught the emptiness of emptiness in order to keep us from grasping at the true existence of ultimate truth. The emptiness of emptiness is practiced on the Mahayana path of preparation, which is the second of the five paths.

The fifth is the *emptiness of the great,* which refers to emptiness without measure or limit. The basis for establishing this emptiness is the ten directions. We can establish the emptiness of the ten directions by understanding that they exist through interdependence. There is no inherently existing east, there is no inherently existing west, and yet a fully functioning east and west certainly do exist. The ten directions are the basis for the emptiness of the great because even though they are beyond the measure of the mind's capacity, there is no doubt that they are empty of inherent existence. The emptiness of the great is taught as the antidote to the mistaken assumption that because a phenomenon is immeasurable, it is therefore inherently existent. This emptiness is established on the first of the ten grounds, or the path of seeing.

The sixth emptiness is called the *emptiness of the ultimate.* "Ultimate" here does not mean ultimate existence or ultimate truth. "Ultimate" here refers to the ultimate goal of the path—the attainment of nirvana.

The seventh and the eighth emptinesses are the *emptiness of compounded phenomena* and the *emptiness of uncompounded phenomena.* Compounded phenomena refers to everything in the three realms of existence that comes into being as a result of causes and conditions. Uncompounded phenomena refers to phenomena that are not pervaded by causes and conditions, such as the emptiness of the three realms. These two emptinesses are the means to counteract sentient beings' diverse habits of grasping at true existence.

The sixth, seventh, and eighth forms of emptiness are established on the second, third, and fourth grounds.

The ninth is the *emptiness beyond extremes.* This emptiness is established on the basis of that which is beyond the extremes of eternalism and nihilism. The emptiness beyond extremes is established on the fifth ground.

The tenth is the *emptiness without beginning or end.* The basis for establishing emptiness in this case is cyclic existence, within which we have been cycling without beginning or end. Just as we come and go in our dreams without really getting anywhere, we have been coming and going in cyclic existence since beginningless time, and there is no end in sight. The emptiness without beginning or end is established on the sixth ground.

The eleventh is the *emptiness of that which is not to be abandoned.* The basis for this emptiness is the Mahayana path, which is not to be abandoned. *Not to be abandoned* is meant in contrast to the path of the individual vehicle, which from a Mahayana perspective is a path to be abandoned. This emptiness is practiced on the seventh ground.

The twelfth is the *emptiness of nature.* This refers primarily to compounded phenomena, which are ultimately empty of inherent existence. This emptiness is somewhat similar to the emptiness of emptiness, the main difference being that the emptiness of inherent existence of a phenomenon is not created by Buddha, or by karma, and so forth, but is in fact the actual nature of the phenomenon itself. The basis for the twelfth emptiness is the ultimate of mode of existence of phenomena. This emptiness is practiced on the eighth ground.

The thirteenth is the *emptiness of all phenomena.* The basis for establishing this emptiness is all phenomena. This also is a subject of the meditative equipoise of the eighth ground.

The fourteenth is the *emptiness of existence by way of its own characteristics.* The basis for this emptiness is the basis, the path, and the fruit. The basis is empty of existing by way of its own characteristics. The path is empty of existing by way of its own characteristics. The result or fruit is empty of existing by way of its own characteristics. This emptiness is practiced in the meditative equipoise of the ninth ground.

The fifteenth is the *emptiness of the unperceivable.* Past, present and future—time—is the basis for establishing this emptiness. Different philosophical schools understand time in different ways. The Sautrantika system asserts that if time is existent, it is the present, and that whatever is past and future is imputed by a conceptual mind. The Prasangika system asserts that time is exactly like the directions in the sense that it is established by dependence, and that there is no time that exists from its own side. According to the Prasangika, past, present, and future can only be designated in dependence upon one another. This emptiness is also an object of meditation on the ninth ground.

The sixteenth is the *emptiness of non-entityness*. The functioning entity itself, a cup, for example, is not the basis of emptiness here. Rather, the basis of emptiness is the cup's ability to hold liquid—its ability to perform its specific function. This emptiness is meditated upon in the equipoise of the tenth ground.

The remaining four emptinesses are subgroups of the sixteenth emptiness. Its divisions are the *emptiness of functioning things*, the *emptiness of non-things*, the *emptiness of self-nature*, and the *emptiness of other nature*. The emptiness of functioning things is established on the tenth ground. The last three emptinesses are established in the state of enlightenment.

A complete explanation of the twenty emptinesses can be found in the sixth chapter of Chandrakirti's *Supplement to the Middle Way*, and also in the first chapter of Maitreya's *Ornament of Clear Realization*.

The Logic of Dependent Arising

What is the difference between the realization of emptiness attained on the Mahayana path and the realization of emptiness attained on the path of the hearers and solitary realizers? In *Illumination of the Thought of the Middle Way*, Lama Tsongkhapa states that the emptiness that is realized on the path of the hearers and solitary realizers is not the emptiness of the two modes of selflessness established through limitless modes of logic and reasoning. The emptiness established on the Mahayana path, however, is particularly effective because it *has* been established on this basis. Thus, it can be said that the selflessness of phenomena and the selflessness of persons in the mind of a practitioner on the path of the hearers and solitary realizers are not established on the basis of the complete form of meditation. This emptiness has not been analyzed using the limitless aspects of logic and reasoning, whereas on the Mahayana path the emptiness realized is meditated upon in the most complete way.

Limitless aspects of logic and reasoning refers in this context to the logic of dependent arising, which is unique to the Prasangika system. In fact, in the Prasangika system, the logic of dependent arising is considered the very king of logic. If, in our meditation refuting the inherently existent "I" or the inherently existent aggregates, we make the mistake of over-negating and lean toward the view of nihilism, we can use the logic of dependent arising to correct ourselves. Of course, as beginners, when we then focus on the reasoning of dependent arising to establish that things do in fact exist, we may swing to the other extreme of perceiving things and events as existing inherently. In the beginning it is quite normal for our minds to fluctuate between the two extremes.

Dependent arising can be understood on two levels: gross and subtle. *Gross dependent arising* refers to the dependent arising of phenomena on the level of cause and effect and in terms of the interdependence of a thing's parts and its whole. This level of dependent arising is accepted by most Buddhist philosophical systems. Subtle dependent arising refers to the existence of phenomena in dependence upon the basis of imputation, the imputed label, and the imputing mind. This is the level of dependent arising asserted by proponents of the Prasangika system, whereby things exist only as merely labeled—through the interdependence of the basis of imputation, the imputed label, and the imputing mind. This more subtle level of understanding of dependent arising allows the Prasangika philosopher to refute a more subtle object of negation.

In *Root Wisdom,* Nagarjuna praised the sublime teaching of dependent arising as follows.

> That which is dependently arisen
> Has no cessation, no production,
> No break in a continuum, no permanence,
> No coming, no going,
> Is not one, nor many,
> And is free from elaboration.

What do these words mean? Nagarjuna is asserting that dependent phenomena are free from all of these modes of existence. Furthermore, Nagarjuna is implying that *because* phenomena are dependently arisen, they are free from such modes of existence.

According to Nagarjuna, the first two modes of existence that dependent arising negates are *cessation* and *production*. These points are meant to be considered in relation to the arising and the disintegration of functioning entities. Of course, if we think about it, we will realize that conventional phenomena actually *do* cease and *are* produced. We can understand this merely by observing the way things work in the world. Cessation and production occur as a result of causes and conditions, and in fact emptiness itself is what makes this possible. So what is Nagarjuna's point? *No cessation* and *no production* should be understood as no *inherent* cessation and no *inherent* production. Thus the statement becomes: "That which is dependently arisen/ has no inherent cessation, no inherent production." This is the meaning of the first two points.

The third and the fourth points refer to time. There is no inherent *break in a continuum* and no inherent *permanence*.

The fifth and the sixth points refer to the movement of objects. There is no inherently existent *coming* and there is no inherently existent *going*.

The seventh and eighth points refer to the fact that it is only in dependence upon imputation that we designate things as *one* or *many*. There is no inherently existent *one* or any inherently existent *many*. However, because things are empty, and because they are dependently arisen, we can establish them as one and many.

All these examples apply to the way that phenomena appear to the mind of an arya being in meditative equipoise. Please keep that in mind. When an arya being is in single-pointed concentration on the ultimate nature of conventional phenomena, in the face of emptiness, conventional phenomena do not appear to him or her. This is not, however, the way an ordinary being perceives conventional reality.

The most important point that you should take away from this quote of Nagarjuna's is that dependent arising and inherent existence are mutually exclusive—they cannot both exist on the basis of a single object. Therefore, if we say that phenomena exist inherently, we automatically eliminate their existing by way of dependence. Conversely, if we say that phenomena exist dependently, it is not logical to assert that they exist inherently. Take, for example, a person and his or her aggregates. We have a person because of his or her aggregates, and we have those aggregates because we have the person. It would not be logical to say that the person is inherently existent and that their aggregates exist in dependence upon that. In the same way, we cannot say that we are an "I" that is substantially existent and that our aggregates are dependent upon this "I."

Even if we talk a great deal about the "I" that travels in cyclic existence

carrying the weight of the contaminated aggregates and the "I" that wishes
for liberation and is trying to achieve that objective, as long as we fail to
determine the interdependent nature of the "I" and the aggregates, as long
as we persistently grasp at an inherently existing "I," everything that we do
becomes a cause for even more delusions and karma, no matter how much
we wish for liberation.

All four Buddhist philosophical schools accept existence through
dependent arising. But it is only the Prasangika system that accepts interdependence through mere imputation. Although the other schools accept
dependent arising, they accept it only as a basis of substantial existence.
The Prasangika system, however, does not accept even an atom of substantial existence. If it exists, according to them, it exists only by mere
imputation. According to the Prasangikas, the imputed label is *not* findable
in its basis at all. In the Prasangika system, the very fact that one cannot
find an imputed label to have any kind of substantial existence—the fact
that phenomena are without essence—means that they are empty of inherent existence. Phenomena exist only through dependence and through
imputation. According to the Prasangika, there is no such thing as something that is both substantially existent and also empty.

I have not given this explanation of the view on the basis of having realized it myself, but rather on the basis of what I have heard through the
course of my studies. In order to facilitate the realization of emptiness, we
should begin by studying extensively, cultivating the correct understanding of what we have studied, and meditating upon it. In addition, in order
for what we have studied to become an experience within our minds, we
should rely upon the instructions of our spiritual teachers and practice
pure devotion accompanied by extensive purification and the accumulation
of merit. If we practice in this way, we will definitely be able to develop the
sure ascertainment of these realizations.

Generally speaking, our understanding of emptiness will improve in
accordance with our intellect as we study and contemplate the teachings.
However, in order for our understanding of emptiness to be truly meaningful, we must be sure to consider whether it is acting as an antidote to
our delusions. We can measure this by checking our behavior and
thoughts—if we are able to apply the teachings and thus distance ourselves
from our delusions and the negative actions that arise as a result of them,

it is safe to say that our understanding of emptiness is having an effect upon our ego-grasping, ignorant minds. If, however, we have studied a great deal yet everything that we have thought about has had absolutely no effect on our ego-grasping, it is clear that our efforts have not produced the desired results.

Sometimes, having gone through a great deal of very difficult philosophical explanation on the view of emptiness, we may feel completely tired, fed up, or totally discouraged. Should feelings like that arise, we should examine the benefits of realizing the view and recall Lama Tsongkhapa's words:

Although you may meditate on renunciation and bodhichitta,
Without wisdom realizing the way things exist
You will be unable to cut the root of cyclic existence.
Therefore, persevere in the realization of dependent arising.

CONCLUSION

IN CLOSING, PLEASE REMEMBER that there is no path to enlightenment that lies outside your own mind. Whatever good qualities there are to be cultivated must be cultivated within your own mind. Whatever negativities there are to be eliminated must also be eliminated within your own mind. In fact, the main objective of Dharma practice is to limitlessly develop the positive potential of your own mind. Your mind can be limitlessly developed because its mental continuum is beginningless and without end, and because you have buddha-nature. Because the delusions, which are the cause of suffering, do not exist in the nature of your mind, suffering can be extinguished by eliminating the ignorance that is at its root. We have discussed this extensively in the preceding pages.

We have also talked a great deal about compassion. Please don't forget about compassion. Compassion is the goodness in your heart that feels for the pain and suffering of others. By suffering I mean the suffering of suffering, the suffering of change, and the suffering of pervasive conditioning. Every ordinary being feels compassion for others at the level of the suffering of suffering, such as compassion for the suffering of sickness, and disease, and so forth. Compassion based on the suffering of change and the suffering of pervasive conditioning is more subtle. And even more subtle than that is feeling compassion for the suffering of sentient beings who have the two obscurations. Even arhats who have attained nirvana become an object of compassion for bodhisattvas who have attained the path of accumulation. The depth of their compassion is unbelievable. We should aspire to practice as they do.

All of you have the basis for generating conventional bodhichitta in your minds. All of you have some basis of compassion—but your compassion at the moment is extremely polluted by your biased ways of thinking. Your compassion is conditional and limited. However, it is this very compassion, this limited compassion of yours, that is the foundation upon which you will develop a more honorable, noble sense of feeling for the suffering of other beings.

Since compassion constitutes the root of the spiritual path, particularly the Mahayana path, as you study the Dharma, as you study the *Lamrim Chenmo,* you should do so with compassion as your motivation. To make your activities of listening meaningful or effective for your spiritual path, your attitude should be rooted in the altruistic attitude of the Mahayana. And although you may have read or listened to many teachings that warn of the infinite failings of the self-cherishing mind, and you know about it, you understand it well, and although you can see that the mind that cherishes others is the basis of all positive qualities and the source of all of happiness, it is not sufficient to merely hear about these things, or even to meditate upon them in solitude. It is also very important for you to put these principles into practice as much as you can within your society or the community in which you live.

Moreover, Buddhism is now moving to the West, and many of you are voluntarily taking your first steps on the path of the Buddhadharma, and are taking ordination, which is the banner of victory on the path to enlightenment. Especially since you are practicing Mahayana Buddhism, the form of the universal vehicle, it is very, very important that the practices of renouncing self and cherishing others do not merely become the subject matter of your meditation sessions alone, but that they are implemented in the form of benefiting others as much as possible in the reality of your lives.

The essence of Dharma practice is being able to recognize your delusions and subdue them. Dharma practice doesn't just mean sitting on the meditation cushion—it has everything to do with the practicality of living and working with your negative states of mind, with lessening them, counteracting them when they arise, and ensuring that, once subdued, they do not arise again. Thus, it is very important that your Dharma training should also entail you actively engaging with society. It is not only a matter of cultivating positive thoughts, or fostering goodness and kindness in your attitude. For every meditation session that you do on cultivating the altruistic mind, you should allocate an equal amount of time in the post-meditation period to the practical engagement of that mind.

There is no doubt that many practitioners have a very clear wish to establish the profound Dharma in the West. In order to do this, you don't need many people. Just *one* person who is proficient in learning, with great perseverance, wisdom, and an extremely good heart can establish the Dharma in the West. So these days, most of the responsibility is on you.

My advice for you is this. First of all, as Westerners, you have to study well. At this time, many texts exist in the Tibetan tradition, so learning Tibetan is helpful. The translation of the Tibetan texts into Western languages is also very important. For us to assume that we should not bother to translate a certain work because it has already been translated once is not correct. It is much too early for us to think like that. Even if it has been translated once, it needs to be translated over and over again until it is completely refined. We should not imagine that just because someone went ahead and did it already, it will not be worthwhile to do it again. A talented runner doesn't stop running just because he or she has won a race—he runs again and again to establish better and better times. Bringing forth the translations of the Dharma in the West is the same thing.

Also, you must ensure that your Dharma practice is well-rounded and complete. You must study, go on retreat, do daily practice, accumulate merit—all of this together. If you put one hundred percent of your energy into studying the texts and never pay attention to purification and accumulation of merit, you are making a mistake. Saying, "Oh, *puja* is difficult—I don't want to pray, I want to study," is not the proper attitude to develop toward Dharma practice.

In the monasteries of Sera, Ganden, and Drepung, we have debating class twice a day. In the morning we debate for an hour, and then we recite the praises of the twenty-one Taras. Sometimes we recite them over sixty times. We make many prayers, and also recite the *Heart Sutra* and the lineage prayers and do some practice for the protectors. It is really essential that you, also, combine your study with the practices of accumulation of merit and purification in this way. When you do so, whatever you listen to and whatever understanding you develop will definitely affect your mind. On the basis of that understanding, whatever course of meditation you undertake will bring results. An individual who has accomplished effective listening, understanding, and meditation is an individual who can establish the roots of the Dharma in the West.

Following a spiritual path fulfills the very purpose of our lives in the very best of all possible ways, and gives great meaning to our existence. As human beings, we are endowed with so much potential. The capacity of our minds is limitless. Sometimes we are lazy, and we don't want to do anything at all. At these times we must think what a tremendous loss it will be if we do not use our minds. When we apply ourselves with effort, so much can be accomplished. And there is no more pure and unmistaken way to apply our minds than to study and practice the graduated path to enlightenment. On the basis of the lamrim teachings, practitioners of the past have achieved incredibly fruitful results. Also, there are many people training in the practices of the lamrim in the present who are now achieving meaningful results. In the future, too, because of the profundity and depth of these teachings, those who have the occasion to study and practice them will enjoy their fruits.

In the *Lamrim Chenmo,* Lama Tsongkhapa, in his infinite kindness, has amassed a manual for practicing the entire graduated path to enlightenment. As I mentioned in the beginning, on the basis of familiarizing yourself with this text, you will have familiarized yourself with all of the major points of practice on the path and all of the major topics that are presented in the philosophical texts of our tradition. With this as your foundation, you have opened the door to your path to enlightenment. All that remains for you to do is to step through it.

On your part, by studying these teachings and attempting to actualize them in your minds, you have made an extensive offering of practice to the buddhas and bodhisattvas, and accumulated vast stores of merit. From my side, although I am completely lacking in qualities, and have no uncontrived renunciation, bodhichitta, or wisdom, I am certain that I have participated in these teachings free of the thought seeking the eight worldly dharmas—better food, better clothing, and better reputation.

Therefore, to ensure that our merit is dedicated in the best possible way, let us dedicate it now to the long existence of the teachings of Shakyamuni Buddha in the world. In particular, let us dedicate it to the long life of His Holiness the Dalai Lama, and that all of his wishes may be fulfilled.

Also, let us dedicate it to the long life and immediate fulfillment of every single wish of Lama Zopa Rinpoche, and to Lama Yeshe's reincarnation, Lama Ösel, so that he may complete his studies with great success and be of infinite benefit to sentient beings.

Thank you very much.

DEDICATION

By Lama Zopa Rinpoche

BY THE VIRTUE COLLECTED from giving this commentary on the lamrim and making it into a book, may the Buddha of Compassion, His Holiness the Dalai Lama—who is the only object of refuge for all sentient beings and the originator of all living beings' happiness—have a stable life for eons equaling the number of drops in the ocean, and may it cause all of his works to succeed immediately without any obstacle.

May the mainland Chinese officials be able to realize what His Holiness is. May they be able to see that his motivation is only impartial, non-discriminating compassion, and that he cherishes the mainland Chinese officials with a compassion and affectionate love that is thousands of times greater than the love they have for themselves. May they be able to realize that the purpose of His Holiness existing in the world is for them—for their peace, happiness and freedom—and may they be able to devote themselves to His Holiness, and do exactly as His Holiness wishes. May they invite His Holiness to mainland China to spread the Dharma like the sun rising, giving opportunity to their own country and their own people, as well as to Tibet. And may there be total religious freedom in Tibet, so that the Dharma can spread even more than before.

May all the holy beings of the different traditions in this world be able to benefit others without hindrance, and may all their holy wishes succeed immediately.

May all the Sangha, who are preserving and spreading the Dharma, receive all the lineages of teachings and may they have realizations by living in pure Vinaya, pure morality. May they receive whatever they need.

May the teaching of Buddha and particularly Lama Tsongkhapa's teaching, especially the lamrim—which is the only medicine for eliminating sentient beings' suffering—spread in all directions, and flourish forever in this world. May everyone in the world be able to meet Lama Tsongkhapa's teaching and actualize it in their hearts.

May anyone who reads this lamrim text, and not only those who read and practice it, but also those who hear, think, or talk about it and those who have this book and listen to its contents have all their heavy negative karmas purified immediately. May they never ever be reborn in the lower realms—as hell beings, hungry ghosts, or animals. May they find unshakeable faith in refuge and karma and immediately actualize guru devotion—the root of the path to enlightenment. And may they also actualize bodhichitta and the highest tantric realization of clear light in this very lifetime.

By this book existing in the world, in any country, area, or house, may the karma of all sentient beings be purified; may they never, ever be reborn in the lower realms, and may all their sicknesses, curable and incurable, be healed. May all those who are harmed by spirits and become crazy, immediately be pacified and free from spirit harm and spirit possession, including those who are suffering from what is called schizophrenia in the West.

May all those painful, disturbed minds of strong desire and anger that create so much turmoil in the world—like a tornado, crazy—and that cause so much violence, so much fear and worry, and so many disasters, be pacified. By generating loving-kindness, compassion and the wish-fulfilling precious thought of bodhichitta—letting go of I and cherishing others—may the whole world be filled with peace and happiness and may every individual's life be filled with much peace and happiness.

May nobody experience war, famine, disease, torture, or poverty, and may this book cause everyone to have wealth, a long life, and health. May this book act like a medicine to heal all heavy mental problems. May those who suffer from depression be healed and may their hearts fill up with bliss. May those who have relationship problems that make their minds like hell immediately have their hearts filled with loving-kindness, compassion and joy, and may they be able to cause each other much peace and happiness.

May those who are looking for a guru be able to find perfectly qualified Mahayana gurus. May those who want to receive teachings be able to receive unmistaken teachings. May those who want to do retreat be able to find a conducive environment with all the facilities they need, and may they be able to receive the realizations of whatever they meditate upon, instantly.

May those who are suffering from failure have success. May all the worries and fears of those who are dying be stopped and may their hearts be filled with immeasurable joy and peace. May they immediately be born in a pure land of Buddha where they can attain enlightenment or receive a perfect human body and be able to complete the path.

In this way, may this book become wish-fulfilling for the happiness of all sentient beings in the world. May it cause all sentient beings to actualize the path to enlightenment in their minds and to quickly achieve enlightenment.

May Yangsi Rinpoche himself have a long life and be able to offer skies of benefit to sentient beings and to the teachings of the Buddha, just as Lama Tsongkhapa did. And may the same thing happen to all the readers of this commentary to the lamrim.

Aptos House, Kachoe Dechen Ling
Dictated to Ven. Sarah, November 2002

APPENDIX:
OUTLINE OF THE TEXT

NOTES

1   The three types of vows are the vows of individual liberation, the bodhi-sattva vows, and the tantric vows.

2   Listening to teachings can refer to listening to oral commentary on a text or to reading it.

3   Lama Tsongkhapa's two heart disciples were Gyalstab Je and Khedrup Je.

4   The Kadampa tradition is an early lineage of Tibetan Buddhism that began with the great Lama Atisha and his disciples. The teachings of this lineage particularly emphasize the practical application of Buddha's teachings, especially the lamrim, in daily life.

5   Becoming a rinpoche refers to becoming a reincarnate lama in the Tibetan tradition. Reincarnate lamas in the Gelug tradition often become teachers as well.

6   The four types of ordained people are novice monks, novice nuns, fully ordained monks, and fully ordained nuns.

7   The five heinous crimes are killing your mother, killing your father, killing an arhat, drawing blood from a buddha, and causing a division within the spiritual community.

8   A *naga* is a type of water spirit that inhabits the earth.

9   If at any time you should happen to experience any delusional sense of pride in your own spiritual accomplishments, the advice of the lamas of the past is to take a look and see whether you have even developed the aspiration of a practitioner of the small or medium scope.

10   Further examples cited to exemplify impermanence and death are a stream flowing downhill, or a flash of lightning in the sky.

11   In tantric practice in particular, the best time to train in the techniques of the channels, winds, and drops is when we are endowed with the vitality of youth.

12   When in retreat, it is common for practitioners to divide the day into four sessions of meditation: the first before sunrise, one in the midmorning, one in the afternoon, and one after sunset.

13   Beings born in the northern continent do have a definite lifespan. An indefinite lifespan is characteristic of the beings of our continent, Jambudvipa.

14   The five great degenerations are the degenerations of life, delusions, view, person, and time.

15 According to the *Treasury of Knowledge*, at the end of the eon a world system is destroyed by the elements.

16 The 10th, 25th, and 30th of the Tibetan month are considered particularly auspicious dates.

17 Differentiating inner and outer paths is usually done from the point of view of philosophy, based on the four seals. In order to be considered a follower of Buddhist tenets, you do not need to realize the four seals, but only accept and understand them.

18 These actions can be from previous lifetimes or an earlier part of this lifetime.

19 A defeat is incurred when a root vow is broken.

20 In tantric practice there are four types of activities: peaceful, increasing, powerful, and wrathful.

21 The eight Mahayana precepts are twenty-four-hour vows that include not taking an evening meal.

22 This is discussed extensively in the section on patience in this text and also in Shantideva's *Guide to the Bodhisattva's Way of Life*.

23 This refers to the cyclic existence in one individual's continuum. This point is argued by some scholars who present the idea that cyclic existence is without end based on the fact that wherever there is space, there are sentient beings. As space is infinite, they reason, we cannot recognize the end of cyclic existence. Before the coming of Lama Tsongkhapa, many great Tibetan masters stated that there is no end to cyclic existence. Those who asserted this generally said that although all sentient beings are suited to attaining enlightenment, it is not definite that they will become enlightened, and hence there is no end to cyclic existence. For example, you can plant a seed in a field, and give it water and so on. Although this seed has the potential to grow, whether it will grow or not is not certain. In the same way, according to this view, all sentient beings have buddha-nature, or the potential for attaining enlightenment, but it is uncertain whether or not they will actually become enlightened. Based on that reasoning, these scholars say that cyclic existence is without end. However, the Prasangika system does posit an end to cyclic existence.

24 The Chittamatras accept the five sense consciousnesses, the mental consciousness, the deluded mental consciousness, and the fundamental consciousness. Vaibashikas, Sautrantikas, Svatantrika-Madhyamikas, and Prasangika-Madhyamikas all accept the grouping of six states of consciousness: the five sensory consciousnesses and the mental consciousness.

25 For further discussion of this issue, see Vasubhandu's *Treasury of Knowledge*.

26 The five Mahayana paths are the path of accumulation, the path of

preparation, the path of seeing, the path of meditation, and the path of no more learning.

27 Absorption at the heart does not refer to absorption in the heart organ, but rather in the heart chakra where the body's channels gather. This is not something that our gross sense consciousness can directly perceive.

28 The thirty-seven limbs of enlightenment comprise four states of mindfulness, four pure forms of abandonment, four types of psychic path, the five powers, the five forces, the seven limbs of enlightenment, and the eight arya's paths.

29 One of two methods for generating the mind of bodhichitta that is explained in the *Lamrim Chenmo.* See part 5, "The Great Scope."

30 This explanation is from Maitreya's *Ornament for the Mahayana Sutras,* which was written in accordance with the Chittamatra school or Mind-Only school of thought. According to the Chittamatra system, an arhat first attains nirvana with remainder, and then attains nirvana without remainder. When nirvana without remainder is attained, it is said that a complete break or cessation in the mental continuum occurs. Because of this, there cannot be a continual flow of virtue. This is the viewpoint of the proponents of the Mind-Only school, who accept three ultimate vehicles. In contrast, the Prasangika system does not assert any kind of break in the flow of virtue in the mind of an arhat.

31 There is an extensive discussion of the way that bodhisattvas "overshadow" arhats in the philosophical texts of the Gelug lineage, such as Lama Tsongkhapa's *Dbu ma dgongs pa rab gsal* and Sera Je Jetsunpa's *Dbu ma'i spyi don.*

32 As a note, although it is advised that we generate spontaneous renunciation of the medium scope before we generate the realizations of the great scope, it is not necessary to generate the spontaneous realizations of the small scope before we move on to the practice of the medium scope.

33 In fact, this is the case even should the Mahayana practitioner incur a wrong view on the path, take rebirth in the hell realms, and then again take a high rebirth and, due to previous imprints, continue on the Mahayana path to attain enlightenment. This is because the practitioner who begins on the Hinayana path will attain the state of an arhat, and as a result of arhathood will remain in a state of blissful meditative equipoise for eons and eons before even entering the Mahayana path.

34 The six basis constituents are consciousness, wind, fire, water, earth, and wisdom.

35 In the Gelug tradition the three great monasteries of Tibet are Ganden, Drepung, and Sera. These monasteries were well-established centers of

study and practice in Tibet, and were reestablished in exile in India after 1959.

36   Shakyamuni Buddha is the fourth buddha of our time.

37   The complete text of the refuge and bodhichitta prayer can be found in *Guru Puja,* by the Fifth Panchen Lama, Losang Chokyi Gyaltsen.

38   This mind is generated on the path of seeing.

39   According to Lama Tsongkhapa, when a fully ordained person gives up on the thought to benefit sentient beings and then utilizes possessions that are above a certain value for only his or her own benefit, a defeat is incurred. This fault is especially serious when other sentient beings *know* that all of this person's possessions have been dedicated to the benefit of others. Other interpretations of Vinaya say that there is no way a defeat could be incurred, because those sentient beings to whom the possessions are dedicated are infinite, and having divided up one's possessions between all of them, there is no way any possession could fulfill the minimum value that is required to incur a defeat.

40   However, in *Supplement to the "Middle Way"* by Chandrakirti, it is stated that merits accumulated over a *hundred* eons by generosity, ethics, and so forth can be destroyed in one moment of anger. The reason for the difference between these two is that when bodhisattvas with lower realizations generate anger toward bodhisattvas of higher realizations, one thousand eons of merit can be destroyed in one moment. In the cases of bodhisattvas with higher realizations who generate anger in relation to bodhisattvas of lower realizations, one hundred eons of merit can be destroyed.

41   The only ultimate antidote to any delusion or obstacle is the wisdom realizing emptiness.

42   The Chittamatra system promotes the "mind-only" view, in which all things exist by the power of the imprints in the mind.

Glossary of Tibetan Names and Terms

afflictive obscurations	Obstacles to individual liberation.
aggregates	The collection of the mind and body of a sentient being.
arhat	A being who has obtained complete liberation from cyclic existence.
arya being	A being who has realized emptiness directly.
Arya Tara	A female buddha whose sadhana is widely practiced in Tibetan Buddhism.
asura, demi god	A higher realm being in the desire realm.
bardo	The state of existence between death and rebirth, also known as the "intermediate state."
bhikshu	A fully ordained monk.
bodhichitta	The wish to attain enlightenment for the benefit of all sentient beings.
bodhisattva	A person who has totally dedicated him or her self to benefiting others.
Brahma	A worldly god.
brahmin	One of the highest castes within the ancient Indian social structure.
buddha-nature	The potential to become enlightened that exists within every sentient being's mind.
causal motivation	The primary motivation for an action.
Chenrezig	The Buddha of Compassion.
conventional truth	Something that seems to be true to an ordinary consciousness but in reality is false.

crown wind	The wind or energy that abides in the upper part of the body.
dakas and dakinish	Male and female deities who offer special support to tantric practitioners.
deity yoga	The practice of generating oneself as a deity.
desire realm	The first of the three realms of cyclic existence; characterized by being a realm of sentient beings who have not eliminated the gross delusions of the three realms; this is the realm we live in.
Dharma, Buddhadharma	The teachings of Buddha.
direct mental perception	The perception of the object by a mental consciousness that observes it without a generic image.
direct yogic perception	The consciousness of an arya being that realizes emptiness directly.
directionally partless particles of atoms	An atom that is unable to be categorized as having parts that have directions.
eight freedoms	Eight states of freedom from the extremes of unfortunate and pleasurable conditions of rebirth that define a precious human rebirth.
eight Mahayana precepts	Twenty-four hour vows for Mahayana practitioners.
eight worldly concerns/ dharmas	The common interests of ordinary beings that are considered hindrances to benefiting others.
emptiness	The lack of inherent existence in phenomena.
Fifth Buddha	Buddha Maitreya.
five aggregates	Form, feeling, discrimination, compositional factors, and consciousness.
five determining factors of a primary mind	Feeling, discrimination, intention, contact, and attention.
five great degenerations	The degenerations of life, delusions, view, person, and time.

five paths	The stages of the bodhisattva path.
form realm	The second of the three realms of cyclic existence; characterized by being a realm of sentient beings who have eliminated the gross delusions of the desire realms.
formless realm	The third of the three realms of cyclic existence; characterized by being a realm of sentient beings who have eliminated the gross delusions of the desire and form realms.
four bodies of a buddha	Nature body, truth body, enjoyment body, and emanation body.
four continents	In Buddhist cosmology the eastern, southern, western, and northern continents that make up our world system.
four immeasurable thoughts	Immeasurable love, immeasurable compassion, immeasurable equanimity, and immeasurable joy.
four levels of meditative absorption	Four levels of consciousness that exist in the mind of a being in the form realm.
four noble truths	The first teachings that Buddha gave after his enlightenment.
Gelug tradition	The fourth of the four schools of Tibetan Buddhism; established by Lama Tsongkhapa.
Guhyasamaja Tantra	One of the main tantric practices in Tibetan Buddhism; one of the three main tantric practices of the Gelug lineage.
Hashang	A famous ancient Chinese master who strongly emphasized the doctrine of no-thought.
hearer	A realized practitioner of the Hinayana who relies upon a spiritual community.
immediate motivation	The secondary motivation for an action, made right before the action is actually done.
impure grounds	The first seven bodhisattva grounds.

individual vehicle	Also known as Hinayana or "lower vehicle;" practitioners of this path seek individual liberation from cyclic existence.
individual vows of liberation	Vows from the tradition of Vinaya.
inferential cognition of belief	A mind that knows things correctly based belief rooted in logic.
inferential valid cognition	A mind that knows things correctly based on logic.
innate grasping at true existence	The mind that spontaneously grasps at things as being truly existent.
Kadampa	A lineage of practice and teachings begun by Lama Atisha in the tenth century.
Kagyu	The second of the four schools of Tibetan Buddhism; established by Marpa.
karma	Cause and effect.
learned grasping at true existing	The mind that grasps at things as being truly existent as a result of the influence of invalid logic and reason.
mahasiddha	A great adept.
main mind	The mind that apprehends the nature of the object.
Maitreya	The Buddha of Love.
Manjushri	The Buddha of Wisdom.
McLeod Ganj	A small town in northern India where His Holiness the Dalai Lama lives.
meditative equipoise	The state of meditation in which there is no duality between subject and object.
mudra	Ritual hand gesture.
naga	A spirit of the natural environment.
nature body of a buddha	One of the four bodies of a buddha.

nine levels of meditative concentration, nine levels of mental placement, nine stages of placing the mind	The steps of practice that result in the attainment of calm-abiding.
noncompositional factors	Any functioning thing that is not form or consciousness.
Nyingma	The first of the four schools of Tibetan Buddhism; established by Guru Padmasambhava.
obscurations to omniscience	Obstacles to enlightenment.
parinirvana	A quality of enlightenment.
path of seeing	The third of the five Mahayana paths, marked by the practitioner experiencing the direct realization of emptiness.
pratimoksha	The ethics of Vinaya.
preceptor	The person who gives precepts.
preta	Hungry ghost; one of the six types of being in the desire realm.
puja	An offering ritual or prayer.
renunciation	The wish for individual liberation from cyclic existence.
root downfall	Actually breaking a root vow.
root guru	The spiritual teacher that has the greatest positive influence on a particular disciple's spiritual life and practice.
sadhana	A daily prayer ritual involving generating oneself as the deity.
Sakya	The third of the four schools of Tibetan Buddhism; established by Khön Konchok Gyalpo.
samaya	Commitment or vow.

Sangha	Conventionally, four or more ordained people, or ultimately, a person who has realized emptiness directly.
secondary mind	The mind that apprehends the attributes of the object.
single-pointed concentration	A consciousness that can hold itself on an object without distraction indefinitely.
six perceptions	The five sense consciousnesses (eye, nose, ear, tongue, and body) and the mental consciousness.
six perfections	The common practice of bodhisattvas: giving, ethics, patience, joyous effort, cocentration, and wisdom.
solitary realizer	A realized practitioner of the Hinayana who does not rely upon a spiritual community.
stupa	A Buddhist shrine that often contains relics of buddhas and great teachers.
sura, god, deva	A higher realm being in the desire or form realm.
sutra	The tradition of teachings given by Shakyamuni Buddha in the aspect of a fully ordained monk.
tangka	Traditional Tibetan painted, drawn, or appliqued images of deities, usually brocaded in silk.
tantra	The tradition of teachings given by Shakyamuni Buddha in the aspect of Buddha Vajradhara.
tathagata	Literally, "one gone beyond:; an epithet for a buddha.
ten directions	The four cardinal directions, the four ordinal directions, above, and below.
ten endowments	Ten harmonious conditions for practicing Dharma in a human lifetime that define a precious human rebirth.
ten grounds	The stages of the bodhisattva path from the path of seeing onward.

ten virtues/nonvirtues	Ten positive and negative actions of body, speech, and mind.
thoroughly established phenomena	A phenomena that is the object of ultimate wisdom.
three higher trainings	The trainings of ethics, concentration, and wisdom.
Three Jewels	Buddha, Dharma, and Sangha.
three poisons	Attachment, anger, and ignorance.
three realms	The desire, form, and formless realms.
three spheres	The agent, object, and action.
three times	Past, present, and future.
three turnings of the wheel of Dharma	The teachings given by Buddha after his enlightenment in accordance with the mind level of three different types of disciples.
three vast collections of the teachings	The Tripitaka, or baskets of Sutra, Abhidharma, and Vinaya.
throwing karma	The main karma that determines future rebirth.
throwing links	The three causal links that bring about the next rebirth within the twelve links of dependent origination.
torma	Offering cake.
tsa-tsa	A small statue of a deity or a holy object made from a mold.
twelve links of dependent origination	The map of the way that sentient beings are born to this life and travel to the next.
ultimate truth	Something that seems to be true to a direct valid cognition and is in reality true.
universal vehicle	Also known as Mahayana or "great vehicle;" practitioners of this path seek enlightenment for the sake of others.

vajra	A tantric ritual instrument that symbolizes indestructibility.
vajra master	The teacher from whom you receive tantric initiation.
vajra position	Sometimes also called lotus position; a meditation posture in which both feet cross and rest on the thighs.
Vajradhara	The form that Buddha Shakyamuni manifested in order to teach the tantric path.
Vajrapani	The Buddha of Power.
Vajrasattva	An enlightened being who manifested for the purpose of helping sentient beings purify broken samaya and negative karma.
Vajrayana	The tantric vehicle.
valid cognition	A mind that knows things correctly.
wrong livelihood	Intentionally making a living from a profession that is not in accordance with the ten virtues.

BIBLIOGRAPHY OF
PRINCIPAL SOURCES

"P" refers to *The Tibetan Tripiṭaka,* Peking Edition, Tibetan Tripiṭaka Research Institute, Tokyo and Kyoto, 1956; and "Toh." to *A Complete Catalogue of the Tibetan Buddhist Canons,* Sendai: Tohoku Imperial University Press, 1934, an index to the Derge edition of the *Kangyur* and *Tengyur.*

Sutras are listed by title in English followed by Sanskrit and Tibetan. Indian, Tibetan, and Modern works are listed by author, editor, or translator where applicable.

A. SUTRAS

Array of Stalks Sutra
Śālistambasūtra
Sā lu'i ljang pa'i mdo
P876, Vol. 34

Condensed Sutra on the Perfection of Wisdom/
Heart of the Perfection of Wisdom Sutra (Heart Sutra)
Prajñapāramitāhṛdayasūtra
Shes rab snying po'i mdo
P160, Vol. 6

Diamond Cutter Sutra
Vajracchedikasūtra
Rdo rje gcod pa'i mdo
P739, Vol. 21

Sutra of the Inconceivable Mind
Akṣayamatisūtra
Blo gros mi zad pa'i mdo
P842, Vol. 34

Sutra on the Perfection of Wisdom
Śatasāhasrikāprajñapāramitāsūtra
Shes rab kyi pha rol tu phyin pa stong phrag brgya pa'i mdo
P730, Vol. 12–18

Sutra Unraveling the Thought of the Buddha
Saṃdhinirmocanasūtra
Dgongs pa nges par 'grel pa'i mdo
P774, Vol. 29

B. INDIAN WORKS

Aryadeva
    Four Hundred Stanzas
    Catuḥśataka: Catuḥśatakaśāstrakārikā
    Bstan bcos bzhi brgya pa
    P5246, Vol. 95

Asanga
    Bodhisattva Grounds
    Bodhisattvabhūmi
    Byang chub sems dpa'i sa
    P5538, Vol. 110

    Compendium of Ascertainments
    Viniścayasaṃgrahaṇī
    Rnam nges rnam par gtan la dbab pa bsdus ba
    P5539, Volumes 110–111

Atisha
Lamp for the Path to Enlightenment
Bodhipathapradipa
Byang chub lam gyi sgron ma
P5343, Vol. 103

Bhavaviveka
Heart of the Middle Way
Madhyamakahṛdayakārikā
Dbu ma'i snying po
P5255, Vol. 96

Lamp of Wisdom
Prajñāpradīpamūlamadhyamakavṛtti
Dbu ma rtsa ba'i 'grel pa shes rab sgron ma
P5253, Vol. 95

Buddhapalita
Buddhapalita's Commentary on "Root Wisdom of the Middle Way"
Buddhapalitamūlamadhyamakavṛtti
Dbu ma rtsa ba'i 'grel pa bud dha pa li ta
P5242, Vol. 95

Chandrakirti
Clear Words, A Commentary on "Treatise on the Middle Way"
Mūlamadhyamakavṛttiprasannapadā
Dbu ma rtsa ba'i 'grel pa tshig gsal ba
P5260, Vol. 98

Supplement to the "Middle Way"
Madhyamakāvatāra
Dbu ma la 'jug pa
P5262, Vol. 98

Dharmakīrti
Commentary on the "Compendium on Valid Cognition"
Pramāṇavārttikakārikā
Tshad ma rnam 'grel
P5709, Vol. 130

Haribhadra
Commentary on the Clear Meaning
Abhisamayālaṃkāravṛtti
Mngon par rtogs pa'i rgyan gyi 'grel pa
better known as 'Grel pa don gsal
P5191, Vol. 90

Kamalashila
Stages of Meditation
Bhāvanākrama
Sgom pa'i rim pa
P5310-12, Vol. 102

Maitreya
Discrimination between the Middle Way and Extremes
Madhyāntavibhāga
Dbus mtha rnam 'byed
P5522, Vol 108

Ornament for the Mahayana Sutras
Mahāyānasūtralaṃkāra
Theg pa chen po'i mdo sde rgyan
P5521, Vol. 108

Ornament of Clear Realization
Abhisamayālaṃkāra
Mngon par rtogs pa'i rgyan
P5184, Vol. 88

Sublime Continuum
Ratnagotravibhāgamahāyānottaratantraśāstra
Rgyud bla ma
P5525, Vol. 108

Nagarjuna
Compendium of All Sutras
Sūtrasamuccaya
Mdo kun las btus pa
P5330, Vol. 102

Eliminating All Arguments
Vigrahavyāvartanī
Rtsod pa bzlog pa
P5228, Vol. 95

Friendly Letter
Suhr̥llekha
Bshes pa'i spring yig
P5682, Vol. 129

Precious Garland of Advice for the King
Rājaparikathāratnāvalī
Rgyal po la gtam bya ba rin po che'i phreng ba
P5658, Vol. 129

Root Wisdom of the Middle Way
Prajñānāmamūlamadhyamakakārikā
Dbu ma rtsa ba shes rab
P5224, Vol. 95

Seventy Verses on Emptiness
Śūnyatāsaptatī
Stong pa nyid bdun cu pa
P5227, Vol. 95

Sixty Verses on Logic
Yuktiṣaṣṭikā
Rigs pa drug cu pa
P5225, Vol. 95

Thorough Investigation
Vaidālayprakaraṇā
Zhib mo rnam 'thag
P5230, Vol. 95

Shantideva
   Compendium of Trainings
   Śikṣāsamuccaya
   Bslab pa kun las bsdus pa
   P5336, Vol. 102

   Guide to the Bodhisattva's Way of Life
   Bodhisattvacaryāvatāra
   Byang chub sems dpa'i spyod pa la 'jug pa
   P5272, Vol. 99

Vasubhandu
   Treasury of Knowledge
   Abhidharmakośabhāṣya
   Chos mngon pa'i mdzod
   P5591, Vol. 115

C. TIBETAN WORKS

Dpad ma rgyal mtshan Blo gling Mkhan zur
   The Golden Spoon: A Detailed Exegesis of the Drepung Loseling Tradi-
   tion of Commentatorial Treatment of Madhyamika Philosophy
   Zab don gdams pa'i mig 'byed gser gyi thur ma

Bsod nams rgya mtsho
   Essence of Refined Gold
   Lam rim gser zhun ma

Dge bshes Glang ri thang pa
  Eight Verses of Mind Training
  Blo sbyong tshigs brgyad ma

Dkon mchog bstan pa'i sgron me
  Collected Works
  Gsung 'bum

Lcang skya Rol pa'i rdo rje
  Tenets
  Grub mtha'

Mkhas grub Dge legs dpal bzang po
  Dose of Emptiness
  Stong thun chen mo

Ngag dbang blo bzang rgya mtsho
  Instruction from Manjushri
  'Jam dpal 'zal lung

Rgyal tshab Dar ma rin chen
  Ornament of the Essence: A Thorough Commentary of the Wisdom Gone Beyond
  Mngon par rtogs pa'i rgyan gyi 'grel pa dobn gsal rnam bshad snying po rgyan

Rje btsun Mi las ra pa
  The Collected Songs of Milarepa
  Mi la'i mgur bum

Se ra Rje bstun Chos kyi rgyal mtshan
  Commentary on Madhyamaka
  Du ma'i spyi don

Thu'u bkwan Blo bzang chos kyi nyi ma
  Crystal Mirror of Tenets
  Grub mtha shel gyi me long

Tsong kha pa Blo bzang grags pa
Essence of Eloquence: Distinguishing the Interpretable and the Definitive Meanings of All the Scriptures of the Buddha
Drang ba dang nges pa'i don rnam par phye ba'i bstan bcod legs bshad snying po

Golden Rosary of Eloquence
Legs bshad gser gyi 'phreng ba

Great Commentary on "Root Wisdom"
Rtsa shes tik chen

Great Treatise on the Stages of the Path to Enlightenment
Byang chub lam gyi rim pa chen mo

Illumination of the Thought of the Middle Way
Dbu ma la 'jug pa'i rnam bshad dgongs pa rab gsal

Lines of Experience
Rang gi togs pa brjod pa mdo tsam du bshad pa

Medium Treatise on the Stages of the Path to Enlightenment
Byang chub lam gyi rim pa chung ba

Praise of Dependent Arising
Rten 'brel bstod pa

Prayer of the Beginning, Middle, and End
Thog mta' ma

Small Treatise on the Stages of the Path to Enlightenment
Byang chub lam gyi rim pai nyams len gyi rnam gzhags mdor bsdus

Three Principal Paths
Lam gyi tso bo rnam pa gsum

D. MODERN WORKS AND ENGLISH TRANSLATIONS

Cabezon, Jose. *A Dose of Emptiness*. Albany, New York: State University of New York Press, 1992.

Cutler, Joshua W.C. ed., The Lamrim Chenmo Translation Committee. *The Great Treatise on the Stages of the Path to Enlightenment*. Vol. 1. Ithaca, New York: Snow Lion Publications, 2000.

———, The Lamrim Chenmo Translation Committee. *The Great Treatise on the Stages of the Path to Enlightenment*. Vol. 3. Ithaca, New York: Snow Lion Publications, 2002.

Hopkins, Jeffrey. *Meditations on Emptiness*. Boston: Wisdom Publications, 1996.

Hopkins, Jeffrey. *Emptiness in the Mind-Only School of Tibetan Buddhism*. Berkeley and Los Angeles: University of California Press, 1999.

Loden, Geshe Acharya Thubten. *Path to Enlightenment in Tibetan Buddhism*. Melbourne: Tushita Publications, 1993.

Pabongka Rinpoche. *Liberation in the Palm of Your Hand*. Boston: Wisdom Publications, 1991.

Rinchen, Geshe Sonam. Edited and translated by Ruth Sonam. *Atisha's Lamp for the Path to Enlightenment*. Ithaca, New York: Snow Lion Publications, 1997.

Sopa, Geshe Lhundrub with David Patt. *Steps on the Path to Enlightenment: A Commentary on Tsongkhapa's Lamrim Chenmo*. Edited by Beth Newman. Vol. 1. Boston: Wisdom Publications, 2003 (forthcoming).

———. *Cutting Through Appearances*. Ithaca, New York: Snow Lion Publications, 1989.

Thurman, Robert. *The Central Philosophy of Tibet*. Princeton, New Jersey: Princeton University Press, 1984.

INDEX

ABOUT WISDOM

WISDOM PUBLICATIONS, a nonprofit publisher, is dedicated to making available authentic Buddhist works for the benefit of all. We publish translations of the sutras and tantras, commentaries and teachings of past and contemporary Buddhist masters, and original works by the world's leading Buddhist scholars. We publish our titles with the appreciation of Buddhism as a living philosophy and with the special commitment to preserve and transmit important works from all the major Buddhist traditions.

To learn more about Wisdom, or to browse books online, visit our website at wisdompubs.org.

You may request a copy of our mail-order catalog online or by writing to:

Wisdom Publications
199 Elm Street
Somerville, Massachusetts 02144 USA
Telephone: (617) 776-7416
Fax: (617) 776-7841
Email: info@wisdompubs.org
www.wisdompubs.org

THE WISDOM TRUST

As a nonprofit publisher, Wisdom is dedicated to the publication of fine Dharma books for the benefit of all sentient beings and dependent upon the kindness and generosity of sponsors in order to do so. If you would like to make a donation to Wisdom, please do so through our Somerville office. If you would like to sponsor the publication of a book, please write or email us at the address above.

Thank you.

Wisdom is a nonprofit, charitable 501(c)(3) organization affiliated with the Foundation for the Preservation of the Mahayana Tradition (FPMT).

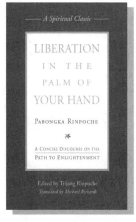

Liberation in the Palm of Your Hand: A Concise Discourse on the Path to Enlightenment

Pabongka Rinpoche
Edited by Trijang Rinpoche
896 pages, ISBN 0-86171-500-4, $24.95

This classic guide for the study, practice, and realization of Budhist teachings is one of the fundamental texts of Tibetan Buddhism. Pabongka Rinpoche, a remarkable teacher who died in the twentieth century, gave a twenty-four-day teaching to a mass gathering of monks, nuns, and lay people in 1921 that was a complete synthesis of all the Buddha's teachings. This book is a translation from Tibetan of the notes from that teaching taken by Trijang Rinpoche, who became the current Dalai Lama's tutor. This book contains most of the famous "teaching" stories of Tibetan Buddhism.

"A comprehensive and straightforward guide on how to meditate on each step of the path."—*Tricycle*

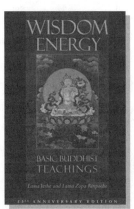

Wisdom Energy—25th Anniversary Edition: Basic Buddhist Teachings

Lama Yeshe and Lama Zopa Rinpoche
160 pages, ISBN 0-86171-170-X, $14.95

"In this wonderful book, Lama Yeshe and Lama Zopa Rinpoche—two highly accomplished Tibetan Buddhist teachers—bring alive the rich tradition of Buddhism in a way that is directly relevant to modern life. Filled with profound wisdom and useful advice, *Wisdom Energy* is a lucid introduction to the key principles and practices of the Buddhism. I highly recommend this exceptional book."—Howard C. Cutler, M.D., co-author of *The Art of Happiness*

**Steps on the Path to Enlightenment:
A Commentary on the Lamrim Chenmo,
Volume 1**
By Geshe Lhundub Sopa
Foreword by Tenzin Gyatso,
H.H. the Fourteenth Dalai Lama
556 pages, cloth ISBN 0-86171-346-X, $39.95

Volume I of a comprehensive and authoritative
five-volume commentary on the *Lamrim
Chenmo*, this much-anticipated work by the
renowned Buddhist scholar, Geshe Sopa, goes into great detail to ensure
the greatest understanding of a lengthy and complex root text.

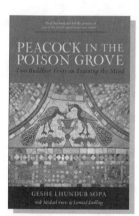

**Peacock in the Poison Grove:
Two Buddhist Texts for Training the Mind**
Geshe Lhundub Sopa with Michael Sweet
and Leonard Zwilling
320 pages, ISBN 0-86171-185-8, $19.95

"The two long poems translated here, attributed
to Atisha's guru, Dharmarakshita, are among the
oldest and most dramatic of the mind-training
texts, woven as they are of startling imagery and a
quintessentially Tibetan admixture of sutra and
tantra practices, as well as conventional and ultimate perspectives on the
world. *Peacock in the Poison Grove* provides lucid translations of the texts,
and a humane and learned commentary revealing why Geshe Sopa has long
been regarded as one of the greatest living scholars of Tibetan Buddhism.
This book belongs on the shelf—and a readily accessible one at that!—of
every scholar and every practitioner of Tibetan Buddhism."—Professor
Roger Jackson, author of *Is Enlightenment Possible?*